CUBA'S BASEBALL DEFECTORS

CUBA'S BASEBALL DEFECTORS

The Inside Story

Peter C. Bjarkman

ROWMAN & LITTLEFIELD
Lanham • Boulder • New York • London

Published by Rowman & Littlefield
A wholly owned subsidary of The Rowman & Littlefield Publishing Group, Inc.
4501 Forbes Boulevard, Suite 200, Lanham, Maryland 20706
www.rowman.com

Unit A, Whitacre Mews, 26-34 Stannary Street, London SE11 4AB

British Library Cataloguing in Publication Information Available

Library of Congress Cataloging-in-Publication Data

Name: Bjarkman, Peter C.
Title: Cuba's baseball defectors : the inside story / Peter C. Bjarkman.
Description: Lanham : Rowman & Littlefield, [2016] | Includes bibliographical references and index.
Identifiers: LCCN 2015037834| ISBN 9781442247987 (hardcover : alk. paper) | ISBN
      9781442247994 (ebook)
Subjects: LCSH: Baseball—Political aspects—Cuba. | Defectors—Cuba—History.
Classification: LCC GV863.25.A1 B525 2016 | DDC 796.357097291—dc23
LC record available at http://lccn.loc.gov/2015037834

∞ ™ The paper used in this publication meets the minimum requirements of
American National Standard for Information Sciences Permanence of Paper for
Printed Library Materials, ANSI/NISO Z39.48-1992.

Printed in the United States of America

In memory of Yadier Pedroso (1986–2013),
who represented everything that was both best
and also most tragic about Cuban baseball . . .

CONTENTS

ACKNOWLEDGMENTS

You see, you spend a good piece of your life gripping a baseball and in the end it turns out that it was the other way around all the time.—Jim Bouton, *Ball Four*

No journey is quite as simple as the twisting highways and byways it traverses; no tale quite reduces itself to the broad plot lines on which it is built; and no human life is adequately capsulized with a mere chronology of the myriad adventures that comprise its months, years, and decades. Built on nearly two decades pursuing (as a devoted fan, sports historian, and working journalist) Cuba's national sport of baseball, both inside the island nation and around the globe, this book offers both a much-needed narrative history and a too-long-absent explanation for the Cuban baseball player "defection" phenomenon that has so dominated North America's big-league headlines throughout the past several seasons.

These chapters explore the daring and often tortuous migrations of some of the better-known Cuban stars who have abandoned low-wage celebrity status in their homeland to endure life-altering (and occasionally life-threatening) pilgrimages in search of multimillion-dollar celebrity status on center stage in the North American major leagues. In the process of pursuing this complex and sometimes sordid tale these pages also expose numerous less celebrated and far less inspiring stories of dozens more who have abandoned family, friends, culture, and profession at home in search of elusive big-league dreams never destined to be realized. In brief, the book explores a phenomenon that now perhaps better than any other exposes both the proud successes and the soft underbelly failures not only of Cuba's little-understood socialist baseball experiment but also of the all-powerful major league baseball (MLB) enterprise itself.

In the process of telling this story it has been necessary to touch on issues far removed from a shared national sporting pastime that has gripped attention in both countries for more than a century. Of necessity this book also addresses perplexing and even perturbing hot-button issues that have divided two neighboring Western Hemisphere nations across the five-decade-long tenure of eleven American presidents (if only one oversized Cuban *caudillo* leader) and in the process have also firmly cemented Cuba in our consciousness as an indelible American foreign policy obsession. In brief the story contained here is about far more than the small world of professional baseball. And it is that very complexity in the end that makes this a tale worth the telling.

Readers will encounter in these chapters a pair of overarching and ultimately intertwining thematic and structural threads. The first has to do with the necessity of defining Cuban baseball itself—its rich history, its indelible legacies, and its inextricably "Cuban" nature, especially in its post-1962 makeover as a bastion of the Cuban Soviet-style socialist sporting system. Just as much as the Japanese and Koreans in the Orient, the Cubans have adapted a self-proclaimed American sport (one transported to their shores in the mid-nineteenth-century) to their own needs and transformed it into a spectacle highly distinct from the North American version today represented almost exclusively by the corporate operation known as major league baseball. Author Robert Whiting once sagely noted that "baseball in Japan appears to be the same as the US version—but it isn't." The same wisdom applies to the Cuban version, in the years both before and after Fidel Castro's arrival. Cuba's current baseball crisis—a self-induced malaise involving far more than the current much-publicized talent drain—only makes sense when set alongside its chaotic if largely glorious past: an evolutionary history stretching from earliest twentieth-century blackball barnstorming winter league seasons, through initial Cuban forays onto the big-league scene in the wake of racial integration and Jackie Robinson, and finally down to bold Castro-era experiments in using the national sport as both an effective instrument for reconstructing socialist society and a potent political weapon for demonstrating symbolic triumphs of the Cuban Revolution itself.

A second equally vital theme underpinning this analysis is one hinted at in Jim Bouton's whimsical if prescient notion that we far too often reduce the national sport of baseball to a childish diversion and, in the process, misapprehend its true meanings and deeply ingrained roots defining our cultural identity. Baseball always seems to emerge as something other than what we first assumed. We often—perhaps in much larger contexts than even Bouton imagined—fail to see that with most of our baseball obsessions it may indeed have always been very much "the other way around." I will argue here that our mainstream media—especially in the wake of Barack Obama's bold December 2014 efforts at placing a belated wedge in a long-standing United States–Cuba stalemate—has rather badly misconstrued and misreported the stories of Cuban ballplayers flocking to the Promised Land of North American big leagues. Popular press accounts have mostly gotten the whole story essentially backwards. Standard procedure has been predictably to frame the entire issue in the guise of yet one more inspired tale about the enticements and glories of an elusive American Dream. The story is thus dressed up as another Horatio Alger "rags to riches" saga of disadvantaged athletes long exploited by a monstrous Castro regime heroically breaking free from their "slave baseball" state while risking life, limb, and painful family separation in order to reap just rewards on lucrative major league playing fields. It is a version of reality that meshes perfectly with an all-too-familiar standard line on Cuba (its eroded politics and collapsing socialist society) that has been regular media fodder in Miami, Washington, and much of the rest of our nation for close to two generations. Nonetheless, this story, like Bouton's own personal history with the game, may well be best viewed "the other way around"—a reverse tale contradicting the one so far popularly told. And in the end, the Cuban talent drain may now haunt MLB's survival every bit as much as it haunts Cuba's own baseball future. My approach here has been to view the saga from not one but two drastically different perspectives: the more familiar (if often misconstrued) view trumpeted by most US media as well as the somewhat different perspectives both found in the Cuban government-controlled press and also voiced by surprisingly knowledgeable fans on the streets of Havana and in ballparks spread across a long-isolated island nation of 11-million-plus hardcore baseball fanatics. From both angles the story remains complex, controversial, and open to a plethora of contrasting interpretations.

Like my previous published works involving the Cuban baseball story, this one has been aided by the invaluable contributions of numerous others at many turns along the way. I have developed many debts that not only demand repayment but also are sometimes risky to acknowledge. It is impossible to credit all those individuals who have taken risks on my behalf or provided valued input to my understandings of Cuba and its national sport. But a few heavy contributors must be singled out for special mention. Colleague Ray Otero has provided me with a home for my reports and opinions over the past seven years—the website www.BaseballdeCuba.com. It has legitimized my work and opened many doors to vital access; Ray also offered advice and updated information for this particular project that allowed me to avoid a number of pitfalls and errors. Ismael Sené in Havana first opened my access to the Cuban baseball scene back in 1997 and remained my most ardent supporter and advocate on the island in all the years that followed. Eddie Artiles has been my valued assistant and traveling companion in Cuba for almost a dozen years and repeatedly turned seemingly impossible quests into successfully completed missions. Martin Hacthoun shared his journalistic expertise and love of the Cuban game, as has Reynaldo Cruz in more recent months. And finally, this book would not have become what it is without the patient, insightful, and adept handling and advice of my editor, Christen Karniski, who adroitly shepherded a complex manuscript through the final stages of production.

The greatest measure of indebtedness of course remains with the ballplayers themselves, many of whom have become my close friends. This group includes (but is not limited to) virtually every member of the senior national team across the past dozen or more years. These superb athletes have been my true family in Cuba, although many are no longer residing on the island and a few have already become household names on the North American big-league scene. They have also been my most valued sources for details informing this complex story, through numerous on- and off-the-record discussions and shared encounters in Cuban ballparks, in their homes and neighborhood restaurants spread across the island, and in hotel rooms and stadiums throughout Europe, Asia, Mexico, and the Caribbean. I have steadfastly avoided breeching those friendships over the years by remaining more a trusted confidant than a detached journalist. Therefore if I now run the risk of violating long-savored trusts by revealing certain back pages of personal stories and experiences candidly entrusted to me—or even only those I have observed from up close—I do so at this juncture in the genuine belief that in telling the tale I do more service than damage. I continue to share with them a passion for both Cuba and Cuban-style baseball. They have already done so much for their millions of fans and countrymen by living this adventure; I hope to do at least a small measure of good in retelling it.

PROLOGUE

The United States government . . . has internalized its allergic reaction to Cuban socialism to such a large degree that any attempt to change course and seek a rapprochement with Cuba will be the equivalent of making a train jump off its tracks.—Daniel P. Erikson, *The Cuba Wars*

Cuba has been a lingering American obsession for more than half a century. For those on the political right, Castro's indefatigable if tarnished empire is the last vestige of a much-despised and brutal communist regime, long fantasized to be a serious threat to American-style democracy. For those of more leftist persuasions, the last tottering American-hemisphere communist experiment still resonates as an inspired model of resistance to increasingly unpopular and outdated American-style imperialism. For the masses of mainstream Americans residing somewhere in the middle, the long-forbidden island nation of Cuba is perhaps, above all else, a highly coveted and hopefully soon-to-be-possessed fantasy tourist destination.

Although Fidel has long since bequeathed the battle of ideas to his successors, the "lone wolf" island nation nonetheless still provides a safe haven for the last-standing tyrant ("dictator" in American parlance) of a now nearly moribund cold war struggle. Vietnam, Iraq, Afghanistan, and George W. Bush's badly bungled war on terrorism aside, Cuba is perhaps the starkest example of misguided, failed, and obstinate American foreign policy. And it is also the place that almost all Americans seem to want to visit. "How can we go there?" is the question I most frequently hear from anyone who inquires about my own widely reported Cuba travels.[1]

Cuba—as both misunderstood reality and overblown fantasy—is indeed the ever-tantalizing forbidden fruit now dangling before a jaded early-twenty-first-century American imagination.

Fidel Castro himself remains a giant if mostly mythical figure looming over the past half-century, and both countries have seemed to base their recent cold war adversarial policies on simply waiting for him to die. Several excellent and quite meticulous biographies (in particular those penned by Tad Szulc and Robert Quirk) detailing every important aspect in the nine-decade life of this most engaging and durable statesman have remained academic curiosities, thus doing little to separate fiction or legend from reality in the American public imagination.[2] There can apparently be no middle ground on either Cuba or its now fading and increasingly invisible supreme leader. And there seems no possibility of letting go. Much of the attention on Fidel and his regularly demonized domain has played out across the decades in the political arena. But an inordinately large part of the saga has also occupied headlines in the much smaller world of North America's organized professional baseball.

The North American obsession with Cuba and its now-sagging communist experiment has come into renewed and sharpened focus since the December 2014 Obama administration announcement that Washington would finally move toward the long-stalled reopening of diplomatic discourse with Cuba. In the process it would abandon six decades of cold war isolation tactics aimed at the demonized communist island sitting little more than 100 miles off the coast of South Florida. Most of the newly aroused public interest has focused sharply on a still-murky if somehow promising future, and much of it has been weighed down with broad misinterpretations and wild fantasies about a new American invasion of the "Pearl of the Caribbean." Only this time it would be an invasion carried out with tourist dollars and weapons of American corporate investment. If Washington operatives could not succeed in their multiple devious plots to kill off Castro and his empire, at long last they might simply be able to buy up what is left.

Also, it would be an invasion carried out in reverse, as *Newsweek* journalist John Walker cleverly suggested in perhaps the single best article so far capturing the essence of a new Cuban invasion baseball story.[3] In his essay "The Bay of Capitalist Pigs," Walker explains how Cuba is now (a half century after kicking out American enterprises controlling the island's sugar, tobacco, mining, and utilities industries) again finally being stripped of one of its most important resources——"strong armed fielders who can go deep."

Our renewed fantasies about an open and "free" Cuba have focused just as much on the shared national sport of baseball as on any hopes for immediate open-ended tourism or simmering latent business investment opportunities. And this is not particularly surprising since the bat and ball sport has always constituted much of the communist nation's post-revolution identity. But it is here, unfortunately, where the disinformation and misunderstandings have been especially unsettling. Cuba is not widely seen through North American eyes as the intriguing alternative baseball universe it actually is. Rather it is imagined only as yet another resource to be tapped, perhaps the last untouched source available to flood MLB ball clubs with the colorful revenue-producing athletes desperately needed to staff rosters suffering from depletions in homegrown talent. This time around it is not tobacco, sugar, or precious metals, but rather talented baseball players that stoke the lust of a cash-rich sector of the American corporate business community. And if the dismantling of Cuban baseball means ruination of one of Fidel Castro's proudest achievements—a socialist-style sports juggernaut—that can be appreciated as further icing upon the cake.

Media outlets—especially those in South Florida and the numerous print and cyber sources covering major league baseball—have rushed to tell a somewhat sanitized version of the story. But most reports demonstrate little understanding of Cuban baseball realities. Tales of human trafficking or violations of Cuban law have often been conveniently buried. Inspired sagas of escape from tyranny and blows for American-style democracy are guaranteed to stir more interest. Front-page headlines have mostly focused on the enrichment of major-league clubs, on the potential of well-deserved windfalls of talented players enlivening the American ballpark spectacle with new Puigs, Chapmans, Abreus, and Moncadas. A subtext, of course, usually also has to do with chasing the American Dream and enjoying the economic freedoms this nation loudly trumpets but denies to increasing masses of its own native citizens. Both treatments seem somewhat off the mark.

The power brokers at MLB could easily enough now talk openly about their fantasies and even their firm plans for upcoming spring-training contests between big-league clubs in long-off-limits Havana. Such developments might also foreshadow television deals for league games broadcast on the island (without much thought to how third-world Cubans might afford to watch them). Big-league general managers might gleefully envision MLB-run academies around the corner and welcome the prospect of soon owning virtually all those budding Cuban athletes without ever pausing to revisit conveniently buried stories about the disasters attached to so much of the MLB academy system recently being run in the Dominican Republic or in Venezuela.

Cuban ballplayers we had never even heard of only a few months back were suddenly becoming American-style millionaires. But behind the scenes a dark-side reality was unfolding. Major league baseball perhaps was never suspected of direct involvement in spiriting young ballplayers off the island—risking the lives of many—and quickly casting aside others who couldn't meet the overripe expectations of greedy player agents who rushed to sign them up. But it did seem that there might be room for at least some culpability for an enterprise (MLB) that seemed to enjoy all the rewards built into the evolving system while at the same time choosing to cast a blind eye on all its emerging evils.

* * *

From a perspective that sees baseball only as American baseball and American baseball as no more than Major League Baseball (MLB), the Cuban invasion of big-league ballparks would be positive in its implications. But there is far more to the convoluted story. Hardly the least important element here is the ominous prospect that the death of Cuban League baseball as we now know it may be but one more sign of critical challenges surrounding the long-term survival of the North American big-league game itself.

There is more than a little irony, perhaps, in the suggestion that the key to salvaging America's national pastime might lie in sustaining vibrant independent international leagues of the sort now approaching its death throes in Cuba. That irony only expands with the recognition that any such rescue will not arrive in the normally expected form—continued streams of high-quality and high-profile foreign prospects are arriving like clockwork to prop up depleted major-league rosters and shore up a sport that today depends on Latinos and Asians for almost a third of its labor force (the number of foreign MLB players reached 28 percent on 2013 opening day rosters, according to the MLB Commissioner's Office). A broader perspective suggests that hope resides instead in the preservation of distant leagues in the Far East and Latin America (even in

Europe, Africa, and Oceania, where the game still struggles to gain a foothold)—leagues existing as independent entities focusing exclusively on their own growth and health as vibrant national cultural institutions. In an increasingly globalized world, prospects are not rosy for growing or even salvaging an exclusively North American sport.

Baseball's salvation as a twenty-first-century sport, I will argue here and in succeeding chapters, depends on the continued health of alternative baseball worlds, ones that remain beyond the reach of the single behemoth professional circuit maintained exclusively on North American shores and known as Major League Baseball. If one wants to know why today's youth, even in the most fanatic of baseball countries, like Cuba and the United States, are rapidly turning toward soccer as the sport of choice, one has to look beyond more obvious factors like soccer's rapid-fire pace of play and hard-hitting violent action, or the expense and availability of equipment.[4] Today's youth gravitate toward a global game in an increasingly globalized world. Soccer (or *fútbol*, as it is known in most corners of the world) is the reigning kingpin of globalized sport; baseball (mainly in the hands of MLB) has miserably failed in its baldly insincere efforts at true globalization.

That the sport today survives at all in a handful of isolated independent pockets (mostly in North America, the Caribbean region, and sectors of Asia and Europe) has certainly not been for any lack of effort on the part of the powerful marketing branches of MLB's corporate headquarters. The big-league game has a lengthy history of exploiting lesser leagues for its own commercial interests and thus of eventually killing off the very corners of the game most likely to contain the best seedbeds for replenishing its own future. The recruiting and marketing practices of the North American big leagues have been especially hard on the survival of coexisting leagues in most of the world's other top baseball-playing nations. Once fertile grounds for developing or fine-tuning big-league talents, Caribbean winter leagues today stand near extinction. In the light of increasing defections of topflight Japanese stars to higher-paying big-league clubs (slowed and controlled, but not ended, by a Japanese posting system later examined in chapter 9), the recent fate of domestic pro circuits in Caribbean baseball centers such as Venezuela, Puerto Rico, and the Dominican Republic should raise strong storm signals for the long-standing and once fully independent Japanese leagues. Surviving

Korean, Taiwanese, and Cuban circuits face similar threats, which seem to promise the unfortunate repetition of an old and all-too-familiar story.

If Cuba's plight is the one highlighted in recent headlines, an equally instructive case is found with the earlier fortunes of Korea's professional version of the sport. In the mid-1990s, the Korean Baseball Organization (KBO) was faced with a crisis of runaway player defections to higher-paying circuits. Ballpark attendance in Seoul and elsewhere within the then-decade-old KBO began to slip significantly after 1994, with the foremost factor being the departure that season of ace pitcher Chan-ho Park to the Los Angeles Dodgers. Suddenly Korean fans were focused on the Dodgers and not their own Haitai Tigers or Lotte Giants. On the heels of Park's defection came the departure of another ace pitching favorite, Dong-yol Sun, who opted for greener grass and greener cash in the stadiums of Japan. Batting champion Jeong-bum Lee quickly followed the same route. Such departures hit especially hard in a nation where it was already a struggle to find sufficient talent to maintain a vibrant national pro game. In both Korea and Taiwan, admitting rented foreign players has been a compromise unpopular with both fans and owners, but is nonetheless necessary if professional baseball is to keep going on the home front.

Cuba has never considered the option of countering defection losses by enticing foreign replacements, since the unique thrust of the Cuban League has always been a purely domestic program designed to develop national teams. Cuba maintains the only pro-baseball league anywhere that has never utilized or even allowed imports—part of what makes the Cuban national pastime so special. It is what generates such pride among Cuban fans—when Cubans brag about "our players" they are always talking about native sons and never rented mercenaries. The wealth of talent alongside a deep-seated tradition in the sport has also so far shielded Cuba from being largely decimated by player losses, although the well is not bottomless and ill effects have already begun to set in.

MLB's absorption policies have not been restricted to foreign lands. It has now been nearly three-quarters of a century since the powerful arm of big-league baseball killed off the thriving institution known collectively as the Negro professional leagues, which were once an important social and economic pillar of black communities throughout the United States (especially in the urban centers of the Midwest and Northeast). Admittedly, the Negro leagues grew out of one of the darkest pages of American sports history. No argument for sustaining a world of racially segregated baseball could be justified, now or ever. From any perspective, the Rickey-Robinson story was one of the brightest pages of both big-league history and the nation's larger social history. And yet the folding of the Negro leagues on the heels of racial integration throughout organized baseball came with a terrible price. Players too old or not dazzling enough to make the few available big-league roster spots (in what were then two eight-team leagues) were left with careers abruptly truncated. Black fans who had flocked to community parks in Birmingham, Memphis, Indianapolis, Newark, and Kansas City and the thriving black neighborhoods of Chicago, Washington, and Pittsburgh now had only Jackie Robinson, Larry Doby, and a few others of their race to cheer for in the distant majors, and in at least one big-league city (St. Louis) they still had to sit in racially segregated bleachers.

An eerily similar story played itself out several decades later in once-thriving leagues throughout the Caribbean region—in countries that were once the cradle of the game in the Spanish-speaking world. Here the circumstances were admittedly somewhat different and the details somewhat more complex. But indiscriminant big-league player raiding of the top local talent and insensitivity to the economic needs of the local leagues were again central contributing factors in the diminished appeal of winter baseball circuits. Astronomically higher player salaries in the 1980s and 1990s meant less motivation for big leaguers to play winter ball. Eventually big-league contracts even actually blocked native Latino stars from returning home for off-season games with special clauses designed to limit a star ballplayer's off-season activities and thus protect the ball club's top-dollar investments from potential career-ending injuries.

Big-league games televised to numerous Caribbean markets further eroded the gate appeal of the local winter leagues, especially once top major-league stars were no longer appearing in San Juan, Caracas, or Santo Domingo. The decision of MLB to establish its own off-season developmental league in Arizona (Arizona Fall League, or AFL) has further undercut the Caribbean's once flourishing culture of winter baseball. Disgruntled with supposedly "deteriorating conditions" in the traditional Caribbean winter circuits, MLB launched the AFL in 1992 as a six-team circuit operating in the Phoenix area. The venture was designed to develop some of the game's top prospects without exposing raw rookies to the supposed pitfalls of playing in a "foreign" environment and outside the tight control of their own MLB clubs. As early as its second season, the new circuit was featuring such future frontline stars as Mike Piazza (Dodgers), Ryan Klesko (Braves), and Mike Lieberthal (Phillies). With all thirty big-league organizations sending their top prospects to Phoenix rather than to Latin ports of call, the overall result has been that Caribbean-based winter ball has been hovering on life-support for much of the past two decades.

In fairness, the failure of baseball in the Caribbean winter circuits cannot be laid at the doorstep of MLB alone, even if the first dismantling might well have begun there. Sagging economic conditions in the Dominican Republic and resulting severe shortages in electricity, potable water, and public transportation have sabotaged league schedules and fan morale. In Puerto Rico in the early 1990s, economic conditions resulted in the curtailing of league schedules from 60 to 48 games and led to the folding of one long-prominent franchise. Bayamón threw in the towel on the eve of the 1993 season, and that same winter unprecedented rains played havoc with what remained of the shortened league schedule. Venezuela fared only slightly better during the same time. In 1999 devastating floods ravaged the country and shut down winter baseball play for five days in mid-December. During that same winter two minor-league prospects were assassinated in separate savage armed robbery incidents.

Despite difficult internal conditions in the leagues themselves, it has been above all else the lack of hot prospects and known veterans on Dominican, Puerto Rican, and Venezuelan club rosters that has largely killed off once-thriving ballpark attendance. In addition, many older Dominican and Puerto Rican ball fans have been spoiled by satellite transmissions and dish antennas bringing them four or five summertime big-league games daily, and younger fans have been lured from ballparks by numerous competing forms of entertainment such as music videos, television dramas, disco bars, American cinema, and action-packed computer games.

Well before the collapse of once-thriving winter circuits, MLB also exerted a direct attack on the competition in nearby Mexico and Cuba. The pre--Jackie Robinson major-league color line long aided Caribbean leagues by driving top black stars to seek winter employment in integrated circuits to the south. During the mid-1940s, recognizing that egalitarian winter baseball was likely the best baseball played anywhere, Mexican League mogul Jorge Pasquel launched the single retaliatory raid still on record against big-league rosters, offering lucrative contracts to white big leaguers as well as black circuit Negro stars in the hopes of competing on an equal footing with the majors.[5]

The short-lived Mexican baseball wars had far greater negative impact on the Cuban League than on big-league teams themselves. Jorge Pasquel's challenge was quickly repulsed, and the careers of only a handful of big leaguers were impacted. A dozen or so recognized major leaguers—pitchers Sal Maglie and Max Lanier foremost in the group—were handed suspensions (eventually revoked) for jumping to Mexican rosters. The summer Mexican League would soon enough crumble under Pasquel's overambitious expansion dreams. For winter baseball in Cuba, however, the immediate impact was more drastic, since two separate circuits were forced to operate in both 1946–47 and 1947–48. Both Cuban and American players fearing their own potential banishment for competing against Pasquel's recruits were forced for the first of those years to take refuge in a separate Liga de la Federación operating out of La Tropical Stadium in direct competition with the traditional Cuban League playing at newly inaugurated Cerro Stadium. A year later (in the aftermath of a peace deal with the MLB commissioner), the MLB-affiliated players returned to the main venue at Cerro and the suspended "outlaw" players retreated to their own soon-failed league at La Tropical. These complexities and their implications for island baseball are taken up in chapter 2, when we briefly review the sometimes chaotic history of professional winter league play in pre-Castro-era Cuba.

The whole Pasquel affair was just the entrée into Cuban and Caribbean winter baseball that big-league owners had long coveted. Soon MLB negotiated agreements with Caribbean leagues (foremost the Cuban League) that regulated and controlled player flow between the majors and the winter circuits, essentially turning the latter into player-development leagues under MLB supervision. Less than a decade and a half later the Cuban Revolution led by Fidel Castro would make the MLB victory moot as far as the Cuban League (closed after 1961) was concerned. Elsewhere, however, the direction and scope of winter league baseball had been drastically altered forever. The summer Mexican circuit would simultaneously shrink to its present diminished stature as a second-tier minor league under a similarly imposed MLB accord. US-based organized baseball was winning all the battles, even if it might have been slowly losing the long-term globalization war.

   MLB's devastation of the competition has not been restricted to international rivals. Organized baseball has never relished or even for long
tolerated the suggestion of business competition. Often the monopolistic
practices of MLB have even been directed squarely at members of its
own extended family—that is, at stateside minor-league baseball. The
spread of televised coverage of big-league games into all corners of urban
and rural America in the 1950s and 1960s was a death blow for once-
thriving lower-level minor leagues and semi-pro or industrial leagues
from coast to coast. Hometown teams—once the very center of the baseball universe for a majority of rural fans in the Far West, Midwest, and
Deep South—faded from the scene, and the minor leagues as a whole
suffered a depression at midcentury that further worked to change the
face of the sport. In 1946, more than 32 million fans attended live minor-
league baseball, a postwar jump from less than 10 million a year earlier.
Before the end of the decade, attendance figures had reached more than
40 million. During the television boom of the 1950s, however, more than
300 cities would lose their minor-league clubs. Forty-three separate
leagues operated in 1952; in 1956, 27 leagues; and by the end of the
decade, there were only 21 operating minor-league circuits. Some overly
pessimistic prophets were foreseeing the final collapse of minor-league
baseball altogether.

   If the notion of history repeating itself is a familiar enough cliché, it
nonetheless carries more than a little weight in the case under consideration. With MLB now milking talent from lesser pro leagues in Korea and
Taiwan and also beginning to entice stars from the rosters of its foremost
rival in Japan (most recently pitcher Masahiro Tanaka, who joined the
top-paying New York Yankees in 2014 on the heels of his record-setting
24–0 campaign with the Rakuten Golden Eagles), Cuba, with its long-
isolated and so-called "amateur" league, now stands alone in resisting any
large-scale and deadly MLB incursions. Cuba remains a solitary island
fortress (metaphorically as well as geographically) housing an anachron-
istic baseball culture—one without even the loosest of formal ties to
North American organized baseball. In the view of at least some (and I
must count myself in that camp), this separate Cuban baseball culture
should be treasured for the very fact of its tenacious isolation. Here is a
league that still refuses to sell off its players to organized baseball and
thus continues to operate outside the clutches of the monopolistic enterprise represented by Major League Baseball and its partners in the North

American network and cable television industries. Cuba has, for far longer than anyone might have reasonably expected, been able to remain a
truly alternative baseball universe.

Of course in an increasingly globalized world of twenty-first-century
sports, economics, and politics, this isolation is now being rapidly eroded.
That this new Cuban League built in the shadows of the Castro revolution
was able to resist all outside intrusions for more than forty years admittedly had mostly to do with accidents brought on by external events—the
cold war political circumstances that drove Washington and Havana in
radically different directions in the 1960s and the decades that followed.
But what MLB could not buy it is now being all too easily and freely
gifted by yet another non-baseball factor, the ultimate and long-predicted
collapse of Cuba's failed experiment with a utopian socialist system.
Defections in recent years of hundreds of young Cuban ballplayers seeking a better economic future are finally collapsing Cuban baseball far
more rapidly than any direct dealings with MLB are reducing the strength
of far-flung Asian leagues. It is, in the end, one of the great ironies of
present-day professional baseball.

If the history of MLB imperialism (and there is no better term) as
outlined here continues to follow its well-charted course, Cuba's independent baseball is indeed living on borrowed time. Only a few years back I
was willing to claim that defections of expendable minor stars were having no more than minimal impact, but that is no longer true. Cuban
baseball is hardly moribund, yet it is clear that a golden age is receding
into the shadows. An immediate death knell may be further off than many
might expect, though I grow increasingly pessimistic on even that projec-
tion. The continued survival of a revolutionary government under Raúl
Castro and his appointed successors will likely forestall rapid change. But
prospects for Cuban domestic baseball retaining any true quality seem to
be dwindling. The Cuban League has survived in its present form for
more than a half century but there are growing indications that it cannot
survive much longer. Politics and the evolving USA-Cuba relations likely
hold a final key to the conundrum.

Two scenarios may yet play themselves out. One is the total collapse
of Cuban baseball as we have always known it. Without some development to end defections and either force or, better still, entice Cuban
players to remain at home for at least a reasonable period of service, there
will soon be a player void on the island so large that all possibility of

keeping a respectable domestic league prospering, or even surviving, will certainly be lost. Cuba will in short order become another Dominican Republic, or perhaps a slightly less chaotic Venezuela, or maybe even the twin face of Puerto Rico's baseball wasteland. An alternative scenario would involve some accord between MLB and the Cuban Federation that develops and supports an existing Cuban League structure and recruits Cuban players at a moderate enough pace not only to keep Cuba's own enterprise in operation but also to facilitate its continued growth. My own crystal ball projections are reserved mostly for chapters concluding this volume. But first we might be best served by exploring, in at least cursory fashion, Cuba's baseball evolution—and especially the interplay of Cuba-USA relations both inside and outside the world of baseball.

* * *

The fascination with Cuban baseball began early in the last century. There were ground-breaking trips by North American pros in the final decades of the nineteenth century and opening decade of the twentieth that brought back news of some astounding players on the island, most of them black men who could have no place in the mainstream North American professional game, but who would have been worth thousands of dollars in bonus money to big-league clubs if they were white.[6]

These early barnstorming visits to the island's newly discovered baseball hotbed were made by groups of big-league all-stars as well as by "outlaw" Negro-league clubs—both groups in search of some quick extra cash and some coveted recreation time in Havana, a city already known as the pleasure port of the Caribbean. The Cubans had commenced a winter professional league of their own as early as 1878 (only two years after the founding of the venerable National League), although during its first couple of decades the Cuban circuit was more like an extended tournament than a full league championship season. Because visiting barnstormers from the North, especially the white big leaguers, were likely to view the tours as a free-wheeling holiday, it is difficult to make too much out of the results of exhibition contests in what by 1908 was being called the "American Season" segment of the Havana winter baseball schedule.

A half century later, baseball's big-league integration opened doors for Cuban stars to finally have a small impact in North America. While penny-pinching owner Clark Griffith and his Havana-based super scout Joe Cambria had inked a small horde of not-too-dark-skinned "Cubanos" in the forties as cheap fill-in labor and hedges against the World War II draft, there were no true Cuban stars in the pre-1950 big leagues except an often overlooked near-200-game-winner named Dolf Luque. There were a few midcentury Cubans who managed to bend the odious color line and it is today arguable that such Afro-Cubans as Tomás de la Cruz (Cincinnati, 1944) and Roberto Estalella (Washington, 1935) have been denied their roles in history as Jackie Robinson's predecessors.

But it was only after Robinson and 1947 that Cubans of true quality began to arrive in fuller force. The first and perhaps most memorable was the original "Cuban Comet" Orestes "Minnie" Miñoso, who flashed onto the scene with the Paul Richards "Go-Go" White Sox of the early fifties. Ironically, the first wave of impactful Cubans was still mostly white and mostly pitchers—Conrado "Connie" Marrero, Camilo Pascual, Pedro "Pete" Ramos, Sandalio "Sandy" Consuegra, Miguel "Mike" Fornieles. But the truly black or perceptibly black Cubans were also not entirely without note and included 1955 World Series hero Edmundo "Sandy" Amoros in Brooklyn, Tony Taylor with the Cubs, Humberto "Chico" Fernández (long mistakenly discounted as the first "black" with the integration-tardy Philadelphia Phillies), glue-fingered if light-hitting shortstop Willy Miranda with the Yankees, Cy Young winner Miguel Cuéllar in Baltimore, and the flashy Zoilo Versalles and the remarkable Pedro "Tony" Oliva, both in Minnesota.

But this early Cuban impact was not destined to be long-lived, as only a dozen years after Jackie Robinson opened doors, Fidel Castro and his revolution would slam them shut again. There were those who had left their island home in the first months of the communist takeover whose big-league careers spanned the 1960s and much of the 1970s—Atanasio "Tony" Pérez, Octavio "Cookie" Rojas, Orlando Peña, Leo Cardenas, José Cardenal, José Azcue, Diego Segui, José Tartabull, and perhaps the greatest among Cuban big-league pitchers, Luis Tiant Jr. But by the late 1970s that wellspring had dried up and the Cuban presence had been reduced to a trickle. While twenty-five new Cubans had reached the majors in the half-dozen years between 1961 and 1967, only seven more arrived during the next fifteen-year span before the first "defector" (Bárbaro Garbey) finally popped up in 1984 (appendix 1).

A more general Latino influence on the big-league scene continued and eventually even exploded; by century's end many talked about Hispanic imports virtually taking over an American national pastime. In

2014 the percentage of foreign-born players on MLB rosters topped 26 percent. By late in the century Latinos were almost without argument the dominant force on the big-league scene, filling annual MLB All-Star Game lineups (Latinos held 15 of the 35 slots on the 2011 American League roster), taking center stage for postseason action, and maintaining an important presence on just about every big-league club. With Cuba out of the picture the field was left wide open for the Venezuelans, Mexicans, Puerto Ricans, and especially Dominicans, who boasted nearly 10 percent of the big-league player population by the end of the new millennium's first decade (to say nothing of the Dominican presence on minor-league teams).

Throughout nearly the entire second half of the twentieth century the suddenly hidden Cuban baseball enterprise remained a mysterious and forbidden alternative universe. Stories filtered back to the American press from time to time, such as in a featured *Sports Illustrated* June 1977 cover story in which Ron Fimrite paints an intriguing portrait of a colorful island baseball scene featuring novel local customs, blaring grandstand salsa bands, aluminum bats, little visible electronic technology, arduous team road trips, primitive and stark, if fan-friendly, stadiums, and a wealth of never-before-heard-of local heroes with names like Miguel Cuevas ("a Cuban Joe DiMaggio"), Lourdes Gourriel (father of today's star Yulieski Gourriel and at the time still himself a developing talent who if found stateside "would have big-league scouts weeping tears of gratitude in backwater Holiday Inns"), and Antonio Muñoz (an oversized slugging first sacker who is best described as "a left-handed Tony Perez").[7] And periodically the Cubans made their presence strongly felt in the outside baseball world, occasionally even on American shores. The latter cases came, for example, with a barely noticed annual "Friendly Series" staged for much of the 1980s and 1990s in Millington, Tennessee, or more noteworthy gold medal triumphs at the 1987 Indianapolis Pan American Games (over a touted American squad featuring pitchers Jim Abbott, Greg Olson, and Chris Carpenter) and the 1996 Atlanta Olympic Games (at the expense of the world's other international baseball superpower, Japan).

Many flowering myths grew out of the baseball and political isolation of the Cuban nation. Easily the most celebrated of those attached to the oversized figure of Fidel Castro himself, who was repeatedly portrayed by American media as a one-time stellar pitching prospect reportedly scouted by numerous big-league clubs and offered contracts by several (the Yankees, Giants, and Senators were the teams most frequently mentioned in this runaway bit of fantasy reporting). The entire tale is nothing but journalistic bunk, of course, as elaborated in chapter 3. But it has long been a favored journalistic trope to mimic the words of Senator Eugene McCarthy and others advancing the notion that if scouts had only been a bit more persistent or observant in pursuing Castro as a neophyte pitcher, then perhaps the full history of late-twentieth-century Western Hemisphere politics might have been altered.[8] Wonderful daydreams, perhaps, but dangerously false history, and worse yet, entirely shoddy journalism.

After four decades of a growing Cuban big-league vacuum, doors again slowly began to crack open in the last decade of the twentieth century. A pioneering trio of mid-1990s journeymen pitchers named René Arocha, Osvaldo Fernández, and Ariel Prieto drew more attention for their novelty as political refugees than for any stellar diamond feats. Liván and Orlando "El Duque" Hernández were postseason sensations at century's end, to be sure, and flashy Rey Ordoñez drew comparisons with earlier stereotypical "good field, no hit" Cuban defensive wizards like Willy Miranda and José Valdivielso. A handful of Cuban stars were finally escaping the world of socialist baseball and making at least small encroachments onto the big-league scene up north. Each new arrival ramped up interest in politically tinged stories about Cuban ballplayer "defections," and the very use of the loaded term was guaranteed to mix the baseball news with anti-Castro and anti-communist politics.

Questions still persisted, nonetheless, about the quality of baseball on the island. Yes, the Cubans dominated all comers in international tournaments, but those were mostly amateur affairs without quality competition involving seasoned pros. A brief glimpse of legitimate Cuban talent was offered by the Atlanta Olympics of 1996. Omar Linares was one player at least who seemed "the real deal" and who justified his glowing assessment as "the best third baseman outside the major leagues, and perhaps even the best third baseman on the planet." But how deep was the talent on the island, and how could you measure sluggers who bashed pitchers with the aid of aluminum bats? Liván Hernández and half brother El Duque enjoyed considerable success once they reached American ballparks, but the small handful of others—mostly pitchers—achieved much more modest triumphs.

The moment of truth seemed to arrive with Major League Baseball's ambitious staging of an inaugural World Baseball Classic (WBC). The Cubans would be invited, but there would be obstacles to their participation as hard-line Bush administration embargo backers fought tooth and nail for continued exclusion of Cuban athletes from competitions on US soil (including Puerto Rico). It would take not only the lobbying power of MLB but also the combined forces of an international sporting community to assure Cuba's presence. The International Baseball Federation (IBAF) threatened removal of its own sanction for the WBC, Puerto Rico promised to withdraw as host, and Venezuela warned of pulling its headlining big leaguers from the games. Most important, perhaps, the International Olympic Committee suggested that Cuba's exclusion might jeopardize America's ability to host any future Olympic events. Under such pressures the Bush administration relented, but only at a price. The Cubans would have to donate their share of tournament proceeds to some humanitarian cause—a condition that Fidel Castro cleverly turned to his own advantage by announcing that those donations would be for US victims of Hurricane Katrina.

Even on the playing field and away from diplomatic maneuvering, the event offered high hopes but also great challenges for Cuba. A lengthy string of uninterrupted international triumphs would now be tested against big leaguers and the illustrious Cuban baseball team suddenly stood in danger of being eliminated from first-round action and sent home with plenty of egg on its face.

But in the end the baseball world would be shocked by Cuban tenacity and the true depth of the Cuban talent. The results—a nail-biting first-round escape in the opener with Panama, a comeback miracle win over host Puerto Rico to cap round two, an impressive semifinal upset of the vaunted Dominicans in San Diego, and an internationally televised title clash with kingpin Japan—produced a resounding success that put Cuba back on the center stage of baseball's international scene. But most American fans did not take it all very seriously in the end. For the American rooter international baseball hardly existed—MLB seemed the only game in town. And even for the largely victorious Cubans, success would quickly bring its own heavy price.

* * *

Cuba's triumphs in the first MLB Classic could only whet the appetites of American fans and big-league talent scouts for access to the apparent Cuban ballplayer gold mine. Slowly over the next half-dozen years the trickle of players escaping the island became first a tiny stream and then a small expanding river. It was acknowledged that the best of the lot were still staying home; there were no Freddie Cepedas or Yulieski Gourriels or Norge Veras or Osmani Urrutias yet pounding on big-league doors. Until recent months, at least, that trickle never became a true flood, like the one long coveted and predicted by defection-instigator Joe Cubas; before he himself faded from the scene, Cubas never did fill up those busloads of defectors he was camped out to corral at each and every new frontline tournament event. But change was nonetheless in the air as economic deterioration began to plague both Cuban society and the Cuban national sport in the wake of Fidel Castro's own long-overdue and health-induced slide from the scene in July 2006.

It is necessary here to explain the Cuban baseball system, at least in its broadest outlines. It is a system quite unlike the one we know here, where professional baseball is first and foremost a profit-generating business aimed as much at producing revenue as at any other entertainment or athletic ends. The game on the field in Cuba is the same in all outward appearances, if a bit shabbier in quality and a bit more old-style in some of its practices. There are few fan amenities in Cuban ballparks, including limited audio or visual electronics, and virtually no marketplace for food, drinks, and souvenirs. The Cuban ballpark experience provides little beyond the rich colors of the game being played on the field. And like the Japanese and Koreans and Taiwanese, the Cubans have adapted the sport to their own cultural and societal needs. Those needs have almost everything to do with trumpeting the powerful Cuban socialist sports machine and little to do with providing livelihoods to hundreds of athletes or peripheral stadium personnel.

Contrasts with the big-league version are quite apparent in a recent volume authored by Mark Armour and Dan Levitt. With their *In Pursuit of Pennants* (2015) the two meticulous historians trace the process by which big-league business models have evolved over the years into sophisticated operations geared to exploit every advantage (on-field and off) in the search for player talent and thus a winning team performance. Armour and Levitt painstakingly demonstrate how big-league clubs have succeeded largely to the degree that they have adjusted to new marketplace realities—racial integration, say, or newly emerging technologies (sabermetrics and baseball analytics) assisting the assessment of athletic

talent or on-field strategies. The best teams over the decades have usually, if not always, been those that most fully exploited such subtle advantages in the search for annual renewals of player talent. And they have
needed to do so, because fielding the best ball clubs and winning the most
championships (or at least competing for those championships) in turn
brought the best ticket sales or radio and television revenues in a sport
that has increasingly become big business over the course of the past
century.

Without understanding this difference in models one doesn't understand much at all about the Cuban game. Cuban baseball after its overhaul
under Castro's reforms in the early sixties (like everything else in the new
socialist society) was not built on any such models of commerce and free
enterprise. Teams were never individually owned by private corporate
enterprises (the new revolutionary Cuba had none) and there was no
competition for gate revenues or media dollars. Winning championships
was only a matter of regional pride and carried no financial incentives.
Ballplayers were not openly recruited across the island, but only developed within the local regions that raised them; Cuban players were not
free agents but instead played only for the native provinces (states) that
nurtured them. (Cuban baseball had no player trades or ballplayer fire
sales.) The ultimate goal was not so much a league pennant (although
those were indeed hotly contested) but rather a slot on the celebrated
national team. The whole enterprise was based, in fact, on two goals. One
was offering quality sports competitions (for both participants and spectators) as healthy and always free activities central to building an ideal
socialist society. A second and more primary goal was creating quality
athletes dedicated to winning international events that might bring glory
to the homeland. Free-enterprise business activity for monetary profit or
any other form of material reward was never the reigning model.

For an impressive span—five-plus decades—the Cuban model worked
quite efficiently. It produced top-level and spirited baseball on the home
front. But even more importantly, it justified the socialist model and the
system that fostered it. And it did so by domination on the international
baseball scene that was like no other form of mastery in the world of
competitive team sports. The term "dynasty" is bandied about shameless-
ly in the world of American sport: a few pennants or league championships won over a full decade seem to be adequate qualification for the
label. But Cuba in the world of international amateur baseball in the mid-

and late twentieth century provided a dynasty like no other before or since. Between 1939 and 2009 (seventy years) and with constantly shifting personnel, Cuban teams captured 25 of the 28 senior International Baseball Federation tournaments in which they competed (finishing second once and third once in the other three outings); between the Amateur World Series of 1961 and the 2008 Beijing Olympic tournament Cuban teams compiled the most incredible "streak" in baseball history, a string of fifty top events in succession in which they either claimed the title or _ reached the final gold medal game. In 28 Amateur World Series appearances between 1939 and 2005 they posted an overall .909 winning percentage across 308 games; and between the 1987 Pan American Games (an early-round inconsequential loss to the Americans) and the 1997 Intercontinental Cup finale with Japan, the Cubans claimed 159 straight victories. All this in a sport in which a mere .600 winning percentage at the professional level usually translates into a league championship.

Finally given the long-desired opportunity in the spring of 1999, the vaunted Cuban national squad even demonstrated it could hold its own against the big leaguers during an historic two-game exhibition set with the American League Baltimore Orioles. Behind the masterful pitching of future defector José Ariel Contreras, the Cuban "amateurs" dropped a hotly contested eleven-inning duel on home soil in Latin American Stadium. Two months later, however, with a young hurler named Norge Luis Vera on the hill—a loyalist who would remain at home and for a time challenge Orlando Hernández's career record for winning percentage—the Cubans coasted to a 12–6 victory in Baltimore's Camden Yards. The triumph was marred only by perceptions that the American Leaguers were only going through the motions and by the histrionics of Cuban-American demonstrators (including one game-interrupting on-field intrusion) that almost turned the whole affair into something of an anti-Castro political circus.

If a second Olympic gold medal and undefeated run during the 1996 Olympics on American soil ended the twentieth century on a definite high note, the first decade in the new millennium was one of rather mixed blessings for Cuba's domestic baseball enterprise. The 2006 WBC triumph appeared to expose the stockpile of raw baseball talent on the island. It also trumpeted an affirmation of the Soviet-style approach to baseball taken over the years by Cuba's governing sports ministry. But in the end it also opened up the proverbial Pandora's box. MLB had created

Future big-league defector Dayan Viciedo in action with the Cuban junior national team at a tournament in Mexico in 2005. Courtesy of Peter C. Bjarkman.

its WBC event in large measure as an "audition stage" for potential worthy imports to fill voids in domestic talent. Once Cuba's own talent reserves became something more than an untested rumor, it was perhaps only a matter of time and circumstance before new raids on the island resources were renewed in earnest.

At the same time the beginning of the new millennium signaled trouble of a different order for the Cubans and their struggling baseball enterprise. Island fans, players, and officials had long wished to demonstrate their nation's prowess against much better competition. But the arrival of that opportunity held deep pitfalls. Beginning with the Pan American Games in Winnipeg in 1999, the playing field was finally leveled. Professionals from the United States, Asia, and the other Caribbean nations entered the scene and changed the nature of the game. Unsurprisingly, the Cuban juggernaut began a noticeable slide. It started in late 2000 in Sydney with a loss of Olympic gold (despite a proud showing against talented future American big leaguers) and then gained momentum with a string of second-place finishes in a Baseball World Cup event where the Cubans had remained virtually unchallenged for decades, having posted nine straight titles between 1984 and 2005 before losing twice to the Americans (2007, 2009) and then to the upstart Dutch (2011).

It was a mere slide and not anything like a genuine collapse, to be sure. Olympic prestige was temporarily regained in Athens (2004) with a hard-fought final-game victory over emerging Australia that turned on an umpire's botched call in the final frame. World Cup titles were successfully defended for the final two times in Havana (2003) and Rotterdam (2005), although Cuba escaped elimination by the narrowest of margins on several occasions. And it remained a dominant force in a trio of final World Cup events despite the upgrade in competition, still managing to last all the way to the finals in Taiwan (2007), Italy (2009), and Panama (2011). But some of the luster had now vanished with this string of silver medal outings after decades of nothing less than first-place gold.

The growing handful of noteworthy and perhaps even a bit surprising successes of players fleeing to the big leagues also began to change the dynamic. Aroldis Chapman not only pocketed $30 million in cold cash, but by his third season in the big time he was standing among the league leaders in saves, becoming a National League All-Star team fixture, and making headlines not only with his radar-gun triple digits but also with the record pace at which he was mowing down big-league hitters. Alexei Ramirez was regularly featured in ESPN *SportsCenter* highlight clips as perhaps the best defensive shortstop playing on North America's biggest stage. Granma's Yoenis Céspedes grabbed numerous headlines with his quick start as a 2012 rookie slugger in Oakland, then added luster with a pair of celebrated All-Star Weekend Home Run Derby crowns.

While most stars were still remaining at home, there were increasing pressures to consider a path to big-league stardom and big-league bank-rolls. And as the economy worsened on the island, more young players fled. The numbers peaked at 23 confirmed cases in 2009 (including future big leaguers Chapman, Maya, and Hechevarría), stabilized briefly (with 16 in 2010, 10 in 2011, and 10 in 2012), and then soared to 36 in the World Baseball Classic year of 2013 (appendix 2). It may have been clear enough that economic conditions and not political dissatisfactions were the driving force. But whatever the motivations, the earlier trickle was rapidly becoming a larger stream, now featuring some top-flight island stars (Leonys Martin in 2010, Céspedes in 2011, Puig in 2012, and then

José Abreu, Erisbel Arruebarrena, Odrisamer Despaigne, and Raisel Igle-sias—all fixtures on that spring's WBC squad—in the landmark 2013 calendar year).

Cuba's long isolation (since 1962) under a US embargo also was finally taking a severe toll. Baseball equipment was in increasingly scarce supply, imported bats and balls, especially, were available only through Mexico and Japan, and the domestic Batos brand products were occasion-ally used in desperation but were not up to league standards. Better com-petition against seasoned professionals from other international leagues—increasingly viewed as vital to upgrading national team performances—seemed to demand a different kind of preparation of the top Cuban stars, perhaps the loaning out of more players to Asia, Europe, or other non-MLB ports of call. More and better year-round competition seemed a top order of business, but this wasn't easy to come by, unless all past tradi-tions were broken and foreign players were imported to shore up the sagging domestic league. The latter was not a likely scenario in a truly national circuit structured solely to hone its own patriotic national team machinery. If the loss of top stars was still so far rather minimal, the drain of large numbers of young prospects (and their forced replacement by teenagers not yet ready or talented enough for big-league status) was admittedly weakening league quality considerably.

This shifting scene on the home front obviously brought morale issues for both fans and ballplayers alike. Cuba owns perhaps the most fanatic fans and (by percentages) the largest domestic baseball following. It is not pure rhetoric to joke that Cuba is an island of 11 million managers (the approximate island population), and baseball has always been as much a Cuban cultural fixture as salsa music, tasty rum, and aromatic cigars. Cuba is perhaps the best place in the world to be a baseball fan, a country where the national pastime is debated daily on nearly every street corner. For years the national team stars were true icons and celebrated heroes to a degree matched perhaps only by soccer heroes in *fútbol* hot-beds like Brazil, Uruguay, Spain, or Croatia. Omar Linares—superstar of the 1980s and 1990s—could legitimately maintain with a very straight face that he valued millions of loyal Cuban fans over millions of big-league dollars. But this now had all begun to change, and seemingly to change more rapidly with each passing winter season.

Fans in Cuba, who once enjoyed the luxury of celebrating annual international tournament victories by veteran squads that rarely ever lost a single match, let alone a cherished gold medal trophy, now found it exceedingly difficult to accept a new reality. This was especially true after the momentary successes of the first MLB-sponsored World Classic, which quickly proved to be more of a last gasp than any signal of continued potency against international opposition now stacked with big-league professionals. A string of second-place silver medal finishes in the 2008 Beijing Olympics (the final hurrah for Olympic baseball itself) and in the final three editions of the IBAF World Cup might have been viewed as indications of just how well Cuban talent was adjusting to a more level international playing field. Instead these results were viewed at home as major disasters and as signals that current Cuban stars just didn't measure up to the legends of past decades.

By the end of the first decade of the twenty-first century Cuban baseball was suffering a rather large crisis in morale. The league was in a constant state of flux as new structures for National Series seasons were attempted as a quick fix for sagging fan interest and sagging international performance. The second season competitions (Super League and Selective Series) had already gone by the wayside in the late 1990s and early 2000s. Now there were more drastic measures taken, like splitting the traditional ninety-game National Series into two stages and eliminating half of the clubs at the midpoint of the pennant chase. A reduced second half of the season required more abandonment of sacred tradition, with top players shuffled to new clubs in a player dispersal draft. A radical plan of loaning top stars out to Japan during the summer off-season (chapter 8) was instituted on a limited basis in 2014 and 2015 but seemed to have little impact as an enticement to keep top stars at home. The defections of celebrated veterans and promising prospects continued to increase, surging to thirty-eight in 2014 and above seventy in the first seven months of 2015.

Perhaps worst of all, a wide majority of Cuba's long-dedicated fan base was now repeatedly bemoaning the sad state of their once-idolized national squad and devoting almost all of their rooting interest and national pride to the daily following of those once-maligned "traitors" now starring on big-league diamonds. The baseball empire that Fidel Castro built and maintained against all odds for nearly a half century was collapsing seemingly overnight. Cuba was looking more and more like the Dominican Republic. The national sport was indeed suffering like never before all across the home front. Its reputation abroad was also morphing from that of an international tournament powerhouse to that of a prime MLB supply route, and the problem of "defectors" was only, apparently, the tip of the iceberg.

But admittedly the devil is always found in the details, and the details here are the very essence of the tale. It is against this broad backdrop of sagging fortunes in contemporary Cuban League baseball, coupled with what seem to be dangerous missteps in the management of contemporary Major League Baseball, that the detailed history of Cuban ballplayer defections can best be recounted. The stage is now set and the various acts of the drama are about to more fully unfold.

I

THE ESSENCE OF "PUIGMANIA"

All things considered there are only two kinds of men in the world—
those that stay at home and those that do not. The second are the most
interesting.—Rudyard Kipling, *Letters of Travel*

Yasiel Puig exploded onto the big-league scene with a flare not witnessed perhaps since the debut of Seattle's Japanese wunderkind Ichiro
Suzuki. There are few more unexpected or dramatic debuts to be found in
big-league annals. The raw twenty-two-year-old Cuban's first trio of
games were headliners on both the offensive and defensive sides of the
field. A single in his very first big-league plate appearance (June 3, 2013,
versus the San Diego Padres) or a debut 2-for-4 batting performance may
not have been all that extraordinary, perhaps, but the novice definitely
turned some heads with a sensational ninth-inning game-saving throw
unleashed from deep right field to double up the potential tying run at
first. For an immediate encore one night later, the heralded rookie ho-
mered twice, collecting three hits and a game-high five RBIs, thus becoming the first Dodger player since Spider Jorgensen, back in 1947, to
drive home that many in his first two big-league appearances.

After being temporarily shut down in his third outing, Puig continued
the onslaught one night later with home run number three, this one a
grand slam that sealed a victory over the visiting Atlanta Braves. But it
wasn't over yet. In his fifth appearance in a Dodger uniform at week's
end, the red hot rookie phenom launched his fifth home run, a game-tying
solo "moon shot" into the left-field pavilion off Braves starter Pat Ma-
holm that was one for the record books. Ten RBIs in the first five career

games tied an existing big-league standard held jointly by Danny Espino-sa (2010 Washington Nationals) and Jack Merson (1951 Pittsburgh Pi-rates). Skeptics could write it all off as one of baseball's occasional inexplicable oddities. One only had to recall that those other two sensa-tional debut sluggers, Espinosa and Merson, were all-too-quickly relegat-ed to the dustbin of baseball's voluminous historical annals.

But what had started with a bang in Yasiel Puig's case would continue with thunderous regularity. For the entire debut month of June, Puig would log numbers that had only been seen once before on big-league diamonds, and in that instance his forerunner in the record books was not a momentary flash but a true giant, the legendary Yankee Clipper, Joe DiMaggio. And Puig was no one-month wonder like Milwaukee's Hurri-cane Bob Hazle (August 1957) or Boston's Clyde Vollmer (July 1951) or so many others who flashed for a few weeks before the league took their measure. At the end of a full calendar year as a big leaguer (June 3, 2014, after 157 games), he owned an unparalleled stat line (.325 BA, .405 OBP, .559 SLG, 30 HR, 191 H, 16 SB) unique in the game's history; no other player debuting in the past half century (not Mike Trout or Albert Pujols or Ryan Braun or Miguel Cabrera) had beaten or even matched every one of those elevated numbers.[1] In the process the dazzling Cuban import overnight captured the hearts of LA fans and the rapt attention of media all around the big-league circuit. But it was not an entirely new story, especially not in Tinseltown.

First there had been Mexican-born icon Fernando Valenzuela, and then a decade and a half later Japan's pioneering Hideo Nomo. "Fernan-domania" gripped America's cinema capital with unparalleled fervor dur-ing the strike-torn 1981 season and Valenzuela's performances were re-markable enough by themselves to transform one of MLB's most embar-rassing summers into one of its most memorable. Of course there were notable differences between the debuts of Valenzuela in 1981 and Puig in 2013. Valenzuela was a pitcher, his highly anticipated outings spaced for dramatic buildup, and not an everyday player, on display daily and thus more subject to fits and starts in performance. He carried no backstory dripping with political overtones and charged with cold war rhetoric. Valenzuela boasted no daring escape from a communist homeland certain to pique general media interest, and there was no subplot involving "po-litical defection" undertaken in search of the celebrated American Dream.

Yasiel Puig enjoyed one of baseball's greatest debut months in June 2013. Courtesy of Byron Motley.

In searching for comparisons to Puig, Hideo Nomo provides perhaps the closer parallel. Like Valenzuela fourteen years earlier and Puig eighteen years later, Nomo took LA by storm, posting a season nearly identical to Valenzuela's (13–6, 2.54 ERA) and duplicating his All-Star Game starting assignment and Rookie-of-the-Year trophy. Nomo was even branded a "defector" by many back in Japan when he became the first of his countrymen in three decades to abandon the homeland in favor of a big-league contract. But obviously the highly charged term did not have the same resonance in this case and was rarely if ever applied in American press accounts. Robert Whiting would label Nomo as such (chapter 5 in *The Meaning of Ichiro* is entitled "The Defector: The Story of Nomo"), but only years after Nomo's career was complete. The huge difference here was that "Nomomania" would reach far more epic proportions back in the pitcher's home country than it ever would in Los Angeles. Nomo was seen by Japanese ball fans as symbolizing the quality if not the superiority of their native baseball and perhaps even their entire nation—a long-standing obsession in Japanese culture. Nomo, with his rookie season in the National League, thus became perhaps the most popular player in Japanese baseball annals, at least until Ichiro Suzuki enjoyed his own stunning big-league debut in 2001. For a brief time in the mid-1990s Nomo stole the spotlight from all previous Japanese baseball greats, including even Eiji Sawamura (Japan's version of Cy Young), Shigeo Nagashima (the country's most popular ballplayer and arguably its best), and Sadaharu Oh (the sport's all-time home run king).

And then there was also the considerable difference in treatment of Nomo and Puig by the US sporting press. Nomo was celebrated as the first true Asian star in the big leagues—there were no forerunners beyond mid-1960s journeyman Mashi Murakami (winner of a mere six games) to live up to or overhaul. His triumph was portrayed as a surprising signal of just how good the Japanese game now actually was. He was thus seen first and foremost as erasing a stigma long portraying Japanese players as too small in stature for the American majors, and also a related prejudice suggesting the Japanese professional game was in every way an inferior product to the big leagues. Those earlier notions had been based on years of off-season big-league barnstorming across Asia (especially Japan), where Japanese leaguers had never offered serious opposition to the more muscular Americans.

But in the case of Nomo, as opposed to Puig or other defectors from Cuba, there was no obvious crowing over blows to Japanese baseball. There were few if any fantasies about the floodgates suddenly opening and all the top Japanese stars fleeing to big-league franchises. (In the case of the Cubans, those fantasies were based as much on hopes of toppling the Cuban system as any desires for actually seeing Cuban stars grab big-league jobs that might otherwise have been filled by American athletes.) MLB had always jealously guarded its relations with the Japanese League (NPB) and its implied if not formally stated policy had been to keep its hands off the Japanese game. The political environment surrounding the respective countries (Cuba versus Japan) was vastly different and MLB-NPB business relations were thus far more cordial, even if some MLB operatives might envision the Land of the Rising Sun as a potential market for future MLB television rights or memorabilia sales.

The Yasiel Puig story carried a different tone entirely. This was not the first Cuban to reject his domestic league and head to America in search of more elevated paychecks and more promising career achievements. Puig was only the most recent in an ever-growing collection of Cuban refugees that had produced other eye-popping debuts over the previous two decades. Liván and El Duque Hernández had also earlier taken the big leagues by storm and earned headlining rookie-year post-season plaudits. Aroldis Chapman had made considerable headlines of his own with his monster bank-busting contract and then his unequaled fastball feats. Most recently, Yoenis Céspedes had also burst onto the West Coast baseball scene in Oakland with his own notable slugging exploits. Furthermore, Chapman had already anticipated Puig when it came to headline-grabbing off-field misadventures (soon a Puig backstory).

By the time Puig arrived in LA, Cuban defectors were no longer mere occasional blips on the big-league scene or novel causes for celebration in the ideological war against Castro's communist regime. It had long been a part of American media policy to cheer on the Cuban baseball defector as more of a political and ideological story than simply old-hat news from the humdrum sports world. Cold war political values could be trumpeted with each and every new defection, especially if the ballplayers were known stars from Fidel's showcase championship national team. MLB lust for available Cuban talent was growing more rapidly as it became apparent that the Cuban system was finally cracking. Fernandomania and Nomomania had both been strictly baseball stories that never stretched very far beyond the sports pages and thus were never truly relevant for a national media occupied by more weighty matters. Puig suddenly seemed the centerpiece for a much larger story that was equal parts baseball news, anti-Castro politics, and a long-awaited and politically tinged MLB takeover of Cuba's coveted baseball dynasty. Public attention would only skyrocket nine-plus months later, once unsavory issues of alleged human trafficking unexpectedly became the new focus of media interest in Puigmania.

* * *

The saga of Yasiel Puig begins in the Netherlands, in the port city of Rotterdam, as have so many of the defection stories. Chapman's earlier convoluted path to the big leagues had also begun there only two summers earlier, when the flame-throwing southpaw walked away from team headquarters in the newly opened Blijdorp Hotel on the eve of the July 2009 World Port Tournament. Future San Diego Padres starter Odrisamer Despaigne's own escape tale would also involve Rotterdam, when the Industriales ace skipped out on the Cuban team at the Paris Charles de Gaulle Airport in transit to the 2013 edition of the same event. The more recent convoluted saga of Yoan Moncada would also have its roots in the same Dutch city and unfold in the same plush hotel that had proved a launching pad for Chapman's celebrated flight to the big leagues. But no defection story is more directly rooted in Rotterdam than the one involving Puig during the summer of 2011. And Puig's tale was—next perhaps only to El Duque's—the most dramatic, intrigue-filled, and well-publicized of them all.

Puig's ball-playing talents and phenomenal athletic skills were first called to my attention back in Cuba by veteran television and print media journalist Jesus "Jeli" Valmaña, who had long covered the junior-level national teams for the communist press. The super-talented teenager had been a virtual phenomenon at the 18-U and 16-U youth league levels, as had Dayan Viciedo several years earlier and as would Yoan Moncada only a few more years down the road.[2] Valmaña was one of the earliest to report that Puig was indeed a multifaceted athlete possessing all five coveted tools (running speed, arm strength, ability to hit for average, power hitting, and fielding adeptness) and therefore clearly destined for can't-miss stardom. What remained unreported early on were such intangibles as raw baseball intelligence and personal maturity.

But for all his early promise, Puig's Cuban League career began on a relatively quiet note. His rookie campaign (2008–09) was plagued by minor injuries, although he did put up respectable numbers (.276 BA, 5 homers, and 74 total bases in 70 of his team's 90 games), and his 11 outfield assists gave hints of a cannon arm that would eventually terrorize big-league base runners. If Puig's arrival was somewhat muted, there was plenty of optimism surrounding his Cienfuegos ball club, a team that already boasted a solid mound corps fronted by veteran southpaw Norberto González, a potent offense anchored by emerging twenty-two-year-old first baseman José Dariel Abreu, and flashy shortstop defense from a third talented youngster, Erisbel Arruebarrena. Then the muscular outfielder's nagging hamstring problems intervened and he was forced to the sidelines for the entire 2009–2010 season, the same year Abreu would surge to the forefront with the first of three consecutive thirty-plus home run explosions. Puig's absence remained something of a mystery, since the nature of his injury was never officially defined and sparse Cuban press coverage rarely comments on such details.[3]

The hiatus was brief and Puig returned with a vengeance for Cuba's celebrated Golden Anniversary National Series of 2010–2011. With its entire trio of exceptional novices back in the fold, Cienfuegos surged to its best finish ever, outdistancing all teams in regular-season victories and surviving until a postseason collapse during a semifinal series with eventual champion Pinar del Río. Puig flashed some renewed brilliance with an 89-game .330 BA and the club's second-best power performance (17 homers). He also trailed only Abreu among his teammates in both total bases (190) and slugging percentage (.581). It was the anticipated breakout campaign Valmaña and others on the scene had predicted, and it provided a special showcase moment during the early February All-Star Game festivities staged on Puig's home turf at the Cienfuegos Fifth of September Stadium. In the Sunday afternoon All-Star Game itself, the flashy outfielder contributed five RBIs during his Occidental (Western) squad's thirteen-inning 15–13 defeat. And in the traditional "Abilities Trials" which are an annual feature of Cuban All-Star festivities, he won the dash to first base (3.56 seconds) and dash around the base paths (14.13 seconds).[4] With his brief league career rapidly nearing its end, that festive All-Star outing would constitute Puig's finest two days on a Cuban baseball diamond.

The breakout performance in the Golden Anniversary National Series earned Puig his first shot at a senior-level national team traveling overseas—the B-level club heading to Rotterdam for the odd-year World Port Tournament event that had been a regular Team Cuba stop for several decades. The Cuban squad selected for this particular trip and managed by Roger Machado was surprisingly solid—given the lesser status of the small-scale Rotterdam event—and actually featured a half-dozen players that would also eventually impact more prestigious A-level national squads.[5] Portly pitcher Yadier Pedroso turned in a top performance that week in Rotterdam as the tournament MVP in a losing cause. Future big leaguers Rusney Castillo, Alexander Guerrero, Erisbel Arruebarrena, and Dalier Hinojosa were all included in a roster also featuring future defectors (and eventual minor leaguers) Yoilán Cerce, Misael Siverio, and rookie-of-the-year pitcher Gerardo Concepción. Concepción—a future bust as a minor-league prospect in the Cubs organization—would in fact jump the Cuban party as soon as it arrived in the Dutch city, before the first tournament pitch was ever thrown. But it was clearly Puig who attracted the small gang of big-league scouts (and smaller contingent of opportunistic player agents, among them Jaime Torres) that eagerly flocked to the scene.[6]

Rotterdam is always a coveted assignment for Cuban players. Trips to the minor tournaments like those in Rotterdam (on odd calendar years) and Haarlem (even years) provide not only baseball proving grounds but also rare opportunities to access coveted material items. Organized shopping excursions on the one free day in the tournament schedule (with the players bussed to a nearby mall for several hours of unsupervised hoarding) become a major focus of any Netherlands visit. As London-native Gawain Owen, a devoted Team Cuba follower during the team's European tours, has deftly phrased it in private conversations with this author, the trips to the Netherlands become "shopping mall outings interrupted by the necessity of playing a half-dozen baseball games." Owen questions whether the players' minds and hearts are always quite as focused on the baseball business at hand as might be desired when traveling in Holland.[7]

It is this reality that reveals a most ugly side of Cuban baseball. The players are adored like celebrity rock stars on these trips, especially in Europe and Asia, and are hounded in the hotel lobbies and ballpark concourses to sell their coveted game-worn Team Cuba jerseys. They are also allowed by team officials to stow boxes of cigars they might peddle to earn a meager allowance of shopping money. A common market for the cigars is often found among the crowds of MLB scouts shadowing the team. A goal for these players is to acquire sufficient euros or US dollars to purchase not only highly desired cell phones or laptops but also scarce household goods and clothing for wives, children, or other extended family members. Pre-arranged shopping trips during the team's single open date have now become common—a single concession to players' personal needs that constitutes a rather recent innovation of Cuban national team travels—and players are given surprising freedom on these controlled outings to roam the city center shopping districts in Rotterdam or Haarlem, as well as in Asian ports of call.[8]

On the morning of the planned shopping outing during the 2011 tournament, I was also in the downtown district enjoying my own time away from the park on Cuba's one free day in the playing schedule. Quite by accident I ran across a group of players out on their shopping adventure. This group included infielders Donald Duarte and William Saavedra, members of the Pinar del Río team and friends over the years during my regular visits to Cuba and to the Pinar ballpark. The trio of players begged my assistance, since they spoke neither Dutch nor English and were thus struggling to negotiate their shopping purchases. I rather reluctantly joined in, against my better judgment but out of some strong sense of obligation. The young men spent several hours in discount outlets featuring mainly athletic gear, loading up on all the cut-price sneakers ("tennis shoes" in the Cuban vernacular), T-shirts, and trinkets their budgets would allow. We eventually parted ways without my encountering any of the other groups of ballplayers also wandering downtown.

It was that same morning that a reported incident took place involving Puig. I knew nothing about it at the time and have uncovered no solid verifications or revealing details since. But subsequent events and piecemeal information suggest that the story is at least somewhere near the truth. Perhaps with very little cash on hand, Puig is rumored to have removed some unspecified items from a Rotterdam shop without paying. Rather introverted, he likely had peddled few if any cigar boxes and hadn't accumulated as much pocket money as most teammates.[9] This is one of the tragedies of the Cuban ballplayer's life. Some have poor luck in raising funds at the ballpark to support their deep-seated shopping wishes. Cuban cigars no longer sell well in Holland, largely an antismoking country and a location where Cuban cigars or Cuban rum can be purchased openly in the village shops. There are also always great pressures from back home to supply family necessities, even in the current era of increased tourism on the island and thus at least slight improvement in the Cuban economy. Sometimes the temptation not to leave for home empty handed is simply too great.

This plight of the Cuban ballplayer traveling overseas is at best a poorly kept secret. Liván Hernández would speak eloquently in the 2014 "Brothers in Exile" film about struggles he experienced attempting to acquire small items necessary for survival back home. He also admitted that the restrictions placed on players by zealous Cuban security officers who blocked those attempts in the name of revolutionary zeal were a major factor in his decision to desert. If there is an ugly side to the Cuban baseball system, for me it is found here. The evil is not that the players are expected to perform solely for love of country and flag and not for any sorely needed material compensation. That seems more admirable than truly destructive. The distortion enters when the ideals of revolutionary purity are pushed so far that players are expected to give blood and sweat to win glory for the nation while at the same time lacking even enough material reward to survive somewhat comfortably at home. These are among the world's best baseball players—some worth millions of dollars in the MLB marketplace—and yet they struggle often hopelessly to purchase an extra set of footwear for a child or wife back home, to acquire a simple cell phone that might not even meet the needs of an average American teenager, or to purchase a beer or snack in the team's European or Asian hotel lobby.

While the Puig story was quietly unfolding, there was also another tangentially related development transpiring on the domestic front in Cuba. I would be among the first off the island to know about a simultaneously emerging story concerning the flight of an even more substantial national team centerpiece, Yoenis Céspedes. At midweek, on the eve of the ballplayers' shopping excursion, I crossed paths with manager Roger Machado enjoying a quick late-night beer at the small hotel bar. After initial pleasantries Machado quietly inquired if I had heard any news about what had just happened back on the island. He then proceeded to inform me that Céspedes had abandoned the pre-selection team training in Havana, had somehow been involved in a fatal automobile accident that had supposedly taken the life of a bicyclist, and had apparently fled justice and was now a fugitive in hiding. The story circulating at the time maintained that Céspedes had been upset by not being sent with the pre-selection group traveling to the preferred Rotterdam destination. Fresh off a career season in which he had led the league in homers (actually tied with Abreu) and RBIs, he believed he deserved that Holland trip and not the one bound for Caracas (which constituted little more than staying in

Havana). Details would later suggest the scenario was much more complicated than what was first rumored, or even what was later publicly reported.

Meanwhile, back in Rotterdam, Puig would suit up for the final championship game, a do-or-die match with spunky Chinese Taipei. Unsubstantiated rumor would latter maintain he had been apprehended by Dutch authorities at the time of the alleged shoplifting incident and quietly turned over to the Cuban camp without publicity. Dutch baseball officials needed the Cubans at their tournaments (it was the Cubans that drew the largest crowds to the park) and worked overtime to guard their warm relationship with the Cuban Federation.[10] Whatever the actual scenario was, Puig was allowed to play and any possible incident away from the park remained well off the radar. Puig would come up big in that final game, although the Cubans would lose a heartbreaker in extra innings and thus squander the championship. While Yadier Pedroso turned in six innings of heroic relief on the heels of an eight-inning outing two days earlier, Puig provided most of the offense with a triple, double, and single, knocking home one of the four Cuban runs and himself scoring two others. It would also be the final game Puig would play in a Team Cuba uniform. Upon return home he would be unceremoniously dropped from his league team for what was announced only as a gross disciplinary infraction committed while on the road in Holland.

Much speculation later arose that the prize outfielder had attempted to defect while the team was still on the ground in the Netherlands, but I was around the ball club until immediately before their airport departure and saw no evidence of any such attempt. Was there a defection attempt, or was there actually a shoplifting incident and a resulting run-in with local law enforcement?[11] Could both have occurred? These remain open questions. Players would later simply deflect the issue or rather unconvincingly claim ignorance when I raised the question back in Cuba. Puig understandably never spoke about the matter. Defection was the more popular theme with US media and that was the story that usually circulated.

Puig himself would remain in limbo in Cuba for the next eleven months. There would later be numerous reports of several failed attempts at illegal exit before he was finally able to leave the island in late April of 2012. Once successfully out of Cuba it was only weeks before the five-tool prospect landed his windfall contract with the Dodgers, a $42 million seven-year package reportedly orchestrated in a Mexico City hotel room by Logan White, Dodgers vice president for international scouting. (Of course a lot had transpired during the two months in Mexico, as we will see below.) The trigger on the lucrative deal (signed on June 28, 2012, with original Puig agent Jaime Torres now on the scene) had to be pulled quickly because of pending MLB restrictions limiting international signings to a maximum of $2.9 million.

Journalist Gwen Knapp one year later sketched the Dodgers' subsequent harried efforts to ready their prize prospect for North American professional baseball.[12] Tim Bravo, the team's director of cultural assimilation, had the original assignment of chaperoning Puig, translating for him, providing English instruction, and shepherding him through a difficult culture adjustment. The Oakland A's were simultaneously employing a similar process with new signee Yoenis Céspedes and had hired former hurler Ariel Prieto for the assignment. (Prieto would eventually take on a similar task for the Arizona D-Backs with 2015 rookie Yasmany Tomás.) When personal issues—school and his son's cancer treatments—obligated Bravo to leave the post, former Cuban big-league pitcher Eddie Oropesa, another early defector, inherited the assignment of handling and grooming Puig.

Before the end of the 2012 season Yasiel Puig was making his minor-league debut in rather spectacular fashion, batting a combined .354 in two dozen games split between the Dodgers Arizona Rookie League ball club and their Advanced A League team at Rancho Cucamonga. But despite another fast start the following spring at AA Chattanooga, there were also early reports of immaturity and some worrisome off-field incidents. Most widely reported was an arrest by Chattanooga police for driving 90 mph in an urban 50 mph zone. It was enough of an alarm signal to have the Dodgers dispatch longtime coach Manny Mota for serious talks with the rebellious youth about "respect" for the game. Bravo also soon returned as Puig's constant companion, translator, and around-the-clock handler.

* * *

If there were early problems they were largely dwarfed by early promise. Few Cuban defectors have enjoyed a faster track to the big leagues. And none beyond Abreu would ever enjoy a more sensational month-long debut once he got there. Yasiel Puig literally rewrote several pages of the team and league record books during his first heady month in the lineup of the Los Angeles big-league club. He would post remarkable numbers and produce even more spectacular highlight film clips with acrobatic outfield catches and laser-beam throws. He became the first Cuban ever to garner National League rookie-of-the-month honors (a feat duplicated that same month by José Iglesias in the junior circuit, and then by American Leaguer José Abreu three times in 2014, and the Dodgers' Alex Guerrero, again in April 2015). At month's end (June 30), he barely missed equaling the debut-month hitting success of the legendary Yankee Clipper, Joe DiMaggio. His forty-four base knocks fell only four short of DiMaggio's standard set in May 1936 but did top the Dodgers club record held by Steve Sax (August 1983) for base hits in any month of a rookie campaign.

Not surprisingly, however, such a performance was impossible to sustain. But the remainder of the season was impressive enough in its own right. He missed out on making the National League All-Star squad by the slimmest of margins, finishing runner-up to Atlanta's Freddie Freeman during an innovative electronic fan ballot to fill his league's final roster slot. Final offensive numbers (19 homers and a .319 BA) were especially impressive given the late start that left him two months short of a full season. Ironically, Puig would lose out for league rookie-of-the-year selection to another Cuban defector, twenty-year-old Florida Marlins pitcher José D. Fernández. Fernández had garnered far less attention early in the year because his own harrowing escape story was at the time barely known to the public.

Fernández had also departed Cuba in search of a better life. But he was a mere teenager at the time and boasted little baseball experience and no reputation for promise in the sport. He had departed the island as a result of his parents' latent dreams instead of any personal visions of baseball stardom. And he would hone his skills not in the spotlight of the Cuban League but in the shadows on Tampa high school fields. Fernández was signed directly out of high school by the Marlins (first round, number fourteen pick) and had enjoyed his own fast-track to the majors. He experienced barely a year of minor-league grooming and jumped directly from A-ball in 2012 into the Marlins 2013 season-opening rotation. And on the heels of his stellar rookie season he would finally reveal details of his own April 2008 flight from the homeland. It was nearly as hair-raising a saga as the one that would eventually emerge five years later featuring his fellow 2013 big-league rookie, Yasiel Puig. All that was missing in the Fernández case was the high-stakes kidnapping of a ballplayer already perceived as a multimillion-dollar gold mine.

Fernández had grown up in Santa Clara, where he began his love affair with baseball before he was five. As revealed in the tale he would later spin for Grantland.com writer Jordan Ritter Conn, his family's defection was a complicated story filled not only with the normal doses of drama, but also with its full share of strange twists and turns.[13] The effort was launched when his stepfather finally decided to leave after being denied permission to join a medical mission bound for Venezuela (as a trained medical technician he had been labeled a defection risk). Ramón Jiménez paid smugglers $1,000 for his own illegal transport and finally reached Tampa after a dozen failed attempts. He was eventually able to save enough money from his new employment to arrange a similar escape plan for his wife and stepson. The efforts of José and his mother Maritza also were at first unsuccessful and the fourteen-year-old José would find himself spending several months in prison detention alongside hardened criminals and other failed defectors. He was finally freed after turning fifteen and the defection attempts were quickly renewed, with more desperation than ever.

The final escape route would involve boarding a speedboat off the southern coast near Trinidad with his mother, stepsister, and eight others. The group was transferred to a larger houseboat used to ferry ransomed refugees to Cancún. The several days at sea were difficult and terror-filled, as might be expected, and nearly ended in tragedy when Maritza was swept overboard by a sudden squall. She was rescued only through the brave efforts of her athletic teenage son. The adventures continued after they reached Mexico, where the family members were put on a bus bound for the US border. Yet another frightening episode occurred when they were stopped by apparent gangsters posing as Mexican police. They were randomly and inexplicably released and finally reached the border town of Reynosa. The trio then crossed routinely into Texas and as dry-foot Cuban refugees were soon reunited with Ramón Jiménez in Tampa.

Puig's own rookie campaign was not entirely a feel-good story. There were reports (sometimes only rumors) of off-the-field incidents rivaling those earlier involving Aroldis Chapman in Cincinnati. The self-possessed Cuban's style of play and on-field bravado would also rub some of his teammates and opposing players the wrong way. (Bat tossing after base hits and failing to run hard to first on routine grounders were signs of Cuban swagger but perceived as "bush league" by the major leaguers.) To fans he seemed to reinforce the stilted stereotype of the flamboyant "hot dog" style Cuban ballplayer. It was far more a stereotype than a reality—there were other Cuban big leaguers who didn't play that way. But admittedly the flashy rookie did often perform with an over-the-top passion and a flamboyance that is often noted as a trademark of the Cuban approach to the game.

The true underbelly of the Puig saga would not be exposed until nearly a year after the breakout season in Los Angeles. The hidden story would begin to unravel with a sensational investigative article penned for *Los Angeles* magazine by Jesse Katz.[14] In a startling exposé, Katz would reveal details of just how Puig finally escaped Cuba, plus the harrowing adventures encountered once he reached an island destination near the coast of Mexico. There the ballplayer and his three companions (Yunior Despaigne, an unidentified girlfriend, and a santero brought along as a hedge against evil) had been made virtual prisoners of the Zeta cartel handlers who had first ferried them to a shabby hotel on Isla Mujeres near Cancún, then quickly jacked up the original fees they were demanding for their valuable hostage. A Keystone Kops adventure—but one with serious consequences—would then transpire. Small-time Miami gangster Raúl Pacheco had originally arranged the smuggling operation that was in turn carried out by Zeta operative Tomás Valez Valdivia (aka Tomasito). The price had been set at $250,000, but once the group reached Isla Mujeres, Pacheco was having difficulty raising the funds and thus so far hadn't delivered. Puig remained a prisoner in the interim and there were reports that he was constantly threatened with bodily injury (such as having his fingers chopped off) by his increasingly frustrated and unpaid captors.

The whole affair came to light when Puig's traveling companion, former boxer Yunior Despaigne (the original contact with Pacheco and the one-time friend who initially convinced Puig to make his April 2012 break from Cuba), seemingly grew frustrated in Miami after never seeing his own promised payoffs. Despaigne, who had been receiving death threats in the aftermath of the affair from Tomasito and his Zeta henchmen, elected in September 2013 (eighteen months after the defection) to visit the office of Miami lawyer Avelino González, who at the time was already building a case against Aroldis Chapman on behalf of a Cuban-American falsely imprisoned in Cuba as the result of Chapman's alleged testimonies to Cuban authorities (see chapter 4). The same lawyer had also recently filed a similar civil lawsuit against Puig, alleging that he too had earlier falsely accused an innocent man in Cuba of smuggling activities in order to buy his own reinstatement with baseball officials and cover his tracks before another defection attempt.[15] Despaigne figured that by spilling the whole story of Puig's defection he could purchase his own protection and perhaps gain a bit of revenge on those like Pacheco who had not delivered as promised. Despaigne's testimony would aid González's planned legal actions against Puig. And it would also now blow the cover off the mysteries surrounding Puig's travels in Mexico and thus provide the basis for breaking stories like the one published by Katz.

In the immediate aftermath of the Katz exposé, I would share a CBS morning news slot with the article's author. Katz was pressed on air about the meaning of his story and asked directly if this was not a tale of human trafficking and thus a huge embarrassment for big-league ball clubs willing to sanction such activities, if only by their silence if not by their complicity in throwing million-dollar contracts at players and agents involved with smuggling rings. Katz replied that indeed there simply was no other way to frame or label it. I would also write my own follow-up piece that same week for the *Daily Beast*, an article in which I extended an identical theme.[16] There now seemed to be substantial evidence that MLB was facing an ugly incident of human trafficking in the explosive Puig case.

Almost simultaneously Scott Eden produced a more detailed story in *ESPN The Magazine*, further elaborating and even correcting the Los Angeles publication.[17] If Katz had registered the scoop through the accident of publication deadlines, it was Eden who laid out much of the backstory, explaining events in Cuba that had preceded the flight of Yasiel Puig. Eden would also go into far greater detail about subsequent events in Mexico. Readers should approach the original article for full details that only need summarizing here. What is perhaps most intriguing in Eden's rendering of the story is a revelation that Puig might not only have been involved previously as an informer aiding Cuban authorities seeking out human traffickers operating on the island, but that the ballplayer might also much later (as a Dodger) have arranged a sting that would land Yunior Despaigne's half-brother Eduardo Soriano in a Cuban prison for alleged ballplayer smuggling activities.[18]

The remainder of Puig's misadventure in Mexico played out something like the following, as Eden details it. While Pacheco struggled to arrange funds needed to purchase Puig's release, another Miami operative known only as "El Rubio" had entered the picture and had begun dealing directly with Tomasito in Isla Mujeres. Unwilling to pay the ransom price that Tomasito had now elevated from $250,000 to $400,000, El Rubio and his associates hit on an ingenious plan of their own. The new Miami group arranged their own audacious heist and managed rather easily to corral the four hostages from Tomasito's incompetent henchmen, who had carelessly left the group temporarily unguarded. Then, despite the lack of any passports or legal Mexican entry documents, they had arranged (likely through bribes) to have the Cubans flown to Mexico City. The Zeta group had been left holding the bag and to this day remains a worrisome threat to the safety of both Puig and Yunior Despaigne. Once in Mexico City, Puig was handed over to agent Jaime Torres and some mid-June showcase workouts were hastily arranged for interested teams (reportedly the Cubs, White Sox, Braves, and Yankees, as well as the Dodgers). Torres only allowed Puig to take limited batting practice, banning any running or throwing, as he didn't want to risk injury to his valuable prospect, who was clearly short on conditioning after a three-month ordeal and previous year-long suspension in Cuba. But it mattered little since the Dodgers were already committed to gambling heavily on Puig's potential.

These were the kinds of details that those championing defectors as heroic pursuers of the American Dream didn't want to read and didn't want to talk about. The story was no longer simple and it no longer fit an MLB-orchestrated script. That human trafficking might be involved was no longer in question. Some would contend in emails and Facebook messages addressed to me personally that the Puig case and others like it could not be defined as human trafficking or even smuggling if those being transported were willing participants. But that is to badly misunderstand (at best) and purposely misconstrue (at worst) what human trafficking actually is—transporting people illegally across national borders and doing so for a profit. And if athletes like Puig (and earlier Leonys Martin) willingly left home, it is now clear that they were not willing participants in the hostage-taking events that followed once they reached Mexico.

It had long been easy to portray a patented "Cuban baseball defector" story in the positive light of heroic flights to personal freedom and the unlimited opportunities of American free enterprise. This was the story line long pushed by Joe Cubas and other flag-waving and profiteering ballplayer agents who followed in Cubas's footsteps. It was also the favored headline story of a jingoistic American press corps. But now that easy, feel-good story had been heavily tainted at best and totally exploded at worst. There was now another far uglier side to the tale. And it appeared to be an extremely sordid and even frightening one. It would also soon prove to be the case that Yasiel Puig was only the tip of the iceberg.

* * *

Leonys Martin's story unfolded a few years earlier, and in retrospect it was almost eerily parallel to the adventure surrounding Yasiel Puig. Much of the same plotline exists—the high-speed cigarette boat ride into Mexico arranged by profiteering smugglers, captivity in Mexico by criminals seeking to cash in on a portion of an expected big-league contract. There were also threats of personal harm and an eventual harrowing escape from captivity that promised to sabotage the dream of someday reaching a big-league stadium.

In August 2010 Martin illegally fled Cuba along with members of his family, departing in a forty-five-foot yacht from an undisclosed location along the northern coast near their home in Villa Clara Province. The party included Martin's father and both his and his father's girlfriends. Leonys was one of the league's better outfielders—a solid hitter who tied Yoandy Garlobo for the league batting crown in 2008 (barely missing out on a .400 season at .398)—and had played on a couple top editions of the national team (including on the 2009 World Baseball Classic) as a backup defensive specialist. He had always posted excellent offensive numbers, although he didn't display a strong power-hitting game. But he definitely had a big-league future, something he knew and those arranging his departure also knew.

Having survived the perilous boat trip, the family was sped to a coastal house, where they initially thought they had reached freedom. But a different fate lay in store. They were taken into custody by a pair of heavily armed gangsters—later identified as Cubans Eliezer Lazo and Joel Martínez Hernández—who announced that Martin was worth big bucks and they were not going to let him go until they were able to fully cash in. The ballplayer was subsequently held for several months in Mexico while his family was removed to Miami—to a house owned by Lazo—where, without proper US entry papers, they were under the constant surveillance of their captors.

Leonys Martin while still with the Cuban League Villa Clara club in 2008. Courtesy of Byron Motley.

Martin himself was moved to a complex in Monterrey, where he was confined with three earlier defectors from Isla de la Juventud—pitcher Israel Soto, outfielder Luis Fonseca, and catcher Joan Chaviano. Martin was then introduced to agent Bart Hernandez (a partner in the Miami Praver-Shapiro Agency) and was told by Lazo and Martínez Hernández that the new agent would now be acting as his official representative. Martin would later contend he never formally agreed to any representation by Bart Hernández and only acquiesced at the time out of fear for his family's safety. Only after Martin (seemingly under duress) agreed to a $15.5 million deal with the Texas Rangers, orchestrated by Bart Hernández, was he at last free to travel to the United States and enjoy a temporary reunion with his family in Miami.

Less than a year after his September 2011 debut with the Rangers, Martin was being sued by the Mexico-based sports agency Estrellas del Baseball (an apparent front for his original captors), which now claimed the ballplayer had not completed his agreement with them two years earlier. The agency claimed he had not paid all it was owed for arranging his escape, and later for housing and feeding both him and his family being forcibly held in Miami.[19] EDB (the agency acronym) claimed Martin had paid it $1.2 million but still owed an additional $450,000 after agreeing to pay the company 35 percent of his future baseball earnings.

In the wake of these latest revelations, former player agent Joe Kehoskie, earlier involved in the defection of Yunel Escobar, as detailed below, but now working as a private sports consultant, would explain to the online news outlet Yahoo Sports precisely how smugglers operated in cases like the one involving Martin. Kehoskie would offer further details that exposed the underbelly of the smuggling operations involving dozens, if not hundreds, of Cuban ballplayers. Still an active agent in 2011, Kehoskie had himself traveled to Monterrey to meet with Lazo and Martínez Hernández and was offered a $90,000 package consisting of the three other Cubans training with Martin at the EDB facility known as the Ranch. He turned down the deal, he told Yahoo Sports, not wishing to work with known smugglers.[20] But Bart Hernández and the Praver-Shapiro Agency appeared not to have such reservations. Details of the Martin lawsuit also made strong connections between traffickers and MLBPA-certified agents who indisputably (as the Puig and Martin cases reveal) work as their partners in the peddling of Cuban players to big-league ball clubs.

Martin would respond to the EDB suit with legal action of his own, filing a civil suit in Miami courts (handled by Paul Minoff of the GrayRobinson law firm) that sought return of $1.2 million already paid to EDB (but only under duress, according to Martin). Martin's suit and its eventual results would supplement the revelations surrounding Puig and throw more light on the widespread extent of ballplayer smuggling operations. One direct outcome was federal charges leveled against Eliezer Lazo (already serving a five-year prison term for Medicare fraud), formally accused of masterminding a human-trafficking ring that had smuggled more than a thousand Cubans out of their homeland and into Mexico. In late August 2014 Lazo would plead guilty to extortion charges, and he now faces as much as an additional twenty years behind bars. One revelation of the Lazo trial was a little-kept secret that while ballplayers are usually better treated because their market value hinges on physical prowess, many other Cubans were beaten, tortured, otherwise abused, and even murdered during the course of smuggling operations. Another outcome was the seizure of cars, property, and bank accounts belonging to Lazo and his Mexican baseball academy "cover" operations.

The Martin case and the Puig story, which would break only a few months before the Miami sentencing of Lazo, both have serious consequences for MLB, even if big-league voices have remained silent or tried to distance themselves from the most uncomfortable facts. There has never been any suggestion that big-league clubs or their representatives (scouts or general managers) have been directly involved in encouraging human trafficking. There has so far been no breaking scandal like the one that involved kickbacks for pocketing ballplayers' bonus money that sunk a number of MLB scouts operating in the Dominican Republic a decade back. But it is just as clear that MLB officials have simply looked the other way. They have supported a popular line that Cuban athletes are prisoners of an evil communist government, and that in opening big-league doors the MLB clubs are only offering "freedom" and a piece of the American Dream.

But it is not that simple. Those Americans who buy or use cocaine on US street corners are as guilty of supporting the crime syndicates that plague Mexico as are any of the frontline drug runners or street dealers themselves. Those who visit prostitutes smuggled into US cities by an illegal sex trade are just as guilty of aiding and abetting sex slavery as the smugglers themselves. It is not a stretch, then, to question the ethics of

MLB clubs paying out enormous sums for defecting Cuban ballplayers when those multimillion-dollar contracts keep Cuban, Mexican, and Miami human traffickers in lucrative business. MLB's billion-dollar entertainment industry does not have entirely clean hands here.

As Scott Eden suggested in his *ESPN The Magazine* treatment, if big-league officials didn't want to know about human-trafficking abuses, the American legal apparatus clearly did. By the winter of 2014 federal authorities were already reportedly interviewing Cuban players on a broad scale about their experiences in leaving their homeland. Investigators from both the US Department of Homeland Security and the Federal Bureau of Investigation were taking part in an expanding probe. The dual investigations were code-named Operation Safety Squeeze and Operation Boys of Summer. MLB authorities remained ever silent as embarrassing circumstances grew up around them. Players were told by the office of the commissioner, by their teams, and by their agents not to talk with the media about their earlier defection attempts. But the players continued to come forward despite any such warnings. Henry Urrutia, for one, would speak openly before ESPN cameras for an *Outside the Lines* segment that first aired in April of 2015 and focused on recent defections at the San Juan Caribbean Series.

Yunel Escobar that same spring would also be unfolding his own tale to the Washington press after he joined the Nationals roster.[21] He had spoken earlier of his sudden decision to flee Cuba while a twenty-one-year-old second-string shortstop with the Havana Industriales, the league's most storied and popular team. It was a move that caught even his family by surprise. He had also revealed his early admiration for a number of big-league stars (Ken Griffey Jr. tops among them) and how his attempt to imitate their batting styles and uniform dress on the field had gotten him into trouble early in his career with his Cuban manager, Rey Anglada. But it was only recently that he revealed the true backstory of his fateful flight from his childhood home in Havana.

There are elements in the expanded tale that bear eerie similarity to some details surrounding more recent top prospect Yoan Moncada (chapter 8). Sometime in the early 2000s Escobar befriended an American women of Peruvian heritage who, at the time, was visiting Havana from Miami, and the two would soon begin casual dating, though she was five years his senior (shades of Moncada and Nicole Banks in 2013). It was not long before she was encouraging him to leave the island and putting him in touch with Miami player agent Joe Kehoskie. A plot was eventually hatched, and on September 24, 2004, Escobar and several teammates snuck away from Havana under cover of night. The players had all faked injuries to explain their absence from practice on the day they disappeared.[22] So guarded was the plot that Escobar never informed his parents, living in the city's Marianao district, that he was leaving.

What followed was another harrowing tale of traversing shark-infested waters. The group had promised a customary fee of $10,000 apiece to their smugglers, money they obviously didn't have but that was likely arranged by Kehoskie and his backers. The ballplayers were quickly added to another group of departing refugees and the combined group, totaling thirty-six in all, made one unsuccessful attempt to depart from the northern coast (it was scrubbed by bad weather) and then was transported to a different remote location before setting out on the rough three-day passage towards Miami. The group was eventually left on a deserted island near Key West on October 4, where they were subsequently picked up by the US Coast Guard. Once reaching Miami and passing through the loose immigration entry point at the Krome detention center, the players were transported to a Miami residence where they lived secluded with the smugglers for another eight months.

The scenario became more complicated when the smugglers insisted on moving the players back out of the United States to take advantage of the third-country provision that would allow signings for higher initial bonus contracts. But Escobar and his companions refused to depart from American soil that they had risked so much to reach. Kehoskie eventually reentered the picture, but refused to pay an additional $200,000 to liberate the six from the now increasingly desperate smugglers. With expenses mounting, the original handlers decided to dump the players on the 2005 free agent draft, where the Braves grabbed Escobar in the second round. When his new agent, Bart Hernandez, was able to arrange a $475,000 contract with Atlanta, Yunel Escobar eventually settled accounts with his handlers to the tune of $50,000, a fee covering the entire group of six ballplayers. Yunel would also eventually pay more than $70,000 to other smuggling groups in order to arrange the transport of his remaining seven family members out of Cuba. The original smugglers, for their part, would eventually all end up in a Miami prison on unrelated charges.

Most recently Adeiny Hechevarría also spoke candidly about personal defection adventures with *USA Today* reporter Jorge Ortiz.[23] Hechevarría had left Cuba alongside Leslie Anderson and Rudy Silva in 2009 and was quite open about the fact that human traffickers had arranged the harrowing adventure that turned out to be just as life threatening as so many others. Anderson, a product of Camagüey, had been a starting first baseman on the WBC team only a few months earlier and would play several seasons of AAA-level baseball for the Tampa Bay organization before winding up with the Tokyo Giants of the Japanese Central League. Silva was a promising young outfielder for Habana Province who would sign on with the Red Sox but then struggle to climb out of the low minor leagues. Hechevarría, the true diamond in the rough among the trio, would soon sign a lucrative free agent deal with Toronto and steadily emerge over several seasons as one of the best defensive shortstops in the big leagues.

The Marlins shortstop would offer few specifics about his arrangements with the smugglers who orchestrated his own escape in Mexico. But he did indicate he was rather obviously lied to about the dangers involved in the high seas journey on a thirty-foot cigarette boat of the type normally used by the *lancheros* (standard Spanish name for the launch operators). He was silent and evasive on the kind of deal he had struck with his smugglers and also about the percentage they eventually got from his original four-year $10 million contract with the Blue Jays.

Over the past two decades the highly lucrative industry of Cuban ballplayer defection and high-stakes Cuban ballplayer smuggling has evolved through two separate stages. While the two phases are somewhat distinct in both sophistication and modus operandi, they both grew from the same perceived opportunities offered by flawed American business and political practices. They were, in the end, similar efforts to exploit opportunities all too easily offered up by the still existing inanities of failed Washington and Havana cold war policies, by flaws in the MLB collective bargaining agreement that treated non-US and non-Puerto Rico-born athletes as unrestricted free agents, and, perhaps more than anything else, by the ongoing lust of MLB team officials and scouting departments for boatloads of new talent obtained at just about any cost.

Phase One, known as "The Joe Cubas Plan"—launched in the summer of 1995 with the opportunistic agent's enticements of pitchers Ozzie Fernández and Liván Hernández (chapter 5)—was born out of Cubas's ingenious assessment that huge sums of money could be made simply by convincing players to abandon Cuba and then whisking them away to some foreign port (in Cubas's case it was usually the Dominican Republic) in order to establish the required third-country residence demanded for free agency. It was a relatively low-tech operation, since Cubas's tools were cell phones, rented vans (which he hoped to fill with dozens of prized ball-playing refugees), boatloads of cash to entice his prospects, and hotel stakeouts adjacent to Team Cuba lodgings in the United States, Canada, Mexico, and even Japan. Cubas didn't operate within Cuba itself, which he saw as far too dangerous. But he did have help on the inside through his cousin Juan Ignacio Hernández Nodar and his future short-term partner Thomas Cronin, both frequent Cuba travelers who maintained regular contacts with players in Havana (especially Orlando Hernández and Germán Mesa) and attempted on numerous occasions to entice them and a few others into leaving home.

The second more sophisticated and more deadly phase known as the *"Bolsa Negra"* ("Black Bag") involved the crime-syndicate-controlled and extremely high-tech human-trafficking ring that was first widely exposed in the case of Yasiel Puig but traced its roots back perhaps as many as fifteen years.[24] It featured highly specialized expertise in marine navigation, bribery, forgery, and money laundering, plus an intimate knowledge of complex immigration policies in several Caribbean Basin nations. The *"bolsa negra de béisbol"* (involving prized baseball prospects like Puig, Leonys Martin, Céspedes, Abreu, and numerous others) was an eventual and inevitable outgrowth of an established smuggling ring which promised to bring any Cuban off the island (usually through Mexico) whose family connections in Miami were willing to pay a going rate (usually $10,000 a head). This was an extremely dangerous enterprise that involved numerous captures and imprisonments in Cuba, countless double crosses and dead bodies on the streets of Mexico, and hundreds if not thousands of stranded Cuban refugees in Mexican coastal cities like Cancún. But for those wishing to flee Cuba it seemed less risky than journeys across the treacherous Straits of Florida on flimsy garage-built rafts or non-seaworthy inner tubes. The focus became baseball players after the Cuban player market exploded in 2010 with a $30 million package dangled in front of Aroldis Chapman.

It was the bull market in Cuban prospects, dovetailed with the questionable ethics of North American baseball business operations, that was the underpinning cause and sustenance of North America's most profitable human trafficking operation. If it is all a dirty and dangerous business, for MLB ball clubs it seems to be one that is best ignored. Journalist Scott Eden provides an eye-opening quote from legendary Cuban-born Dodgers scout Mike Brito (directly involved in the signing of Puig) that captures the very heart of the matter: "How he got from Cuba, I don't care," remarked Brito. "I don't want to find out either. . . . Only thing we care about is when a guy is in a territory where we can sign him. Sign players and keep my mouth shut. The less you talk the less you get in trouble."[25] It is not a stretch to claim that Brito here speaks as the majority voice of Major League Baseball.

* * *

Puig and Martin—the most celebrated cases of cartel-connected human-trafficking victims—didn't have an exclusive corner on stories involving harrowing escapes across the high seas. Within three months of the Puig revelations details would also begin emerging about an even bigger island star risking his own life as well as those of family members in equally desperate efforts to flee Cuba. Only days after capturing a second Home Run Derby crown in Minneapolis and on the eve of his trade to Boston, Oakland slugger Yoenis Céspedes would provide a story to the *San Francisco Chronicle* that was remarkably similar and every bit as full of twists and turns.[26] The only difference in the end was the direction of the escape route.

The early accounts of Céspedes's problems with Cuban legal authorities turned out to be not quite accurate, at least not according to the personal accounts he provided to reporters once his family had been safely reunited stateside. There was indeed a fatal accident on the national highway in Granma Province, but the true circumstances were different from the ones first leaking out of Cuba. What also became clear in the end was that the accident was merely one unanticipated detour in a previously hatched escape plan. It was not, as some thought, the ballplayer's motive for fleeing in the first place, but only an unfortunate diversion.

Céspedes, like so many other modern-era Cuban Leaguers, was born into a baseball family and gifted with the athletic genes of his parents. His father, Cresencio Céspedes, was a former Cuban League catcher who had played only a single undistinguished season and had nothing like the talent his one offspring would eventually display. That father had also separated from his wife, Estela Milanés Sálazar, when his son was still an infant and was therefore never a presence during Yoenis's upbringing. Milanés was herself a skilled athlete, a talented pitcher on the women's national softball team and a participant in the 2000 Sydney Olympics. Her extended family would have a hand in raising her son while she traveled frequently to represent the country in international tournaments. But the doting mother did help mold her son as a ballplayer and coached him as a hitter in his preteen years. She even crafted his first crude bat out of a tree branch and carefully fashioned it by extensive polishing with a broken piece of glassware.

The youngster would develop rapidly into one of the country's top stars as a slugging outfielder with the Granma Province National Series team. By the mid-2000s he was teaming with Alfredo Despaigne to provided one of the league's top power duos. For a few seasons he was the more outstanding of the pair, debuting one year earlier (2003–04) with a solid .301 BA and then outdistancing Despaigne in homers during their first three joint seasons. He also reached the national team level ahead of his stellar teammate. In the second WBC (2009) Céspedes shone in the outfield alongside Freddie Cepeda as half of Cuba's top slugging duo. Cepeda and Céspedes were also the only Cubans tapped for the all-tournament team. He also starred in the September 2010 World Cup Qualifier in Puerto Rico, keying a vital win against Canada with a booming game-saving double. But his biggest season was the one immediately before his departure, when he tied José Abreu for the league lead in homers and also walked off with the league RBI crown. That latter achievement blocked Abreu from becoming Cuba's first National Series slugger to claim a still-elusive Triple Crown in batting.

As so often is the case, the promising ballplayer would make it out of Cuba ahead of his family. It was again only a matter of months (less than nine) before he was signed to a $36 million deal by Oakland in mid-February 2012. But the defection process itself was similar to but also a bit more complex than that of dozens of others. Fixers for agents operating in Latin America had approached the slugging star on numerous occasions over a period of several years, and he had always turned his back on them. But then Céspedes apparently had a sudden change of heart after what he took as an unwarranted snub left him stuck on a third-level training squad headed for exhibitions in Venezuela rather than on either of the World Cup pre-selection teams headed for Canada or Holland. It was at that point in July 2011 that he first made surreptitious contact with a Dominican-based agent named Edgar Mercedes. Inevitable steps leading toward defection then quickly took place.

The entire family put together elaborate plans for a secret illegal departure and rented a house on the coast near their Granma Province home as a potential staging area. Things then went horribly wrong when Cuban authorities, apparently alerted to the plot, apprehended Milanés Sálazar and several unidentified companions on a shoreline adjacent to the rented beach house. Yoenis was ensconced in a nearby car at the time and apparently witnessed his mother's arrest. He remained hidden in fear and spent at least one night sleeping in the vehicle. His mother was held for four days but refused to give up any information about her missing son's whereabouts.

It was at that point that Céspedes, apparently heading back to training camp in Havana in the wake of the busted escape plot, was involved in the freak accident on the national highway that resulted in the death of an aged bicyclist. Céspedes did not immediately flee as was earlier rumored, but complied with questioning by authorities and was quickly cleared of any culpability. The injured victim made a formal statement to authorities before succumbing to a heart attack and that statement was apparently enough to clear the ballplayer. But Yoenis, still hoping to flee, did not immediately return to the Havana training camp and instead told baseball officials that he was too upset by the accident to begin playing again immediately. That delay provided just enough time for the defection plot to be reorganized, and within a week Céspedes and six others were on a small boat bound for the nearby Dominican Republic.

Things didn't get much easier on a personal level for the prized ballplayer once he was free from Cuban clutches and being showcased by Mercedes for enthused MLB teams. In the wake of his own flight, several family members were detained at home for further interrogations and one was temporarily jailed. The ballplayer's mother and two female cousins were soon able to escape and join Céspedes in the Dominican, where the agent promptly set up the new arrivals in a rented house. But things only got more complicated after Céspedes signed his deal with Oakland, shortly after establishing official Dominican residence in January 2012, and then promptly departed for Arizona and spring training in March. The trio of family members was left behind without proper visas needed for US immigration. Their residence status in the Dominican also remained in limbo, and the group feared the worst—deportation back to Cuba.

Matters were further complicated when a bitter dispute arose between the ballplayer and his agent/smuggler over the precise cut that Mercedes would receive from the lucrative Oakland contract. Eventually the contentious issue was resolved by a Dominican court (Céspedes was ordered to pay Mercedes 22 percent after taxes) but not entirely to the satisfaction of either party. Stuck in the crossfire, Milanés later would report feeling threatened by her son's agent, who might have the power to sabotage all their visa hopes. It was at that point that Milanés and the other family members decided to risk another treacherous boat ride and try to reach US shores via one of the standard routes chosen by many fleeing Cuban rafters.

The ballplayer's family fled on a small boat financed by friends in Miami and headed for the Turks and Caicos islands, British territory 600 miles south of Miami and a known transfer point for Cubans and Haitians heading toward South Florida. Their subsequent adventure—as reported by the *San Francisco Chronicle*—would read like something scripted for a made-for-television docudrama, or even perhaps a popular primetime reality show. Joining the desperate family contingent were several additional cousins who had also found their way to the Dominican. The ten travelers on the vessel, one a baby, soon found themselves adrift at sea and finally became stranded on the small sandy strip of an uninhabited islet. Without food or water, they resorted to capturing a lone iguana in order to provide a sparse meal. The intrepid group was eventually rescued by a passing yacht, although details remain sketchy. Further complications arose once the family group (soon expanded to twelve with the arrival of another boat direct from Cuba) was settled at Turks and Caicos awaiting permission for legal US immigration. What followed was a mysterious arrest and more than 100 days of incarceration for several of the family members (including Milanés) in a refugee detention camp while British officials further investigated a suspected human-trafficking operation. Without much proof, Céspedes and Milanés suspected that former agent Mercedes had somehow been behind the arrests and detentions. It would then take nearly two more years for the family members to be reunited with the star ballplayer on American shores.

Other legal troubles were in the making as Céspedes struggled on the field during a second Oakland season that didn't measure up to his rookie summer. Cuba-based family members of the unfortunate Granma highway accident victim sought to file a lawsuit aimed at recovering damages from the now wealthy athlete, but the issue quietly died outside the Miami court system. The combined weight of off-field issues nonetheless seemed to impact on-field performances, and Céspedes was surprisingly dealt to Boston in the middle of a third Oakland season, only weeks after a second straight winning Home Run Derby performance at the MLB All-Star Weekend extravaganza. The layover in Boston at the end of the 2014 season—where he briefly teamed in the outfield with fellow Cuban Rusney Castillo—would prove shorter still, as he was traded again to Detroit in the off-season. Early in 2015, legal issues now apparently well behind him and his family safely established in Miami, Céspedes was again enjoying a pleasant career rebound in the heart of a Tiger lineup (also featuring Victor Martinez and Miguel Cabrera) with considerable pennant prospects.

But travels were not quite over for a ballplayer whose career seemed defined by vagabond journeys. Detroit languished by midseason and all hopes for remaining competitive in the American League Central Division were abandoned when slugging star Miguel Cabrera was forced to the disabled list by a calf strain at the season's traditional July 4 midpoint. On the eve of a July 30 trading deadline the Tigers announced a fire sale that included not only newly arrived staff ace David Price, but also Céspedes. Despite his continued elevated offensive production and almost nightly *SportsCenter* video clips showcasing his spectacular outfield throws, the prized Cuban moved on again, this time to the National League New York Mets, a surprise postseason contender at the top of the pack in the NL East.

Questions were again raised in the media about potential clubhouse issues lurking behind the scenes that seemed to keep the valued slugger and top defender on the constant move. "What's wrong with Céspedes that no one apparently wants him?" seemed a common refrain. The truth was that Yoenis Céspedes was now living the other side of the two-faced American Dream. All the recent moves had their explanations: Oakland had been seeking a showcase pitcher (Jon Lester) for a stretch run; Boston simply had an overly crowded outfield filled with young talent; Detroit found it expedient to unload the Cuban on the eve of his free agency year while they could still get something decent in return. Baseball was a business, pure and simple, and even rich American ballplayers didn't control their destinies. It was Céspedes's top-heavy contract, and not his production, that made him expendable for teams that owned him; and it was that same talent that made him desirable for teams in need. It was now only a different master pulling the strings.

2

CUBA'S HIDDEN *"BÉISBOL PARADISO"*

In no field of American endeavor is invention more rampant than in baseball, whose whole history is a lie from beginning to end. . . . The game's epic feats and revered figures . . . all of it is bunk, tossed up with a wink and a nudge.—John Thorn, *Baseball in the Garden of Eden*

The recent phenomenon of high-profile Cuban League baseball defectors that has so dominated headlines in the past several seasons is not entirely a ground-breaking event. The roots lie deeply imbedded in Cuba's baseball history, and in at least one important sense it is little more than the extension of a phenomenon that has long been at the heart of the island nation's ball-playing history. The circumstances have undeniably altered in the early twenty-first century, and the heavy overlay of cold war trappings has created a rather novel manifestation. But the Cuban baseball player viewed as an exile estranged from his homeland is only a continuation of a lengthy saga that has for more than a full century defined the sport and its central role within the passion-filled and baseball-obsessed nation.

The notion of the Cuban baseball player as an itinerant mercenary frequently isolated from his native homeland is one that stretches not merely throughout the twentieth century but actually back to the sport's very roots in the final decades of the nineteenth century. And the intimate bond between baseball and national identity within Cuba is hardly the creation of the modern-era mid-twentieth-century Castro revolution. From the very dawn of Cuba's arduous late-nineteenth-century struggle for independence from Spain, baseball has been the most useful instrument for defining Cuban nationhood.

In an intriguing, if sometimes strenuously academic, study of baseball's central role in Cuban identity, ethnologist Thomas Carter (*The Quality of Home Runs*) has adroitly traced the evolutionary history of generations of Cuban baseball players as itinerant migrants shuffling between homeland and foreign soil to ply their trade, and in the process carrying a special notion of Cuban native identity (*cubanidad*) with them. Carter draws on writings by the late MLB commissioner and Yale University president A. Bartlett Giamatti for the central metaphor of baseball as symbolic migration.

Giamatti visualizes the game's inherent structures and repetitious actions as a symbol of man's search for the lost "homestead" that provides his true identity. In one sense the sport seems little more than an elaborate "passion play" (as Carter terms it) capturing man's eternal quest for a return home (to childhood roots). In its playing structure of batters setting out on dangerous journeys around the base paths the sport seems to stand ideally as a classic symbol of epic journeys and circular migrations toward this lost homeland. In a central passage quoted by Carter and summing up the transparent metaphor, Giamatti waxes poetic about the game's deepest nineteenth-century symbolism:

> The journey begins at home, negotiates the twists and turns at first [base], and often founders far out at the edges of the ordered world at rocky second—the farthest point from home. Whoever remains out there is said to "die" on base. Home is finally beyond reach in a hostile world full of quirks and tricks and hostile folks. There are no dragons in baseball, only shortstops, but they can emerge from nowhere to cut one down. And when it is given one to round third, a long journey seemingly over, the end in sight, the hunger for home, the drive to rejoin one's earlier self and one's fellows, is a pressing, growing, screaming in the blood.[1]

Carter painstakingly expands on Giamatti's clever trope to better illustrate the vital connections among baseball, homeland, and national identity for native-born Cubans. Cubans as a population have been repeatedly forced to flee their homeland throughout a century and a half of nationalistic struggles that began with an anti-Spanish revolution in the late nineteenth century and culminated with an anti-American revolution at the midpoint of the last century. Cuban abandonment of the homeland and a subsequent desire (often blocked) to return to native soil is—as Carter stresses—ideally reflected by baseball's central metaphor of adventure on the circular base paths. But the connections are far deeper than merely symbolic. Cuba's baseball history itself is a full-blown tale of constant comings and goings, of ballplayers spending large chunks of their athletic careers in either temporary or permanent exile from the cherished homeland.

The game, in fact, originates on the island as a result of immigration stories. It was first brought to Cuban shores by a pair of native sons—brothers named Nemesio and Ernesto Guilló (often misspelled Guillot)—returning from a temporary exile as students at an Alabama secondary school.[2] The seeds of the sport planted in Havana in 1864 would blossom into a popular pastime, with ceaseless immigration at its very roots. Throughout the first half of the twentieth century Cuba's fledgling professional league represented a constant interplay between arriving immigrant ballplayers from the north during winter months and hometown Cuban athletes who themselves became exiled itinerants (either in the States, Mexico, Venezuela, or the Dominican Republic) across the summer seasons. There was a large racial component to this story, since many of the Cuban stars (after 1900) were blacks or mulattos drawn from the lowest ranks of Cuban society, and their ball-playing lives were episodes of constant enforced travel.

One central irony of Cuba's baseball evolution remains the fact that the sport began as a social diversion or "pastime" for the members of Cuba's nineteenth-century elite. Games were staged as weekend gentlemen's entertainments by social clubs that formed the first teams and enjoyed ball-playing diversions as part and parcel of social outings resembling modern-era church or fraternity picnics—affairs drawing well-dressed female spectators and featuring elaborate postgame banquets and dances as a highlight. In this sense Havana's earliest baseball mirrored the game's similar origins as a gentlemen's spectacle in pre–Civil War America. There were also intimate ties among baseball, dance, and the literary arts that Roberto González Echevarría has intricately traced.[3] The earliest league "seasons" were not seasons at all but a series of short weekend tournaments, which accounts for the lack of any early efforts at tabulating and recording individual ballplayer statistics. But, as in the States, once the novel game gained widespread popularity, it quickly transformed itself into a professional venture replete with the hiring of skilled mercenary athletes to assure victories and thus advance club pride, as well as to spike the interest and profit of those who wagered on such matches, or sold admissions to popular games as a fledgling business venture.

In Havana, the more mercenary forms of baseball activity that could be truly called professional first emerged in the early 1890s, and the most visible outward signs of the recasting of the game as "spectacle for profit" were the increased number of contests held, the first visits by teams of North American professionals, the recruitment of some of the better American visitors to fill local lineups, and, most significantly, the gradual appearance of black-skinned Cubans who at first had been excluded from strictly segregated social club team rosters.

The notion has long persisted that Cuba's winter league of the early twentieth century represented something of a baseball "*paradiso*" where whites and blacks would play together in complete racial harmony. But this notion was always an elaborate distortion of Cuba's actual baseball history. Amateur leagues centered in Havana and spread across the island were, from the beginning of the century, restricted to whites only and drew many of the island's most talented players. Those teams, eventually sponsored by business enterprises (the telephone and electric companies and other industrial corporations) as well as exclusive white-only frater-nities (the Vedado Tennis Club and Havana Yacht Club), were the true spiritual inheritors of the game's origins among Havana's elite social clubs. The small group of professional teams playing an organized winter league season in Havana drew heavily, if not exclusively, from the left-overs found in Cuba's largely African communities and also housed tour-ing black clubs from the North. Many of the North American Negro ballplayers who first visited as barnstormers soon signed on with Havana teams for extra paychecks in the winter months. These visiting American blackballers were athletes whose sporting lives were first and last an ongoing saga of constant migration.

Cuba's white (amateur) and integrated (professional) baseball leagues often crossed paths with the island's third early baseball manifestation, the barnstorming sugar mill leagues. There players from both circuits were often recruited as temporary mercenaries for games staged at "*cen-trales*" (cane processing factories) and played by teams patched together during the non-harvest dead months by wealthy mill owners as morale-building entertainment for resident plantation laborers. But it was the amateur circuits (most especially the Cuban National Amateur Baseball League active from 1914 through 1960) stretching across the entire island that proved the heart of the domestic sport. Cuban baseball thus knew racial segregation from its earliest years, although the lines were not usually as rigidly drawn as they were on American diamonds. The story of racial mixture in Cuba's prerevolution baseball has always been far more complex than popular notions of a color-blind *"béisbol paradiso"* might lead one to believe.

The overriding aim of Thomas Carter's monograph is to establish the connections between the island's long-established baseball traditions and the sense of national belonging that he calls *cubanidad*. Baseball's central role in the late-nineteenth-century struggle for independence, and thus true nationhood, anchored the connections between the imported American sport and a Cuban's sense of self-identification. And in a more recent postrevolution era of diaspora, Cubans living abroad (especially in the United States) still identify the bat and ball game played on their native island (and the triumphs of Cuban teams in international events) as an essential means of retaining their own sense of "Cuban-ness." Baseball and Cuban identity are hopelessly intermixed, which helps to explain the sometimes perplexing paradox that finds Americans and Cubans sharing the same national sport. It explains, in the phrasing of Roberto González Echevarría, how the national game of the threatening imperial power to the north (America) can at the same time shape and define the Cuban nation itself.

My own goal in this chapter is to underscore this central role of island baseball, and to amplify Carter's notion that the Cuban game, from its earliest nineteenth-century roots down to the final twenty-first-century hurrahs for the Castro revolution, has been first and foremost an immigration saga. At the dawn of island professional play in the opening decades of the last century (1900s and 1910s), native Cuban stars inflated national pride with victories over itinerant immigrant visitors from the north (both black leaguers and big leaguers); and the economic realities of the time then forced these same pioneering Cuban stars to take their craft on the road during summer months to earn their keep in neighboring Caribbean lands as well as on American shores. Once the odious color line finally collapsed for organized baseball in 1947, for a brief dozen years a muted but noteworthy Cuban invasion of big-league diamonds produced the likes of Miñoso, Pascual, Ramos, Consuegra, and more than a dozen others who earned their fame as summertime exiles playing outside their native land. And in turn American big leaguers continued to fill the rosters of the Marianao, Cienfuegos, Almendares, and Habana ball clubs for the final decade of the Cuban winter circuit.

The 1959 revolution and its immediate cold war aftermath ruthlessly ended one half of the immigrant story and temporarily curtailed the other. North American ballplayers (and other foreigners, including Dominicans, Mexicans, and Venezuelans) were no longer welcomed in the domestic postrevolution Cuban League launched in 1962; and for thirty or more years the flow of Cuban players off the island and into organized baseball was also severely, if not completely, curtailed. But the revolution did not end the ongoing saga of Cubans themselves playing overseas as immigrant mercenaries and therefore as either temporary or permanent exiles. The new regime would now send its best stars into battle overseas wearing national team uniforms and earning glory for the state in international tournaments abroad. Cuban baseball continued its history of triumphs on foreign shores.

Nor did the flow of itinerant Cuban ballplayers into organized baseball remain curtailed for long. Economic realities and even the strong-arm strategies of INDER (the Institute for Sports, Physical Education and Recreation) bosses themselves would eventually force open a new escape valve as a trickle of Cuban stars began—rather slowly at first—abandoning homeland domestic play for far greater economic opportunities in the North American professional ranks. The initial slow leaking of Cuban talent in the mid-1990s and early 2000s had grown significantly by the second decade of the new millennium, making two facts obvious. Cuban baseball players, despite the best efforts of the revolutionary government, would eventually renew their long history of pursuing fortunes overseas as exiles and immigrants. And more important still, the latest wave of island emigrant athletes would become true "exiles" in the most painful sense—they would be prevented from returning home by the realities of the Cuban-American cold war divide. Extending Bart Giamatti's cogent metaphor, these latest "defecting" Cuban immigrant ballplayers are now being stranded on the base paths and thus are unable to complete a successful journey homeward. It is not at all a new phenomenon, but instead a new reflection of the entire history of baseball as a defining measure of Cuban identity.

* * *

If the arrival of baseball in Cuba was itself something of a standard immigration story—the return home of a pair of temporarily exiled students enthused about an exciting new bat and ball game they had discovered during their half-decade in America's Civil War South—Cuba's discovery of the sport nonetheless remains clouded in lore and half-truths. Cuba's version of baseball Eden is every bit as fanciful as the long-discarded tales about Abner Doubleday and a miraculous immaculate conception for the sport in the pastures of Cooperstown. [4]

For years the standard legend involved a first-ever game on December 27, 1874, between two teams that had somehow miraculously sprung forth full-blown without antecedent. There were also tales of the American game making its first appearance in 1866 (nearly a full decade before the anointed first game at the Palmar de Junco field in Matanzas) when US sailors demonstrated ball playing for local dockworkers in the same northern seaport city. The factual record about origins would be eventually set straight with emerging details about the efforts of the Guilló brothers to spread their enthusiasm for the sport among their companions in Havana's Vedado neighborhood two years before the American naval visit to Cuba's north coast shipping port.

The December 1874 game at Palmar de Junco did indeed take place and was assuredly an important historical event; if not the first baseball game ever played on the island, it still assumes its indelible spot in the history books as the first known game to be documented (along with primitive box score) by the Cuban press. [5] One of the standouts of that early contest (Esteban Bellán) had already played professionally up north and today is recognized as the first Latino big leaguer. American sailors also most likely did bring bats and balls to Matanzas and thus further stimulate awakening interest in the novel game. Americans thus admittedly had a hand in the sport's quick blossoming in both Matanzas and Havana, but baseball's success in Cuba was hardly the mere result of American visitors who transplanted their native game for purposes of "Americanization," as they did during approximately the same time period in Japan, in China, or in the Philippines.

The central truth is that Cuba's baseball origins, like America's several decades earlier, were from the earliest moments bound in a hopeless blend of inaccuracies, facts, folklore, and partial distortions, and they today hold their main significance precisely for that very reason. As

González Echevarría effectively explains, myths about origins (especially origins of a national game) provide a culture's "collective bonding," and thus baseball in Cuba—coinciding with independence from Spain and the birth of a national identity—remains somehow central to the very notion of Cuban-ness. It is indeed baseball's role in the nation's initial independence struggle that goes a long way to explaining the game's continued durability during a modern era when Americans became the main cold war rivals and so much else of US capitalist origin would become officially taboo on the communist island.

The bats and balls in the Havana-bound luggage of Nemesio and Ernesto Guilló, as well as in the gear of Matanzas-bound US merchant marines, was a most fortuitous historical accident. Cubans at the time were immersed in a bitter and long-standing rebellion against their Spanish overlords that would last for most of the nineteenth century's final three decades and culminate in what Americans now falsely label as the Spanish-American War of 1898. The ongoing military campaigns spawned a strong identification among Cuban rebels with almost everything American, everything that seemed part of a coveted modernistic future and thus rejected the distasteful backward-looking Spanish past, including the modern game of bats and balls. Cuba's emerging love affair with the game thus closely mirrored a parallel contemporary process in Asia, where the Japanese, Chinese, and Filipinos also latched onto the novel sport brought to their shores by the American imperialist invaders. It was all part of what one scholar has labeled the "motive of imitation" strategy that might be one explanation for baseball's rapid evolution as the first modern-era team sport.[6]

The new sport of baseball not only underscored Cuba's supplanting of all things old and Spanish (like bullfighting) with all things new and distinctly American. It was also quickly bound to the rebel movement itself. Baseball games, and especially the early professional league launched with the brief winter tournaments at the end of the 1870s, actually became an effective tool aiding guerilla warfare against the Spanish. Many of the early ballplayers were active participants in the anti-Spanish hostilities, and some earned their reputations as much through revolutionary activity as through their weekend exploits on the diamond.[7] Baseball contests (through small admission charges) were even used by the anti-government combatants to raise needed cash for their rebel cause. The Spanish governors retaliated by temporarily banning all ball playing on the island after the 1868 outbreak of the Ten Years' War (the first major phase of the independence skirmish). Other similar interruptions to the sport cropped up between 1868 and 1898, with professional winter games suspended by ongoing warfare during 1880–1881 and 1883–1884, and championship seasons finally canceled altogether for three years (1895–98) during the war's final phase.

Emilio Sabourin was perhaps the most notable example of a celebrated baseball-playing rebel, but there were others. Several star players took up arms with rebel groups and did not survive the hostilities. A number of early inductees to Cuba's Baseball Hall of Fame, formed in 1939, earned that honor more for their status as heroes of the rebellion than for outstanding feats on the actual baseball diamond. One was José Manuel Pastoriza (a champion pitcher instrumental in leading Almendares to the 1894 league title), who was dragged from his home in Guanabacoa in December 1896 and publicly executed by a Spanish firing squad. Another was Ricardo Cabaleiro (famous for smacking three homers, two doubles, and a single in eight trips to the plate during one memorable February 1893 game), who also fell heroically with his outnumbered rebel battalion in September 1897 on the outskirts of Pinar del Río.

But none earned a greater place in island baseball lore than Sabourín, again more for patriotic heroism than for diamond theatrics. His playing career was modest and his baseball prowess was most often displayed as a successful manager, in which role he would be later credited with the innovation of the modern "squeeze play" as an offensive strategy. He also served as Club Habana's left fielder, playing alongside catcher Steve Bellán, during the historic December 1874 pioneering game at Palmar de Junco. Much of Sabourín's attention, however, was focused on acting as rebel fund-raiser and funneling revenue from his Habana ball club into dangerous anti-Spanish causes. In early December 1895 his home was raided (he had been suspected of providing secret refuge to a popular rebel general) and he was arrested and formally tried for treason in February 1896. Serving out a twenty-year sentence in the dreaded Moroccan dungeons of far-off Ceuta in North Africa, he died under the prison's inhumane conditions the following July (1897). His martyr's death earned Sabourín a posthumous spot within the pantheon of Cuba's most celebrated patriotic heroes.

The lengthy rebellion fostered connections between baseball and immigration as much as it cemented bonds between baseball and nationhood. Many privileged landowners and sugar barons fled the island during the Ten Years' War and carried their fledgling baseball passion with them to other Caribbean ports. Baseball's transfer to the Dominican Republic, Puerto Rico, Venezuela, and Mexico can be largely traced to those wartime events (as explained in the book's epilogue). Cubans, not Americans, would become the true apostles of baseball throughout the Caribbean region, just as the Japanese (not the Americans) would adopt that same role throughout neighboring countries in Asia.

And despite the late-century years of disruptive warfare, there were also reverse movements throughout the nineteenth century as immigrants from English- and French-speaking neighboring islands (the Bahamas and Haiti) were drawn to employment on Cuba's emerging sugar plantations. Most Haitians arrived in the wake of the 1804 slave rebellion and effectively launched Cuba's role as a principal sugar producer. They brought the British game of cricket with them and thus indirectly fostered future generations of ballplayers once their descendants gravitated toward the new American-style ball-playing passion at the end of the century. It was that early immigration that would eventually produce modern-era Cuban League ballplayers (most from the island's far eastern provinces of Santiago, Guantánamo, and Las Tunas) with odd-sounding Anglo or French names like Bell (Alexei), Anderson (Leslie), Jhonson (Jorge), Montieth (Frank), and Videaux (Robelquis).

The early years of Cuban professional play also provided constant intercourse between Americans and Cubans on the baseball diamond. The earliest big-league barnstormers, seeking both a Caribbean holiday and some extra off-season income, were already arriving before the first decade of the twentieth century. The earliest documented Havana visit by "white" pros can be fixed in December 1879, when the Hops Bitter Club, representing a soft drink company, defeated the newly minted Almendares Baseball Club.[8] A more celebrated whirlwind tour in January 1891 sponsored by part-time pitcher and full-time promoter Al Lawson featured a contingent of Baltimore Orioles, including future Hall-of-Fame manager John McGraw. The first Negro "invasion" came with a squad of US blacks in 1900, when the New Jersey–based and curiously named Cuban X-Giants staged an eighteen-game tour, playing against both regular island league teams and assorted all-star squads.

This increased interaction between Cuban and American ballplayers rapidly led to a new feature of Cuban baseball that would be known widely as the "American Season" and that often cemented financial solvency for the developing island winter circuit. Preceding each Cuban League championship campaign, usually in the early fall, exhibitions were scheduled with barnstorming US clubs (usually ragtag outfits of big leaguers). Those competitions with visiting American teams were played out against growing resentment of the de facto American military, commercial, and political control that had followed the ouster of the Spanish. And the highly charged games were further spiced by the fact that Cuban team rosters were usually heavily supplemented with top US Negro leaguers already plying their winter trade in Havana.

Cuba's first true baseball heroes earned their stripes with victories over the visiting American barnstormers during these fall exhibition matches, especially those with celebrity big leaguers. Foremost in the group of emerging island stars stoking national patriotic zeal was a young black pitcher named José de la Caridad Méndez (popularly dubbed Cuba's "Black Diamond"), who would ring up an impressive string of victories in 1908 and 1909 that were enough to make him a full-blown island legend and eventually (a full century later) earn a belated spot in Cooperstown. Almendares teammate Eustaquio ("Bombín") Pedroso was another black pitcher who fired national pride with his dominant fastball, especially with his November 18, 1909, no-hitter against a visiting squad of Detroit Tigers. The wins over American visitors were celebrated as sorely needed emotional lifts for a small nation chafing under yet another unwelcome foreign occupation.

Just as in Asia during precisely the same era, what had been first a "motive of imitation" for Cubans would quickly evolve into what Joseph Reaves terms an "impulse of rejection" explaining how the sport soon became a means for resisting and combating US imperialist interests. Victories by Cuban teams over American players during the "American Season" could be celebrated as blows against an unwanted oppressor. This closely mirrored what was also happening in Japan during the very same decade when students of the First Higher School of Tokyo (*Ichiko*) stimulated local nationalistic pride with wins over visiting American baseball clubs. Following a similar pattern, the Koreans and Taiwanese would much later employ baseball as a method of striking blows at the Japanese themselves after decades of unwelcome military occupation.

In addition to cash-hungry white big leaguers, blackball stars soon began to visit the island in increasingly large numbers. While no white major-league stars showed up on Cuban League rosters until the 1940s (and then they were mostly marginal players like Rocky Nelson, Max Lanier, or Forrest "Spook" Jacobs), top-drawing American blacks had been doing so since the 1910s. The Cuban League would in fact soon have as many American stars (albeit "outlaw" Negro leaguers) as native Cubans themselves. Oscar Charleston, Willie Wells, Josh Gibson, Rube Foster, Cyclone Williams, Ray Brown, Preston Hill, Spottswood Poles, Dobie Moore, John Henry "Pop" Lloyd, Chino Smith, Johnny Wilson, and dozens more would shine through the years and often distinguish themselves as league-leading pitchers and hitters. In effect the Cuban circuit had become largely a league built around temporary immigrants from up north. But it was a two-way exchange, with black athletes— Cubans as well as Americans—also regularly heading northward for the summer stage of their regular year-round migrations.

By the third decade of the twentieth century, Cubans consistently filled rosters of Negro league teams across North America as well as integrated squads in Mexico's summer circuit. And a handful of Cubans who were light-skinned enough would also reach the major leagues during the summer months. Several dozen Cubans made big-league lineups in the first half of the twentieth century, beginning with a pair of recruits (Armando Marsans and Rafael Almeida) signed by the Cincinnati Reds in 1911. Of the Cuban big leaguers only Adolfo Luque, winner of twenty-seven games for Cincinnati in 1923, became anything like a household name for American fans. Some, including Luque, would even play in both the big leagues and the blackball circuits, where racial lines were much less carefully and consistently drawn.[9] Soon Cuban rooters at home in Havana were as focused much of the year on native players performing abroad as on the shorter season when their heroes played on native soil.

The Cuban ballplayer—often black or mulatto—was forced by the economics of his profession to become an accidental immigrant, and for much of his playing life he would also therefore be a virtual exile. Due to the racial restrictions that ruled their world (and also the undeniable linguistic barriers for monolingual Spanish speakers), many Cuban stars found their exiled home in the Mexican League or in Venezuela and not in North America. But wherever they performed, they left legends, sometimes of expansive proportions. Given the shorter span of the winter league, most of their lives were spent on the road as journeymen athletes living out large chunks of their active careers far from native soil. Among the most notable was Martin Dihigo, a star at eight positions who would eventually enter the halls of fame in four nations.[10] There were others like Ramón Bragaña, Santos Amaro (father of big leaguer Ruben Amaro), Pedro Orta (father of big leaguer Jorge Orta), Lázaro Sálazar, Luis Tiant Sr. (father of big leaguer Louie Tiant), and Manuel "Cocaina" García, who all wrote larger legends abroad (both in Mexico and the States) than at home. A few would even settle permanently in Mexico at the end of their lengthy playing days.

Racial restrictions affecting baseball both stateside and in Cuba would also impact the Cuban scene in yet another form. Many of the better Cuban players somewhat less African in appearance chose to remain in thriving segregated amateur circuits, where rewards were far more lucrative. AAU league players earned decent salaries for cushy (sometimes nonexistent) desk jobs and only had to take to the playing fields twice on weekends. They pocketed far more than pro leaguers, for whom salaries were still anything but hefty (a reality causing pros to barnstorm on foreign soil each off-season just to earn living wages). The preference of some Cubans for the amateur circuit either permanently kept them out of the majors or long delayed their appearance. Such a case involved one of the island's top pitchers, Conrado Marrero. Marrero only migrated to the pros in the early 1940s (already in his mid-thirties), when he was suspended from the better-paying amateur league for illegally pitching for two teams at the same time. It was Marrero's late decision to turn pro that explains his tardy 1950 arrival in the big leagues as a grizzled thirty-nine-year-old rookie with the American League Washington Senators.

In the mid-1940s, on the eve of big-league integration, an odd development would briefly transform at least some Cuban stars into virtual exiles within their own country. Open recruiting wars between MLB and Jorge Pasquel's summer Mexican League had a deep and unexpected negative impact on Cuba's winter season baseball. When big-league commissioner Happy Chandler banned players who had signed on with Pasquel in Mexico, that action would quickly throw the post–World War II Cuban circuit into temporary chaos. An immediate result was a pair of rival Cuban leagues operating simultaneously and desperately vying for Havana's fan support.

The first season (1946–47) in the wake of Chandler's edict, the banned players (Cubans and imported Americans like Max Lanier and Sal Maglie who had also gone to Mexico) moved into the newly constructed Cerro

Stadium and drew the largest crowds, if only because their circuit commanded most of the top ball-playing attractions. Meanwhile those signed on with organized baseball who feared expulsion if they performed on the same field with the "outlaw" Mexican Leaguers remained in recently abandoned Tropical Stadium and played under the banner of a hastily constructed alternative league known as the National Federation League. Future big leaguer Conrado Marrero would make his pro winter season debut with Oriente of the Federation League, but he soon skipped over to Cerro Stadium and the popular pennant-winning Almendares club when the alternative league was forced to fold before its scheduled campaign had been completed.

The following winter the complex scene shifted dramatically with the banned "outlaw" players escaping to La Tropical and the group from organized baseball now occupying the new showcase venue in Cerro Stadium. This time both circuits completed a full schedule of planned games and the parallel teams named Habana captured both pennants. But the MLB-sanctioned circuit now regained the spotlight with a number of top American (Sam Jethroe) and Cuban (Claro Duany) Negro-league performers and such future big leaguers as Marrero and ebony-skinned Orestes Miñoso.

When an accord finally came, there were loud outcries at home that the new peace deal orchestrated by MLB was forcing many Cubans out of their own league, only to be replaced by an excess of American players

Cuban baseball's proudest venue, Havana's historic Latin American Stadium, built in 1946 as Cerro Stadium, later expanded and renamed in 1971. Courtesy of Peter C. Bjarkman.

for whom big-league clubs wished extra winter seasoning. It was at this point that the Cuban circuit was actually taken into the fold of MLB and in the process lost something of its native Cuban flavor. But at the same time the integration breakthrough up north had opened new doors for Cuban players to ply their trade and demonstrate their talent on foreign soil. The tale of Cuban baseball as essentially an immigration saga would thus continue, with the only real changes to be found buried in the details.

* * *

It was one of the most remarkable stories of the twentieth century and it happened right under the noses of disapproving Washington politicos. The Fidel Castro–led revolution not only was destined to reshape all of Cuban society and thus write the most crucial chapter in the country's chaotic social history; it would also transform the Cuban baseball landscape. Professional leagues were soon shut down on the island and a new revolutionary baseball took their place. For many in the eventual Miami exile community, the change would be seen as the loss of a Golden Age and the virtual death of the cherished island sport. A more reasoned view finds Cuba after 1960 finally reaching the true apex of its glorious baseball history.

A first profound impact of the changing environment was the loss of the prized Havana Sugar Kings minor-league franchise, Cuba's one visible connection to organized baseball. The baseball-crazed island had officially entered the realm of North American professional leagues in 1944 with formation of the Class C (later Class B) Havana Cubans (Cubanos) of the Florida International League, largely through the machinations of Washington Senators super scout and liaison "Papa Joe" Cambria, and then remained a prominent fixture for a decade and a half. The Cubanos produced a handful of superb teams and also a few native pitching stars, namely Conrado Marrero and Jiqui Moreno. This initial club gave way a decade later (1954) to the renamed Sugar Kings (Reyes de Azúcar) after the franchise was bought by Havana businessman Roberto "Bobby" Maduro and elevated to much higher status with entry into the AAA International League. The Sugar Kings would enjoy a single moment in the sunlight by capturing a surprise league title and hosting a prestigious "Little World Series" against the American Association champion Minneapolis Millers (events detailed in chapter 3). A bit of fortuitous timing found this franchise peak occurring in the immediate aftermath of Fidel's January 1959 rise to power. But that same season also included events that would signal a rapid demise, since the team would not survive another season.

Immediate impetus for the departure of the Havana franchise was Fidel's July 8, 1960, nationalization of all US companies on Cuban soil. MLB commissioner Ford Frick was under considerable pressure in the aftermath of Castro's actions to pull the team—a Cincinnati Reds affiliate—from its Havana home. MLB officials had been making considerable noise about the unsafe environment surrounding baseball on the island in the aftermath of a July 1959 Rochester-Havana game interrupted by gunfire (see chapter 3). It was true enough that Havana was not the calmest of locales during the turbulent twenty-four months of sporadic counterrevolutionary outbursts following Fidel's takeover, although Washington paranoia was likely exaggerated. Stripping Havana of baseball might be better explained as retaliation than precaution. Steps would also be taken that same summer to pull all American players from the Cuban winter circuit scheduled to begin in November. That added action (or overreaction) would also signal a further and even more resounding death knell since the 1960–1961 Cuban winter league season would be the last hurrah for the island's long-standing professional baseball.

Most shocking to the Cubans was the heavy-handed manner in which the six-year-old Sugar Kings franchise was yanked from Havana under cover of night and relocated to Jersey City with virtually no formal warning. The surprise action came swiftly on July 13, 1960, while the club was in the midst of a stateside road trip. League president Frank Shaughnessy, given sweeping powers to effect such a move only months earlier, announced that his decision was made merely for "the protection of the players." MLB commissioner Frick had already driven a first nail in the coffin with his spring 1960 directive to club owners that they cease allowing players to compete in the Cuban and Dominican winter leagues.[11] In a flash, the boasting point of claiming a team in organized baseball had dissipated. It was no doubt a personal blow to Fidel, who had taken obvious pride in the team and who had been a fixture at Sugar Kings games during his first summer at the helm of the new revolutionary government. As much as anything else, the break with organized baseball underscored a final step in the deterioration of normal relations between Washington and Havana.

The loss of professional baseball attached to the stateside big leagues would turn out to be anything but a death blow for the sport on the island.

Fidel would quickly seize upon these events as a final motivation to reshape island baseball and all other sports activities in a form more appropriate to the ideals of his rapidly evolving reconfiguration of Cuban society. Within seven short months (February 1961) legislation would create a new sports ministry and launch a socialist-style sports mechanism that, among other actions, would ban professional baseball. A most immediate and visible consequence was a January 1962 inaugural amateur baseball championship that would evolve over a handful of winters into the showcase Cuban National Series. The decision to kill off organized baseball on the island, launched by Shaughnessy and Frick and cemented by Fidel himself, would thus turn out to have some rather surprising unintended consequences. Foremost it would unleash events eventually producing MLB's greatest international rival—a single holdout alternative baseball universe which would survive the entire coming half century.

But there were more immediate consequences from a dismantling of Havana's minor-league ball club. Suddenly a number of Cuba's top homegrown stars were forced into choosing exile from their homeland. A sizeable portion of native Cubans comprising the Sugar Kings elected to cast their futures with professional baseball in the North, even though it quickly became apparent they might have to permanently abandon their homeland and families in order to do so. Among future big leaguers caught in this crossfire were Orlando Peña, Octavio "Cookie" Rojas, Joe Azcue, Leo Cárdenas, Miguel Cuéllar, and Raul Sánchez. Coach Nap Reyes also elected to remain with the relocated International League club and promptly took over as interim skipper in Jersey City, a decision that made him an unpopular outcast back home in Havana. Choosing to resign from the relocated team and return home were manager Tony Castaño and bench coach Reinaldo Cordeiro, the latter a former manager of Cuba's 1940 Amateur World Series champions. Castaño would be rewarded for his decision with selection as one of the four original National Series managers (with Azucareros) when the new domestic league opened a year and a half later. But the half-dozen emerging prospects opting to continue their careers on American soil were soon permanent exiles from the land of their birth.

In addition to the handful of Cubans affected by the forced move of the Sugar Kings, there were several dozen others already playing in the big leagues or with other minor-league clubs in the States. One especially heart-rending story was that of 1955 Brooklyn Dodgers World Series hero Edmundo (Sandy) Amoros. Returning home to Cuba for the winter months (and playing in the Cuban winter league with both Habana and Almendares), Amoros would run into unexpected problems during the winter of 1960–1961 when a reported confrontation with Fidel left him stranded and penniless in Havana and effectively put an abrupt early end to his already fading big-league career. As Amoros would relate the tale to *Sports Illustrated* writer Nicholas Dawidoff in July 1989, Fidel had pressured him to remain at home and manage an island pro league reportedly in the planning.[12] But Amoros refused, wishing to revive his career in organized baseball that summer with a stint in Mexico. The result was the confiscation of the ballplayer's personal assets (a car, ranch, and considerable cash), which left him marooned in Cuba for more than a half-dozen years. When he was finally allowed to depart in 1967, his baseball dreams had ended and he would live out the final quarter-century of his life largely forgotten and mired in poverty. He battled first alcoholism and later the diabetes that would cost him a leg and eventually take his life in Miami by mid-1992. The Sandy Amoros tragedy would remain one of the more painful tales of the Cuban diaspora.

Orestes "Minnie" Miñoso—entrenched at the height of his big-league career in Cleveland when the revolution triumphed—would never return to his homeland in the aftermath of Castro's rise to power. Nor would Washington Senators mid- and late-1950s mound aces Camilo Pascual and Pedro "Pete" Ramos. First-generation postrevolution Cuban-born big leaguers who would never return home, or only did so after decades of separation, also included Pedro "Tony" Oliva, Humberto "Chico" Fernández, Luis "Little Louie" Tiant Jr., Julio Bécquer, José Valdivielso, and Zoilo Versalles. A few—most notably slugger Borrego Alvarez—hesitated too long before leaving and lost out on even a "cup of coffee" big-league career. These players also became largely forgotten figures back home, especially as far as the revolution-oriented Cuban sporting press was concerned. Even among the general public memories of them would fade as an older generation of baseball fans slowly died off. Nevertheless they were never entirely forgotten in a land that so passionately treasures its baseball legacy.

When a much-belated December 2014 effort was finally made in Havana to reestablish a long-dormant Cuban Hall of Fame, both Miñoso and Pascual would be illustrious members of the inaugural ten-man class.

Inducted were five stars from the pre-revolution professional era, as well as five from the epoch of revolutionary baseball, itself a rather shocking shift in official Cuban thinking. [13] But neither of the living old-timers was granted permission by Cuban authorities to return home for the official ceremonies during an All-Star Game event staged in Granma Province. If the government voice represented by INDER had not yet entirely softened, the general tone on the island definitely had. This was signaled by the very possibility of electing two big leaguers to the new Hall of Fame in the first place. When Miñoso died eight months shy of his ninetieth birthday and only weeks after his election to the new Cuban baseball Valhalla, his passing was widely announced in the Cuban press and his legacy for Cuban baseball was at least mildly celebrated, if only dimly remembered, across the island.

The diaspora that separated Cuban families when the exile flow from Havana to Miami began in the early sixties had obviously played out on a smaller scale for many ballplayers. Tony (Pedro) Oliva and Preston (Pedro) Gómez were only two more pressing examples. Oliva's younger brother remained in Cuba and was a star national team pitcher (1979 Pan American Games) as well as a career 100-game winner for the Pinar del Río National Series team. The less-than-satisfactory result was that two elite ball-playing brothers were destined to play out their careers in two far different baseball universes. Juan Carlos Oliva remains a pitching coach in Pinar del Rio to the present day. Gómez provides an equally poignant case. Once manager of the Sugar Kings, he became the first full-time Cuban manager in the big leagues when he took the reins of the San Diego Padres in 1969. Over the years he worked at fostering a Cuban-USA baseball détente (see chapter 3) that never actually materialized. He also returned to the island frequently in the 1990s to visit a Havana-based brother who had eventually been freed after serving a lengthy prison term for anti-revolutionary activity. Gómez would maintain a personal if not always cordial relationship with Fidel over the decades and would even speak briefly with the Cuban leader about potential thawing of relations during the Baltimore Orioles 1999 visit to Havana. [14] But despite these exceptional cases represented by Oliva and Gómez, a wide gulf always remained for Cuba's baseball exiles.

The diaspora effects on Cuban families living out lives of Miami exile would also spawn another telling baseball-related phenomenon. As Thomas Carter would elaborate in his own treatise on Cuban identity, physically exiled Cubans would develop a strong tendency to reshape their notion of Cuban-ness, or *cubanidad*, as their altered situation demanded. For them being Cuban didn't require residence on the home island; it all had to do with historical roots, cultural associations, and family connections. One telling manifestation of the phenomenon involved an exiled Miami community of former professional ballplayers, whose numbers swelled over the years. Those aging exiled former athletes eventually set up their own formal "association" and established their own Hall of Fame to replace the one that had disappeared after 1960 in Havana.[15]

The Miami-based Hall of Fame would quickly evolve into something that had more to do with politics than with the history and traditions of the sport itself. It would often be confused by stateside journalists as a sanctioned continuation of the pre-revolution original. But the Havana-based honor roll never enjoyed any formal museum building and was little more than the plaque still hanging in Havana's Latin American Stadium. For a short time the Miami group did occupy a specific fixed location, a small Miami showroom opened in 1986 but no longer operating a decade later. There were annual old-timers games staged for much of the 1990s at the Florida Marlins National League ballpark. But the organization eventually evolved into a self-promotional farce. To celebrate an anti-Castro stance and also raise funds, by the late 1990s the group was inducting onto its honor roll virtually every former ballplayer, coach, sportswriter, or loosely connected official who had subsequently exiled himself in South Florida. A June 1997 banquet attended by this writer featured the installation of sixty new inductees, including a number of island-born former big leaguers (Tito Fuentes, Bert Campaneris, and Tony Perez among them) who had never played professionally on Cuban soil. The idea seemed to be more about selling induction banquet tickets than anything else.

There was also a novel tendency among exile-community baseball enthusiasts to reshuffle the very notions of a Cuban identity. Many began claiming second- or third-generation offspring as "Cuban" big leaguers even if that term might more appropriately be reserved for ballplayers actually born somewhere on the island. Inventories have been published listing the offspring of US-based exiles as legitimate Cuban players: namely Alex Gonzalez (Blue Jays shortstop), Fernando Viña (Cardinals infielder), Jon Jay (Cardinals outfielder), Alex Fernandez (White Sox pitcher), or, more recently, veteran outfielder Raúl Ibáñez and Kansas City slugger Eric Hosmer. But no one would claim Joe DiMaggio or Mike Piazza or Yogi Berra in this same vein as being genuine Italian big leaguers. It was a clear example of what Carter explains as the phenomenon of Cubans faced with a diaspora legacy trying to redefine the very nature of being Cuban, or of owning genuine Cuban identity. These flag-waving exiles had simply carried their abandoned homeland and its treasured identity with them on the road.

* * *

The new revolutionary government rapidly revived and even advanced already long-existing connections between baseball and nationalism. The adoption of a Soviet model in 1961 envisioned national sports teams as instruments for propping up national propaganda. Victory might be far easier and equally effective in the athletic areas, even if it might be difficult to achieve on the battlefield or in international political circles. But this notion of baseball in the service of national identity was not at all novel for Cuban leaders. It stretched back to an earlier revolutionary struggle against Spanish colonial overlords, when baseball was already seen as a political weapon as much as a sporting entertainment and public pastime. And it took new shape when early-twentieth-century Cuban pro teams, behind the brilliant pitching of homegrown heroes like Méndez and Pedroso, first fired full-blown national pride by defeating barnstorming big-league American squads at their own declared national game. It was equally present when World War II–era national squads began claiming regular dominance with the earliest versions of a newly inaugurated competition known as an amateur "World Series" that riveted national attention during summer months in the late 1940s and early 1950s.

It was an American named Leslie Mann who had first come up with the idea of staging international baseball world championships.[16] But it was the Cubans, already boasting a deep amateur-league tradition, who seized upon the possibilities offered by Mann's first limited effort staged in London in 1938. Cuban sports officials had already pushed international tournaments as early as 1926, when the struggling Machado regime underwrote an inaugural Central American Games competition in Mexico and then restaged the fledgling event in Havana four years later to divert attention from growing domestic unrest surrounding an unpopular corrupt administration. It was the 1930 Havana Central American Games that also provided a motive for construction of a state-of-the-art stadium on the Tropical Brewery grounds that would serve as a showcase venue for Havana pro and amateur games until the 1940s. But it was three initial Amateur World Series (AWS) events at La Tropical in 1939, 1940, and 1941—featuring epic matches with the rival Venezuelans—that not only indelibly inscribed Conrado Marrero in Cuban baseball lore but also launched Cuba into a position of prominence in international baseball circles that would not be relinquished for more than a half century.

Cuba would fade from the international tournament scene in the late 1940s but return to earlier prominence with three titles in 1959. Cuba's fifty-year grip on Amateur World championships actually began in Havana in September 1952, six months after military functionary Fulgencio Batista grabbed power (March 10) and suspended constitutional government. Cuban national teams thus had been winning important victories bathed in national pride for two decades by the time Fidel arrived on the scene as Batista's replacement in the late 1950s. Those victories gained little notice outside Cuba and a handful of its Caribbean neighbors. Asian teams had not yet become major players in international tournament play—Japan, South Korea, and Taiwan would not enter their first AWS until they simultaneously appeared in Cartagena in 1976. And that level of non-professional baseball was totally off the radar for stateside players and fans. The few American teams—usually university or industrial league clubs—sent to these early international events were anything but competitive and certainly not representative of baseball's leading standard-bearer. No one in the States seemingly cared about that brand of baseball. The pro game was the national pastime's only true measure for most Americans and even collegiate or scholastic versions of the sport had relatively little following on the North American sporting scene.

Cuba had always boasted a strong amateur-league tradition and amateur leagues and sugar mill leagues arguably outstripped the Havana professional league in popularity throughout the entire first half of the century.[17] One of the great myths surrounding baseball on the island is the notion that the Havana winter league represented an epicenter of the island's baseball legacy. While the amateur game remained popular, the winter pro circuit often badly floundered. Pro seasons were often interrupted by political unrest or financial meltdowns—occasionally even canceled—and frequently appeared quite different in size and structure. The popularity of the traditional winter circuit rivals—the Habana Reds and Almendares Blues—was real enough, yet flourished mainly in Havana and was often a mere rumor elsewhere across Cuba. National pride focused more on the few native Cubans who flourished in the big leagues and on the national squads that carried the local flag against regional rivals from the Dominican, Puerto Rico, Mexico, and Venezuela.

If a focus on international triumphs at the amateur level was not novel by the time Fidel and his revolutionary regime arrived on the scene, it would soon take on heightened dimensions. Accidents of history also helped to up the ante. The loss of the minor-league Sugar Kings and then the MLB-connected winter circuit played equally significant roles. And so did a fortuitous conflation of military and sporting history during April 1961. A first great triumph for Cuba's post-revolution national team (chapter 3) overlapped the aborted Bay of Pigs invasion, a US-directed strategic debacle that cemented the hold of the revolution among the Cuban population. A group of amateurs pulled from the ranks of the just-completed first National Series swept the AWS field in Costa Rica while battle flags were being raised during the repulsion of an American-sponsored invasion in what became known as the glorious Victory at Girón. Just as in the States, baseball victories and military triumphs were often intricately and hopelessly intertwined. [18]

The new INDER-run domestic Cuban League launched in 1962 would itself undergo many transformations over the next half century. The length and format of seasons would shift; the number of teams grew from four to a high of eighteen in the late seventies, before normalizing at sixteen in recent decades. There would sometimes be two distinct championship seasons within a single calendar year. But the focus was always clearly on providing training grounds for national team victories. Cuba would compile a remarkable record in international tournaments in the decades of the sixties, seventies, eighties, and nineties, one that featured an overall winning percentage (in individual games) above 90 percent and that I have elsewhere labeled as unparalleled at any level of known organized sports competition. [19] There were always naysayers who pointed to the low level of non-professional opposition in such events as the AWS or Pan American Games, but the record was phenomenal nonetheless.

During this era of four-plus decades, few talented ballplayers ever left the island. There was much indeed to keep them at home—if salaries were low, revolutionary fervor was still high and national team membership brought true rock-star status. But Cuba's embargoed cold war struggles also meant that domestic baseball became almost entirely isolated from a North American baseball universe where past-generation itinerant Cuban ballplayers had for so long traveled. One result was the lost opportunity for American fans to glimpse several generations of great Cuban stars—sluggers Agustin Marquetti and Antonio Muñoz, batting magicians Wilfredo Sánchez and Armando Capiró, mound aces Braudilio Vinent and José Antonio Huelga, most likely all surefire big leaguers. Another was that Cuban baseball would remain cloaked in mystery that lent intrigue but shrouded credibility. Only an occasional rumor reached American shores, sketchy reports that the game was alive and well on the island and also being played at a level that now outstripped those better-publicized pre-revolution days. [20]

Many of the greatest raw talents Cuba ever produced now played in a distinctly different universe of aluminum bats (introduced in 1976) and their numerous exploits are thus quite difficult to judge in retrospect. But they were still migrants, although migrants with a different mission. Developed and honed on the island, the best of the Cubans traveled overseas with a juggernaut national team that regularly swept through international rivals in events wildly celebrated in Cuba and ignored altogether by American fans. Cuban ballplayers may have largely disappeared from the MLB scene in the seventies and eighties. But they were now building a different legacy on diamonds in Europe, Asia, and throughout the Caribbean.

The interaction with North American baseball was briefly reopened on a small scale in the late 1980s with a novel "friendly series" hosted occasionally on North American soil. It was yet another opportunity for strong Cuban squads to beat their Yankee rivals at their own game on the baseball diamond. The series of matches between the Cuban "nationals" and the select squad of US collegians actually began in July 1987 in Cuba (Havana and Artemisa), with the hosts taking the rubber match of a five-game set serving as a warm-up for Pan American Games matches in Indianapolis. The series moved to Millington, Tennessee, the following year and would be staged at that same locale (the official USA Baseball training site) several times in coming years. Over the first half-dozen years the games were highly competitive and provided at least a small window into the quality of Cuban talent. Cuba claimed seven of the first nine series and twenty-eight of forty-seven total games, with the 1991 six-game set ending in a tie.

Team Cuba celebrates a 2003 IBAF Baseball World Cup Gold Medal victory at Havana's Latin American Stadium. Courtesy of Peter C. Bjarkman.

A first small crack in this new baseball détente and in the "sugar cane curtain" isolating the island sport came during the single renewal that failed to produce an on-field winner. It was in the midst of a mid-July 1991 series, split between Millington and Santiago de Cuba, that star Cuban pitcher René Arocha broke new ground by abandoning the Cuban team (chapter 4). Arocha would be followed by a handful of others across the next several years. A trio of future big leaguers (including Rey Ordóñez) would bolt from a 1993 Cuban junior team competing at the World University Games in Buffalo. Pitchers Osvaldo Fernández (again in Millington), Liván Herández (in Mexico), and Ariel Prieto (who faked injury to arrange a legal exit) would flee two years later. And most significantly, star hurler Rolando Arrojo would escape the Cuban squad en route to the 1996 Atlanta Olympics. This final defection (following a tune-up series, again staged in Millington) would bring a temporary halt to the USA-Cuba "Friendly" matches. But more significantly, perhaps, these sudden cracks in the isolated world of post-revolution baseball meant that a small batch of Cuban players were now once again opting for the role of ball-playing exiles that had long defined the island's national pastime.

Arocha was not actually the first post-revolution Cuban Leaguer to find his way north. A single pioneer had arrived in 1980 as part of the Mariel Boatlift exodus (yet another Cuban ball-playing exile), and his tale was a bit more shadowy in detail. Bárbaro Garbey was banned in Cuba for game-fixing but welcomed by organized baseball as a Castro defector, exposing a potential dual standard in MLB policies governing exiled Cuban ballplayers. Open-armed acceptance of fleeing Cubans, despite known criminal activities possibly connected with their desperate flights, now gave a different twist to the exile phenomenon. It also couched a potential hypocrisy enveloping MLB actions that would raise an even uglier face three decades later with the human-trafficking events exposed by the saga of Yasiel Puig.

With the explosion of new defectors from the Cuban system in the new millennium, the tradition of Cuban ballplayer as exile would be reborn with a new urgency. But it would be only another chapter of a saga that was not at all unique to Cuban baseball or its storied history.

3

SUGAR CANE CURTAIN FIASCOS

One thing appears to be clear: Cuban national, cultural, and political identities can only be carved out of their involvement with the United States.—Roberto González Echevarría, *The Pride of Havana*

Surprise developments in the final weeks of 2014 hinting at a long-overdue détente between Washington and Havana were quick to inspire predictable responses from both camps when it came to the admittedly somewhat less important baseball side of the equation. A newly en-throned MLB commissioner wasted little time in gushing with optimism about island-based academies, imminent spring training junkets, and boatloads of new Cuban-bred talent floating to American shores. And a freshly minted Cuban commissioner also took to the airwaves, but with much more muted and guarded prognostications for possible long-range cooperation between the two baseball epicenters. It was the same old familiar song, but only a new set of well-conditioned crooners.

MLB commissioner Rob Manfred was quick to issue a number of carefully crafted statements that were all too familiar in their implicit message. MLB, of course, desired and was even planning for exhibitions next spring in Havana. It was obvious that such events (at least in the commissioner's view) would be a rousing success given the Cuban na-tion's own deep-seated love for baseball. Manfred's off-the-cuff pro-nouncements concerning newly perceived opportunities on the commu-nist island merit exact quotation (with my own italics for emphasis):

I can envision a situation, assuming that it is consistent with the government's policy on Cuba, where we could have ongoing exhibition game activity in Cuba. . . . Cuba is *a great market for us* in two ways. It's obviously *a great talent market*. We've seen enough of that during the off-season [*clearly a reference here to the signing frenzy surrounding Yoan Moncada, Héctor Olivera, and other recent defectors—PCB*]. It's a country where baseball is embedded in the culture. . . . It is someplace it would be feasible for us *to do business in* an ongoing basis.[1]

There were two particularly noteworthy features of Manfred's statements. First was a familiar bombastic assumption about total US control, a bald-faced conclusion that the only possible block to MLB's plans would be Washington's own evolving policy on Cuba. Never is there a consideration here of Cuba's role in accepting and sanctioning such exhibitions. And then there are also the repeated references to Cuba as an exploitable "market"—a strong signal that nothing had changed in MLB's approach to baseball imperialism.

Major League Baseball had altogether transparent interests in Cuba: it was by any measure, in Manfred's eyes, a spectacular new marketplace (a place to buy ballplayers—if not steal them at bargain basement prices—and eventually to sell memorabilia and maybe even television broadcast rights). Cuba for decades had been off-limits, virgin territory blossoming with raw ball-playing talent and protected by an impenetrable wall of cold war politics. But with the shifting political scene it was now possible to brand Cuba as the new Japan, Dominican Republic, and Venezuela all rolled into one. In short, little had shifted in the longstanding MLB position. Nary a mention could be found anywhere of opportunities for exploring cooperative programs that might help the Cubans upgrade their sagging baseball infrastructure or strengthen their own role in the international baseball community. Cuba was a new business opportunity to be fully exploited—pure and simple—and the waiting was now apparently over. MLB was ready to pounce on one of the last remaining opportunities for rampant talent strip-mining, one that had long eluded its grasp.

The Cuban commissioner was far more guarded and only slightly less realistic in his own reactions to a changing landscape. Heriberto Suarez Perera—only a month in office—would candidly admit in an early January *Mesa Redonda*, a Cuban national television program, that of course Cuba was changing and the country was of necessity prepared for a new reality that would find it now sending some of its top players around the globe. It was a statement that clearly reflected Cuba's new rhetoric under the economic shifts put in place by Raúl in the wake of his own succession to power in 2006.

But Suarez was careful to couch his terminology and veil his message. Cuba would consider all possibilities, he announced, and there was mention of Japan, Taiwan, and Canada as realistic possible locales for outsourcing Cuban players. MLB would remain a possibility, as well, but only if circumstances were right and conditions were favorable. What remained largely unsaid (and therefore not fully appreciated by American interpreters) was the implicit message that Cuba would always remain in full control of its ballplayers; Cuban stars would not simply be turned over to big-league clubs that would then own their contracts and control their services.[2] Suarez was suggesting that the American big leagues were clearly not the only player in the picture or the only alternative for the future. Cuba's own conditions and demands would have to be met—such as the need for top stars to return for winter service at home and for duty on Cuban national teams. This echoed the stipulations also alluded to in San Juan one month earlier, when Suarez delivered an almost identical message to ESPN cameras. And it signaled the wide divide between the two systems, a divide that Cuba most likely still did not fully appreciate.

It is important perhaps to note here precisely who Suarez is and why—at this critical juncture in the island nation's baseball and political history—he has so suddenly and rather unexpectedly emerged on the scene. Even for those close to the Cuban baseball scene he is something of a mystery, someone previously unknown in Cuban baseball circles. Nothing has been published to date in Cuban media outlets about his previous connections (if any) with the sport. So what explains the change? Admittedly, long-standing fan and ballplayer dissatisfaction with Higinio Vélez (in office since 2008) had peaked in recent years.[3] But it was the internal concerns about a changing political scene that most likely seemed to mandate a shift at the top; with political hard-liner Suarez Perera given the reins and Higinio Vélez also allowed to remain on the scene as something resembling a thinly disguised co-commissioner. Therefore these statements about a possible new accord with MLB were now being made by an official spokesperson for a revamped set of INDER caretakers, who were obviously not, in large part, baseball people motivated by any pure baseball interests. Cuba's motives are as much driven by politics and economics as are the interests and strategies of MLB.

The statements by Suarez in his San Juan ESPN interview are perhaps the most revealing. He reiterated the progress of INDER in developing and training its own athletes (namely, baseball players). He did express a willingness to listen to overtures from MLB officials and admitted the door was ajar for possible future cooperation, but he was also quick to emphasize that Cuba would always demand complete control of its ballplayers. In other words, read here "no MLB-style academies on the island that leave American ball clubs poised to scoop up free-agent talents and train them for MLB's own purposes." Julia Sweig and Michael Bustamante's analysis of the new Cuban realities is relevant here: "Cuba's basic political and economic structures appear as durable as the midcentury American cars still roaming its streets."[4] The changes (in philosophy if not yet in overt action) that were now occurring on the island were indeed significant. But at the same time they hardly signaled anything like wholesale abandonment of long-reigning socialist principles.

On the eve of a seemingly possible, much misunderstood, and certainly long-overdue thaw in USA-Cuba relations, several latent developments seem almost too easy to predict. Changes in Cuba will be painfully slow when it comes to any revamping of a well-entrenched communist social and political system; although the desperate need for at least small private enterprise has been recognized in Havana, there is no reason to expect that the guardians of the communist regime will simply throw in the towel completely on humanitarian ideals that underpin their revolution, or adopt wholesale any odious form of an American-style capitalism which they have so long resisted. Whatever modifications might unfold in the current Cuban system will play out against a well-established backdrop of communist party control. It will not look anything like the sweeping adoption of US-colored democracy envisioned by the Cuban-American exile community.[5] Cuban leaders will compromise only in areas where Havana does not find its own continued independent existence compromised, or continued control of its own destiny threatened. And if this is the case, MLB seems so far to be playing all the wrong cards.

* * *

History is written by the victors and news always has a local and nationalistic slant. Cuba has rarely, if ever, been portrayed the way it actually is by the North American media. And in entire fairness the Cubans have always suffered their own slanted view of the United States and its policies toward their homeland. The America known on the streets of Havana is largely shaped by popular gangster movies that remain a staple of late-night Cuban television; the Cuban state media wastes no opportunity to headline North American racial unrest and inner-city violence, and the abuses of capitalism. A long-standing travel ban limiting Americans' access to a neighboring country only ninety miles off its southern coast has continually reinforced the growing information vacuum. Neither Havana nor Washington has ever been able to see very far beyond its own wall of propaganda during an ongoing fifty-year war of ideologies.

Cuba has long been portrayed by Washington and its allies in the US fourth estate as a rogue terrorist nation. But it is Cuba and not the United States that has suffered the occasional invasions, the repeated acts of terrorism, and the constant incursions against its presumed right to self-determination. There is no record of any attacks by Cubans on US soil or against any US properties in any corner of the globe. Cuba, for several decades, has had virtually no military force capable of such provocative overseas activities. It has been nearly a half century since there has been any Cuban military involvement in far-flung territories like Angola or any subversive guerrilla activity in neighboring Latin American outposts like Bolivia. While the Cuban armed forces plays a major role in administering the island—controlling 60 percent of the country's economy—its effective power to engage in any form of combat was severely reduced by the loss of Soviet subsidies. The present Revolutionary Army force of less than 39,000 men and women (not enough to fill Havana's Latin American Stadium) is focused exclusively on resisting any potential invasion from its mega-neighbor to the north.

The US attacks on Cuba, by heavy contrast, have been quite well documented and quite substantial. Some of these onslaughts have been plotted in Washington inner circles and others have been carried out by Miami-based and US-backed terrorist groups. While the United States continued to carry Cuba on its list of nations supporting terrorism (a stance only recently dropped by the Obama administration) it was the Americans themselves who orchestrated terrorist plots targeting Cuban assets.[6] There were numerous early efforts to eliminate Fidel Castro by the most devious of means—poisoned meals and drinks, exploding cigars, and other adventures seemingly more appropriate to Hollywood filmmaking than serious late-twentieth-century foreign policy. A more than four-decade Washington embargo of Cuba is best described as a hostile, warlike act designed directly to facilitate regime change.

One of the most concise summaries of American-orchestrated covert warfare against Cuba is found in the opening chapter of Margaret Randall's recent engaging report (*To Change the World: My Years in Cuba*) detailing her dozen years spent personally experiencing Cuba's remarkable social experiment. Randall catalogs the one-way aggression directed at Cuba and provides some firsthand insight into what the isolated island nation was actually like during that time (1969–80), years that represented the highest point of its bold experiment in building a more just and equitable type of society. She also elaborates on the stark distinction in priorities between the neighboring countries. Socialist Cuba devoted less than 5 percent of its GNP to military expenditure (compared to 50 percent for the United States); Cuba spends nearly 10 percent of its national wealth on education and long ago (1960s) largely eliminated illiteracy; medical services in Cuba ranging from dentures to heart surgery are free to all citizens, and while the country, with its present sagging economy, spends only $230 per capita on health care, that entire amount goes directly to beneficiaries and not to pharmaceutical companies or insurance providers.[7]

Perhaps Randall's most biting critique comes on the issue of repeated US condemnations of Cuba's human rights abuses and its lack of American-style democracy. She finds it an all-too-easy target to stress Washington's own record on the mistreatment of political prisoners in the wake of 9/11 (prisoners ironically held off Cuban shores at Guantánamo Bay) and the flaws in an American electoral system. This system, she claims, is built largely on gerrymandered voting districts, documented recent efforts (especially by the Republication Party) to suppress voter registration under the guise of combating imagined voter fraud, and the hypocrisies surrounding recent American presidential elections in which George W. Bush "won his first term through a judicial coup and stole his second through voter mismanagement and manipulation."[8]

Of course there were many who supported the early dreams of the Cuban Revolution yet eventually became disillusioned and turned against Fidel and his communist-style social reforms.[9] It was indeed part of Fidel's genius to let most of that opposition migrate north, a strategy that clearly allowed the revolution to survive. Had a vibrant opposition remained on the island, Fidel would likely not have long remained in power and Western Hemisphere history would have followed a far different course. The failure by the first waves of Miami-bound immigrants to risk personal fortunes and stand their ground at home is one of the rarely discussed aspects of the Cuban Revolution and its survival.

The mostly idyllic socialist society that Randall and others have remembered from the 1970s and the era of highest Soviet support for the Cuban enterprise would be transformed into something quite different in the final two decades of the twentieth century. There is little question that Castro-led government control became far more rigid over the "Special Period in the Time of Peace" (the late 1980s) and personal freedoms were consequently severely restricted. Randall not unreasonably explains this less positive evolution as resulting to some large degree from the Cuban government's perceived necessity to survive at all costs. Two major outside threats to that survival were in part responsible for the entrenchment. One was the devastating collapse of Soviet support that sent the national economy into rapid free fall. Another was the persistent threat from American aggression, both overt and covert in nature.

The notion of a nation restricting the liberties of its citizens due to perceived outside threats to its reigning political system should not be such a hard concept to grasp in the wake of post-9/11 developments here on the American home front. Despite its long-standing reputation as a supposed bastion of individual liberties, this country has witnessed an unparalleled assault on valued American personal freedoms (especially personal privacy in matters of phone calls, emails, and Internet and library usage) under the guise of a necessary war on terrorism. We hear much about the Cuban regime's assault on human rights (imprisonment of active dissidents), while at the same time our own government carries out similar abuses on detained enemies of the state. And ironically the worst of these abuses (torture techniques such as "water boarding" imposed by the Bush administration on suspected terrorists held for unlimited terms and without benefit of due legal process) have occurred along Cuba's own shores at the controversial American military prison camp on Guantánamo Bay.

There have indeed been some massive failures of the Cuban system in the post-Soviet era. It is quite difficult for even the most dedicated supporters of the Cuban experiments in socialist society to blithely ignore those failures. But if increasingly tight control of its population by Cuba's government in recent decades is not palatable to most Americans, it might be better understood in the context of the outside pressures that have caused the defenders of the revolution to retrench in the pursuit of survival. Cuba's sagging socialist government has spent much of the last quarter century simply trying to stay afloat.

* * *

No world leader has ever been more directly involved with his country's national game than has Fidel Castro; nor has any political figure enjoyed longer or more pronounced impact on the sport of baseball—or any other sport, for that matter. [10] Since the onset of his power in the early 1960s, Fidel has been intimately identified with Cuban baseball in a manner unprecedented in the United States or any other baseball-playing nation. And much of that identification has been based on irresistible mythology hiding the Cuban leader's actual role in molding the forms and goals of post-revolution baseball on the island.

Few have not heard one version or another of the myth touting the young Fidel as a blossoming baseball prospect, a phenomenal pitching talent with a recognized big-league arm. As the story goes, the young Castro was supposedly scouted by a number of big-league clubs and even offered several pro contracts. There are a handful of early North American journalistic reports that gave quite specific—if highly fictitious—accounts of Fidel's baseball talents and budding baseball career. [11] Many over the years have bought into those fictionalized accounts (including at least one US senator, Eugene McCarthy); they have also served as background thematic material for at least two popular novels set in Cuba, and one can still expect the embellished tale to pop up periodically in North American press accounts, despite its widespread dismantlement by a number of reputable scholars. [12]

The source of the nine-lives myth seems to have been a single pitching exhibition staged in July 1959, only six months after the initial triumph of the revolution. Fidel would appear with his Barbudos ("Bearded Ones") team in a staged event preceding an International League game involving the Rochester Red Wings and Havana Sugar Kings. The setting was a weekend series in Havana timed to coincide with the first post-revolution celebration of the July 26, 1953, Moncada attack that had launched Fidel's campaign against the despised Fulgencio Batista regime. That game has often been built into something it never was and photos from that exhibition appearance have been regularly employed to spread the myth, sometimes even suggesting that they are action shots of Fidel pitching in an actual league game. One US firm (Blue Marlin Corporation) even chose to market Cuban replica ball caps with a brochure claiming the photo represented Fidel in action during his "minor league career." A glossy 1994 ESPN poster promoting Sunday- and Wednesday-night MLB telecasts also featured the same familiar 1959 photo of Fidel delivering a pitch in his Barbudos uniform, superimposed with the bold-print headline "The American Game That Once Recruited Fidel Castro."

Far more significant for baseball's future on the island were the events that transpired one night after that misunderstood exhibition. On the first post-revolution anniversary of the Moncada attack (July 26, 1959), chaos broke out in the late innings of the Saturday evening Rochester–Havana game. Further elaboration on those events can be read in *A History of Cuban Baseball, 1864–2006* (chapter 9: "The Myth of Fidel Castro, Barbudos Ballplayer") and only a bare summary is needed here. A planned celebration of arms-toting revolutionaries erupted at midnight with the game still in progress. Gunfire sent both teams scurrying for cover, and in the middle of the melee Rochester third base coach Frank Verdi and Havana shortstop Leo Cardenas were actually grazed by stray bullets. The Havana–Rochester series was promptly suspended and the tone set by that game would eventually lead to the transplanting of the Sugar Kings franchise in New Jersey the following summer.

The bottom-line result of that eventful weekend—which first saw Fidel take the mound and later chaos overtake the ballpark—was the perhaps inevitable demise of International League baseball on the communist-controlled island. But the death knell would be slow to peal for the Havana franchise. The International League Governor's Cup championship playoffs (with surprising third-place finisher Havana defeating the fourth-place Richmond Vees) and a Little World Series showdown with the Minneapolis Millers of the American Association (featuring a hot prospect named Carl Yastrzemski) would both transpire in Havana later that same fall. And Fidel the baseball fan was a fixture at both events, although later reports of Comandante Castro and his comrades toting firearms, strolling uninvited inside and atop the dugouts, and even intimidating first Richmond and later Minneapolis ballplayers with threats of violent intervention have likely been mildly (if not wildly) exaggerated across the years.

Fidel Castro's pitching exhibition with the Barbudos team on July 24, 1959. Courtesy of Peter C. Bjarkman.

In the middle of the following season the Havana franchise would finally be pulled from Cuban shores by International League officials in an atmosphere of worsening tensions between Havana and Washington and also sometimes violent anti-revolutionary unrest in the streets of Havana. There has been subsequent speculation that the franchise removal (orchestrated under the direction of league president Frank Shaughnessy) was a blow that severely alienated Fidel, both as a fan and as a national leader recognizing the importance of baseball to the Cuba people. One thing is certain, however. Despite all the rhetoric about Fidel killing off professional baseball on the island with his legislative directives establishing the new INDER sports ministry in February and March of 1961, the actions of organized baseball officials themselves in closing down the Havana franchise in mid-1960 were every bit as much to blame.

Fidel's legendary status as ballplayer was mostly, if not entirely, spawned by the Barbudos game of July 24, 1959. But it was also firmly entrenched in the American imagination by a single article published in *Collier's* magazine and based on a supposed account by former big-league infielder Don Hoak. The article, penned by Myron Cope in June 1964 (only months after Hoak's career-ending release by the Philadelphia Phillies), provided the ballplayer's blow-by-blow account of batting against "the future Cuban dictator" in a winter league contest that the former Pirates star conveniently misremembers as occurring in the off-season of 1950–51. The supposed backdrop to the story was political unrest against the Batista regime and a spontaneous student protest that broke out just as Hoak, playing for league team Cienfuegos, stepped into the batter's box. Hoak's account has the charismatic student leader— Fidel Castro himself—marching to the pitching mound, seizing the ball from an unresisting Marianao pitcher, and then delivering several wild fastballs before Hoak's protests have the intruder chased from the field.

The article was one of the most widely swallowed baseball hoaxes of the modern era. The falseness of the entire episode was first laid bare several years back (1994) in a Society for American Baseball Research (SABR) journal article, but that initial exposure got relatively little notice.[13] The story was more thoroughly dismantled in González Echevarría's 1999 book (*The Pride of Havana*) and with my own accounts in my 2006 volume (*A History of Cuban Baseball, 1864–2006*), which contains an entire chapter on Fidel's elaborate baseball connections. Holes in the Hoak account are numerous and easily exposed. Most significant is the fact that Hoak's actual single season in Havana was 1953–54 (not 1950–51), a time when Fidel was already imprisoned on the Isle of Youth in the immediate aftermath of the failed Moncada invasion; furthermore the 1950–51 date cited by Hoak would have anachronistically placed the event before Batista actually took power in a 1952 coup. Numerous misspellings of names central to the reported events and total mischaracterizations of umpire Amado Maestri (a severe disciplinarian who never would have permitted such a game interruption) and ballplayer Pedro Formental (a supporter of Batista and not a pal of Fidel as implied) eventually sink the wild story completely.

But the story of Fidel as budding baseball star would never go away entirely. Eminent baseball historian John Thorn would anthologize the Hoak report without any hint of disclaimer in various editions of his edited *Armchair Book of Baseball*. Tom Miller repeats the legend in his popular Cuba travelogue (*Trading with the Enemy*) with a sense of wonder and the true voice of authority. NBC broadcaster Bob Costas would once inform me in a hand-scrawled note that it was just too good a story to stop telling, despite its questionable veracity. And the embellished legend in one form or another still persists and still pops up periodically. In a most recent book, Gary Cieradkowski (*The League of Outsider Baseball*) acknowledges that Fidel was certainly not a true prospect, yet he then reveals his own gaps in knowledge by asserting that Fidel (rather than the forces of organized baseball) killed a vibrant professional baseball league on the island.[14]

Perhaps more damning still, Cieradkowski implies further that the legend of Fidel as pitcher was long promoted by the Cuban media, supposedly in an attempt at glorifying the prowess of the supreme leader. Neither claim is true. Cubans have always laughed off the tale, which remains a favorite only of the American media and not at all of the Cuban press. Fidel alone did not kill off the winter leagues; they were dismantled by policies of organized baseball that pulled out the American players for the last Cuban League winter season of 1960–61 and then sent the Sugar Kings packing from the island. And at any rate, the Cuban winter league was anything but a vibrant concern at the time and the Sugar Kings drew rather poorly in Havana after the early seasons of 1954 and 1955. Rather than sounding the death knell for Cuban baseball, the new communist regime would soon replace what by 1960 had become a sagging professional enterprise with what would soon become a truly successful island-wide amateur baseball enterprise.

* * *

If Fidel was never in truth a recognized baseball star or a realistic pro pitching prospect, he would nonetheless soon emerge as a central figure in the island's baseball history. Perhaps pushed by the departure of the Sugar Kings and the abandonment of the island by organized baseball, Cuba's powerful new *caudillo* would act decisively to transform the island's national game into something consistent with the principles of the recently empowered revolution itself.

The first step was the February 1961 creation of a revamped sports ministry with the acronym INDER (Instituto Nacional de Deportes, Educación Fisica and Recreación), molded to take on the role of Batista's old DGND (Dirección General Nacional de Deportes) and designed to oversee all of Cuba's future "socialistic" sporting activities.[15] Within a month the new government entity had legislated via its National Decree Number 936 what amounted to a total ban on all professional athletic competitions, including, most prominently, the once-popular winter league affiliated with US organized baseball. Plans were also announced for an annual amateur national championship to begin within the coming year. Another novel innovation was the decision that there would no longer be admission charges for sports contests, a policy that lasted almost until the end of the twentieth century.

A new league had been formed virtually overnight and was now to be based on very different principles than those governing professional versions of the sport. And in the earliest years Fidel himself played a major role and was a constant presence within Cuba's new baseball enterprise. An opening season was launched in January 1962 with considerable ceremony and Fidel himself would appear for a ceremonial first at bat (dressed in his familiar military garb) and "officially" stroke the first league hit, a single off a soft toss delivered by Azucareros (Sugar Harvesters) starter Jorge Santin. A similar ceremonial act would be staged to open the second National Series in Havana's Cerro Stadium (later rechristened Latin American Stadium) later that same fall, with the season's symbolic "first hit" this time gifted by another Azucareros pitcher named Modesto Verdura. It might seem ironic that Fidel chose to stage these events as a batter and not as the pitcher he was often reported to be.[16] It was all grand theater, of course, and it continued the vital link between

Cuba's national identity and the central role of its long-standing national game. Over the next few years Fidel would continue to be a notable presence in Cuban ballparks, and there are numerous available photos of the national leader taking ceremonial swings at the plate or hurling ceremonial pitches from the mound at stadiums spread around the country.

The league Fidel inaugurated in January 1962 began on a small scale, with but four teams (Azucareros, Orientales, Habana, and champion Occidentales) playing twenty-seven games each, and thus looked something like the Havana-based winter circuit it had replaced. That initial National Series lasted little more than a full month and followed by less than nine months the clandestine unsuccessful US-backed invasion at the Bay of Pigs. The players were mostly rank amateurs (a few had starred in the popular pre-revolution Amateur Athletic Union circuit) who worked other jobs and approached baseball as a recreational sideline. But the circuit rapidly expanded into an island-wide structure with all provinces involved, jumping to six clubs for the fifth season, twelve for the seventh, and fourteen by 1972 (National Series XII). The new Cuban baseball had some special features that distinguished it from leagues found elsewhere. By 1975 the ball clubs represented each of the island's thirteen provinces and ball players would be locked into playing on their native provincial squads. While the players were soon full-time baseball men, they were paid little and salaries reflected socialist standards; star players did not negotiate higher salaries and the athletes were government employees and not mercenary athletes signing on with corporate franchises (the professional baseball model). And the league, as well as the Cuban season, would take several forms over the ensuing years, often including a second (sometimes longer and sometimes shorter) "super-provincial" season known variously as the Selective Series (1975–95) or the Super League (2002–5).

Perhaps the most defining feature of the new Cuban baseball league structure was its motive of producing and training strong national teams. The revolutionary government and its INDER sports ministry saw baseball as occupying numerous roles within a new societal structure. Obviously nationwide high-level competition would offer entertainment (and thus build morale) for a population long addicted to the bat and ball sport, and thus baseball (and all sports, with their inherent values of instilling good health and a spirit of vibrant competition) was to be seen as the acknowledged "right of Cuban citizens" under the revolutionary regime.

This was the philosophy that also dictated dropping admission fees for all contests, now valued as free public spectacle. But the league structure was also to be a training ground for teams which could carry the national banner in one arena where the small nation might score large propaganda victories and underscore the superiority of its new Soviet-style sports machinery. Baseball was now a way to demonstrate the power of the new socialist structure by beating the Yankees at their own game.

The earliest triumph would come in the shadow of the Bay of Pigs. Mass tryouts in Havana produced an exceptionally strong Cuban team for the first international competition after the installation of Fidel's revolutionary government. At the mid-April 1961 Amateur World Series in San José, Costa Rica, the Cuban ballplayers ran roughshod over the competition at precisely the same moment when Fidel's army was repulsing the Bay of Pigs invasion forces. By the end of that decade Cuba was winning international events with amazing regularity, posting a string of successes that would find Fidel's teams winning (or at least reaching the finals) in nearly every major world competition (Amateur World Series, Pan American Games, Central American Games, Intercontinental Cup, and Olympic Games) for the next four decades. The Cuban national squad became a juggernaut in the international arena across the final four decades of the twentieth century, capturing all fifteen of the Amateur World Series events entered before 2000, winning gold (and not losing a single ball game) at the first official Olympic baseball competitions in Barcelona and Atlanta, and capturing better than 90 percent of all individual international games played. With a string of 159 individual game wins between 1987 and 1997, the Cubans built a legacy almost difficult to fathom. But there was also always the caveat that they were playing against inferior non-professional competition.

The connection between baseball and Cuban national identity certainly did not begin with Fidel Castro and his 1959 revolutionary triumph. Nor was the use of baseball by government officials as a symbol of national superiority strictly a communist-era innovation. As historian Roberto González Echevarría has eloquently elaborated, baseball was present at the birth of the Cuban nation. The Cuban national identity was largely molded in the thirty-year struggle for independence from Spanish colonial rule in the last decades of the nineteenth century, the precise time when the diamond sport also took hold on the island. Baseball flourished there largely due to its all-too-easy reflection of everything new, modern, and American, and thus it became a perfect antidote to everything archaic, backward-looking, and Spanish (like bullfighting). Many of the nation's earliest celebrated ballplayers of the 1880s and 1890s were also patriotic rebel soldiers during the anti-Spanish independence struggle (chapter 2). And as González Echevarría stresses, strong-arm military leaders from President Machado in the 1930s through Batista in the 1950s clearly anticipated Fidel's later uses of baseball as a mechanism for shoring up and glorifying Cuban national identity.[17]

But as in Japan and other Asian nations, the game would soon become not only a means for aping coveted American modernism, but also a tool for rebelling against an encroaching American influence itself. As noted in the previous chapter, this was first witnessed in Havana with the so-called "American Seasons" played against the backdrop of American military control late in the first decade of the dawning twentieth century. The island's first true domestic baseball hero was a black pitcher named José Méndez, who won significant victories in 1908 against touring teams of American big leaguers. Exactly three decades later, in the midst of a Second World War, the earliest Cuban national teams would begin winning major victories, mostly on home soil. These triumphs came in the late 1930s and early 1940s in inaugural sessions (mostly Havana-based) of an Amateur World Series event that would grow into a true Baseball World Cup competition by the late 1980s. This early midcentury stage for Cuba's international dominance in the amateur game only ended with the chaos of the Castro revolution in the second half of the 1950s. But it would not disappear from the scene for very long.

* * *

Castro's triumph in January 1959 drove an ever-widening and eventually unbridgeable wedge between Havana and Washington. By the mid-1960s the countries were headed in very different directions and were destined not to reverse course or even slow the estrangement for more than half a century. One of the long-buried secrets of the cold war divide has been the large number of behind-the-scenes attempts over the decades at reconciliation and some form of détente between Fidel and his Washington adversaries. That story has only begun to emerge with the recent scholarship of William LeoGrande and Peter Kornbluh, published in 2014 as *Back Channel to Cuba*. Drawing on hundreds of formerly secret US government documents and fleshing out their accounts through searching interviews with dozens of Washington and Havana negotiators and policy makers (including Jimmy Carter and Fidel himself), Leo-Grande and Kornbluh have successfully challenged the conventional wisdom about ceaseless hostilities between the adversarial countries.[18]

This revealing research has uncovered several long-hidden efforts by Fidel Castro to secretly reach out to Washington with olive branches and to find some grounds on which a palatable program of cooperation might protect stability for his evolving revolution. It was most often a perceived matter of survival for the Cuban leader, who faced tough sledding in keeping his socialist experiment alive, even at the height of Soviet economic and military support. But Castro's vain efforts—we now know—were consistently rebuffed by Washington's top intransigent hard-liners. Successive US governments under Eisenhower, Kennedy, Johnson, Nixon, Ford, Carter, Reagan, Bush the elder, Clinton, and especially a younger Bush all wanted nothing short of a complete elimination of Fidel Castro.

The futile efforts at an accord began during the Eisenhower administration, as early as Fidel's guest appearance at a Washington luncheon hosted by acting secretary of state Christian Herter in April 1959. Efforts by ambassador Philip Bonsal to seek amicable relations grounded in economic mutual interests could not overcome growing distrust of Castro by Bonsal's State Department colleagues. A remarkable near breakthrough, however, came on the very eve of the Kennedy assassination in November 1963. French journalist Jean Daniel was in Varadero dining with Fidel and carrying a personal message of reconciliation from Kennedy on the evening of November 22, 1963, when the Cuban leader received the shocking phone call announcing events in Dallas and putting an abrupt end to what might have been a history-altering doorway to détente.[19] Another recently revealed eye-opening event reported by LeoGrande and Kornbluh was the secret interviews with Fidel carried out by a member of the Warren Commission panel.[20]

While the two governments struggled in secret for a political accord of some sort, there were also periodic efforts at some workable form of baseball détente. Those hidden efforts reached a peak during the 1970s, as detailed in declassified documents released in a National Security Archive electronic briefing booklet published on the eve of the Baltimore Orioles historic March 1999 exhibition game appearance in Havana.[21] San Diego Padres manager Preston Gómez launched attempts to stage games with the Cubans in the early and mid-1970s, but his hopes were

Tony Castro, one of Cuba's highest-ranking baseball officials, poses with a photo of his father Fidel inside Havana's Latin American Stadium. Courtesy of Peter C. Bjarkman.

dashed by the State Department, with Secretary of State Henry Kissinger deeming "politically inappropriate" what Gómez had optimistically promoted as a plan akin to earlier "ping-pong" diplomacy with China. In May 1975 George McGovern visited the island and talked with Fidel about potential baseball diplomacy as well as more serious political diplomacy. The Cuban leader himself acted to warm the waters during those meetings by announcing he would permit Luis Tiant Sr. to visit Boston for a long-overdue reunion with his son, then a star pitcher for the World Series–bound Boston Red Sox.

That same year the Cubans invited the New York Yankees, reputedly Fidel's favorite team, to visit the island for spring exhibitions. Baseball commissioner Bowie Kuhn initially endorsed the plan and there was even a promise that the big leaguers would not attempt to recruit disaffected Cuban players. But this overture was also blocked in Washington, again by Henry Kissinger, who seemed to have a particular ax to grind with the Cubans. By March 1977 a temporary thaw in Cuba policy under new president Jimmy Carter encouraged renewed talk of a possible Havana visit by the Fidel-favored Yankees, but this time Commissioner Kuhn canceled the plan as unacceptable, since it might give the New York team an unfair advantage in scouting or recruiting Cuban talent. And in November of the same year a group of Houston Astros, including manager Bill Virdon and all-star players Bob Watson and Ken Forsch, visited Havana to offer a series of clinics for the Cuban national team. [22]

It would be another two decades before baseball diplomacy would take even momentary hold and détente would become a brief reality. In early 1999 Baltimore Orioles owner Peter Angelos was able to convince the Clinton administration to sanction a home and away exhibition series between his own big-league club and the reigning Olympic and IBAF World Champion Cuban national team. The Cubans quickly agreed and the historic first game was staged at Latin American Stadium in March, during the height of Grapefruit and Cactus League spring training and to much hoopla and near-euphoric anticipation all across the island. While there was mild stateside interest in the historic event, Cubans were far more enthused by this first visit of a big-league club to Cuban shores since then-commissioner Ford Frick had canceled a scheduled March 1960 series between the same Baltimore club and the Cincinnati Reds and thus put a final halt to spring big-league junkets.

The Orioles–Cuba match in Havana involved intricate preparations and aroused a certain degree of criticism—even cynicism—especially in Miami. MLB had to upgrade ancient and decaying Latin American Stadium, retrofitting it to big-league specifications with outfield wall padding and a regraded infield. As part of the process the Cubans were also supplied with a large shipment of wooden bats fit for professional competition. [23] The game was scheduled in the midst of the Cuban League playoffs (Industriales, Santiago, Isla de La Juventud, and Guantánamo were engaged in the semifinal round) and therefore a number of top stars—including flashy Industriales shortstop Germán Mesa and Santiago sluggers Orestes Kindelán and Antonio Pacheco—whose teams were still in action did not perform. Some critics noted that a jammed stadium for the March 28 game in Havana consisted almost exclusively of invited party loyalists and that few "regular fans" got to enter. But the same would have to be said about big-league All-Star Games or World Series matches, where tickets are at a premium and doled out mainly to high rollers and those with family or business connections to the thirty big-league ball clubs.

The game on the field in Havana was a thrilling affair which saw the Cubans hold their own and surprise their opponents with the actual quality of their all-star squad. While future big leaguer José Contreras provided eight frames of stellar two-hit shutout relief (striking out ten), the Cubans edged back into the game with a pair of late rallies (one sparked by icon Omar Linares) and forced extra innings. Baltimore's Harold Baines saved the day for the big leaguers with an 11th-inning single off Pedro Lazo, plating Will Clark with the final 3–2 victory margin. The Orioles may have won on the scoreboard, but it was also a moral victory of grand proportions for the Cuban forces, since the locals demonstrated rather convincingly that they could indeed play head-to-toe with the big leaguers.

The May 3 rematch in Baltimore (played on a Monday evening open date in the MLB schedule and delayed for almost an hour at the start by rain) caused expected tensions away from the field as hordes of anti-Castro forces converged outside the park to protest the Cuban regime and the presence of the Cuban team on American soil. A hefty number of player agents also surrounded the park and the team hotel and openly encouraged hoped-for defections.[24] There was even a single ugly on-field incident when an exile-community protester raced onto the field during the fifth inning and was quickly felled by the Cuban umpire (César Valdés) manning second base. Another tarnishing blot was the public whining by several Orioles players (especially B. J. Surhoff and Albert Belle) upset about being forced to play "a meaningless exhibition" on a rare day of respite from regular league action.

The second game provided little of the competitive excitement of the first and quickly turned into a Cuban fiesta for television viewers back home. The Cubans—strengthened by the insertion of sluggers Kindelán and Pacheco in the heart of the lineup and enjoying a stellar four-for-four batting outburst by Linares—thoroughly outslugged and outpitched the uninterested American Leaguers, who appeared to be only going through the motions. Albert Belle displayed particular disdain on the field, waving haphazardly at the first pitch in his three at bats. And there were some further expressions of unhappiness among Orioles players when Cuban Andy Morales danced around the bases (the Americans took it as bush-league showboating) after a late-game homer that iced the 12–6 victory.

To the disappointment of Miami protesters and also many in the US media, the Baltimore match resulted in no ballplayer defections from the Cuban roster.[25] One of the off-field highlights of the whole affair came in a pre-game press conference with Cuban stars Omar Linares and Luis Ulacia. Pressed about their interest in playing in the majors, both declared they would welcome such a challenge as long as they didn't have to abandon their country to achieve it. Ulacia raised eyebrows when he added he would even play for free (no salary needed) just for the thrill of such an experience, a statement that had to leave MLB players' union officials shrinking in horror. With those unexpected pre-game statements the Cubans had already scored a major public relations triumph every bit as large as the one earned on the field of play a few hours later.

Rather than diminish the Cuban team and its accomplishments, the sloppy performance by bored Baltimore players in Camden Yards only seemed to enhance the image of Cuba's "play-for-pride" national baseball. Andy Morales's over-enthusiastic late-inning trot around the base paths—showboating for the big leaguers but merely the raw joy of national victory for the Cubans—also provided a final and indelible contrast between two clashing baseball universes.

4

NINETY MILES OF SEA, ONE HUNDRED MILES OF "HEATER"

They wait. . . . They wait at the bus stops, the bodegas, the cinemas, the taxi pools, the *agromercados*, the *tiendas*, the hospitals, the currency exchange booths, the banks and schools, in the *panaderias*, *lecherias*, *carnerías*, *relojarias*, *cafeterias*. You see the disorganized files and columns everywhere, the bodies twisted in posture, arms leaning on blistering laminated counters, disgruntled looks, resignation, pants and sighs, groans and grumbling, small talk issuing from frustrated lips in the Cuban run-on sentence of fragments that winds and rambles and ambles on for years upon years through heaps of bureaucratic slips of paper and top-brass decisions yet to be made in the trail of time that Cubans have nothing but.—Ben Corbett, *This Is Cuba*

Baseball diplomacy and baseball détente were both filling the air in the spring of 1999 with the announcement of a friendly exhibition series between the big-league Baltimore Orioles and the Cuban national team. At last an apparent breakthrough was on the horizon—for the baseball cold war, at least, if not for the larger and far more significant four-decade stalemate between Washington and Havana. For the first time in precisely forty years a big-league team would be visiting the island for an exhibition match.[1] And the Cuban national team was also scheduled to play a return engagement in a big-league stadium, this time not merely in off-the-radar amateur Olympic competitions (as had occurred three years earlier with the Atlanta Games) but at the invitation of Major League

Baseball and thus against top American big leaguers. The winds of change definitely seemed to be radically shifting.

But for the hard-liners at the forefront of an anti-Castro movement nothing had seemingly changed. Anti-Castro Cuban Americans and their numerous allies in a conservative stateside media fretted over these small steps toward baseball détente as signaling unwelcomed Washington capitulation in the long battle against a hated Castro government and its communist trappings. And Joe Cubas was also still very much in business, seeing this latest turn of events as still another welcome opportunity to score perhaps his biggest self-enriching defector haul yet, as well as his most dramatic assault so far on the communist regime.

Cubas was not a lone disruptive presence in Baltimore for the Cuban team visit in early May. Other opportunistic protestors—mostly, but not exclusively, based in Miami—would quickly turn the Cuban delegation's visit into a full-blown anti-Castro theatrical sideshow. On game day (May 3) the streets surrounding Oriole Park at Camden Yards witnessed tense face-offs between banner-toting groups haranguing the Castro regime and only slightly smaller contingents calling for an end to the US blockade. Joe Cubas himself set up a street corner soapbox to promise the festive if highly charged crowd still another bus-load of ballplayer defections. There would even be a brief interruption of the game when one audacious protester sprinted onto the field during the fifth inning draped in a Cuban flag, only to be felled with a body slam near second base by enraged Cuban umpire César Valdés. That incident alone elicited far more media commentary than any details concerning the game itself, a lopsided 12–6 Cuban victory over big leaguers who didn't seem to be playing the match with any real seriousness. In fact the North American press and electronic media seemed more focused on protestors in the streets surrounding the ballpark, or on the constant rumors about possibilities for defections of star players, than they were on the true historical significance of the Camden Yards baseball game itself.

There were also some other significant changes in the air. The upcoming Pan American Games slated for Winnipeg, Canada, in the final week of July would represent a seismic shift in international tournament format. Professional players, mostly minor leaguers with a sprinkling of former cup-of-coffee major leaguers, were now for the first time being allowed into the competition. Winnipeg would also determine two Western Hemisphere qualifiers for the 2000 Sydney Olympics. Ash wood instead of aluminum bats—authentic pro-style major-league wooden bats—would return for tournament play after an absence of nearly a quarter century. This was a shift that impacted the Cubans most heavily. Cuban Leaguers (like American collegiate and scholastic teams) had used aluminum since 1977. But the larger factor was the introduction of professionals, not only from the States, but also from hotbed ball-playing nations like the Dominican Republic, Mexico, and Venezuela. No longer would the reigning amateur world champions simply feast upon underage collegians or squads of second-level semi-pros and ragtag industrial leaguers. A new international era was definitely dawning.

Winnipeg would also signal a modern era for Cuban defections. El Duque (1998) had only recently followed Liván (1997) in establishing that Cuban pitchers could indeed make an immediate impact on the big-league scene. Ever-crusading agent-smuggler Joe Cubas had already enticed a handful of at least moderately successful Cuban pitchers, first with Ozzie Fernández and Liván, and then Rolando Arroyo. Now he was hungry for more and Winnipeg seemed the ideal target. On a more personal note, the Winnipeg baseball competitions held in newly opened Canwest Global Park on the banks of the Red River would also represent my own first trip to watch the Cubans abroad as an official member of the working baseball press. It was the landmark event that first placed me in close personal contact with both the elite Cuban ballplayers and the pro scouts and talent-hungry agents that were constantly shadowing them.[2]

The Winnipeg Games would turn into an event dominated by defection obsessions within both the local and national Canadian press. The reigning theme of the competitions, at least for local scribes, seemed to be "The Free World versus Fidel Castro" and the top-floor windows in a building directly across from the press media center featured an oversized and daily changing scoreboard of unofficial defector counts—Defectors 4, Fidel 0, etc. There was also continuous harassment of the Cuban delegation that included one nasty incident outside the venue of a wrestling match when several protesters entered into brief fisticuffs with some senior INDER officials, including former Olympic track and field star Alberto Juantorena. When one local newspaper scribe searching for a story found out I was an American following the Cuban team, he requested an immediate interview on a most predictable topic: the fictions behind the legend of Fidel as a one-time pitching prospect. And then there was also Joe Cubas (as well as his competitor in the hunt, Gus

Domínguez), camped outside the Cuban team quarters, haunting baseball practice facilities, always awaiting possible contacts with disaffected ballplayers he hoped were now primed to abandon their flag and their teammates.

* * *

The eyes of Joe Cubas and a handful of his rival agents, as well as dozens of big-league scouts, were focused primarily on a newly arrived and highly touted flame-throwing phenomenon named Maels Rodriguez. In his few appearances in Winnipeg, Maels indeed turned some heads during his handful of outings. He won the opener against Mexico with 3.2 innings of stellar relief in which he allowed a single hit and struck out five. He closed out the ninth inning of the gold medal finale with the Americans by striking out the side. He did falter in a first outing against Team USA, giving up five earned runs and suffering the loss. But during the week he struck out ten with his blazing fastball and walked only four in six innings of work. A true highlight of the week would remain Maels's first entrance from the bullpen in the Mexico game (I was sitting alongside a stunned Mets scout, Omar Minaya, at the time), when his first several warmup tosses (all registering ninety-nine on several Jugs guns) sent an entire home-plate-area scouting contingent scrambling for their report sheets. The biggest news was that Maels remained solidly entrenched in the Cuban camp.

In the end Cubas would have to settle for what appeared at the time to be a far lesser prize. On the morning of a USA-Cuba final the least-known and least-heralded pitcher on the Cuban staff, a twenty-two-year-old righty with untested potential, slipped away from the Cuban team quarters at an adjacent Canadian air force base. Danys Baez (often spelled "Denis" or "Danis" in Cuban League guidebooks) had a limited-enough Cuban League resume to escape previous notice; he was the number nine hurler on the current Cuban nine-man staff and had made only a pair of brief appearances in Winnipeg, working a total of 2.1 innings, facing only eleven batters, and escaping without yielding an earned run. Cubas had his limited prize—one that would turn out in a few years to be much bigger than anyone perceived at the time—but that week in Winnipeg it did not make the headlines he might have been hoping for.

Like others, Baez wouldn't remain in Cubas's camp very long. But he did prove one of the bigger surprises among the string of early Joe Cubas successes. Unlike the half-dozen defecting pitchers before him, he had virtually no visible record of accomplishment in Cuba, having claimed only six wins spread over two seasons for Pinar del Río. He may have boasted plenty of raw promise based on size and natural fastball alone, but he was also clearly a true diamond in the rough. Cubas had little enough trouble peddling his prize to Cleveland, landing a hefty $14.5-million deal, and within two years the hard-throwing righty had reached the big leagues. Two more summers and he would begin a three-year stretch of most impressive saves numbers (25, 30, 41) as a closer, the final two seasons of that stretch with Tampa Bay. Baez would turn out to be one of the more effective Cuban pitchers of his decade, earning a 2005 All-Star Game nod, lasting ten seasons with a half-dozen big-league teams, and racking up more than one hundred games saved. These were big-league accomplishments matched by few of his countrymen, before or after the revolution.

In retrospect one had to wonder what might have been the outcome had Maels bolted in Winnipeg instead of Baez. The next couple of National Series campaigns back in Cuba would reveal just how much the agents and bird dogs had missed out on. Maels Rodríguez was about to become the biggest short-term sensation the Cuban League had ever produced.

A little more than a decade later the big-league universe would be enthralled by the remarkable triple digit fastballs of Cuban southpaw Aroldis Chapman. By 2010 and 2011 Chapman was already etching his spot in big-league lore alongside a handful of super arms like Bob Feller and Walter Johnson and Nolan Ryan, and perhaps only a few others, who might lay legitimate claim to the most explosive "heaters" ever witnessed. "The Cuban Missile" (as styled by the Cincinnati Reds) would also draw comparisons to the legendary Steve Dalkowski, a failed minor leaguer who never did make "The Show" but reportedly launched the greatest fastballs ever witnessed in an early-1960s era, when radar guns were not available at minor-league parks to verify velocities some claimed might have topped 110 mph. But in large part those lavish raves were propped up by the fact that an American baseball universe never witnessed Chapman's Cuban forerunner, Maels Rodríguez.

Maels was easily the best pitcher I ever witnessed in Cuba. He was also the hardest thrower, Chapman included. He was first to top the century speed mark on the island, the only one to author a perfect game in post-revolution Cuban baseball, and a truly untouchable hurler who struck out hitters at a rate rarely paralleled anywhere in a legitimate top-level pro league.[3] The big rawboned country boy from Sancti Spíritus was something of a Chapman plus Dalkowski, all rolled into one package. But Maels was also more than a mere overbearing thrower cut in a Chapman mold. He got batters out on a consistent basis, not in limited one-inning stints but in seven-, eight-, or nine-inning full-game labors. His blazer was usually in or tantalizingly close to the strike zone. He was also a right-hander.

One—perhaps two—of the greatest seasons in Cuban baseball lore were posted by Maels Rodríguez at the outset of the new millennium. Fans of old-time Cuban baseball love to spin the legend of José de la Caridad Méndez (el Diamante Negro) and regale his 1900s-era performances against touring pros. It is not possible in a shifting baseball world to adequately judge Méndez, who pitched in a Dead Ball epoch and earned his stripes against vacationing big leaguers who may well have seen those games as a lark rather than as serious competitions. But there are many around today (including this author) who watched Maels up close for that all-too-brief spell at the outset of the new century. And it was, in truth, pure magic to behold.

A breakout season for the Sancti Spíritus phenom during National Series 39 (1999–2000)—already Maels's third league campaign despite the fact that he was barely nineteen—witnessed the island's first officially measured 100-mph heater, recorded December 8, 1999, at his home park, José Antonio Huelga Stadium. Two weeks later, on the same field, Maels authored the league's first-ever perfect game, a 1–0 blanking of Las Tunas featuring 12 Ks among the 27 consecutive putouts. This rarest of masterpieces was assured when the Sancti Spíritus club punched home a lone run in the bottom of the ninth to prevent extra frames. Maels's 177 Ks on the campaign (62 walks) tied teammate Yovani Aragón for the league's lead.

The encore campaign at age twenty (2000–1) elevated his game several more notches. He broke into the double-figure column in victories for the first time and his fifteen wins represented the league's top mark, as did his totals for innings pitched (178.1), starts (23), and ERA (1.77). Most notably, he virtually obliterated the league strikeout record, his 268 Ks eclipsing Santiago "Changa" Mederos's three-decade-old standard (208) by nearly 30 percent. In a single season and barely out of his teens, Maels had established himself as one of the most dominant ever on the island. Meanwhile, he was also building impressive credentials on the international scene. A year after the impressive debut in Winnipeg, Maels anchored the national team bullpen at the Sydney Olympics, blanking the opposition for 13.1 innings and striking out twenty-two while permitting only nine hits and six walks. The highlight in Sydney was an excellent no-decision outing in the gold medal final (4.2 scoreless innings with 7 Ks) despite a heartbreaking loss (charged to José Ibar) to Ben Sheets and the Tommy Lasorda–managed Americans. Although used sparingly in Cuba's first Olympic gold medal setback, Maels still stood among top tournament performers, ranking third in strikeouts and tying American Ryan Franklin for the best ERA.

The following season brought more of the same. Again Maels would top 200 strikeouts (219 with 85 walks) while posting a 14–3 National Series ledger. He was also again the staff workhorse (with Yovani Aragón), leading Sancti Spíritus to its first-ever league finals appearance during the era (launched in 1986) of postseason play. But that second year of further record-busting statistics was also the beginning of the end. Rodríguez, despite his robust physical stature, was clearly being over-used, laboring 165 innings in regular-season action, plus 46.2 more in the postseason (four starts and seven relief appearances) and another 43.1 in the follow-up short-season summer Super League. In that later competi-tion, pitching for the Centrales team, he would toss the first-ever Super League no-hitter, a 1–0 blanking of Habana marred only by three walks and one hit batsman. His coaches, and eventually even the baseball com-mission itself, were already stretching and burning out a potential star—a not-infrequent scenario in Cuba before the introduction of pitch counts several years down the road. And there was also a bizarre injury added to the mix.

A straw that broke the proverbial camel's back would occur during the spring 2002 postseason. Maels would be heavily relied upon by Sancti Spíritus manager Lourdes Gourriel as perhaps no hard-throwing young-ster ever should be. His longevity was being jeopardized in a desperate effort to win a single coveted National Series pennant. And if that was not enough, the star pitcher was also being put on display to score some important propaganda points. On the eve of late-May playoffs he was ordered to pitch in a staged exhibition hastily arranged by Fidel to tout the national game for visiting former US president Jimmy Carter. Billed as an All-Star contest between teams representing the two league divisions

(Occidentales and Orientales) and played before an overflow crowd of 50,000 that gathered for the festivities in Latin American Stadium, the match was no more than a trumped-up opportunity to show off Fidel's prized stars; the league's actual All-Star Game had been held months earlier in Pinar del Río. Carter was invited to throw out a ceremonial first pitch and national team ace José Contreras took the hill for Occidentales. Although his own team was housed in the same Western Division as Contreras's, Maels was nonetheless shifted to the Orientales lineup, where he could display his arsenal of fastballs for Carter in a *mano-a-mano* tussle between Cuba's top two pitchers. Sigfredo Barros would report in the daily edition of *Granma* that Maels threw a steady diet of ninety-plus fastballs for five full frames, struck out seven, and permitted only a pair of scattered hits (ironically enough, to future defectors Kendrys Morales and Yobal Dueñas).

The league postseason would begin only four days later and in those playoffs Maels would set new standards for workhorse effort. He earned two victories in the quarterfinals (where he also dropped a third decision) and another pair in semifinal games. He was called to the hill for closer duties in Game Seven (one night after starting Game Six), securing a coveted ticket to the finale for longtime league doormat Sancti Spíritus. (The last out of the historic semifinals came when Omar Linares, in his final Cuban career at bat, crushed a Maels fastball to deepest center field, where only a spectacular defensive effort by a less-heralded Gourriel brother—Yunieski—prevented sweet victory from evaporating into sudden painful defeat.) Already largely spent, Maels was then used in all seven games as his team dropped a tense championship series with Holguín; two of those final efforts were starts (both losing decisions) and the others involved short relief assignments.

There was also a hidden backstory to the whole affair. It wasn't just that the mainstay pitcher was being disastrously overused. He was also being trucked out day after day while suffering from a painful injury incurred weeks earlier and never disclosed to the Cuban press corps. Apparently Maels had been assaulted with a malicious blow across the shoulders by a bat-wielding teammate during an altercation marring a rowdy practice session. It was this injury, never allowed to heal properly during the heat of a pennant race, that was the dark secret behind the collapse of one of baseball's great unknown natural talents.

A year later Maels was nearly finished. He labored through sixteen starts and posted a still impressive 8–3 won-lost mark, but his strikeouts (117) dropped nearly by half and his ERA soared to 3.11. He still got batters out regularly enough and was generally effective, but he simply was not the same magical pitcher. The drop in strikeout numbers was the most alarming, from 13.3 per nine innings two years earlier to a still impressive but not so exceptional 9.3 average. And then by year's end, still only a twenty-two-year-old youngster, he was done. Maels could no longer throw above 85 mph and thus had lost his one dominant pitching weapon. In late summer he was left off the national team training for the World Cup games that Cuba would host at split venues in Matanzas and Havana.

Those missed World Cup games provided the final sad chapter. On the night Cuba was claiming another championship with its nail-biting victory over Panama, word spread in the press box that Maels had secretly fled the country. (I was present in the Havana press box at the time and was one of the first to hear the spreading rumors.) He left with another former national team star, Yobal Dueñas, who had also fallen out of favor with league officials and had similarly lost a national team slot to a rising phenom named Yulieski Gourriel. Maels was bound to attract the major attention of MLB scouts given his demonstrated brilliance only a few seasons earlier and his brief trials on the international stage, most especially in Winnipeg and Sydney. Agent Henry Vilars was soon showcasing the latest pair of defectors for thirty clubs in Costa Rica while one rival agent was already suggesting that Maels would soon demand more money than the $32 million José Contreras had lately garnered from the Yankees. Agent Jaime Torres also chimed in, opining that Maels was the only pitcher on the planet worth more than his own client, Contreras. Maels himself would issue statements to the press implying that Cuban officials had exaggerated the degree of his injury as an excuse for leaving him off a pair of national teams. Maels claimed the real reason was that Cuban authorities feared he would defect.

But it was all a smoke screen. Both players would experience a rocky path toward professional baseball. Dueñas had been a national team star for several years, beginning in the same 1999 Winnipeg tournament where Maels had debuted. He enjoyed his own biggest moment on the international stage with the 2002 Intercontinental Cup in Havana, where he blasted one of the longest homers in the history of Latin American

Stadium to clinch a gold medal win over South Korea. But at the advanced age of thirty-one he had been left off the 2003 World Cup squad in favor of the nineteen-year-old Gourriel. Dueñas did land a hefty contract with the Yankees, reported to include a $60,000 signing bonus, but in the end never got out of the minors. His AAA cup of coffee in Columbus as a fading thirty-two-year-old consisted of a mere six at bats. By career's end he had experienced anything but a gilded American Dream. Playing days squandered, he soon ran afoul of the law and in late 2008 served brief prison time for stealing jewelry in South Carolina.[4] It was a classic cautionary tale that highly touted Cuban League stars do not always translate into can't-miss professionals.

Maels Rodríguez would be a flameout of still grander proportions. It appeared in short order that he was not as healthy as he had claimed before his Costa Rica showcase and that perhaps the Cubans had, in fact, not exaggerated the extent of his arm damage. There were no takers, since no one in the MLB marketplace was interested in a recently sidelined hurler now sporting no more than a high-80s fastball. Setting up shop in Miami, Maels attempted to rehabilitate his arm and rescue his fading dream. Reports circulated that he was on the mend and that the injury had only been damaged rib cage muscles (perhaps from the rumored bat attack) that had caused him to lower his elbow during delivery and thus also lowered his velocity. But the arm condition was obviously far more serious. In a 2014 interview with *Miami Herald* writer Jorge Ebro, Maels would finally admit that there had been three unsuccessful surgeries to repair the damage, the first as early as December 2003, on the heels of the Costa Rica workouts.[5] The Houston Astros would gamble a twenty-second round amateur draft pick (2005), but there was never a contract offer or a single inning of minor-league baseball.

Maels served as yet another stern warning to those young prospects back home who might be willing to heed it. Gambling everything on a slim hope for big-league riches and fame was always a shot in the dark. Careers could end at any moment; injury could instantly wreck even the most exceptional athletes, and pitchers especially were fragile creatures. In this case, a youngster who a few years earlier had been a magnet for every big-league scout that ever saw him toss a flaming fastball would find himself building a very different life on American shores than the one he had once anticipated.

Maels would be back in the headlines half-a-dozen years later, but under far different circumstances. He would stir controversy and produce fallout when he briefly and surreptitiously visited a pair of his former teammates at a major international tournament in San Juan (chapter 8). One had to wonder, after Maels came forth in the Miami press with the details of his involvement that led to the unpopular suspension of Team Cuba captain Freddie Cepeda, if the overreaction of Cuban officials in that instance might have resulted as much as anything from the residue of guilt and bitterness surrounding the original circumstances under which Maels had been motivated to leave his homeland.

In the end Maels Rodríguez provides one of the saddest tales of failed baseball dreams and failed baseball policies within Cuba. Likely the best natural talent the island ever produced—certainly the most electric arm I ever witnessed in my nearly twenty years of traveling there—he was unarguably abused by the system that had spawned him. Maels eventually found his way out of Cuba, but when he did there was no baseball life left for him. Even the dreams that might have been on the island had been ruined. It seems that Cuba all too often kills off its brightest talent, or at least squanders it in a sea of excessive suspicion or excessive exploitation—nearly as fast as it uncovers it.

* * *

As difficult as the concept might be to grasp, Chapman—the famed Cuban Missile—was not Maels Rodríguez when it came to pure pitching talent. At least not back in Cuba for the brief spans during which they both tantalized Cuban League hitters. That might be hard to believe, given what Chapman would eventually accomplish on the big-league stage in Cincinnati, but it is true nonetheless. If Chapman had a leg up on Maels it was simply the fact that the Holguín southpaw, for all his own personal missteps along the way, was simply much, much luckier.

The Aroldis Chapman saga—almost as might have been predicted—began in Rotterdam at the 2009 edition of the biennial World Port Tournament. Chapman reappeared on the international scene as part of a second-level Cuban team that had traveled to Rotterdam under the control of first-time national team manager Roger Machado. The hard-throwing Holguín southpaw had been assigned to the squad as perhaps a final shot at redemption after his poor March showing during World Baseball Classic outings in Mexico and San Diego. When he abandoned the Cuban delegation before the first Rotterdam pitch was thrown, it was perhaps not that great a surprise, maybe not even to the Cubans themselves. It did leave Machado's club rather short on pitching, and yet the Rotterdam games would provide an opportunity to showcase a new flock of rising stars including José Dariel Abreu, Leonys Martin, Adonis García, Freddy Asiel Alvarez, and Vladimir García. The loaded Cubans waltzed to another expected title behind their 9–1 overall slate and despite the loss of their prized southpaw starter, drubbing a Dutch squad 9–3 in the finals. This was the same Netherlands roster that had received such rave reviews at the earlier 2006 World Baseball Classic. If Chapman's departure didn't seem to unsettle Machado's club on the field, and perhaps at the time wasn't even viewed by the Cubans as that great a loss, it did establish something of a dangerous new trend.

Rotterdam would soon become a main departure point for Cubans seeking the alternate life of a professional career and the promise of hitting big-league pay dirt. Two summers later Odrisamer Despaigne would flee in the Paris airport en route to the 2013 Rotterdam edition. That July 2013 Rotterdam tournament (another Cuban victory on the heels of yet another WBC disappointment earlier that spring) didn't witness any further on-the-scene defections, but events would be set in motion there that eventually led to the loss of prized prospect Yoan Moncada (chapter 7). Geraldo Concepción, recent National Series rookie of the year, would bolt from that same port city in 2011, only days before Puig ran afoul of Dutch authorities (chapter 1). Puig and Abreu would also make their final national team appearances in Rotterdam, as would the aforementioned Moncada.[6]

Thus it would later pan out that Chapman had launched an unprecedented European wave of Team Cuba defections when he walked away from the newly opened Domina Hotel with such relative ease. The hotel sits on the same grounds as the Rotterdam Zoo and Neptunus Family Stadium ball park.[7] Cuban ballplayers are under little watchdog security there since the site is a relatively isolated one. Chapman would later report that he walked away from the hotel entrance carrying only a pack of cigarettes and his passport and stepped into the car of an unnamed friend who had arranged to pick him up. All this transpired less than two hours after the team had arrived, eaten lunch, posed for credentials photos, and then retired to their second-floor quarters (where Chapman was scheduled to room with fellow pitcher Vladimir García). When Aroldis told García he was stepping out for a short smoke, he surprisingly found himself alone at the hotel entrance, no security or delegation members to block or even notice his departure. One has to wonder if the Cuban contingent actually expected him to leave and perhaps didn't care that much if he did. Chapman seemingly was becoming less valued as a national team contributor. Yet the strangest part of the story and the part that raises the most questions was that Chapman had left with his valuable passport in hand. For yet-unexplained reasons, Cuban Baseball Federation officials had not followed normal protocol and confiscated passports after immigration check-in at Schiphol Airport. Cuban players rarely, if ever, have such documents in their possession.

Once free of the island, Chapman would have a relatively short but circuitous route to the big leagues and the big dollars. Hidden away with his unnamed friend in Amsterdam, the ballplayer was joined three days later by a second childhood friend (whose identity also remains undisclosed) and by player agent Edwin Leonel Mejia (working for the newly formed Athletes Premier International), with whom he quickly signed a working agreement. The group then drove straight to Barcelona, a trip of slightly less than twenty-four hours. Needing to find a third-country residence, but also fearing efforts by other agents to entice Chapman into seeking alternate representation, Mejia abandoned any plan to take his prize athlete to the Dominican Republic, instead arranging to house him in the most unlikely locale, the tiny independent principality of Andorra just outside the Spanish border.

While awaiting his Andorran residency papers Chapman worked out privately and also for scouts at the former Olympic baseball park in Barcelona, sessions also attended by ESPN writer Jorge Arangure.[8] The processing of his clearance by the Office of Foreign Assets Control (OFAC)—the action necessary for official free agent status—was accomplished in relatively short order, which has not always been the case with many of the Cubans once they have established their required third-country residence. By the end of November the story broke that Chapman had already fired Mejia and signed on with brothers Randy and Alan Hendricks as his new official representatives, a development reported by the *Miami Herald* without much explanation. But many scouts remained dubious, especially considering the big money the new agents were bandying about as a price tag. I would have a number of telephone discussions with prominent scouting directors (from the Red Sox and Royals in particular) who contacted me for my own assessments of Chapman's potential and market value. I had my own doubts, based on what I had seen on the ground in Cuba over the past several winters. And apparently so did many others far more experienced within the professional scouting community. There were troubling questions about the pitcher's mental make-up, his maturity and stability, both on the mound and away from the ballpark. A meltdown against the Japanese in San Diego during a crucial WBC match had not been an impressive signal. There was the issue of how consistently he could control that marvelous fastball. And then there were also concerns about just how big a risk a hard thrower like Chapman actually might be. Pitchers like that can suffer injuries that end careers in a heartbeat. Maels Rodríguez was the poster boy for such unanticipated setbacks. Professional baseball is in fact littered with such storied burn-outs.

I had first encountered Chapman outside Changa Stadium in Havana in late September of 2007. He had been working out with the pre-selection national team preparing for the upcoming IBAF World Cup in Taiwan and we were briefly introduced by Cuban journalist Jeli Valmaña. It would be our only face-to-face encounter on Cuban soil. That 2007 event would be the tournament in which Cuba would finally lose its long stranglehold on the IBAF event, dropping a 6–3 final to a Davey Johnson–managed American team featuring Evan Longoria, Andy LaRoche, and Jayson Nix. But the nineteen-year-old Chapman showed brilliance there in his two brief outings, posting the tournament's lowest ERA (1.20), striking out twenty in fifteen innings during a pair of dominating performances, and earning a post-event all-star selection as the top southpaw hurler. It was after that Taiwan outing that big-league scouts (to say nothing of bottom-feeding player agents) had Chapman fixed firmly in their sights.

In the following couple of years the Holguín southpaw would wrap up a somewhat uneven four-year National Series career. He would work almost exclusively as a starter in three of four seasons and he would lead the circuit in strikeouts on two occasions (2007 with 100 and 2009 with 130). He won barely more than he lost (24–21), which might in part be explained by team support, but his career 3.71 ERA was not eye-catching. He was the second Cuban flamethrower to top 100 mph on the Jugs radar gun, equaling Maels's feat of a few years earlier. But he frequently struggled with his command and never proved overwhelming, even in a league short on big league–quality opposition hitters. His strikeout totals never

Cuban ballplayer jerseys on display at the National Shrine Basilica of Our Lady of Charity near the village of El Cobre in eastern Cuba. Included (top right) is the World Baseball Classic jersey of defector Aroldis Chapman. Courtesy of Peter C. Bjarkman.

matched those of previous greats like Maels (whose single-season record doubled Chapman's best year), or Changa Mederos and Manuel Alarcón (who also both topped the 200 mark). And in the summer of 2008 he would pitch his way off the Olympic team with several wild displays on the mound during the José Huelga Memorial Tournament staged in both Havana and San Jose de las Lajas as a final audition for the upcoming Beijing Games. Chapman's absence in Beijing would later often be attributed to punishment for an early 2008 defection attempt. Yet if that were the sole reason, it is not substantiated by the fact that Aroldis was a member of the pre-selection group picked to compete for roster spots during the June Huelga Tournament matches.

Rumored earlier defection attempts and the Beijing absence aside, Chapman was back on the scene when Cuba headed to Mexico City for the second edition of the World Baseball Classic. If there had indeed been a thwarted effort back in 2008 to abandon the island, the pitcher had seemingly worked his way back into good graces with Cuban officials. Just how all that had occurred was a murky tale that would remain hidden for a couple more years. By March 2009 Chapman was obviously still being counted on as a potential fourth or fifth starter in the Cuban national team pitching arsenal, behind aces Norge Vera, Yunieski Maya, Yulieski González (15–0 a year earlier in league action), and Vladimir García. He performed well in an opening round match versus Australia, working four strong innings as the starter, striking out seven, and allowing only one walk and one run. But when he got his chance in the spotlight with a repeat start for a crucial second-round game versus Japan in San Diego, he did not show well. He never made it out of the third frame, allowing a trio of base-loading singles while seemingly losing both his self-confidence and composure, prancing around the mound and suddenly appearing most unwilling to challenge Japanese hitters. It was becoming painfully clear that he might not have the makeup to be a big-league starter.

But if there were warning signals, there were also plenty of enthusiastic suitors once the unproven flamethrower was on the free agent market. After an impressive December workout in Houston there were rumored bids in the $20 million range from both the Red Sox and Marlins. By mid-January, six months after Chapman had bolted, it was small-market Cincinnati that was willing to bust the bank and gamble a $30.25 million deal that included a $1.5 million signing bonus. José Contreras had received slightly more eight years earlier ($32 million over four years from New York), but that might be explained away. Contreras was a proven international star (undefeated in his thirteen Team Cuba outings) and the undisputed cream of the crop when he left the island. Chapman was a potential late-inning closer, but only if the Reds minor-league instructors could find a way to tame his wildness, adjust his delivery, and polish his raw physical tools. The Yankees had invested in a savvy pitcher while the Reds appeared to be gambling on a rifle arm alone.

On the heels of Chapman's eye-opening contract with Cincinnati, I weighed in with my own measured assessments of his potential in a three-part blog site interview also republished on www.BaseballdeCuba.com.[9] My views were immediately and widely misunderstood and thus caused a good deal of controversy, generating charges on social media that my doubts about Chapman arose only from my apparent disappointment he had defected in the first place. My opinion of Chapman had nothing to do with any "political" stance, as several of my critics would loudly contend at the time. (One blogger, falsely assuming I was based in Havana, labeled me a shill for the Cuban government.) My words of caution had everything to do with what I (and others) saw as his perceived makeup as a potential big-league starter. And if he would be limited to a closer's role, was the money (even for wildly rich MLB teams) in the end justified? Certainly anyone potentially throwing 100 mph at big-league hitters had to be seen as a legitimate prospect. I only questioned whether or not Chapman truly was a $30 million prize.

Given the elevated price tag and the ear-piercing hype, Chapman did seem to start rather slowly in Cincinnati. He appeared in fifteen games out of the bullpen as a late-season call-up in 2010 after spending most of the year with AAA Louisville, where he had won nine as an early season starter and then settled into a closer's role with eight saves. He stuck with the parent club a year later and was used exclusively in middle relief, but in those earliest trials the strikeout potential (12.8 per nine innings both years) was already obvious. The Reds had obviously decided that his makeup and his fastball dictated short relief stints. Over his first two seasons he won six games and saved one, and while his SO/BB ratio was impressive enough, one still had to wonder if he was paying enough dividends on a $30 million gamble. It was the radar gun feats primarily that grabbed the headlines and made the *SportsCenter* highlight reels. Less than one month after his big-league debut, on September 25, 2010, in Petco Park (on the same mound where he had disappointed against Japan eighteen months earlier), Chapman unleashed the fastest recorded pitch (105.1 mph) ever witnessed on a big-league diamond.

There were also highly celebrated off-the-field incidents that cast a good deal of cold water on the Reds' optimistic plans for Chapman. There were several arrests for reckless speeding in fancy new sports cars, the most celebrated coming when Chapman was nabbed by troopers in May 2012 topping 93 mph on an Ohio interstate while carrying a suspended Kentucky driver's license. Reports also surfaced the same week of Chapman being robbed in his team hotel room by a woman he had rather unwisely picked up during a club road trip to Pittsburgh. Both incidents, along with breaking news about possible legal troubles stemming from events back in Cuba, unfolded just as Chapman was launching what would soon prove to be his breakthrough big-league season. At first it was reported that the ballplayer's room had been ransacked by intruders who stole valuable jewelry, with the alleged women "companion" left bound and in tears in the aftermath of the apparent heist. But the truth would soon leak out that the woman herself was the actual culprit, having staged the whole affair with several accomplices. She was eventually charged with the robbery and with filing a false police report. The entire bizarre affair left Chapman tarnished with charges of hopelessly naïve decision making; few and far between were those who saw him as merely a sympathetic or innocent victim.

Worse news was on the way and was in fact already circulating at the time of the speeding arrest and hotel break-in. Chapman was now being sued in Florida courts by a Cuban American, Danilo Curbelo García, who claimed the ballplayer had directly caused his own false imprisonment and resulting torture by giving false testimony to Cuban officials in the aftermath of the widely rumored and apparently all-too-real initial 2008 defection attempt. The suit was filed by Miami attorney Avelino González, who would also soon be launching a similar case against Yasiel Puig (discussed in chapter 1). As Scott Eden fully elaborates in his *ESPN The Magazine* article detailing smuggling operations involving Puig, Curbelo was a Florida resident who disappeared while visiting his family in Cuba during July 2008 (immediately after Chapman's meltdown at the Huelga Tournament in Havana). He had apparently crossed paths with Chapman while traveling in Holguín Province with a friend and had casually inquired (perhaps in jest) about why the ballplayer had not found a way to escape the island. It was a foolish and costly mistake on the part of the boisterous tourist.

Curbelo's version of events claimed that Chapman seized on the opportunity and, along with his father (a boxing trainer and city employee), reported the incident to authorities, but with the added suggestion that Curbelo had actually approached the ballplayer with a specific plan for arranging his defection. The lawsuit would rest on the contention that Chapman, like Puig a few years later, had agreed with Cuban authorities to report possible human traffickers as a means of paying his penance and earning his way back onto Team Cuba in the wake of his own early 2008 unsuccessful defection effort.[10] It was with the Curbelo lawsuit that details would now finally begin to emerge concerning the young pitcher's first rumored efforts to flee Cuba several months before the mid-summer Olympic tryouts, efforts that were often rumored but never previously detailed. As a result of that suit—eventually settled out of court in Octo-

ber 2014 when both parties agreed to a motion to dismiss the action—
Chapman would now begin to appear as something of a fastball-heaving
double-agent, not merely a defector from the Cuban system, but also (like
Puig) an informant working at least part-time for the elaborate Cuban
state intelligence apparatus. [11]

As all this ugly off-field publicity was weighing on Aroldis Chapman,
his on-field career finally took off. Starting with the 2012 campaign, he
rang up three straight seasons of 35-plus saves. He quickly became the
most effective closer on the major-league scene and perhaps one of the
best in the game's history. He rang up a string of records in the process
and appeared in four consecutive MLB All-Star Games. In mid-July 2014
he broke Bruce Sutter's big league mark for the most consecutive relief
appearances (forty) with at least one strikeout; he extended that string to
forty-nine by the end of the campaign. The Chapman investment had
indeed paid off, even if the Reds had to suffer a handful of public relations bruises in the process, and even if his outsized contract was stretching the Reds' budget enough by late in the 2015 season to spark trade
rumors. [12] But big-league fans and sports fans in general are always willing to look the other way if the on-the-field stuff is sensational enough.
And on today's American celebrity sports scene, bad-boy images sometimes actually pay some added dividends.

One writer for *ESPN The Magazine* would publish an intriguing in-
depth report on Chapman's lifestyle five years into his big-league adventure. The piece by prize-winning journalist Eli Saslow would question if
Chapman was indeed truly happy with his decision to leave Cuba. [13] The
ace pitcher was pictured as finding his new off-season life tedious, sleeping through daylight hours at his Davie, Florida, mansion surrounded by
the extended family he had now extracted from Cuba, fighting boredom
by returning to his roots through a financial and personal interest in a
half-dozen Cuban boxers training in New York and Miami. (Chapman
had begun his athletic career as a boxer and his father had trained amateur
fighters in Holguín.) He missed some of the simplicities of rural Cuba
that he had left behind, and, as Saslow told the story, to compensate the
ballplayer was soon taking up a series of new diversions, some of which
were not always of the healthiest kind.

The Saslow article would raise all of the pluses and minuses of a rags-
to-riches story typical of several Cuban imports who had found overwhelming success in the American big leagues but had not always known

how to handle the lucrative trappings that seemed to come all too easily. Saslow would underscore a major theme of the emerging Cuban defector story. As he phrased it, Chapman and many of his countrymen spent so much effort in plotting and planning their escapes to the American Promised Land that they apparently never spent any time considering what life would be like once they got there.

I had definitely been wrong about Chapman. And I would soon prove to be even further off target with my assessments of the big-league potential of one-time national team ace Yunieski Maya. My initial predictions had been that Maya, a hard-throwing right hander with Pinar del Río who possessed a large warrior's heart, would almost certainly be a far bigger success in the majors than Chapman. I had based that assessment on Maya's achievements both in the Cuban League and on the national team, where he had been one of the most dependable performers for several seasons.

Maya had shown considerable grit in his three outings at the 2009 WBC, the very event in which the more celebrated Chapman had faltered. He lost the elimination game versus Japan, but largely because of a first-inning dropped fly ball by Yoenis Céspedes; he yielded no earned runs during the brief outing. Later that same summer he had attempted to leave the island with his five-year-old son in tow, a violation that resulted in brief incarceration. But Maya had found a way to flee to the Dominican Republic by September, where he then languished for more than nine months awaiting OFAC clearance. Finally freed to sign as a certified free agent, Maya landed a late-July four-year deal with the Washington Nationals reportedly valued at $8 million. He was all-too-quickly brought to the big leagues for an initial cup of coffee in early September. But in the end the entire three-year Washington big-league career would consist of no more than sixteen games and a single 2011 victory.

In Maya's case the promise never paid off. Perhaps he had simply languished far too long on Dominican soil before finding his way back into competitive action. He would spend the next couple of years laboring in AAA, first in Syracuse, and then with Gwinnett, after being released and picked up by Atlanta. Maya was clearly a major disappointment for both Washington and Atlanta and he was gone from organized baseball before the end of the 2014 campaign. But there would be one last largely invisible hurrah for the former Cuban ace. Signing on in the Korean pro league in late 2014, during the following spring Yunieski Maya would toss a no-hit, no-run game for the Doosan Bears (the second ever by a foreigner in the KBO) that had to rank near the top of his quickly diminishing career resume.

Maya would not be the only Cuban pitcher to miss badly at living up to scouts' big-league expectations. Strapping Artemisa right-hander Miguel Angel González would prove an even larger disappointment with the Philadelphia Phillies. During 2009 and 2010 González had been at least the top righty if not the all-around best pitcher on the island, leading his 2009 Habana Province club to a rare National Series title. For several seasons with Habana he was the mainstay of one of the best National Series staffs ever; his Habana Province team at one point featured five hurlers all performing for Team Cuba—the corps also including starters Yadier Pedroso, Jonder Martínez, Yuliesky Gonzalez, and Miguel Lahera (not to mention career-saves leader José Angel García) González was a national team ace during the 2009 World Cup as well as the 2010 Puerto Rico World Cup qualifier. Then he suffered a career-slowing shoulder injury that was never clearly identified. Scouts who had once rated him highly were surprised to find that he was simply not the same pitcher during the 2011 World Cup in Panama.

On injured reserve with a new Artemisa team during the 2012 season, González was apprehended and jailed after a first defection attempt went awry, one in which he and several companions were reportedly caught offshore by Cuban coastal patrols in a small escape vessel containing an arsenal of illegal firearms. A second February 2013 effort at flight through El Salvador and into Mexico proved more successful. When he became available on the free agent market, there were still lingering questions about the arm/shoulder injury that had halted his Cuban League career. But the Phillies were willing to gamble, initially offering a reported $48 million but subsequently dropping the bid to $12 million when doubts about arm strength lingered. It was a gamble destined to be unrewarded. González blew his initial chance to make a weak 2014 Phillies pitching staff by surrendering a dozen runs in only fourteen innings during his initial spring training trial. A shot at redemption during a late-September call-up resulted in only a couple of innings in the big leagues. By 2015 spring training the Phillies had given up entirely, placing the Cuban on waivers. There were no takers among the remaining twenty-nine big-league clubs.

Far more promising was the debut in Cincinnati early in the 2015 season of Raisel Iglesias, a young right-hander who had emerged seemingly overnight as the new Cuban closer during the March 2013 World Baseball Classic.[14] Iglesias pitched alongside another top young prospect, Yoan López, in Isla de la Juventud. He would impress international scouts in Tokyo at the Classic and then again during midsummer outings at both the Rotterdam World Port Tournament and the follow-up tour by a Cuban squad playing the USA Baseball Collegiate All-Stars in Omaha, Des Moines, and Durham. A lanky righty with an elastic arm, Iglesias was quickly grabbed by the Cincinnati Reds when he appeared on the free agent market in early 2014. After only a brief stint in the Arizona Fall League, he paid immediate surprise dividends by making the National League club's opening day roster.

Iglesias not only impressed with his debut April 12 start versus St. Louis in Cincinnati (a five-inning no-decision effort), but he also claimed a piece of big-league history as the first Cincinnati Reds player in three decades to appear in a major-league game with no previous organized baseball minor-league experience. And another first was also accomplished in that mid-April debut game at the Great American Ballpark. Iglesias hooked up with veteran catcher Brayan Peña to become the first Cuban all-defector battery in big-league history.

Other promising pitchers also would make at least small waves on the big-league scene over the recent handful of seasons. Guantánamo's Roenis Elias enjoyed a strong rookie year with Seattle in 2014, making the club's starting rotation out of spring training and posting 160 innings and twenty-plus pitching decisions after only brief seasoning in the minors. Odrisamer Despaigne also surprised after his sudden rise to the parent club in San Diego. Despaigne started fast after his June call-up and barely missed tossing the first hitless masterpiece in ball club history. In only his fifth big-league start on July 20, the former Industriales ace hurled 7.2 innings of no-hit baseball at the New York Mets before Daniel Murphy broke the magic spell with a dream-ending double. Early in the 2015 campaign the Boston Red Sox summoned hard-throwing Dalier Hinojosa from AAA Pawtucket, another former Guantánamo starter who holds a unique distinction as the only pitcher ever to hurl two perfect games in top-level international tournament play. Hinojosa made only a single appearance in Boston but was claimed off waivers by the Philadelphia

Future Cincinnati Reds top prospect Raisel Iglesias warms up in the Cuban bullpen at the Rotterdam 2013 World Port Tournament. Courtesy of Peter C. Bjarkman.

Phillies in mid-July and finished the campaign seeing spot duty in the National League.

And there are more on the way, more than can fit into the present account. Yoen López, a young prospect who labored briefly with the Isla de la Juventud club, now waits in the wings after signing in January 2015 with the D-Backs in what proved to be a record deal (an $8.2 million bonus) under newly imposed MLB international signing guidelines. And as the final version of this book was being drafted in late May of 2015, news broke that another prized pitching prospect, twenty-one-year-old Camagüey right-hander Norge Luis Ruiz, had also fled Cuba. Norge Luis was likely the best pitcher still left in Cuba and he would flee to Haiti the very weekend he was supposed to report to Havana to begin national team training for the upcoming Pan American Games in Toronto and a US Friendly Tour in North Carolina. It was yet another severe blow for a Cuban national team whose arsenal of quality pitchers and sluggers was seemingly dwindling at an unsustainable pace.

They just seem to keep coming. The floodgates have now truly opened. A documented total of 75 defectors in the first seven month of 2015 alone represent nearly 22 percent of the entire crop reaching back to the Mariel exodus of 1980; 113 since January 2013 was nearly one-third of all the ballplayers that had abandoned the island across the thirty-five years separating Bárbaro Garbey from Norge Luis. The dream of baseball in Cuba was now apparently dying on the vine, being strangled by a faltering economy and too many years of tightening restrictions on the lives of Cuban athletes. Fidel himself—the one constant for half a century—was no longer on the scene to beat the drums. Raúl was making glacially slow changes on the economic front and even in the area of limited private enterprise, but they just couldn't come fast enough. The desire to play for personal honor and the glory of the revolution, even for the national flag, had by early 2015 largely been replaced by the dream of cashing in on the good life and the dreams that could be bought with American dollars. Three decades of a collapsed revolutionary ideal and a severely taxed Cuban economy had at long last taken their full toll.

* * *

The first wave of defectors almost entirely consisted of pitchers, and the bulk of the new arrivals did not have anything like a sensational major-league impact. At the time of Maels Rodríguez's defection near the close of the 2003 MLB season, the thirteen pitchers who had already defected from the National Series during the previous decade could boast only a subpar 289–299 composite big-league won-lost ledger. Only Orlando Hernández, at that point, stood more than five games above .500 with a 53–38 mark. There had to be considerable skepticism about the quality of the Cubans, despite the brief postseason splashes in 1997 (Liván) and 1998 (El Duque) by the Hernández brothers.

This phenomenon seemed to mirror the situation with Japan. The first wave of Japanese big leaguers (Murakami, Nomo, Irabu) and Asians in general (Chan Ho Park) was also all pitchers. In fact, there was no significant everyday Japanese big leaguer before Ichiro Suzuki tested the waters with Seattle in the first season of the new millennium. A reigning conceit, as Robert Whiting would point out, long had been that the Japanese were simply too small and too fragile to succeed in a big-league lineup as consistent hitters or even as deft fielders.[15] But with the Cubans there seemingly had to be other explanations.

Why only Cuban pitchers? It wasn't as if the Cuban League was a pitcher-dominated league with a scarcity of true sluggers. Those few American journalists who made surreptitious visits to the island (like Ron Fimrite in the late-1970s and Tom Boswell in the early 1980s) raved about some hefty sluggers named Muñoz, Marquetti, and Victor Mesa, and not about hidden Latino versions of Nolan Ryan or Catfish Hunter. Of course there might have been some skepticism about Cuban hitters since they used aluminum bats and weren't facing big-league arms. But after a first Olympic tournament in Barcelona there was suddenly plenty of interest in wunderkind Omar Linares and muscular Orestes Kindelán. Among top Cuban defenders, Germán Mesa turned enough heads at shortstop to draw comparisons with "The Wiz" Ozzie Smith. Perhaps it was simply that no talented hitters or glue-gloved defenders chose to leave, although that seems more of a happenstance than explanation. It may in the end have been an inexplicable accident of history. But it was likely also that a pitcher always sensed he might have a quicker path straight to the majors. Pitchers don't have to adjust to big-league hitters in quite the same way that position players must adjust to crafty big-league hurlers.

The pioneer among modern-era defectors was, not surprisingly, one of Cuba's most celebrated pitchers of the 1980s, once a member of one of the strongest youth teams the island had ever produced, later a national team star for several seasons, most recently a popular figure with the Havana Metropolitanos, and at age twenty-five still heavily relied upon as an ace hurler in top international competitions. When René Arocha suddenly decided to bolt from the Cuban team at the Miami airport in the midst of the 1991 USA-Cuba Friendly Series, his departure sent considerable shockwaves through the Cuban baseball establishment. When the veteran pitcher failed to report for the team's scheduled flight back to Havana, panicked team officials scoured the Miami airport, believing he had either somehow gotten lost or inexplicably been kidnapped. The team's charter flight was held up for nearly two hours and only departed after a near revolt broke out among the remaining players, frustrated at the lengthy and seemingly futile delay.

The details of the Cuban pitcher's unexpected departure from his homeland provided a dramatic story in its own right. Nothing like this had happened before and at first INDER operatives were thrown into a panic by the realization that Cuban baseball had now perhaps changed forever. Meetings with the returning players were held immediately in Havana and for the first time a Cuban ballplayer was officially labeled by a top party official (INDER vice president Reynaldo González) as a "traitor" to the nation and to the revolutionary cause. National team members were for the first time harangued on the need for remaining strong and loyal and demonstrating that any such "defection" by a weak teammate meant nothing to the revolutionary cause. As authors Fainaru and Sánchez would later suggest, the reality was that for the bulk of the players it was far more likely that Arocha would appear to be something of a pioneering Jackie Robinson figure, one who overnight changed their perceptions about what might be a new way of thinking and possibly a new way of reacting to the harsh conditions under which they were forced to play. [16]

Meanwhile details surrounding Arocha's flight were not long hidden from the US media and were already being reported within three weeks of the actual event (which took place July 10) by Ft. Lauderdale–based journalist Sharon Robb. [17] Long disturbed by Special Period conditions at home and still steaming about his overuse as a junior-level pitcher, which had damaged his arm and earlier cost him three National Series seasons— more upset still by breaking game-fixing scandals of the early 1980s that had led to the banishment of his teammate and idol Rey Anglada—Arocha had plenty of reasons for growing disillusionment with the Cuban system. It had all come to a head when he was briefly reunited with his aunt and father (René Sr., who had fled to Florida in the 1980 Mariel Boatlift) at the Miami airport during the team layover. On an impulse, built on years of apparent exasperation back home, the disaffected pitcher decided he was leaving with his estranged relatives and not returning to Cuba.

Arocha's bolt from his team during the July 1991 US tour was a totally unexpected event. Nothing like this had occurred previously and unpreparedness for dealing with such occurrences was as palpable on the big-league scene as it was in Havana. There were no existing regulations governing how big-league clubs might handle Cuban defectors, since so far there had never been any. (There had been Bárbaro Garbey a full decade earlier, but he was a different kind of case altogether.) Not born in either the United States or Puerto Rico, Arocha did not fall under the stipulations of the normal annual amateur player draft; as a political refugee now residing on American soil he also didn't fit the profile of a foreign player available for free agent status. There were as yet no well-defined third-country residence requirements and thus no precedents of bidding wars for well-scouted Cuban stars. Ultimately the decision was made by commissioner Fay Vincent to stage a special lottery draft in which the St. Louis Cardinals pulled the lucky draw and signed the refugee prospect for a bargain-basement $15,000. It would take the Cuban little more than one year (after a stellar 1992 AAA campaign in Louisville) to work his way to the roster of the big-league club, where he debuted in the first week of the 1993 National League season.

Arocha had enjoyed a stellar eleven-year Cuban League career after joining the hometown Havana Metros club for National Series action in 1979 at the raw age of only fifteen. While most of his National Series career was spent with the Metros, he moved to the capital city's more popular Industriales club by 1988 and became the ace of that team's staff over his final years on the island. In total (including Cuba's second annual season, known as the Selective Series) he would win over 100 games and post a near-.600 winning percentage. He was the league's ERA champion in 1987 and hurled the most complete games in his final Cuban National Series season. His impact was perhaps greater still with the national team, where he served as part of a most formidable rotation alongside Lázaro Valle, Omar Ajete, Osvaldo Fernández, and El Duque Hernández. There was not much doubt that the Cubans were counting on Arocha as a reliable starter for the first official Olympic baseball competitions in Barcelona during the late summer of 1992.

Arriving on the scene at a rather advanced age of twenty-seven, Arocha would experience a largely uneven and definitely truncated big-league career. His rookie season was by far his best showing, providing 60 percent of his career victories and more than 80 percent of his career starts. He would start twenty-nine games and break into the double-figure victory column with an 11–8 mark. But for two succeeding campaigns he was largely relegated to bullpen duty and struggled to stay above the break-even point in the victory column and below 4.00 in ERA. By season number three he was the least used among the team's regular five-man relief core. Then arm troubles that had marred each of his final two St. Louis campaigns would shut him down entirely. After a year of desperate rehabilitation there would be one last largely unsuccessful attempt at a comeback with the San Francisco Giants.

If Arocha never made it big in St. Louis, he did capture hearts in Miami, where some fans switched allegiance to the rival Cardinals. His first start in front of the Cuban exile community at Joe Robbie Stadium drew considerable attention. Sporting a 5–3 record and having served a short April stint on the disabled list (after breaking a finger on his glove hand), Arocha made his first hometown Miami start in late June (a 4–3 victory in which he lasted 5.1 innings) and the contest drew a healthy crowd of nearly 38,000. While Arocha was never much of a success and certainly not a headliner in the American big leagues, he did seem to accomplish something of lasting significance. His rookie season alone was solid enough to answer the many doubts of the skeptics and to demonstrate that at least the top Cuban League pitchers could indeed make the grade at the highest levels of professional baseball.

Another Cuban pitcher attempting to follow in the path blazed by Arocha was not anywhere near as fortunate, nor even that much noticed. Euclides Rojas, Arocha's teammate on that fateful 1991 Miami getaway junket, was already acknowledged as the best relief pitcher in island history when he and his family made the dangerous choice to depart from the mouth of Havana harbor on a flimsy raft, in a desperate attempt to reach Miami and pursue a more promising life. It was the low-point summer of 1994, when thousands were fleeing the Cuban coastlines and unparalleled mass protests (near-riots) had broken out along Havana's waterfront Malecón. Rojas had apparently scrimped and saved for several years to buy materials for a makeshift seaworthy craft that might aid his escape. There seemed little enough reason to stay; both his career and future prospects for his family seemed to be dwindling. Rojas had enjoyed a successful career as a ballplayer in Havana, but life was increasingly difficult for all Cubans during what became known as the "Special Period in the Time of Peace," which unfolded in the wake of the Soviet collapse and the loss of economic support from Cuba's Russian benefactors.

Rojas was still in mid-career with the Industriales club at the time he made his life-altering decision. He had already broken the league's career mark for saves and figured at twenty-six he was still young enough to have a big-league future if he could only get to the US shores less than one hundred miles to the north. It was an arduous trip for the group of ten refugees (including his wife Marta and two-year-old son Euclides Jr.) that departed from Moro Castle on the morning of August 17, 1994. In the end the intrepid group, like so many of their desperate countrymen, was lucky merely to survive the perilous five-day undertaking. Some reports suggest that as many as 8,000 Cubans may have died trying to make similar rafting escapes that same summer.

Rojas would claim in later interviews that he did not come to the United States to simply play baseball, but rather merely to obtain freedoms unavailable in his homeland. [18] There certainly were severe enough restrictions on all Cuban citizens in a country where domestic travel was restricted (more by infrastructure than mandate) and foreign travel virtually impossible for the overwhelming majority. And Rojas had other reasons for leaving. He had come under suspicion of having known about Arocha's plans three years earlier. He was interrogated repeatedly about Arocha in the months surrounding the summer 1991 Pan American Games (from which he had been excluded), then suspended from the 1992 team that would capture gold at the first official Olympic baseball tournament in Barcelona. His future on the national team was obviously finished, and without national team status there were few remaining perks at home.

Rojas never did quite fulfill any fantasies he might have harbored regarding a prosperous big-league career. He was drafted by the Florida Marlins shortly after his arrival, but only in the thirtieth round. He bounced around on four minor-league teams that first summer but did eventually reach the AAA club in Charlotte before year's end. The following season there was yet another brief stint in Charlotte before he was finally cut loose. But Rojas would eventually find a slot in pro baseball as a successful pitching coach with the Marlins minor-league organization, where he served for six years. And he would belatedly reach the majors, first as 2004 Red Sox bullpen coach, where he earned a World Series ring, and then as full-time big-league pitching coach for manager Clint Hurdle's 2011 Pittsburgh Pirates. In the end Rojas was anything but disappointed in his decision to pursue the elusive American Dream. He did grasp the bright future he had sought for his family, even if it didn't materialize on the big-league pitching mound as he might have once anticipated.

A new wave of refugee pitchers was soon on the way, with a half-dozen Cuban League hurlers abandoning home between July 1993 and July 1995, and with all destined for at least brief stints in the majors. The fresh group included youth team standouts Eddie Oropesa, Alberto Castillo, Hanzel Izquierdo, and Michael Tejera, plus more established veterans Ariel Prieto and Osvaldo Fernandez. There was also a rare sprinkling of position players led by flashy shortstop Rey Ordoñez and journeyman outfielder Alex Sánchez, both also stellar members of a Cuban junior national team. Two of the earliest non-pitchers would carry with them rather bizarre "backstories" suggesting that at least some of these defections were not so easily reducible to familiar feel-good tales about brave and sorely disadvantaged Cubans seeking the American Dream and striking blows at Fidel Castro's evil empire.

Stateside at least, René Arocha was widely celebrated as a true pioneer when he suddenly chose to abandon the Cuban League and cast his fortunes with the North American big leagues. But Arocha was not technically the first ballplayer to flee Fidel's iron reign and show up on US soil. A full eleven years earlier the first disgraced Cuban Leaguer had already washed up on American shores, and in this particular case the alleged sin was far more serious than actual or rumored attempts to abandon the Cuban socialist system. The player's name was Bárbaro Garbey, and it was not mere accident that he arrived in the States alongside actual boatloads of Fidel's undesirables, misfits, and rejects during a mass 1980 exodus known as the Mariel Boatlift.[19]

The Mariel story has different versions depending on who is doing the telling. Fidel's key to success in surviving so many US-generated efforts to sink his government had long been linked to astute policies of clearing his island of all large pockets of threatening opposition. This had commenced in the earliest years of the revolution and was periodically repeated on numerous later occasions of similar internal crisis. Indeed, had so many of Cuba's professional class not opted to abandon the island, especially during the unstable transition period of the early sixties, Fidel's reign might well have been a short one. Opposition was again peaking in 1980 and Fidel took a similar stance when he announced that any disaffected citizens wishing to depart for the United States were free to leave. The immediate trigger had been an Easter weekend 1980 incident in which as many as 10,000 Cubans had stormed the property of the Peruvian embassy seeking political asylum. In response to the worsening upheaval Fidel announced the Mariel port west of the city would be opened and all Cubans who wished were free to leave as long as there were boats available to pick them up. Cuban exiles in South Florida immediately rushed toward Miami and Key West dock sites seeking to hire boats capable of transporting the expected mass exodus of stranded relatives.

The incident took a sudden twist when Fidel decided to free prisoners (hardened criminals as well as political dissidents) and mental patients for the exodus, in part to rid his island of a large social burden, but also to discolor the image of the Cuban exile population up north. Most Mariel emigrants, blue-collar laborers in the main, were not criminals by any measure, but some obviously were. The expected flotilla arrived from Miami to aid the departures, which lasted more than six months before the two governments jointly agreed to call a halt to the exodus. In all, more than 125,000 Cubans reached South Florida, but the bulk (approximately 70 percent) crossed the Straits of Florida during the first six weeks. Fidel's latest and perhaps most innovative strategy of cleaning house would also have a rather dramatic impact on future American immigration policies regarding Cubans. Washington and the American population as a whole were not quite ready to welcome a tidal wave of often less-than-desirable Cuban refugees.

Bárbaro Garbey had been a talented player in Cuba, if not quite a genuine superstar. He had admittedly accumulated a small collection of entries in league record books; he paced the circuit in RBIs the year before his sudden downfall, and he served on the national team on several occasions. He was a valued pinch hitter and backup outfielder at the 1976 Amateur World Series in Cartagena. But he was also a principal contributor to one of the darkest moments in league history. He had been accused on the heels of the 1978 season of belonging to a ring of players involved in a three-year plot to fix league ball games for cash payoffs. Gambling had always been rather prevalent in Cuban ballparks and it apparently persisted even under a new social order spawned by Fidel's revolution. Garbey was banned, along with two dozen others, from all future island baseball and also served a brief prison term for his transgressions.

Another prominent figure caught up in the unfolding scandals was the popular Industriales second baseman Rey Anglada. Anglada and Garbey had been teammates and Anglada, still an active ballplayer at the time, would be present to see Garbey depart from the shores of Mariel harbor during the great migration of May 1980. Yet Anglada would choose a far different path, electing to stay at home and seek eventual redemption. He would soon be banished from the sport (blackballed for two full decades) during a second wave of game-fixing arrests in 1982 and sentenced to a jail term that lasted more than two years. He would later work himself back into INDER's favor, however, and eventually became an Industriales manager and national team skipper, directing Cuban squads in both the 2007 World Cup (silver medal) and 2007 Pan American Games (gold medal). Anglada, like Germán Mesa, was one of a small number of disgraced ballplayers who remained loyal, underwent the system's version of formal rehabilitation, and years later regained prominence at the pinnacle of Cuban baseball.

Once safe on American shores, Garbey soon caught the attention of the Detroit Tigers scout Orlando Peña, himself a former big leaguer and one-time member of the Havana Sugar Kings. Peña stumbled upon Garbey at a refugee resettlement camp in Pennsylvania and offered the new refugee a $2,500 contract to join the Detroit farm club in Lakeland. But the potential success story would eventually sour when past transgressions came to the attention of MLB officials via a May 1983 *Miami Herald* article in which the minor leaguer confessed to his run-shaving activities while still a Cuban Leaguer.[20] Once the story broke, the Detroit farmhand (then playing at AAA Evansville) was summoned to an interview with John H. Johnson, president of the National Association body that oversaw organized baseball's minor-league operations. At that session Garbey would explain (as he had earlier admitted to the press) that he had never attempted to lose games on purpose, but only worked to keep scores close for the benefit of the gamblers that were funding him. Life was hard in Cuba under the restrictions of the revolution, the ballplayer admitted, and he was only trying to survive and support a family that was still, a half-dozen years later, stuck in Cuba. The explanation apparently seemed sufficient to National Association officials (and apparently to MLB commissioner Bowie Kuhn) and Johnson responded with no more than a temporary suspension.[21] Past sins on Cuban soil were overlooked and Garbey was freed to play for the big-league organization.

It was perhaps understandable to some that Garbey might have turned to the distasteful business of consorting with gamblers to survive the harsh conditions of the Cuban economy. It might be a bit more difficult to grasp the hypocrisy implied by so quickly excusing his treacheries toward the sport simply because they occurred on Cuban soil. If nothing else, the Garbey case exposed an egregious double standard on the part of the MLB commissioner and organized baseball in general. Pete Rose would only a decade later offer a similar excuse that he had never purposely lost games in his own gambling endeavors, but that line of defense never worked for baseball's all-time base-hits leader. After all, Rose had struck a blow at the presumed integrity of the sacred American pastime, and not at the despised communist sports system of Fidel Castro. Game-fixing was apparently not game-fixing if it could be viewed as having some sanctioned political motive.

Bárbaro Garbey would turn out to be anything but a model big-league citizen, however much the big-league public relations machine tried to paint him as an admirable anti-Castro warrior. Before reaching the majors and while still under suspension during investigations into his Cuban League misadventures, he was suspended for attacking a heckling fan outside the ballpark in Louisville, striking the offender with a fungo bat. He did impress with a torrid big-league start during Detroit's record 35–5 early season streak, but slumped badly as a DH against the Padres (he was hitless in twelve tries) during the year-end lopsided World Series. Apparently no longer as concerned with the family left behind in Cuba after his brief big-league successes, he was remarried to a Michigan woman in August 1985. When Garbey demanded a role as an everyday starter after his disappointing 1985 campaign, Detroit management quickly unloaded him to Oakland, where his big-league career largely ended with a March 1986 release. (He later had a brief 1988 trial with the Texas Rangers that spanned only thirty games and produced nothing noteworthy.)

Before a final big-league stint in Texas, while performing in the AAA Mexican League, Garbey faced further embarrassment when he was involved in an off-season drug-related incident. Pulled over for speeding in Miami, he was charged with cocaine possession. Those charges were eventually dismissed when the ballplayer agreed to enter a pretrial drug intervention program. In the end Garbey's entire career seemed to be filled with embarrassments. And the way it had all started seemed in retrospect to foreshadow yet another kind of MLB hypocrisy, one that would emerge decades later, when human smuggling rather than game-fixing would become the backstory sullying the big-league arrivals of some of the most coveted Cuban ballplayers.

The saga of New York Mets all-star defensive whiz Rey Ordóñez would prove to be every bit as complex, and by some accounts a bit more disturbing. Ordóñez would abandon his Cuban teammates at the July 1993 World University Games in Buffalo, New York. Escaping with him was young lefty pitcher Eddie Oropesa (also spelled Oropeza in Cuba). Both had already appeared briefly in the National Series—Oropesa as a hotshot pitching prospect with Matanzas and Ordóñez as a slick-fielding but lame-hitting Industriales benchwarmer stuck behind legendary short-stop Germán Mesa. Ordóñez had apparently prearranged his own escape with a phone call to his father-in-law, who had earlier left Cuba and settled with a new family in Miami. And therein would lay the founda-tions for a rather sordid tale.

Eddie Oropesa would eventually have his own brief big-league career, although it took him the better part of a decade to reach his brief trials with the Philadelphia Phillies, Arizona D-Backs, and San Diego Padres. He was twenty-one at the time he decided to bolt from those World University Games in Buffalo and leave his wife and family back home in Cuba. In something that might have appeared like a slapstick comedy routine had it not been so serious, Oropesa fled from the Buffalo ballpark in full game-day uniform, jumping a fence and escaping in a car driven by a cousin who had also appeared on the scene from Miami.

Ordóñez was destined for a more noteworthy career in the big leagues. Breaking in with the Mets, he was soon hailed as a new Willy Miranda, a modern-era version of the midcentury "good field, no hit" Cuban infield-er cut from the identical mold as Miranda, José Valdivielso, Chico Fernández, and a handful of others. Ordóñez would hit barely well enough to sustain a decade-long career with the Mets, but it was always his glove that was his meal ticket. Some of his ESPN *SportsCenter* high-light "web-gem" scenes were legendary in the 1990s.

Ordóñez had not been the best shortstop back in Cuba, however, and in fact he may have left largely because of Germán Mesa and Eduardo

Paret, two talents looming ahead of him in the pecking order for a prized slot on the senior national team. Many still argue that Mesa was the best that Cuba ever produced. Those who saw him in his prime regularly make comparisons with Ozzie Smith. When Mesa briefly fell out of favor before the 1996 Olympics, it was Paret who took his place. Paret would hold down the middle-infield position for more than a decade and eventually became a national team captain. Ordoñez was likely correct to assume that he would never have much of a shot at replacing either of those legends.

But there was more to the picture. Slowly stories would come to light concerning the price that Ordoñez and especially his family back in Cuba had paid for the ballplayer's budding big-league dreams. Those stories would even raise questions about whether or not there were more than simply baseball ambitions motivating the teenage athlete to leave his Havana home. The bulk of the backstory would be laid out in some detail by S. L. Price in his book *Pitching around Fidel*, a 2000 treatise exploring the dark side of athletics under Cuba's communist sports system.

The story began with Rey's father-in-law, Arnaldo Fiallo, who also left his family behind to build a new life as a contractor in Hialeah, Florida. Fiallo had departed in the same Mariel Boatlift exodus that had transported Bárbaro Garbey to the States. Soon that father-in-law would remarry in Miami without divorcing Rey's mother-in-law back in Cuba. It was not an uncommon story, but in this case it held a few extra twists. Rey and his young wife Hilda had themselves plotted an escape from Havana and had actually divorced in order to deflect attention from her and their infant son in the aftermath of the ballplayer's defection. She applied for legal exit papers while Fiallo hired an accomplice to facilitate Rey's escape in Buffalo and then purchased his plane ticket to Miami.

Rey promptly moved in with Arnaldo's family and was soon dating his father-in-law's eldest stepdaughter, Gloryanna. The future big leaguer would eventually follow a similar course as Arnaldo and remarry without informing his Cuban wife back in Havana. He subsequently cut off all contact with Hilda and his infant son, and the jilted ex-wife would be left husbandless and blaming her own father for betraying her and deviously manipulating the entire messy situation. At least this was the version of an all-too-believable soap opera scenario that Hilda would relate to the American journalist S. L. Price during their personal interviews in Havana.[22]

Long before Yasiel Puig or Aroldis Chapman or late-breaking revelations about sinister plots involving human trafficking, there were already elements of the Cuban ballplayer story that were better swept out of sight. These were stories that no one wanted to hear in Miami. But they were also stories that many were all too eager to tell, with more than a little bitterness, in Havana.

5

BROTHERS IN EXILE

I know what everyone knows: Cuba is the worst place on the globe to be an athlete today. But I'm sure I know something even stranger. It is also the best.—S. L. Price, *Pitching around Fidel*

A vexing problem with most of the stories surrounding Cuban baseball defectors such as Orlando "El Duque" Hernández and José Contreras (a pair of ace pitchers who both ended up starring for the Yankees and also teamed up to bring Chicago its first World Championship in nearly a century) is that in many cases the stark truths have been embellished by journalists and player agents. For the journalist, there were scoops to be found and newsprint to be sold; for the agent, high stakes attached to the player's promised MLB payday. El Duque's desperate December 1997 "freedom flight" from Cuban shores on a makeshift leaky raft was later exposed by intrepid *Sports Illustrated* writers (November 1998) to be a heavily fictionalized version of how manipulative agent Joe Cubas had arranged and carried out the star pitcher's clandestine removal from his homeland and into the lucrative MLB free agent market. Defector stories have also heavily distorted the picture of baseball talent on the island of Cuba, forestalling any accurate portrait of the modern-era Cuban League as a legitimate alternative baseball universe.

Cuban baseball officials, not surprisingly, view the present situation from an opposite perspective. For them big leaguers are the true "baseball slaves" no matter how highly they are rewarded at the pay table. Major-league players, INDER apologists emphasize, are owned by corporate management and traded as valued property. Cuban players never changed teams (at least until the modifications of recent seasons that now include a championship-round player dispersal, with stars moving from eliminated teams to contenders) and didn't sell their skills to the highest bidder; rather they played nobly in the service of a local provincial team and were rewarded for their talents in relative uniformity. The owners and athletes alike in US organized baseball are viewed by Cuban loyalists as selfishly motivated capitalists driven by dollar profits alone and not by love of sport or the traditions of a cherished national game.

Both sides have long taken an admittedly oversimplified view of the other's ideologically opposite baseball structures. Soaring profit and excessive greed have become an issue even for some of the more enthusiastic supporters of the North American big-league baseball scene. "It is not a game, it is a business" has long been a familiar mantra. Author Robert Whiting, in his excellent book (*The Meaning of Ichiro*) on the "defection" of Japanese leaguers to MLB in the 1990s and 2000s, remarks at some length (chapters 4–6) on the less avarice-based approach of the Asian players and stresses that single factor as accounting for much of their endearment to American baseball aficionados.[1]

For an American press corps devoted to the capitalist free-enterprise economic and political model, the expanding story of Cuban athletes abandoning a socialist sports structure fits all too perfectly into the deeply imbedded Horatio Alger myth—the classic American success story and archetypal American character arc, with its pilgrim's progress from rags to riches. It is the replaying (in this case with an enriching anticommunist political overlay) of the search for the true American Dream. And the American Dream, by anyone's reading, always equates directly to the search for American dollars.

The saga of El Duque Hernández and his hair-raising escape from unjust Cuban oppression thus reads exactly like an expected Hollywood script. There were, indeed, suggestions during the ballplayer's earliest months in the States that film rights to the adventure, with its heartwarming overtones of a desperate search for the great American success story, were actually being marketed to Hollywood producers. It had all the elements of a masterful drama, after all, one designed to sell well throughout Middle America. There was the unjust INDER suspension that took away a star ballplayer's rights to his livelihood in Cuba. Then the staged show trial by the Castro government that transformed the former national hero into a shunned pariah and social exile. There was the thrilling escape by a handful of refugees who somehow survived shark-infested waters and a dangerous marooning without food or water on an isolated cay in the Straits of Florida. Add an unlikely fortuitous rescue by the American Coast Guard. And for extra drama there was also a true knight in shining armor, the crusading ballplayer agent Joe Cubas, who was able to head off possible deportation back to Cuba. Finally comes a fittingly climactic dreamlike big-league season with the anointed "America's Team"—the storybook New York Yankees—and a full dose of World Series heroics thrown in for good measure.

The actual story of El Duque's flight is not that much less enthralling. Most of the details as originally reported were essentially correct if one only tones down some of the "knight in shining armor" rhetoric involving profit-minded and opportunistic agent Joe Cubas. The movie would never materialize as a Hollywood thriller, starring perhaps Denzel Washington (a near look-alike) as the intrepid El Duque. But there was eventually a full-length film version of the escapade provided in the form of a gripping documentary treatment by producer/director Mario Diaz, made for the 2014 ESPN *30 for 30* series. That version ("Brothers in Exile") would focus on the story of both El Duque and his half-brother Liván and would expose many of the details of Cuban baseball defections across three decades. But it would not appear until nearly seventeen years after the original events, and several years after the Hernández brothers had both retired from the big-league baseball scene.

The El Duque Hernández story would be laid out much earlier, in great detail, in a largely accurate book-length treatment penned by award-winning journalist Steve Fainaru and his collaborator Ray Sánchez. Fainaru's book (*The Duke of Havana*) was legitimately an "inside story" by a writer who had spent time with El Duque on the ground even before the developments that led to his Cuban League banishment. Fainaru traces El Duque's adventure through the World Series heroics that were the culmination of his first big league season. He provides considerable insider's detail on the events that led to Fidel's last-minute decision allowing El Duque's mother, daughters, and former wife to travel freely to New York in time for a joyous World Series celebration. The Diaz documentary covers essentially the same ground as the Fainaru book written fifteen years earlier. Both treatments reach a climax with the 1998 World Series triumphs and thus entirely ignore El Duque's later seasons (and second World Series) in Chicago, as well as the long wind-down of Liván's far more extensive big-league career. Fainaru's book was written long before either Hernández had played out his full MLB career. Producer Mario Diaz, for his part, was understandably gripped by the high-drama defection stories and not the successful big-league careers that ensued.

* * *

Steve Fainaru spares little in his often bleak portrait of the Cuban sports system that produced El Duque and then later attempted to crush him as a suspected traitor. It remains unquestioned that Fainaru himself is a champion of the capitalist sports system which the Cubans rejected on the heels of their socialist revolution. But author Fainaru is also balanced and fair-minded in the large bulk of his reporting. He is hardly complimentary in his treatment of Joe Cubas and peels back all the motives underlying the agent's crusade to liberate Cuban ballplayers from the clutches of what he sees only as a malevolent Castro regime. Fainaru also details many of Cubas's underhanded plots to entice players to defect for his own considerable financial profit, as well as similar efforts by his associates like Gus Dominguez, Tom Cronin, and Juan Ignacio Hernández. At the time the book was written there were no better portraits of the devious ways in which player agents like Cubas were repeatedly attempting to seduce high-profile Cuban stars away from the traveling national team during annual international tournaments.

Fainaru remains justly balanced in presenting other details as well. He reports on suspicions that Industriales teammate Germán Mesa had "sold out" El Duque during the Havana trial of accused player agent Hernández Nodar, allegedly in order to save his own skin. But he then reveals his own reasons for not entirely buying that version of events. He details Fidel's surprising role in freeing El Duque's family in what amounted to a significant humanitarian gesture, and he portrays the Maximum Leader as a remarkable politician who is far more complex than the Miami crowd always wants to paint him. And he ends his book with an intriguing report of a poolside Miami discussion in which one Cuban exile explains with some passion why El Duque and other ex-patriots had, in many respects, enjoyed a far better life in Havana than they ever could on American soil. His presentations of the Cuban sports system are hardly positive, but he finds more fault with some of its incompetent administrators than with the socialist system itself. His report on Cuba of the late twentieth century is certainly far less one-sided and distorting than others offered at essentially the same time by his fellow American journalists S. L. Price (*Pitching around Fidel*) and Milton Jamail (*Full Count*).

The most detailed account of El Duque's escape from Cuba on Christmas Day of 1997 remains the one provided by Fainaru and Sánchez (chapters 12 and 13). An essentially identical version, enhanced with reenactment video, would also appear in the more recent ninety-minute ESPN documentary. A similar account, more jazzed up in unrestrained red-white-and-blue hagiography, was penned for *Cigar Aficionado* magazine in April 1999, largely prompted by El Duque's 1998 postseason Yankee pitching heroics.[2] But much earlier, a mere month after the World Series and less than a year after the dramatic events themselves, *Sports Illustrated* would publish a somewhat different account. Authors L. Jon Wertheim and Don Yaeger suggest that there was a good deal of amplification to the tale as US media attempted to dress up the El Duque adventure for popular consumption. Apparently the waters outside of Cuba were calm, there were no shark sightings, and, contrary to a circulated *Newsweek* report, there was no dangerous leaking on the stout fishing vessel. But if there were contradictions in the contrasting accounts, they seemed to live largely in the details.

The basis for the *SI* story was a late-1998 lawsuit filed in Costa Rican courts by one of El Duque's "freedom raft" companions, boat pilot Juan Carlos Romero. Romero, still stuck in Costa Rica (and perhaps coveting a piece of El Duque's World Series earnings), would claim that Hernández had promised to aid him in reaching a better life in the States and then had failed to deliver despite all his own newfound wealth and celebrity. Romero's revelations to the *SI* writers would shed faint light on the exact nature of the voyage for readers not yet exposed to Fainaru's more ample book version. About the best that could be said back in early 1999 was that, whether Romero's legal claims about El Duque's subsequent actions had merit or not, there was at least some evidence that the desperate escape journey had early on been subtly—even dramatically—amplified for the public.

Fainaru would later dismiss the *SI* article as a "particularly cynical assessment," and, while admitting that some of the escape details might have been exaggerated along the way, he saw no evidence that El Duque himself had done so to "exploit the event for profit" as Wertheim and Yaeger seemed to suggest.[3] Fainaru reasonably observed that the escape "hardly needed to be embellished," given the nature of what it represented. Whatever the factual realities, this flight across the sea, like so many others made by desperate Cubans over the years, was by almost any measure a risky enterprise. No matter the details, anyone setting out on such a route was faced with numerous possibilities of disaster. Many athletes have made the voyage unscathed in recent years and may or may not have struggled in the process. But it is a matter of record that literally thousands of Cubans have perished across the decades on just such ventures. The precise details of such risky voyages in the end may matter little.

Fainaru's incisive portraits make it altogether clear that one simply can't know El Duque's early life in Cuba without grasping the background story of a colorful father and a pair of equally talented ballplaying brothers. Arnaldo—the father and the original "El Duque"—had himself been a considerable baseball talent in his youth. But a domestic-league career never went far for the less-than-serious Arnaldo Sr., and his subsequent vagabond lifestyle would convert a potential pitching phenom into a living legend of a very different order. The elder Arnaldo fathered two future ballplayers (Arnaldo Jr. and Orlando) with his first wife and then another, Liván, during a second marriage. He would spend decades as an apparently carefree drifter enjoying his aura of irresponsibility and passing briefly in and out of hi children's lives. Fainaru would eventually track him down in 1999, now residing in the central province of Las Tunas with yet another son and all too eager to reminisce about a squandered youth and boast that his youngest offspring—fifteen-year-old Marlon—was most likely now destined to become the actual supreme pitching talent of his rather star-crossed family.

Arnaldo's eldest son and namesake—Orlando's senior by two years—was occasionally reported to be the most gifted athlete of the clan. But an accident with a machete during his teenage years had scarred his wrist and stolen his fastball. When a second son came along, the proud patriarch also wanted to name him in his own image (a third Arnaldo), but, bowing to his wife's objections, he settled on a close approximate, Arnoldo. Family legend (reported by Fainaru) claims that the headstrong Arnoldo as a preteen himself insisted on rearranging the letters to Orlando. Arnaldo Jr., his pitching career sidetracked and sabotaged by the childhood injury, would eventually find his way into the National Series for a single modest season as a first baseman with Havana's second league team, Metropolitanos. He was desperately trying to resurrect the pieces of a broken baseball dream when, in April 1994, he was tragically struck down by a fatal aneurysm only a few months after turning thirty. The family's poverty at the height of Cuba's Special Period clearly contributed to the untimely death. The lack of a family phone, available gasoline and electricity, or a nearby ambulance all conspired to delay medical assistance that might have saved Arnaldo's life. Orlando was devastated by the tragic death of his idolized older brother.

Orlando would ironically prove to be the lesser natural talent among Arnaldo's three ball-playing offspring, outshone in the early years not only by Arnaldo Jr. but also by the late-arriving Liván. Orlando's arduous path to the National Series was anything but an avenue paved with immediate successes. He was exposed to the sport as a toddler, watching his father and later his more promising elder brother play. His mother María Julia would regularly drag her two sons to Latin American Stadium to watch the original El Duque pitch, even though the marriage had already been dissolved. Baseball was in the youngster's blood from the start. But when he tried out for the provincial EIDE (elementary level) sports academy at age eleven, he was promptly rejected and told he had few aptitudes for the sport. Undeterred, he plugged on with the encouragement and occasional schooling of an uncle who had also played during early National Series years as a spunky shortstop of limited skills. Through constant application El Duque had developed enough promise by the age of sixteen to be accepted into a high school–level sports academy (ESPA). He finally debuted at age twenty-one with the Havana Industriales, the team his father had once briefly played for. It was not a particularly young age for a Cuban League rookie. And it would then be another half-dozen seasons before Orlando would truly blossom as a recognized pitching ace.

By the mid-1990s El Duque had finally carved out his niche as one of the most talented and idolized pitchers on the island. A first season of double-figure wins came in 1992–93 (12–3) and would be followed by stellar 11–2 and 11–1 ledgers. He enjoyed an especially heated rivalry with future defector Rolando Arrojo (then starring for a Villa Clara team in the process of posting three straight league titles) and also with Industriales teammate Lázaro Valle. By the time of the 1992 Barcelona Olympics both Valle and El Duque were mainstays on a potent Team Cuba staff. And on the domestic front, after ten full seasons El Duque had compiled the best won-lost record (126–47, .728 pct.) in island league history. It is a mark that has since been challenged several times but today still stands unsurpassed.[4]

El Duque's troubles begin with Liván's defection in Mexico in September 1995, an event overlapping with the flight of another top pitcher, Osvaldo Fernández, who also skipped out on the Cuban team during a July exhibition series in Millington, Tennessee. Paranoia about such defections was suddenly growing by leaps and bounds in the Cuban camp. El Duque was placed under immediate surveillance, since his own possible defection was apparently widely suspected within INDER's inner

"El Duque" celebrates a gold medal victory for Team Cuba at the 1992 Barcelona Olympic Games. Courtesy of Peter C. Bjarkman.

circles. The harassment wouldn't stop there. In March 1996 he was dropped from Team Cuba's roster for the upcoming Atlanta Olympics, a severe personal blow made more painful by the fact that the star pitcher received the news only via a television broadcast announcing team selections. Germán Mesa had also been suspected of defection plans and was consequently booted from the Olympic squad headed for Atlanta. Mesa's exclusion would unexpectedly open the career door for another talented shortstop, Eduardo Paret, who was destined to be captain of Team Cuba throughout the entire first decade of the new millennium. [5]

Then Juan Ignacio Hernández Nodar entered the scene and things got much worse in a hurry. Juan Ignacio had once worked closely with his cousin Joe Cubas, but there had been a bitter falling out, spawned mainly by Nodar's refusal to follow his cousin's edicts against traveling openly to Cuba. In the aftermath Juan Ignacio decided to set himself up in the ballplayer agent business, with a particular focus, of course, on Cuban defectors, since that is where the big bucks could most quickly be found by a novice hoping to crack the agent business. Juan Ignacio stepped up his travels to Cuba, but was not the smoothest of operators. He flaunted his presence on the scene by flashing wads of cash and making bold public display of his lavish lifestyle. Cuban state security rapidly had him on their radar, and he was soon arrested at a youth tournament in Sancti Spíritus. It quickly came to light that he was carrying a number of false documents and an illegitimate passport with El Duque's name on it. That—along, perhaps, with stellar shortstop Mesa—was the big fish he was hoping to land.

Onetime Cubas associate Tom Cronin, now Juan Ignacio's full-fledged partner, had just landed in Havana at the time of Juan Ignacio's arrest and was also immediately taken into custody, then quickly sent packing back to the States. But consequences would be far worse for others caught up in the web. The subsequent Hernández Nodar trial (opening on October 28, 1996) was pure disaster for El Duque, Mesa, and national team catcher Alberto Hernández. (Alberto had seemingly come under suspicion when his roommate, Ozzie Fernández, fled the Cuban camp in Millington.) All were called to testify, and it was a grueling and frightening experience. El Duque was first up and stoically refused to brand Juan Ignacio a dangerous smuggler rather than merely a casual friend; Mesa, by contrast, pointed his finger at the American as an enemy of the Cuban state. A terrified Alberto evasively answered questions about his own past contacts with Cubas during overseas trips. Hernández Nodar was promptly convicted and sentenced to prison for thirteen years, a term he would serve out in full.[6] His crime had apparently been plotting to carry out illegal defections (those of El Duque, Mesa, Alberto, and possibly Pedro Lazo), but the truth was that he was being punished as much for the actual defections previously orchestrated by his now estranged cousin Joe Cubas as for any of his own bumbling activities.

There were several smoking guns in the Hernández Nodar affair that led to the downfall of the three Cuban players. The wannabe agent had become the link that allowed Liván to aid his impoverished brother back in Havana with gifts of much-needed cash. Nodar on several occasions had carried large bundles of American dollars not only to El Duque but also to Liván's mother, Miriam Carreras, still living in Isla. And he did so with little discretion or even minimal caution. Fainaru would later quote El Duque's own claims about just how foolish and careless his benefactor had been. Worse still, Nodar had foolishly decided he could pry both El Duque and Mesa away from Cuba with a scheme that was more James Bond than Joe Cubas in its outlines. And so on his final, ill-fated visit he carried with him forged Venezuelan work visas in the names of both ballplayers that he thought would facilitate his efforts. Such documents are highly illegal in Cuba, as they are in just about any country. In the end, that was the evidence that sealed his own fate, as well as theirs.

And then, in the wake of the trial, the biggest blow of all came when El Duque and Mesa were summoned to the Latin American Stadium INDER offices for an ominous high-level meeting. They optimistically expected they might perhaps receive some stern warnings about future behavior and be left home during an upcoming scheduled tour of Mexico by their Industriales team. But instead both, along with Holguín catcher Alberto Hernández, were informed that they were now being permanently banned from Cuban baseball. The "Pride of Holguín" (Alberto) would return home to his own embarrassment and disgrace, including the dismantling of a shrine at the local ballpark displaying his hard-earned trophies and gold medals. Mesa, suspected by many of cooperating at the trial to secure his own hoped-for pardon, disappeared into a quiet obscurity from which he wouldn't reappear for two years. But it was the star Industriales pitcher—condemned in the wake of his brother's heresy—who suffered the most severe banishment consequences.

El Duque was now suddenly a shunned man. The sport he loved had been stripped away from him. He could play ball only in a weekend recreational league where, because of his skills, he was not allowed to pitch. Instead he played the infield in a treasured souvenir New York Yankees T-shirt. His failing marriage to Norma Manzo quickly dissolved. He was assigned to work as a physical therapist at the psychiatric hospital in his neighborhood, near Havana's Jose Marti International Airport. Life seemed to have hit rock bottom.

Mesa was eventually pardoned by INDER authorities, but the friendship was by then irrevocably ruptured. Fainaru would later report that El Duque claimed to understand how Mesa might have been squeezed by officials and thus might have felt a need to protect his own family. Ironically, only weeks after El Duque's 1998 World Series triumph Mesa would be back in an Industriales uniform for an emotional welcome by fans, teammates, and even opposing players at Latin American Stadium. Milton Jamail describes the boisterous scene during that November 1998 season opener with Pinar del Río and characterizes Mesa's reinstatement as an "unparalleled and important symbolic gesture" obviously orchestrated by Fidel Castro himself.[7] Mesa also returned to Team Cuba for the Pan American Games in Winnipeg (August 1999) and Sydney's Olympic Games thirteen months later. He would play out the last several years of his legendary career back in INDER's good graces and, like another once-disgraced Industriales star—Rey Anglada—he would in time emerge as manager of the Havana ball club, and he would also enjoy a stint as skipper of the Cuban national team. Unfortunately his reign as manager would not equal his storied career as one of Cuba's greatest shortstops.

* * *

El Duque's escape from Cuban shores on the Christmas weekend of 1997 was a secretive and deftly plotted affair, largely orchestrated by his close friend Osmany Lorenzo. The group would include new girlfriend Noris Bosch, Lorenzo himself, all-star catcher Alberto Hernández, and several fellow travelers, including boat pilot Juan Carlos Romero.[8] After several reportedly harrowing (but apparently not life-threatening) hours the group successfully reached Anguilla Cay. But the trip became more complicated when a prearranged pickup launch promised by Duque's great uncle Ocilio Cruz never arrived from Miami. After three tense days filled with fears of being hopelessly lost or perhaps fatally marooned, the frightened and hungry refugee group was eventually located by an American patrol helicopter, then loaded onto a 110-foot US Coast Guard cutter based out of Miami, and finally delivered to authorities in the Bahamas.[9] That is when the real complications set in.

It appeared for a time that the refugees might be sent back to Cuba. It was at that crucial juncture that opportunist Joe Cubas (alerted to El Duque's plight and also grabbing his own sudden opportunity to cash in) arrived on the scene. It is reported in some accounts (including the ESPN documentary) that a US visa had already been arranged for the highly valuable baseball pitcher (along with his girlfriend and catcher Alberto). According to those versions, El Duque nobly refused to leave the Bahamian refugee encampment without his entire contingent of companions. (As Fainaru eventually unfolds the tale, that selfless decision would have negative consequences in the future when it came to seeking Washington aid in arranging transport of El Duque's mother and daughters out of Havana on the eve of a 1998 World Series victory celebration.) Cubas, in the end, was able to arrange the transfer of all members of the party to Costa Rica, where they would eventually receive the required third-country residence visas.

Within six months Cubas had arranged a deal with Steinbrenner's Yankees, who had missed out on brother Liván three years earlier, and by late spring El Duque was already proving his skills at AAA Columbus. The Yankees contract was not what Cubas had hoped for but was substantial enough: $6.6 million for four years with a $1 million signing bonus.[10] In short order the thirty-two-year-old rookie reached New York for his big league debut, a five-hit, seven-inning victorious effort against the Tampa Bay Rays. One colorful rookie-season incident that has become legend has Hernández questioned by New York media about the pressures of first facing the Red Sox and Pedro Martínez in "The House That Ruth Built" (it would have been the game of September 14, in which El Duque tossed a three-hit shutout). El Duque is reported to have laughed off the question by responding that no pressure could compare to what he had already known pitching against rival Santiago de Cuba with 50,000 fanatics crammed into Havana's Latin American Stadium.

El Duque would waste little time in nearly matching Liván's first-year postseason heroics.[11] And this time it would happen on a grander stage, in baseball's anointed media capital of New York City. The Cuban import posted a dozen rookie victories (against but four losses), emerging overnight as one of the aces of a deep Yankees staff. He would then author several crucial victories in a postseason charge to the American League pennant. None was more vital than a brilliant seven-inning shutout effort during a do-or-die Game 4 ALCS victory over the Indians at Cleveland's Jacobs Field. In his single World Series outing, Hernández breezed to a 9–3 victory as the Yankees easily dispatched the San Diego Padres with a four-game sweep. The dream season would then be crowned by the most personally important moment of all, when El Duque was tearfully reunited with his mother and two daughters just in time for the traditional New York City victory ticker-tape parade.

That emotional family reunion provides one of the strangest twists of the entire El Duque Hernández saga. Orlando had been deeply depressed over the ten-month separation from his daughters (eight-year-old Yahumara and the younger Steffi), a deep void that could never be filled by newfound freedom or any headline achievement on the big-league diamonds in the United States. Through the heroic behind-the-scenes labor of Joe Cubas's personal aide René Guim (pronounced "gimm") and City University of New York international relations professor Pamela Falk, efforts had been mounted to convince Fidel Castro that it might serve his own interests to make yet another goodwill gesture and allow El Duque's family to freely and quickly leave Cuba. Such an action would repeat a concession Fidel had made only a year earlier by releasing Liván's mother to join her son for a World Series celebration in Miami.

Fainaru (chapter 17) again provides an elaborate account of the reunion efforts and their eventual happy outcome, and it was that event, played out on a private airstrip in New Jersey, that provides a feel-good conclusion for Mario Díaz's 2014 ESPN documentary film. John Cardinal O'Connor, the archbishop of New York, would be a main player in the unfolding events, along with his emissary Mario Paredes, who personally carried the cardinal's letter of request to Fidel. The pivotal heroine had been the tireless Pamela Falk, who first enlisted the cardinal's aid and then fought to convince initially uncooperative Clinton administration officials to provide the needed US visas. Joe Cubas and George Steinbrenner—two men not especially celebrated for their altruism or humanitarian gestures—also would have significant roles to play in the unfolding drama. Cubas had originally initiated the entire plot to bring his star client's missing family to US shores and, at the eleventh hour, it was also Cubas who enlisted aid from the Yankees owner in the form of a private jet needed to rush the new arrivals from Miami to New York for the time-sensitive reunion.

Fidel's gesture was a lone bright spot when it came to the Cuban government's role precipitating and then following El Duque's fall from grace in Havana and his eventual resurrection in the US big leagues. El Duque had been treated by INDER officials and the communist government mechanism with what can now only be viewed as a fully unwarranted savagery. He and Mesa and Alberto Hernández were stripped of their small livelihoods, their much larger prestige and blossoming careers, and their valued reputations as loyal Cubans, for no crime that they had actually committed, but rather for some imagined infraction that paranoid officials believed they might have considered committing. They, in fact, were not in the end convicted of any specific crime against either the state or its baseball machinery. They were instead the ill-fated recipients of a merely symbolic act. They had been held up to the public as examples of suspected (even if not actual) disloyalty in what was quite transparently a desperate and irrational government effort to stem the tide of a growing annoyance that no one had the slightest solution for.

In retrospect one might understand and even sympathize with the frustrations of INDER officials and perhaps of Fidel himself as they witnessed what, from their perspective, was an illegal and immoral effort to destroy their national sport for the mere profit of outsiders—intruders they viewed as capitalist villains. And it was not entirely unreasonable for the Cubans to also see the raiding of their players on home soil and overseas as connected to ongoing Miami and Washington efforts to bring down their entire revolution.

The reasons behind the growing paranoia were indeed understandable. But that in no way could justify the tactics that were used to try to stop it. There is a great underlying irony here. For years before and after the El Duque saga the US government had employed a cruel and highly unsuccessful economic embargo strategy to bring down a hated Castro regime. Not only was that strategy a complete failure, but it actually had the reverse effect of strengthening Fidel's ironclad grip at home. The same was now true of the strategy adopted by INDER in the late 1990s to end the defections by its athletes. The entire effort was misguided and repeatedly bungled. Not only did it simply not work, but it weakened the government's position among its own citizens, made martyrs of the ballplayers, and only served to speed up the defections themselves. [12]

That even the Cuban officials might have realized the error of their ways in the treatment of El Duque was soon apparent. The INDER administration was shuffled within a year, partly due to corruption scandals, but also, as Fainaru would later suggest, perhaps at least in part because of its mangling of the entire El Duque affair. And maybe even Fidel's gesture of releasing El Duque's family was another clever effort on the part of a savvy Maximum Leader to turn a major political blunder into something of a face-saving propaganda victory.

* * *

While El Duque's tribulations and eventual escape plan were unfolding in Havana, Liván in the summer and fall of 1997 was writing a most dramatic script of his own. Called to the Miami big-league club in June, the young Cuban produced an immediate breakout performance that would launch the Marlins into their first ever postseason appearance. Liván was still a developing prospect with only a trio of National Series seasons under his belt when he departed Cuba. Although already a privileged member of the national team pitching staff when he fled in Mexico from the select squad preparing for a late-October Intercontinental Cup event on tap for Havana, he was still barely twenty. He had won but twenty-seven league games with the Isla de la Juventud team and thus his promising career was barely underway on his home island.

He was also a much different type of pitcher from his equally successful elder brother. Simply put, he was a pure natural, with a hopping fastball and smooth delivery that would be the envy of any pro prospect. El Duque had worked hard to develop and polish his art; he had possessed neither the speed on his pitches nor the same smoothness and effortlessness of delivery. Liván found it all came easy—too easy, in the eyes of some. What he displayed in natural gifts he notably lacked in self-discipline. Coaches and the sporting press early on complained loudly about the degree to which he was seemingly squandering his immense talents. [13]

There had been little contact between the half brothers while they grew up on different corners of the island; Liván was already ten when they first met. El Duque was born to a different mother (Maria Julia Pedroso, Arnaldo's first wife) a decade before Liván; he had already logged a half-dozen National Series seasons by the time Liván made his rookie debut with the Isla team. Liván was born in Villa Clara Province (to Miriam Carreras, the third of four women with whom Arnaldo fathered children) but moved to the isolated special territory of Isla de la

Juventud (Isle of Youth) as a youngster when his father served a brief stint there as a manager and pitching coach.[14] But the two brothers would see each other occasionally in the late 1980s and the relationship was always quite warm despite the wide differences in age, circumstances, and personalities.

Liván became frustrated with his hardscrabble Cuban life earlier than El Duque, who at least lived in the more stimulating surroundings of the capital city. There might be a number of explanations for why Liván choose defection as early as he did. Fainaru reports on one theory that the final spur was perhaps an incident involving a missing television tube.[15] But Fainaru also observes that this was likely no more than a symbolic element in the larger drama. Life was especially hard for a ballplayer marooned in Isla, even by the standards of Cuba's "Special Period" of deprivation in the early 1990s. Liván himself would eventually speak eloquently during the ESPN documentary filming about his reasons for leaving. They mostly had to do with the repressive treatment of Cuban players by their own state security and repeated bans on carrying home even simple items like hotel toiletries. Demands to remain ideologically pure by sacrificing oneself for the revolution's notion of idealized sport were increasingly difficult to stomach as family members went without even the most basic necessities on the home front.

The escape—played out in Monterrey in September and once again orchestrated with the aid and plotting of Joe Cubas—was a tearful cloak-and-dagger event. It was also severely traumatic for the young athlete, despite his own months of secret plotting to bring it all about. Fainaru recounts how Liván was so distracted when he fled the team hotel that he almost ran directly into the path of a speeding car.

Drama would only heighten when Cubas began shopping Liván and Osvaldo Fernández to big-league scouts. Teams rolled out a red carpet all around the MLB circuit for the prized pitchers that Cubas had hidden for several months, mostly in the Dominican Republic, but also with his cousin Juan Ignacio on Venezuela's Isla Margarita. The Marlins were the most desperate for a Cuban defector to stimulate recently sagging attendance, and because of his age Liván was easily the bigger prize.[16] Cubas eventually worked out a deal with the Marlins, one that may well have been orchestrated behind the scenes and in advance of an official bidding lottery. It apparently involved Cubas accepting a slightly lower bid from the Marlins (the Yankees had tendered a $5 million offer to Florida's $4.5

million), but Rudy Santin, who had his own axe to grind with the Yankees (see below), would later tell Fainaru that he believed the fix was in and that the deal likely brought the conniving agent a large secret bonus of his own.

Cubas, for his part, was angling to finally cash in big time. But there would be repercussions, since it was the money from Liván's contract that soon sabotaged the increasingly strained relationships between Cubas and a number of his earlier partners and aides. None got what they were expecting from the deal. There would soon be more fallout to boot. If Liván was Cubas's first big score, he would also become, within little more than a year, his first big setback. In July the young and suddenly rich Marlins property, unhappy with the size of the cuts his agent was taking, broke off their agreement and signed on with Cubas's former silent partner Juan Iglesias, who was now also active in the agent business. The Liván Hernández signing sent the whole pursuit of Cuban ballplayers spinning in a new and complicated direction.

Liván, for all his talent, would have major problems adjusting to life in the United States. A youngster who had known only poverty and who had developed little in the way of self-discipline was suddenly thrown into a land of plenty, with seemingly unlimited resources at his command. He gorged himself on fast food, especially McDonald's hamburgers. He reportedly bought a fancy new sports car every three months of his first year on American soil. His extravagance almost ruined his budding career and squandered his hard-won opportunity. Liván ballooned in size and seemed to lose the edge on his natural fastball. The Marlins brass watched helplessly while his promising future careened toward self-destruction. During his initial minor-league season with AA Portland and AAA Charlotte, the over-talented and out-of-control Cuban phenom had become a major reclamation project for his immediate handlers and for the entire Florida Marlins franchise.

Nevertheless, reclamation efforts won out. Slimmed down enough to again be effective, and clearly rededicated to his nearly lost pitching craft, Liván enjoyed a truly sensational summer as a 1997 Marlins rookie. He reeled off a midsummer victory skein that grabbed headline attention around the country. In the process he played a major role in lifting his newly minted National League ball club to its first-ever division title and postseason appearance. The regular-season performance (a 9–3 ledger) was not enough in the end to garner senior-circuit rookie-of-the-year

(ROY) honors, but it was more than enough to capture hearts in Miami. The Cuban exile community at long last had its own hometown hero among the recent waves of defectors striking a blow at the despised Castro government. This one was not pitching in St. Louis (like Arocha), Oakland (like Prieto), San Francisco (like Osvaldo Fernández), or nearby Tampa Bay (like Rolando Arrojo one year later), but right here in front of his fellow exiled countrymen a stone's toss from Miami's Little Havana.

Postseason heroics would cap the phenomenal 1997 debut National League season for the first Cuban in decades to play a significant role in an MLB pennant race. There was an MVP performance in the National League Championship Series to kick things off. Liván claimed the NLCS opener in Atlanta with three scoreless relief innings. Then as an emergency starter in crucial Game Five, the Cuban novice authored a complete-game, three-hit, fifteen-strikeout masterpiece. Two more effective outings earned a second MVP trophy during an historic Fall Classic triumph over Cleveland. Struggling at times, Liván outlasted veteran Orel Hershiser in the opener, the first World Series game ever played in Florida. And in the Game Five rematch with Hershiser, Hernández again was more gritty than brilliant, barely holding on down the stretch to win 8–7 with some nail-biting ninth-inning relief help from closer Ron Nen.

It would be the first World Series success for a still-young Miami franchise, and one made extra special for hordes of Cuban exiles by the heroics of one of their very own. The aftermath of a Game Seven extra-inning Series-clinching win was a spontaneous love feast for both Miami's Cuban community and its own adopted hero. In a surprise goodwill gesture, a baseball-loving Fidel had allowed Liván's mother, Miriam Carreras, to travel to Miami for the Series finale. Flushed with the victory and the unexpected family reunion, Liván would raise his MVP trophy high overhead before a national television audience and shout into the microphone in heavily accented English the words that would make video newsreels around the nation: "I love you, Miami!" It had to be a painful moment indeed for any INDER officials who might later catch a video glimpse of that Miami celebration and hear those potently defiant words.

Liván would never again reach that same pinnacle of big-league success. His days in Miami would also be relatively limited—less than two added seasons. But he would nonetheless experience true longevity as a big-league pitcher during a career taking him to numerous stops (ten teams) around both the National and American Leagues. In the end Liván would run up career numbers (178 wins, 355 decisions, 3,000-plus innings worked, and nearly 2,000 Ks) that would quietly place him among the top Cuban big-league hurlers of any era. Only an illustrious quartet (Luque, Tiant, Pascual, and Cuéllar) can claim higher or even approximate totals for victories, career decisions, innings pitched, or strikeouts. If Liván's seventeen-year career did not boast quite as many highlights or etch as many headlines as that of his older brother, in the end it stands as a near-equal monument to the quality of modern-era Cuban baseball.

* * *

The central role played by José Ignacio (Joe) Cubas in the real-life dramas of El Duque and Liván—and in most other early high-profile defection sagas—shaped the developing story. Cubas from the beginning had his own agenda, one that Fainaru would label "the Joe Cubas Plan" and that would eventually become the modus operandi of the entire ballplayer-smuggling industry. Cubas had figured out that there was big money to be exploited from marketing top Cuban players to big-league clubs always in search of fresh talent. He also had a family history that drove him to strike whatever blows he could at what, for him, would always be a wickedly evil Castro communist regime.[17] It was thus a dual mission, and Cubas also knew precisely how to play the media and cover his tracks. It was easy enough to cloak his crusade in trappings of flag-waving American patriotism. But the lust for revenge against Fidel aside, a more obvious goal from the start was always the motive of personal enrichment.

Cubas (known to his friends and clients as "El Gordo") first hit on the ingenious "Joe Cubas Plan" with a good deal of early help from his small coterie of allies in opportunistic capitalism. He had initially found an easy entrée to the player agent business via a childhood friend named Rudy Santin, who set him up with his first client, Yankees prospect Bobby Muñoz. Santin worked briefly for George Steinbrenner's Yankees, rising to the post of Latin American scouting director, and quickly saw the venture Cubas was talking about launching as a huge perk for his celebrated employer. In the end it would not quite work out as planned, since Santin had parted ways with Steinbrenner's operation and moved to a post with Tampa Bay by the time Cubas had landed his first prize Cuban recruits. That was the one largely unexpected turn in a plot that Santin and Cubas originally laid out in detail. The idea was simple enough, and it still forms a basis for most trafficking of Cubans seeking a big-league payday. Get players off the island by whatever means possible, establish a third-country residence to avoid both an MLB free agent draft and OFAC embargo restrictions, and then let the bidding wars begin. Santin had originally envisioned the Yankees as having an inside track (given his own post at the time) in this new windfall of already-seasoned talent. Peeved at a 1995 playoff loss to Seattle, Steinbrenner had, however, gutted his front office, and Rudy Santin departed in the process; it was an upheaval in New York that later cost the Yankees a crack at the first wave of Cubas's Cuban clients.

Cubas had the requisite drive and persistence but initially lacked the cash to fund his budding operations. He relied on numerous friends and family members to support his ventures and thus built up considerable debts along the way. He borrowed profusely in the early 1990s to hop around the globe, shadowing the Cuban national team on its tours in Asia, Europe, Canada, and the States. One of the major early players in the emerging scheme was a flamboyant cousin, Juan Ignacio Hernández Nodar; another was Cape Cod real estate agent and enthusiastic Cuba traveler Tom Cronin. In the end most of Cubas's debts were not repaid as expected, and that would become a major factor in eventually splitting the Cuban defector enterprise into a number of competing factions.

The Hernández Nodar part of the tale would provide a revealing subplot. Juan Ignacio started out working for his cousin, believing in his own mind that he was somehow a full-fledged partner in Cubas's operations and unfolding schemes. Unlike Cubas, he was actually Cuban-born, and he also maintained a residence in Venezuela. It was Juan Ignacio, a former freight company truck driver, who drove the getaway car during early defection attempts staged in Millington, Tennessee. But then there was a falling-out, in part over money, as Hernández Nodar didn't feel he got his fair share of hefty commissions on the big-league contracts of Ozzie Fernández and Liván. And Cubas was also furious at his cousin's open and risky travels to Cuba to carry gifts and money from Liván and Fernández back to family members on the island.

Juan Ignacio left Cubas at precisely the same time that another early partner, Tom Cronin, also left the operation. While Hernández Nodar was funneling cash on a regular basis to Liván's mother in Isla and half brother El Duque in Havana, Cronin had developed a similar relationship with Germán Mesa. Eventually Hernández Nodar and Cronin would join forces in their own poorly conceived and even more poorly executed play to somehow entice the friends—El Duque and Mesa—off the island as the latest pair of high-valued Cuban imports. The scheme would quickly unravel as a result of Juan Ignacio's careless and boisterous activities on the ground in Cuba. One irony was that the bungled efforts would eventually land El Duque squarely in the hands of cousin Joe Cubas, a double blow to Hernández Nodar's own dreams to strike out on his own.

Gus Domínguez was another pioneering agent soon entangled in the budding business of smuggling Cuban ballplayers. Domínguez also had fallen into a newly created niche as an agent for defectors quite by accident when he was fortuitously hooked up with the first modern-era refugee pitcher, René Arocha. Once Arocha suggested that the former Miami marketing executive represent him, he also started recommending his novice agent to other Cubans following the same path. Domínguez grasped the potential opportunities even before Cubas and quickly expanded his own operations. He was soon not just representing more than 100 athletes but also actively smuggling potential clients out of Cuba. It was a practice that eventually landed him a five-year prison term when he was convicted in April 2007 of transporting and harboring aliens. The conviction resulted from a charge that he had paid to have several Cubans smuggled off the island in 2004, but Domínguez received early release when a circuit court of appeals in Atlanta overturned his conviction in October 2011.[18]

Cubas played a large role in the escapes of two other Cuban pitching mainstays who had preceded the Hernández brothers out of Cuba. Ozzie Fernández followed the path of René Arocha when he also bolted from the Cuban camp in Millington, Tennessee, on the eve of the July 1995 USA-Cuba Friendly Series. The big right-hander was an ace for the Holguín National Series team and a member of the 1992 Cuban squad that had earned gold in the first official Olympic baseball tournament in Barcelona. Fernández was sharing a hotel room with catcher Alberto Hernández—a Holguín teammate—at the time he elected to bolt with Cubas. It would turn out to be a most unfortunate circumstance for Hernández, who would later be condemned alongside El Duque and Mesa in the Hernández Nodar trial and would subsequently accompany El Duque in his own fateful December 1997 flight to Anguilla Cay. Cubas and Fernández had apparently been discussing the possible escape plan for some time during furtive meetings at past tournament events, and there had also been reported meetings on Cuban soil between the pitcher

and Cubas's silent partner Tom Cronin.[19] Once Fernández fled Millington, Cubas quickly spirited him away to the Dominican Republic, with
formal plans already made to enter him in the big-league free agent market.

Fernández's departure came only days before Cubas received the surprise phone call that Liván was also ready to jump in Mexico. What was
at first a trickle was now becoming a steady stream. An even bigger loss
for the Cubans would unfold during the next USA-Cuba Series a year
later when another ace, Rolando Arrojo, walked out of the team quarters
at the Albany (Georgia) Quality Inn. Again it had all been orchestrated by
Cubas, including a secretive smuggling operation that had already spirited the pitcher's family (a wife and two young sons) out of Cuba. Coming
on the eve of the Atlanta Olympic Games, Arrojo's stunning defection
would result in a lengthy suspension of the USA-Cuba Friendly Series; it
would not be reestablished until almost two decades later.

Another national team ace hurler sought a quite different route of
escape from worsening island economic conditions. Only months before
the sudden departures of Fernández and Liván in the summer of 1994,
Ariel Prieto faked injury and was able to arrange a legal emigration exit,
two full decades before Yoan Moncada would follow a similar and far
more celebrated path. Pitching for the Isla de la Juventud National Series
team at the time, Prieto had also decided that life in the Special Period
was not a life that he wanted to continue. But Prieto went about plotting
his own escape in a more ingenious and somewhat less risky manner. He
faked an arm injury and created the appearance that his career as a pitcher
was over; he even engineered a fall from his bicycle that produced minor
bruises and kept him out of the league All-Star Game. Of no further
apparent value, he was dismissed by the INDER Baseball Federation and
allowed to apply for legal emigration to Puerto Rico.[20] Arriving in Miami
in April 1995, he entered the MLB free agent draft and quickly found a
home with the Oakland A's as the fifth overall first-round selection in the
1995 lottery. Prieto enjoyed only a handful of seasons in the majors,
logging six years of limited duty. But he had in fact suffered actual arm
damage in Cuba that eventually curtailed his big-league career.

Most of these early arrivals among pitchers were at least somewhat
damaged goods before they ever reached the States. All had developed
arm stress during an era of aluminum bats and inferior locally produced
Batos brand baseballs. They had spent a career trying to throw breaking

pitches with balls lacking the standard stitching that allows a solid grip. But their loss hurt the Cubans nonetheless. Arrojo had been the biggest blow in the 1990s and had been expected to front the Cuban staff during the Atlanta Olympics. Liván was not yet a true star at home with Isla or a fixture on the national team, and his loss to the Cubans was more a matter of "what might have been" than what currently was. Fernández also stood somewhat short of megastar status when he departed his home in Holguín, a national team member but hardly a celebrated squad ace. The same could be said of Prieto, who was solid on the island but never quite in the upper echelon that at the time included El Duque, Lázaro Valle, and southpaws Omar Ajete and Jorge Luis Valdés. El Duque had already been banned and thus his domestic career was finished when he fled. And El Duque's loss was also one that the Cuban baseball machinery had quite clearly inflicted upon itself.

But the coming decade would provide a very different story. Perhaps the most devastating setback to the Cuban system was the sudden and highly unexpected departure of José Ariel Contreras. Contreras was an established part of the best one-two pitching punch in the entire domestic league and indisputably the anchor of any national team mound staff. He was the reigning ace of a strong Pinar del Río team and worked alongside Pedro Luis Lazo, himself destined to be the league's all-time winningest hurler within a decade. Lazo, a starter in Pinar and something of a Lee Smith clone, emerged as a closer for Team Cuba but never quite matched Contreras when it came to international events. The latter never lost a single senior-level international game. But his brilliant 13–0 tournament ledger was also at least in part due to the fact that he never seemed to pitch the biggest games against the toughest teams (especially the Americans).

Contreras was the pitching hero of a Pan Am Games tournament in Winnipeg that earned the Cubans a ticket to the Sydney Olympics. He did indeed best the Americans in the gold medal match, but the truly crucial semifinal contest versus Canada, with the Olympic bid hanging on the line, had been turned over to José Ibar. And in Sydney the following summer Contreras was tapped for the semifinal tussle with Japan—important, but not the grand finale. He sat and watched from the dugout as Ibar was outdueled by Ben Sheets and Cuba lost Olympic gold for the first time after two previous successes. But if he wasn't handed the ball for what some outsiders saw as the biggest games, he never failed to deliver in those contests the Cubans needed to reach a coveted slot in the championship showdown. As the Cuban brass saw it, they were indeed relying on Contreras for what, in their view at least, were indeed the most vital games.

But more important perhaps was Contreras's special status back home. He was a flag-waver for revolutionary loyalty, a position he inherited from Pinar del Río teammate Omar Linares. He often appeared on podiums alongside the Comandante when national team triumphs were celebrated and he was rumored to be among Fidel's personal favorites. His sudden decision to leave therefore stunned INDER authorities as well as a nation of Cuban fans. It had to be a major blow to morale for all who bought a government line about placing love of game and loyalty to Fidel's revolution above mercenary interests represented by the capitalist North American big leagues. Contreras would finally bolt on Mexican soil during a Team Cuba training session in October 2002, just as Liván had seven years earlier. More painful still, he was joined by one of Cuba's top baseball officials, Miguel Valdez, which made the loss cut even more deeply for Cuban authorities.

Contreras would debut in New York on the same team with an aging El Duque, where he would win in double figures during his second season. But his greatest success came in 2005 with the Chicago White Sox, where he again teamed with El Duque to bring the long-suffering Sox their first world title in eight decades. Contreras would win the opening match of a four-game World Series sweep of the Houston Astros. He would register double figures in the win column three straight years in Chicago and make his only American League All-Star Game roster the year after the team's historic world championship.

A lengthy career drop-off would follow before a final brief stint in Pittsburgh, where he was finally released in the spring of 2014. In the end the career numbers certainly did not match those of El Duque or Liván, yet the big-league career was substantial enough, with a decade-long winning ledger. Among defecting pitchers, only Liván and El Duque still outrank Contreras in overall stature. Away from the field he would acquire and maintain a large cattle spread in rural Tampa, Florida. Alexei Ramírez would later credit Contreras for convincing him to sign with the White Sox. And as late as 2015 Contreras would still be nursing pitching dreams, laboring in the Mexican League at age forty-three and still trying to work his way back for perhaps one final shot at big-league glory.

* * *

The defectors saga began with pitchers, and for most of the early decades Cuban refugee pitchers garnered the bulk of the moderate attention paid to the phenomenon. There were numerous reasons, not the least being that pitchers seemed to have slightly better chances of beating the odds. A talented thrower with dominating speed or tantalizing "stuff" didn't, perhaps, have as many adjustments to make as did a batsman trying to upgrade his game against big-league hurlers. There were a few exceptions, to be sure, like fancy-fielding Rey Ordóñez with the New York Mets. But the non-pitchers were not only in a large minority, they also were not prime-time established Cuban stars. A teenager when he bolted, Ordóñez was never an elite performer on the island and likely would never have become one, since Germán Mesa blocked his path not only on the national team but also with the hometown Industriales club in Havana. Bárbaro Garbey had perhaps been an exception as the original arrival, but once again Garbey was, at best, a second-level star during his brief five-year run in the National Series. Alexei Ramírez, the first true paragon among position players, would not appear until well into the first decade of the new millennium. Joe Cubas was never successful—although certainly not for lack of trying—in enticing top position players like Linares, Kindelán, Antonio Pacheco, or Germán Mesa to join his promised busloads of defectors.

It was a scenario similar to Japan's more moderate big-league invasion. There also it was first pitchers—Murakami (1964), Nomo (1995), Hasegawa and Irabu (1997), Yoshii (1998), Ohka (1999), Sasaki (2000)—who gambled as free agents seeking American big-league success. It was likely a bit easier to fathom in the case of the Japanese circuit. Physical size was a major factor, for one thing, as pointed out by Robert Whiting (*The Meaning of Ichiro*). There was a long-standing taboo attached to Japanese players and a reigning myth about their inadequacy due to lack of bulky frames and resulting power. Sadaharu Oh and Shigeo Nagashima might have been MLB targets, but they peaked during an era when owners seemed unwilling to recruit the Japanese for rumored political reasons.[21] The same stereotypes never existed about Cuban hitters; if there had been doubts over the years, they were about aluminum bats and not muscular prowess. And politics vis-à-vis Cuba was of a far different order. If anything, it favored pushing for defections, not discouraging them.

The absence of a star Cuban position player would all change with the arrival of Kendrys Morales, initially a three-season cup-of-coffee big leaguer (2006–8), but a full-fledged star with the Los Angeles Angels by 2009. The irony was that while Kendrys (sometimes spelled Kendry in Cuba) was not a pitcher, he was not much of a position player either. He never found a true defensive slot in Cuba and most big-league suitors saw him as an offensive prospect only—a classic DH. He also was a potential star needing a good deal of polishing before being considered big-league ready. Kendrys would spend most of his first several years on US soil simply trying to make the grade with the Los Angeles franchise. After a single transitional summer in the lower minors (2005), several brief call-ups over the next three campaigns resulted in only 127 big-league games and a dozen homers. It was clearly the defensive side of his game that held him back.

Morales had produced a sensational rookie season in Cuba back in 2001–2002, one of the best ever in the Cuban National Series. He posted several top slugging marks (21 homers, 82 RBIs) and was a runaway choice as the league's top novice player. A .324 BA was second-best among rookies, although it didn't crack the top thirty in an offense-oriented Cuban circuit. His hefty bat and abilities from both sides of the plate also immediately lifted him onto Cuba's select roster for the upcoming 2003 September IBAF World Cup to be held on Cuban soil. And his wide popularity was only enhanced by his location in Havana with the island's most popular team, Industriales. Kendrys had, in fact, been a promising pitching prospect at the Cuban junior-level, throwing in the low nineties as a sixteen-year-old. But his switch-hitting prowess was simply too good for a career limited to appearances once or twice a week out on the pitcher's mound.

That 2002 debut year was also a centerpiece in the award-winning Ian Padron documentary film *Fuera de Liga* (Outside the League), and in retrospect part of the charm of Padron's video today remains the candid shots of a young Kendrys Morales in the crude Industriales dugouts, on the arduous cross-country team bus treks, and in the second-rate team hotels. The film captures the beauties and simplicities of Cuban domestic baseball, yet it also provides all the rationale needed by American viewers to grasp why a prospect like Morales (and so many others soon to follow) would abandon the hardscrabble life of the Cuban ballplayer for the potential luxuries of the American big leagues.

From the beginning there were problems both on and off the field for the multitalented Havana rookie prospect. In brief, Morales appeared to be something of a discipline problem in the eyes of his coaches and manager. I personally witnessed one small incident that may have been indicative of larger breaches on the part of the budding phenom. I had arrived early at Latin American Stadium for a February 2002 game between Industriales and city rival Metropolitanos. Cuban journalist friend Jesus Valmaña had planned to corral the rookie star for an early pre-game interview and I was intending to accompany Valmaña onto the field as an uninvited eavesdropper. But when we arrived at the home club dugout we learned Morales had already been sent packing by manager Rey Anglada for what seemed a humorous, if serious, disciplinary infraction. Arriving at the park on his rickety bicycle from the downtown team hotel several miles away (a not-usual mode of transportation for Cuban players), Kendrys apparently had forgotten to include a home club jersey in his gym bag and reached the park without the needed playing gear. This is an oversight impossible for big leaguers or most North American minor leaguers, who have all their equipment handled for them by team staffers, but an everyday snag for Cuban baseball. This apparent lack of self-discipline on the part of the eighteen-year-old rookie would foreshadow larger issues that would later give rise to questions about his readiness for North American–style professional baseball. And there was also the question of where to play the iron-fingered wunderkind. Despite his hot bat, Kendrys was a daily liability at almost any defensive post in either the infield or outfield. He had started the year at third base, which didn't go well, was moved to the outfield briefly (he did have a great arm—an obvious plus at the hot corner or in the pasture), and finally wound up at first, where he might do the least damage.

Cuban baseball always seems to produce the most unlikely confluences of memorable events. Kendrys would enjoy his grandest Havana triumph during a tense moment of the 2003 Havana World Cup. With the heavily favored Cubans facing a shocking elimination during a quarterfinals match with unheralded Brazil, it would take some true heroics from still-developing first-year prospects to save the evening, and indeed the entire showcase event, for the beleaguered home forces. A loss would have ended a string of eight straight World Cup titles, and most embarrassing of all, it would have done so on home soil. The teams battled at 1–1 into the ninth inning, when a surprise opposite-field home run by one

Rookie star Kendrys Morales during his first national team performance at the 2003 Havana-based Baseball World Cup. Courtesy of Peter C. Bjarkman.

of the light-sticking Brazilians dropped the heavily favored Cubans into a 2–1 hole with a single half inning remaining. A throng of 30,000 Latin American Stadium loyalists were stunned into sudden silence and disbelief.

But in one of the many great comebacks in team lore, the slumbering Cuban giant would be awakened with breathtaking suddenness by the heroics of a pair of heavily hyped national team rookies. Brazilian ace pitcher Kleber Tomita was spent after a laudable effort across eight innings, but he remained in the game as his club's only reliable option. Nineteen-year-old Yulieski Gourriel opened the home ninth by stroking Tomita's first delivery off the right-field foul pole for a ringing triple that ignited stadium pandemonium. Kendrys stepped to the plate next, swinging from the left side, and watched one pitch sail wide of the strike zone. A second delivery was then crushed into the upper reaches of the right-center-field grandstand, and a suddenly inspired Team Cuba was miraculously rescued on the road to another world championship. The on-field celebration and grandstand jubilation in the aftermath of Kendrys's heroics were as wild as anything I have witnessed over the years at Latin American Stadium.

That 2003 Havana tournament would provide a launching pad not only for Morales, but also for Cepeda and Gourriel, two emerging stars destined to remain at home as the heart and soul of Cuban national teams over the next dozen years. Cepeda's two late-inning solo homers would provide the narrow margin of victory in a 4–2 gold medal triumph over Panama later that same week. Ironically Morales would drop a pop fly near first base in the ninth frame, giving Panama unexpected life and setting the stage for a bang-bang game-ending twin killing that also launched a brief on-field melee delaying Cuba's final victory celebration. It would also be on that same night—as Cuba was winning yet another coveted international title—that rumors would begin filtering through the stadium press box that injured ace hurler Maels Rodríguez had fled the island earlier in the day. It couldn't be known at the time that the hero of the moment, Kendrys Morales, was himself also launching his own secret escape plans.

Problems surrounding Kendrys lay right around the corner, in Panama City, where the Cubans traveled a mere week later for scheduled Western Hemisphere qualifying matches preceding the upcoming Athens Olympics. Morales would be sent home early by Cuban officials for what was later described in an INDER press release only as a severe disciplinary infraction. The Cuban press offered no further details, but there was soon word on the street that the infraction was having an underage female admirer visit his hotel room. There were additional rumors (none verified) of an actual defection attempt. It would later be known that Morales had merely been observed chatting innocently enough with an MLB scout in the hotel lounge. Once again the continuous paranoia of Cuban team bosses would set in motion the precise chain of events that overzealous security officials were supposedly trying to squelch.

If Kendrys had not intended to abandon the Cuban team in Panama, it was not long before he did successfully flee the island. If potential big-league dollars and attached celebrity were not enough to entice the prospect, it seems that increased harassment by INDER officials and constant scrapes with his Industriales manager and coaches were reasons enough to drive him from home. Once more we would witness a self-fulfilling prophecy, just as with the past cases of El Duque or Liván or the future scenarios surrounding Aroldis Chapman, Yoenis Céspedes, and so many others. As paranoia grew for the INDER bosses about increasing defections, their strong-arm tactics aimed at controlling a worsening situation only tossed gasoline onto the fire. Kendrys would soon decide he had had enough, making a dozen unsuccessful attempts to flee according to his own later accounts.[22] He reportedly even served a brief jail sentence in Havana after one early abortive effort at illegal flight. But persistence would pay off and eventually yet another established Industriales star performer (shades of El Duque a half decade earlier) would be able to sneak off the island in one more daring bolt for what was perceived as a shot at dignity and freedom.

A big-league windfall was quick enough in coming for a hitter of Kendrys's obvious potential. Six months after his June 2004 arrival by raft on Florida shores, and on the heels of several impressive showcase workouts in the Dominican Republic, the Los Angeles Angels would tender a six-year package that featured a $3 million signing bonus. For all his obvious talent the route to the majors wasn't destined to be direct or easy. There was no immediate insertion into a big-league lineup as with Abreu, Céspedes, or Ramirez, and no fast track through the minors in a matter of months as with Puig, José Iglesias, or Alex Guerrero. There was an initial 2005 campaign split between Advanced-A and AA-level farm clubs and then three summers of moving up and down repeatedly between the parent club and AAA Salt Lake City. It was the obvious lack of defensive skills that kept him stuck in the minors much longer than might have otherwise been necessary. But any questions of maturity and character were quickly answered by a surprisingly strong work ethic and immediate progress at adapting to the professional game. That had always been the overriding issue for this writer and for other naysayers among big-league scouts, especially given so many reports of the young Kendrys's somewhat erratic behavior as a Cuban League rookie.

Then came a sudden breakout season with the Angels in 2009 that transformed Morales into an unexpected American League MVP candidate. It was one of the best offensive seasons ever for a Cuban-born player and groundbreaking among the modern-era defectors. Morales posted one of the highest home run totals (34, with 108 RBIs) for any Cuban slugger, one that would not be approached again until José Abreu came along a decade later. Only pre-revolution Cuban stars like Tony Pérez, Tony Oliva, and Orestes Miñoso had ever put on that kind of offensive display in the big leagues.

But just as suddenly as he had emerged, he would be sabotaged by a freak injury. It was the kind of odd injury that reflected well the aberrations of the modern baseball era. Circling the bases after a dramatic walk-off grand slam homer on May 29 versus Seattle, the Angels slugger was mobbed by teammates who piled on the game's hero in an excessive and costly display of celebration. This was not a hit that clinched a pennant, after all, but just another game in a long summer season. But it was destined to be the final game that year for Morales, whose left leg was fractured in the enthusiastic display.[23] The season was over long before the strong Morales comeback might have reached yet a new plateau. He would miss the final 100-plus games of 2010 and then also lose the entire 2011 campaign due to complications in the healing process.

A return to action in 2012 was highlighted by a rare July 30 batting feat in which the Angels switch-hitting slugger became only the third batter in big-league annals to launch homers from both sides of the plate in the same inning. Nonetheless a December 2013 trade would leave Kendrys reviving his career in Seattle (not LA), where for a single summer he continued his onslaught against rival pitchers as one of the most productive designated hitters on the American League scene. Then in the early winter off-season of 2013, Morales made a poor career decision, likely one pushed by overaggressive agent Scott Boras, to test the free agent market. His attractiveness was limited as a one-dimensional designated hitter. Any interested club would have to display specialized needs that could excuse gambling another top-dollar contract on an aging veteran (he had turned thirty the previous June) with a limited window on productivity. Turning down what seemed to be a generous offer from the Mariners, Morales found himself sitting on the sideline without a team at the outset of spring training. The gamble had failed miserably, and it looked like an often ill-starred big-league career might be over even earlier than expected.

Morales was eventually picked up by the Minnesota Twins, where he logged only thirty-nine games and smacked a single homer before finding himself back in a Mariners uniform by mid-season. Seattle had reacquired his now one-year contract at a fraction of their original free agent offer and at the additional cost of nothing more than a single minor-league pitching prospect. And by season's finish he had once more been cut loose, as a fading career took yet another downturn.

But Kendrys would keep bouncing back, despite the numerous delays, injuries, and miscalculations comprising a rollercoaster career. Early in 2015 he had been resurrected in Kansas City and was again contributing heavily, and this time with a team seemingly bound for a serious American League pennant run. Morales began the season with an April and May offensive surge that reminded one of the earliest years in Cuba or that one phenomenal 2009 season in Los Angeles. There was even serious buzz by midyear of an All-Star Game slot that never materialized. The end of the trail had not quite yet arrived for thirty-two-year-old Kendrys Morales, pioneering muscular slugger among the defectors and a noteworthy foreshadowing of the likes of Céspedes, Puig, and Abreu looming on the horizon.

6

"THE BEST THERE EVER WAS"

All I want out of life is that when I walk down the street, the folks will say, "There goes the greatest hitter that ever lived."—Ted Williams, *My Turn at Bat*

I was able to stir considerable controversy on the streets of Havana in early 2015, although I wasn't personally present on the island at the time. The event was the appearance of a polemic article in the popular monthly Cuban arts and culture magazine *La Calle del Medio*. It was an interview I had done with journalist Reynaldo Cruz, based in the eastern province of Holguín. The original piece had earlier appeared online but was now surprisingly being excerpted in one of the more visible and avowedly conservative hard-line government publications.[1] The fact that the Cuban press would print such an item was in itself a somewhat landmark occurrence. It was printed with a prominently displayed headline disclaimer that the editors were not in entire accord with the sentiments of the interviewee but still found his views thought provoking and well reasoned. But what stirred up heated debate on the streets of Havana was not the ground-breaking political stance of the editors or a surprising choice of editorial subject, but rather the controversial opinions I was expressing about the beloved national sport.

The part of the original interview chosen for excerpt in the national magazine was my outspoken views on the elevated quality of current Cuban baseball stars. It was a position I had been arguing in private conversations with Cuban friends in ballparks, in hotel bars, and on Havana street corners for a number of years. My contention was simply that

Cuban ballplayers—especially the celebrated stars on the national team—
had never been better than during the past dozen or so years. It was a hard
sell to push such a point with Cuban fans now so disappointed in the long
string of setbacks the national team had been suffering for several years.

For most new-millennium Cubans, it seemed illogical that players like
Cepeda, Despaigne, Gourriel, and the bulk of their Team Cuba mates who
had dropped so many titles of late could possibly rank as superior to (or
even equal) those heroes of a decade or two back who brought so much
honor to the nation and who won so many glorious victories with such
relative ease. Wasn't the proof in the record books? Few, if any, opponents ever subdued the slugging of Linares, Kindelán, Casanova, and
company, or roughed up pitchers like Braudilio Vinent, Faustino Cor-
rales, or Rogelio García. But I was not alone in this seemingly radical
view that post-2000 Cuban ball clubs were superior, all recent World Cup
or Olympic stumbles aside. It was an opinion that had also been voiced
by several well-respected Cuban ball-playing old-timers themselves during a recent informal gathering staged that same month with a group of
Canadian and American baseball fans in the bowels of Latin American
Stadium.[2]

What was not well understood by most Cuban fans was precisely how
much the landscape had changed and how isolated they had been from the
realities of a new brand of international baseball. The situation was reminiscent of one found in Japan four or five decades back and so artfully
described by Robert Whiting.[3] Those earlier Cuban icons of the
1970s–1990s shone so brightly at home and on the road largely because
of the uneven playing fields on which they performed. They were not
playing the same game as today's Cuban stars who find themselves repeatedly matched against the world's top professionals, many of whom
are already established big leaguers and not raw recruits still in training.
Teams fronted by the likes of "Cheito" Rodríguez, Lourdes Gourriel, and
the lionized Omar Linares were carrying aluminum bats into battle; they
were a much older and far more seasoned group than the bulk of the
teams they faced in international tournaments, and they were squaring off
repeatedly against university and industrial-league clubs, not the potent
rosters their successors faced with the arrival of a new millennium.

Everything had changed with the Pan American Games in Winnipeg
during August of 1999 and with the follow-up Olympic tournament one
year later in Sydney. Professionals were for the first time sanctioned for

such Olympic-style venues, and Asian and Latin American clubs (let alone the Americans) would now be using high-level minor leaguers and a sprinkling of former major leaguers. USA teams now boasted AA or AAA prospects for events like the late-season IBAF World Cups of 2003, 2005, 2007, and 2009. The Dutch (long claiming athletes from the baseball hotbeds of Curaçao and Aruba as naturalized citizens) emerged as a true powerhouse once their stash of Caribbean minor leaguers and sprinkling of big leaguers became available for national team duty. The tenacious Cubans survived despite the opposition upgrade for more than a half-dozen years, claiming the first two of those four early 2000s World Cups and finishing first once (2004) and second twice (2000, 2008) in three Olympics before baseball was so unfortunately dropped from that showcase venue. But by the final years of the new century's first decade the retooled Americans and upstart Dutch had taken control as the new reigning senior-level tournament powers.

The logic seems irrefutable that ballplayers in the majors are better today than ever before—bigger, stronger, perhaps even more dedicated to their year-round craft and physical conditioning. Of course the game may not be as artistic as it once was, and there is merit to the argument that young ballplayers are today short on some of the game's fundamental skills and strategies. But athletes in baseball today, as in all professional and amateur sports, are head and shoulders above those of any earlier generation. Almost any top college hoops team of the current era would run circles around Bill Russell's dynastic NBA Boston Celtics of the sixties. NFL stars of today would physically crush those of two decades back in every aspect of offensive and defensive play. And in the major leagues contemporary players are not only superior physical specimens, but they train better, eat better, and outstrip their predecessors in all physical dimensions. Even if we acknowledge that baseball (especially stateside) no longer has a corner on the best available athletes, any MLB scout or front office honcho will affirm the advantages of today's professional ballplayers.

The case with the Cuban Leaguers is equally obvious. This is especially true since we now have a far more convincing basis for detailed comparisons with the major-league game. One simply could not imagine Cuban stalwarts of the fifties or sixties competing in something like a WBC event against all-star American-bred big leaguers—even in a low-stakes exhibition series. For one thing, the Cuban big-league contingents of the pre-1960 epochs were always rather miniscule in size when it came to body counts. Outside of Miñoso and Luque and Cuéllar and Oliva, there were very few Cuban headliners during the decades before or immediately after the Castro revolution. Players like Atanasio (Tony) Perez and Tony Gonzalez and Tony Oliva (throw in another Tony named Taylor) actually learned their baseball skills largely in the stateside minor leagues and not on the soil of their native homeland. The list of pre-revolution (or even 1970s-era) Cuban pitchers who were true big-league headliners can easily enough be reduced to only four: Luque, Pascual, Tiant, and perhaps Cuéllar. And with the first "defectors" of the 1990s and 2000s, only El Duque and briefly Liván and José Contreras earned top billing. But in the past five years the trickle has become a steady stream, if not a true flood tide. More than a small handful of these latest Cubans have become immediate frontline stars (Puig, Abreu, Céspedes, and Chapman for starters) or at least stellar prospects (Raisel Iglesias, Yasmany Tomás, Jorge Soler, José D. Fernández), and they have notably done so in an age literally crammed full of the best big-league talent ever assembled. The recent defectors alone are proof enough that Cuban players have never been better.

No decade or even any full era of several decades has witnessed a greater impact of Cubans filtering into the big leagues—despite all the roadblocks to their presence since Fidel Castro emerged a half century back. Pure numbers tell the story. Nearly 30 percent (see appendix 1) of all Cubans to make big-league rosters have done so in the twenty years since René Arocha emerged as the first modern-era defector. It is a widely held conclusion that without the revolution and the isolation it quickly caused, Cubans entering the big leagues would have continued to dwarf the numbers of Dominicans and Venezuelans. But there is a countertheory as well, since some might contend that it was precisely the INDER-designed and highly regimented socialist sports system keeping Cubans home in their own domestic league that, in the end, helped the island produce such an overabundance of raw baseball talent.

And if we need more solid proof beyond mere numbers, we can point first to Chapman, Puig, and Céspedes—or to a long list of recent impact rookies that now includes Jorge Soler, Rusney Castillo, Alex Guerrero, and Odrisamer Despaigne. And for the top exemplar we obviously have Jose Dariel Abreu. No Cuban import—Miñoso or Oliva included—has had the same kind of immediate overnight impact on a big-league diamond. None, with the possible exception of Oliva alone (MLB's first rookie batting champion), has ever posted a better rookie big-league campaign.

Abreu's first American League season was stunning by every measure, and it might have been even more so if Yasiel Puig had not made a nearly parallel, if not quite equally heavy, splash a mere year earlier. For over two decades the handful of successful Cuban defectors had almost all been pitchers—Arocha, Osvaldo Fernández, Arrojo, the Hernández half brothers, Contreras, and more recently Chapman. Alexei Ramírez and Rey Ordoñez earlier had been exceptions, but they were both more noted for defense and thus fit a long-familiar Cuban stereotype. Céspedes had shown plenty of raw power at the plate (20-plus homers in each of his first two seasons) but hardly took the majors by storm and also tailed off dramatically as a sophomore big leaguer (a 50-point drop in batting average). Kendrys Morales developed rather slowly in the minors, held back by the lack of a well-defined defensive position. But now with first Puig and then Abreu, it became clear that Cuba was capable of producing quality hitters as well as big league–ready pitchers.

Abreu's rookie month topped even the one enjoyed by Puig, who nine months earlier had burst on the scene in Los Angeles with quite a bit more flair but not as much staying power. Both would win rookie-of-the-month honors in their respective leagues (Alex Guerrero would do the same a year later); both would ring up a string of debut-month record book entries.[4] But Abreu's list of rookie records was longer and thus more impressive; it overshadowed even the recently celebrated novice Mike Trout (2012 AL Rookie of the Year) and may well turn out to be a record-book bonanza that will remain unequalled for quite some time.[5]

After Abreu sprinted out of the gate with a torrid April, he did suffer a minor and fortunately quite temporary derailment. A mid-May injury (tendinitis in his left ankle) kept him cooling on the sidelines for two weeks before a dramatic return coinciding with the club's first important West Coast road trip: in his second at bat of the reinstatement Abreu slugged his eleventh homer of the season off Dodgers southpaw ace Clayton Kershaw. What turned out to be a minor injury didn't slow the big first sacker for long, and by the All-Star break the Chicago novice seemed a lock for rookie-of-the-year honors, despite an almost equally impressive opening two-plus months for New York Yankees Japanese import, hurler Masahiro Tanaka. Tanaka himself would post a dozen victories by All-Star week and owned the advantage of playing in media-heavy New York; but by July the Yankees ace was himself on the disabled list, with both his season and his hopes for rookie honors largely dismantled. Abreu's own batting average surged dramatically in the final weeks before the All-Star Game, thanks to one of several lengthy hitting streaks he would enjoy over the course of the full summer.

Abreu's second half season offered something of a puzzle, however, as the power numbers dropped drastically and many who remain enamored of the long ball were outspokenly suspicious that the long campaign had already begun to take its inevitable toll. Or perhaps the pitchers had made the necessary adjustments by the second and third time around the league. I had early on predicted that Abreu would get even better under hot weather conditions. That hunch would eventually prove prophetic, despite the outcome (a plummet in home runs and a dramatic spike in batting average) taking a slightly different shape than I had expected. If many misunderstood the power outage, they also likely misgauged its true cause. Down the stretch, Abreu demonstrated just how gifted a pure hitter he actually was, and how selective a batsman he could be. It had always been his game plan to hit the ball where it is pitched, to pepper the defense with endless line drives to all fields (and especially to the opposite side), and never to merely swing for the fences. The switch in power numbers was in fact the finest measure of his true offensive game.

By season's end there would be a host of awards and recognitions, although a coveted MVP was not destined to be part of the package. The Chicago ball club was too far out of the pennant race and stars with tail-ender clubs rarely get serious consideration. Viewed as an entire body of work, Abreu's rookie campaign was surely one of the best ever, even if his ROY award would remain somewhat tarnished for many traditionalists by a single technical consideration. Abreu's top award would again raise the issue of whether mid-career Cuban defectors, just like Japanese-league free agents, should actually be viewed as legitimate rookies. Abreu had already played seven seasons in a circuit that I have long contended is largely equivalent to the AAA or AA level in North American organized baseball.

* * *

February 2013 offered up one of my more extraordinary "baseball adventures" on the ground in Cuba. I was again touring as an unofficial guide and resident Cuban ballpark expert with Kit Krieger's Cubaball group based out of Canada, and a quirk in the schedule had provided a rare opportunity to take in two games in two different locations on the same day. Both ballpark visits would—largely through the hand of fate and the role of odd circumstance—turn out to be exceptionally memorable.

The official group tour agenda included an afternoon contest at quaint "26 de Julio" ballpark in the historic village of Artemisa, a new league member after the restructuring of provinces in August 2010. It was actually the first time I witnessed an official league game in this particular venue, one of the island's most charming, if somewhat rickety, playing grounds, and one that all-too-obviously reflects its 1930s vintage. Like many of the Cuban parks, the Artemisa grounds are reminiscent of minor-league venues in the States during the years immediately preceding and following World War II. But "26 de Julio" (named for Cuba's post-revolution "Independence Day," marking the 1953 Moncada uprising) also has an inescapable rundown quality that says much about the deteriorating state of league baseball on the island. The game itself, pitting the league-leading Matanzas Cocodrilos (Crocodiles) against the hometown also-ran Artemisa Cazadores (Hunters), also turned out to be an exceedingly rare one.

For starters there would be an odd delay that pushed a one o'clock starting time back by almost three hours. I spent much of the unscheduled hiatus chatting in the Matanzas dugout with an old friend, national team manager Victor Mesa. No one seemed aware at first of what was causing the unscheduled suspension, but it soon became clear that there were no umpires on the scene—a most likely explanation. A rumor began to circulate in the dugouts and grandstands that car problems (perhaps even an auto accident en route) had interrupted the crew's thirty-mile journey between Havana and Artemisa. Only later that evening at Latin American Stadium would I learn (during a chance encounter with a league official charged with umpire scheduling) the true reason for the delay that finally ended with a first pitch being tossed well past mid-afternoon and with only three hours of daylight remaining in a park with no functioning light towers. Apparently it all had to do with commissioner Higinio Vélez back in Havana, who had suspended the crews' departure until his office was paid some outstanding funds long overdue from the local Artemisa IN-DER commission. Only in Cuba could a big-league ball game be delayed and even jeopardized for such an unlikely and seemingly trivial reason.

Once action finally started there would also be a historically significant pitching performance, the last ball game ever worked on native soil by one of the nation's brightest and most ill-starred young mound prospects. Twenty-six-year-old Yadier Pedroso had been one of the most intriguing pitchers on the island for several years, a league ERA leader back in 2009 and a potential national team closer in the absence of recently retired Pedro Lazo. He had been part of a pitching staff in Habana Province a few years earlier that featured five of the nine national team hurlers; once the aforementioned provincial realignment occurred on the eve of the 2010–11 season, the entire stellar staff (also including Jonder Martínez, Miguel Lahera, southpaw Yulieski González, league career saves leader José Angel García, and future big-league defector Miguel Alfredo González) had been transferred to the replacement Artemisa team. Still a relative youngster, Pedroso had recently recovered from a nagging shoulder injury and there were questions about whether he would make the final cut for the soon-to-be-named 2013 World Baseball Classic squad.

Pedroso was Artemisa's scheduled starter that rare afternoon, and it was a fittingly impressive performance. He worked six innings and allowed only a single run, leaving with the game still tied. He certainly appeared healthy enough and had obviously made a strong case that he indeed belonged on the WBC roster, or at least remained a legitimate candidate. It was also a game that would, in retrospect, carry a far deeper and sadder significance. Pedroso's short life would be snuffed out in a horrific automobile crash less than two months later, only a few miles from this very ballpark. That tragic ending to a promising career to this day remains the saddest among my large storehouse of accumulated Cuban memories.[6]

The day's second game carried what would prove in retrospect to be equal significance. With the Artemisa-Matanzas game finally suspended due to failing light after eight frames (the score still knotted), the tour group returned to downtown Havana before 7:00 pm, providing me with the rare gift of a second evening contest now on tap in the capital city. After racing to the Cienfuegos–Industriales game in Latin American Stadium, my longtime Havana driver and ballpark companion Eddie Artiles and I were able to witness José Abreu slug two mammoth homers (the second a tiebreaking, extra-inning grand slam) that decided a crucial late-season clash. I visited briefly with the Cienfuegos slugger in the visitor's dugout after the contest and we talked casually about seeing each other in Japan within the month for the opening round of WBC action. Entirely unknown at the time, of course, was the fact that I had just seen Abreu perform on Cuban soil for the final time.

I had over a handful of years witnessed several slugging displays by Abreu, yet none matched the one I had witnessed on an earlier trip (2011) while guiding the same Canadian Cubaball group. Playing the Havana Metros in rickety Changa Metros Stadium on the grounds of the Havana Sports City training academy, Abreu would belt the longest homer I had ever seen in six decades of baseball watching. It was a mammoth blast that easily traveled beyond 550 feet, cleared both an interior and a secondary exterior concrete wall in dead-center field, and landed on the roof of a packed city bus motoring along a nearby busy thoroughfare.

I was expecting to see Abreu, on the field in action if not off the field for some personal contact, when I returned to Havana in September. I was

Jose Abreu on the field in Havana's Latin American Stadium with the author in January 2013, during his final Cuban League season. Courtesy of Peter C. Bjarkman.

part of an ESPN filming venture focused on interviews with Tony Castro and others and aiming to capture something of the current state of flux in Cuban baseball. Our first day in town we headed out to the very same Changa Stadium, where ESPN investigative reporter Paula Lavigne was planning to begin a series of formal interviews with the younger Castro, Fidel's son, former national team doctor, and recently named vice president of both INDER and the World Baseball and Softball Confederation.[7] The backdrop would be a morning preseason practice game between Industriales and Cienfuegos. I was surprised on the field before the contest to find that Abreu, Erisbel Arruebarrena, and Yoan Moncada were all missing from the Cienfuegos traveling squad. It was not generally known at the time, but Abreu and Arruebarrena had already left Cuba, and Moncada had secretly announced to authorities that he was no longer interested in playing with his hometown club.[8] One of the ironies of the moment was that failing to find Abreu for a brief visit, I instead chatted with a number of Industriales players I had long considered off-field friends (Gourriel, Alex Mayeta, Carlos Tabares). One of those replacement "*saludos*" (friendly greetings) included Yasmany Tomás, also about to play his own final season at home.

Tony Castro's lengthy interviews with Paula Lavigne during that abbreviated visit would signal the changing winds on the island. Ironically, at the very time Castro was expounding before ESPN cameras, Cuba was, unbeknownst to most, suffering its largest and most impactful defection losses ever. And in an unfortunate later development, ESPN producers back in the States would eventually decide not to use the bulk of Lavigne's interviews with Castro and national team manager Victor Mesa, nor an interesting filmed session with Yulieski Gourriel in which the longtime star talked openly about his Cuban salary (providing details not often spelled out for the US press) and his own possible aspirations to someday don a big-league uniform with his favorites, the New York Yankees (see chapter 8).

At the time of his quiet departure in September 2013, Abreu was still largely an unknown up north, even after several of the best seasons ever posted by an island slugger. But he did not escape the eyes of all stateside Cuban baseball watchers. MLB scouts had definitely taken a bead on the young slugger after the 2009 Europe World Cup, although he was still viewed by most as a work in progress. But at least one observant North American baseball writer had also noticed Abreu (in the stat sheets, if not in the ballpark) and attempted to spread the gospel. Jonah Keri, then writing for Grantland.com, revealed that the Cienfuegos slugger was "putting up god-like numbers in the closed-off world of Cuba" and sang the praises of an athlete he labeled "The Best Hitter You've Never Heard Of."[9]

But mystery remained. Despite its unmistakable enthusiasm and inventory of impressive stats, Keri's article doesn't begin to reveal the full impact of Abreu on the island over his last several seasons in a Cienfuegos uniform. Perhaps only Osmani Urrutia enjoyed such a string of dominant performances when he won five batting titles in the span of only six years and batted above .400 for the entire streak. Few who had seen them both would have ever contended, however, that Urrutia was in Abreu's class. The former was a stereotypical singles hitter who didn't run well and barely held his own in the outfield. I never heard MLB scouts talking Urrutia up during the years he was with the national team, which included the inaugural World Baseball Classic. Abreu dominated in all hitting departments, not just one. Keri had not seen him play up close and personal, but the stats alone were enough to turn readers' heads and pique the enthusiasm of American journalists.

Abreu was born in the rural village of Cruces, a town of several hundred sitting to the north of the provincial capital of Cienfuegos. It is a locale owning a legacy in the island's baseball lore, since it is today the final resting place of the greatest Cuban ballplayer of them all, Negro Leaguer and Cooperstown Hall of Famer Martin Dihigo. Abreu would make his early debut (a month shy of turning seventeen) as an oversize and overtalented teenager in December 2003, at the outset of National Series 43. Omar Linares—for many the greatest revolution-era slugger—had also debuted at that tender age, and future big-leaguer Dayan Viciedo was still fifteen when he first struggled in a Villa Clara uniform. Abreu's first season showed promise (he slugged 5 homers and batted .271 across 71 games), but he enjoyed nothing that resembled the immediate impact earlier experienced by Linares. It wouldn't be until his third league campaign that it became apparent that the statuesque Cienfuegos first sacker would indeed be one of the island's true greats.

Abreu first appeared as a top international prospect in September 2009. Traveling with the national team to the 2009 Europe World Cup as a backup first baseman, he showed immediate flair in the pretournament Italian Baseball Week, where he paced all hitters (.556 in four games) and pocketed an MVP award. But for much of the actual World Cup event he remained on the bench while the veteran lefty swinger Ariel Borrero manned first base. Overall it seemed a rather quiet national team debut, but things wouldn't remain that way for very long.

The breakout season came in the shadows of that 2009 World Cup event in Europe. For the first of three straight campaigns, Abreu would slug thirty homers and trail Alfredo Despaigne down to the wire in that popular department. He would also miss out on a rare .400 season by the barest of margins (a single base hit) on the season's final day. It was a clear demonstration that Abreu was a pure hitter and not just a long-ball slugger. The following year there would be no falloff, but an actual surge in production (33 homers, 93 RBIs, .453 BA). For much of the year it appeared that Abreu was on course for an unprecedented Triple Crown, something that had never before been witnessed with a Cuban National Series.[10] Such an achievement might have been fitting and even poetic during the league's Golden Anniversary year. In the end it was not his normal rival in the slugging department, Despaigne, but rather another Granma basher, Yoenis Céspedes, who would sabotage the effort. Céspedes finished with a rush, tying the big first baseman in homers and sneaking by him the final weekend in the RBI department. Nonetheless Abreu owned the batting title, and his RBI and home run numbers were among the loftiest in league annals.

There was an additional pair of remarkable performances yet to come. During the following National Series (51) the RBI totals surged to 99, but still not enough to pace the league. Despaigne rang up 105 and also upped the league home run standard to 36, a record that still stands. Another .400 batting average was lost only down the season's final stretch. Winter 2013 witnessed a drop in raw numbers (.345 BA, 60 RBIs, and 19 homers). But it was a campaign in which all slugging waned on the island for a combination of reasons, including a softer Japanese-made baseball and a new format concentrating the league's best pitching on eight surviving teams during the second half of a split season. Even with only nineteen round-trippers Abreu stood at the top of the league pack. He had by then not only emerged as the starting national team first baseman, but also the cleanup hitter in a power-packed lineup that included the likes of Despaigne, Gourriel, and Cepeda. During the March 2013 World Baseball Classic in Japan, it was Abreu who led the Cubans in the power department, posting club bests in homers (3, tied with Despaigne), RBIs (9), and total bases (19).

Over several short years Abreu left a remarkable legacy in the Cuban record books. He was indeed proving to be another Linares or Kindelán (perhaps the two wrapped into one), but he was doing it in an age of arguably better competition and with wooden bats, and thus on a playing field that might be more easily measured against major-league standards. And he did, in fact, regularly test his skills against big leaguers overseas, an opportunity not enjoyed by Cuban sluggers of earlier decades. The peak moments came with the third edition of the WBC in Japan, and that tournament convinced MLB scouts that they were watching a true big leaguer. It also equally convinced Abreu himself, a fact that destined the Japan tournament to be the slugger's final glorious hurrah in a Cuban uniform.

Abreu would travel with a Cuban squad to Rotterdam later that summer, and he was also scheduled to perform in the States during the renewal of the USA-Cuba series in July. But he was almost immediately injured (a strained oblique muscle while batting) in the second game of the World Port Tournament and saw no further service. He sat quietly on the sidelines for the final week of Rotterdam action. Never very outgoing, he seemed more withdrawn than usual in the team hotel, where we frequently crossed paths. The reason was later rather apparent—the decision to leave had already been made. There were eventual suggestions that his injury was also perhaps exaggerated to aid escape plans. Whatever the brewing scenario, the injury left Abreu off the Cuban roster and at home during the USA tour at month's end. His last several at bats in Rotterdam would also be his last in a Team Cuba uniform.

* * *

The 2014 American League season was a true breakout year, not only for Abreu but for Cuban ballplayers en masse. The recent campaign witnessed the most Cubans debuting in the big leagues in four-plus decades.[11] The White Sox would inaugurate the year with four Cubans on their roster and thus make their own bit of league history.[12] No team had opened with that many since the Cleveland Indians played their 1969 lidlifter with an equal number of Cubans, not only on the twenty-four-man roster, but actually in the starting lineup.[13] Abreu highlighted the Sox March 31 season opener (at U.S. Cellular Field) with a ringing first-inning double off Minnesota Twins starter Ricky Nolasco on the very first big-league pitch he ever saw. It was a signal of even bigger and better things to come.

Alexei Ramírez, the most veteran among Sox Cuban imports, had been the first successful modern-era position player among his country-men to strike pay dirt in the majors. Alexei had played in the outfield for the Cubans during the inaugural World Baseball Classic and later moved to the infield on the Cuban national team. A slender if exceptionally athletic figure, his great wrist action with the bat had even produced a league home run title late in his Cuban career (twenty round-trippers in 2007, his final National Series). But for all his promise on the island, Alexei simply blossomed beyond all expectations in the big leagues. He immediately wowed teammates, scouts, and the press with his acrobatic infield play during his first spring-training session of March 2008. Within a mere handful of years he was widely acknowledged as the best defen-sive shortstop in the majors. And unlike his 1950s-era predecessor Willy Miranda—or equally flashy Rey Ordóñez in the early 2000s—Ramírez quickly proved a dangerous big-league batsman. In his White Sox debut season he batted .290 and slugged twenty-one homers, including a roo-kie-record four grand slams.

Ramírez had left Cuba under rather extraordinary conditions back in the fall (September) of 2007. He had been given official permission by then league commissioner Carlitos Rodríguez to visit the Dominican Re-public after his wife (a native Dominican who had recently completed medical studies in Havana) returned home with the couple's two infant children. There was some speculation that the Cubans were actually more than willing to let him go, with promising youngster Héctor Olivera sud-denly emerging on the scene. But the player's decision not to return home would have some serious consequences for the baseball commissioner who had allowed him to depart so easily. Rodríguez, who had survived for a full decade in the hot-seat post, was soon relieved of his duties, and the Ramírez "defection" was rumored to be a primary cause for his fall from grace.

Alexei would eventually tell the full story of his departure from Cuba to the American press during his second Arizona spring camp, in the process shedding needed light on prevalent US media misconceptions about playing baseball in his homeland.[14] It was quite a different tale, and one altogether unique for its time period, especially when compared to the saga on the high seas surrounding the departure of Orlando

Hernández, or the escapes from team hotels under cover of nightfall reported in the cases of Liván Hernández, José Contreras, or Osvaldo Fernández. There was no dangerous adventure at sea, no sneaking out under cover of darkness, no history of numerous previous failed attempts, no shark-infested waters or marooning on a tropical island. It was all pretty mild stuff and in some ways not really a defection at all. Alexei did not consider himself a traitor; he had always dreamed first and foremost of playing for the Cuban national team and playing in the Olympics, and once that was accomplished he simply wanted to test his skills against the very best in the big leagues.

A second Cuban member of the 2014 White Sox was Dayan Viciedo, a hefty twenty-five-year-old outfielder who had been around for four full big-league seasons but had experienced a rather roller-coaster career, first in Cuba and then in the majors. Viciedo was every bit the prospect as a teenager that first Puig and later Moncada would eventually be. He was a legitimate star at the junior national team level and broke in with the National Series Villa Clara club as a somewhat unpolished fifteen-year-old third baseman. Viciedo was touted as a most promising prospect; he flashed signs of brilliance with a .337 BA as a sixteen-year-old league all-star, but soon faltered under controversial and sometimes overbearing Villa Clara manager Victor Mesa. That contentious relationship might have explained Vicicdo's slow development in the Cuban League.[15] But also entering into the negative equation was the relentless pressure of constant comparisons to Cuba's greatest third baseman, Omar Linares. Despite his single All-Star Game appearance, Viciedo never made the roster of a senior national team, and his career had definitely stalled by the time he fled the island (with his family, on a boat bound for Mexico) in late May of 2008.

The final Chicago rookie on the 2014 Opening Day roster was a "defector" of far different ilk. Catcher Adrian Nieto was also a native Habanero, but he had left the island at the age of only four with his parents and thus with no possible budding baseball ambitions. The future ballplayer and his family were indeed sociopolitical refugees and the trip they made to US shores was an admittedly difficult and frightening one.[16] But Nieto never played any baseball in Cuba. He learned the game as a youth in Florida and quickly blossomed as a big-league prospect while an all-star at American Heritage High School in Plantation. There would be some detours en route to "The Show" that almost sabotaged his career, including an embarrassing fifty-game suspension from minor-league play in 2011 after testing positive for anabolic steroids. But by 2014 (after playing for the Spanish national team in the 2013 World Baseball Classic) he had made it to the top, although under somewhat quirky circumstances. As a Rule 5 Draft selection plucked from the Washington Nationals, he had to be kept on the big-league roster for a full year or returned to the Washington club. Nieto would be used sparingly during the long campaign and appeared in only forty-eight games as an occasional replacement for starting receiver Tyler Flowers. By the following spring, no longer projected by Rule 5 Draft provisions, he had already lost his big-league job in Chicago.

One of the strongest indications of the surge in Cuban big-league presence was the election of five recent defectors to league rosters for the 2014 All-Star Game in Minneapolis. It was the highest number of Cubans in years and the most during the post-revolution defector era that had effectively begun with Arocha and a slim handful of other refugee pitchers in the early 1990s, surged with the Hernández brothers and Contreras in the latter part of the same decade, and then exploded after Chapman's arrival in 2010. Abreu and Ramírez would represent the Chisox and Céspedes the Oakland A's. The pair of National Leaguers would be Puig (the only starter) and Aroldis Chapman, the latter making his third straight appearance.

Céspedes would grab most of the headlines with successful defense of his 2013 Home Run Derby crown on the eve of the All-Star Game. The Derby had become over recent years almost a bigger television spectacle than the showcase ball game itself.[17] The Minneapolis Derby was hardly a nail-biter, however, as some of the more reputed sluggers disappointed. Giancarlo Stanton's meltdown (the Miami Marlins basher failed to reach the seats even once in his National League semifinals match) allowed Cincinnati's Todd Frazier to reach the final slug-off; Céspedes edged AL rival José Batista (Blue Jays) by a 7–4 count. With his easy victory over Frazier in the finale (9–1), Céspedes joined Ken Griffey Jr. as the only back-to-back Derby winners and Griffey (3) and Prince Fielder as the only trio of repeat champs. It would ironically be something of a last hurrah for Céspedes in an Oakland uniform, as he would be dealt off to Boston within less than a month.

If the five Cubans had made some history with their combined appearance in Minneapolis, they did little outside of Céspedes's staged performance to turn the affair into any kind of showcase. Puig, after missing the event in a final fan-vote runoff election as a rookie, was a major flop in his All-Star debut. The flashy outfielder went hitless in the official game and looked totally lost as the worst performer among the dozen entrants in the showcase made-for-TV Derby. Puig rushed his swings, lining seven quick outs into the shallow outfield during the opening round, and was the only performer in the original ten-man field never to reach pay dirt. Chapman provided his accustomed late-inning spark, closing out the game for the victorious National Leaguers. Ramirez also had his brief moment in the television spotlight when he replaced Cooperstown-bound Derek Jeter, who was making his final All-Star curtain call. Abreu had one brief plate appearance and flied out tamely to left field. The night's highlight for Cuban fans undoubtedly came in the eighth, when Céspedes squared off against Chapman and lined sharply to shortstop for a bang-bang infield out. [18]

The biggest question surrounding Abreu, at least once it became apparent he could indeed make adjustments to big-league hitting, was how well the hefty first sacker might stand up to the rigors of a full 150-plus-game MLB season. The power numbers would inevitably drop as the season extended into the dog days of late summer. At mid-year Abreu seemed a lock to obliterate Mark McGwire's rookie home run standard of 49, with 30 already in the books at the season's halfway point. It appeared for a while that he might even have a shot at the more difficult target of a seemingly unassailable 1939 rookie RBI mark (145) owned by Hall of Famer Ted Williams. The nagging question was not only how well Abreu could stand up over a season that was almost 40 percent longer than any he had ever played back home in Cuba, but what would happen the third and fourth times around the circuit when savvy big-league hurlers began to figure out how to pitch to the untested if rather mature Cuban rookie?

Abreu's power production did indeed sag as the year wore on; there would be only six homers after the All-Star break. But pure hitting skills actually spiked after the Midsummer Classic and Abreu's second half was by all other measures (outside of the long ball) even better down the season's final wilting stretch. With an initial eighteen-game hitting string broken on the very day of the traditional July 4 midpoint, Abreu immediately launched a second skein that lasted twenty-one more days. The lengthy hitting onslaught (there also would be a third fourteen-game string in late August) lifted his average by nearly 30 percentage points between mid-July and mid-August, and by early September there were only two American League rivals outpacing him in the batting race. (In my July 2014 article for *Baseball Digest* I had warned that Abreu was, after all—like all Cubans—a hot-weather hitter seasoned by a tropical island environment.) In the end his .317 BA stood sixth overall, topped only by José Altuve (Houston), Victor Martínez (Detroit), Michael Brantley (Cleveland), Adrian Beltre (Texas), and National League pacesetter Justin Morneau (Colorado).

With his eye-catching early-season power numbers and his "second-half" surge in hitting proficiency, José Abreu would eventually stand in truly rare company among hordes of earlier standout rookies found across the game's lengthy annals. Of course it might well be debated that Abreu (like Japanese ROY-winners Ichiro Suzuki, Kazuhiro Sasaki, and Hideo Nomo) was not a legitimate "rookie" by strict measure. He arrived in the big leagues with plenty of seasoning in a foreign professional league of admittedly high standards (a league that features forty or fifty likely big leaguers alongside uneven talent ranging from Class AA to university-level performers). But there is another side to that coin, since if one considers performances by players breaking into "The Show" without any previous MLB playing time (true rookies, and not those who qualify by the technicality of fewer than 130 previous at bats), then Abreu's numbers look even that much better. Only twenty-six big-league "official" rookies have ever reached the thirty-home-run plateau, and Abreu, with thirty-six, would end up in the number six slot (edging out four others with thirty-five on the season's penultimate day). But it has to be noted that of the five previous "rookies" claiming more than thirty-six round trippers, only three (Wally Berger, Frank Robinson, and Albert Pujols) did so without at least a modicum of previous big-league playing time.

There are other measures of Abreu's remarkable year also worthy of mention. Bursting on the scene in April, he quickly joined former Cienfuegos teammate Yasiel Puig as the only two players in big-league baseball history to earn overlapping "rookie-of-the-month" and "player-of-the-month" plaudits for their spectacular first thirty-day spans of big-league action. Abreu would earn these same honors on several more occasions, as the month's top American League performer in July and as top rookie in both June and July. He would post three of the longest consecutive-game hitting streaks of the campaign, strings of 18 (June 15 thru July 4), 21 (July 6 thru August 1), and 14 games (August 19 thru

September 5). A single dry outing on July 5 interrupted a hot spell in which Abreu hit safely across 39 of 40 consecutive outings. And several other historic landmarks were also reached along the way, as Abreu became only the second rookie in the past sixty-five seasons (following Ichiro in 2001) boasting multiple eighteen-plus-game hitting strings, and the first White Sox player (rookie or otherwise) to do so since Hall of Famer Eddie Collins turned the trick back in 1920. Abreu also joined former Boston star Nomar Garciaparra as the only two big leaguers ever to slug thirty homers and author a pair of eighteen-plus batting streaks in the same campaign.

While Abreu had been heavily hyped in Chicago as an AL rookie-of-the-year shoo-in, there was also expected to be heated competition for the honor from Yankees import Masahiro Tanaka. Tanaka was coming off perhaps the best season ever enjoyed by a pitcher in Japan, and he held the distinct advantage of playing with the Yankees in New York's media capital.[19] Tanaka would experience an early season start almost as outstanding as Abreu's, but injuries would shut down the challenge at midseason. Abreu's runaway rookie-of-the-year award would not only be the second straight for a Cuban native (José Fernández preceded him a year earlier in the National League), but also only the third ever claimed by a newcomer who had never played in the US minors. The other two were both Japanese imports, and the old question of whether either the Japanese or Cuban defectors were in truth legitimate rookies might again arise. But that issue aside, the rookie-of-the-year award would be a fitting cap to a remarkable and better-than-anticipated big-league debut. And there were a few other year-end recognitions as well, including nomination for the prestigious Hank Aaron Award. The Sox slugger had been shortlisted for this additional honor as the league's best overall hitter—a rare rookie distinction—but in the end had been edged out by league MVP Mike Trout.

* * *

By the end of the 2014 summer season player agent Barry Praver would no longer talk with me or answer my emails.[20] I had hoped that we might discuss, if only in general terms, some of his excellent work with those Cuban players he and his Miami-based partner Scott Shapiro represent. I had enjoyed a number of brief conversations the previous summer with both Praver and Shapiro in Chicago. My opinion was always that he was one agent, at least, who had the best interests of these players at heart and had in recent years done an excellent job of representing their inter-ests. But despite making it clear in a number of emails that I was not at all interested in pushing for precise answers about how some of his clients had left Cuba surreptitiously, Praver had apparently decided that he wanted no interviews with me and that he no longer cared to respond to my overtures.

The response (or lack of it) was not particularly surprising. Cuban players were now largely under wraps, and reports circulated that they were in fact being called to testify individually before federal officials regarding those illegal exits from Cuba (aided in one form or another by human traffickers) that many of them had endured. Scott Eden of *ESPN The Magazine* would report in September that federal officials had re-quested permission for such interviews from clubs with Cuban players and that teams were cooperating.[21] All this was playing out against the backdrop of a new Florida trial of Gilberto Suarez, a low-level Miami crime figure accused of involvement in the smuggling operation that had moved Yasiel Puig to Mexico and eventually onto the Los Angeles Dodg-ers roster. Puig was, in fact, one of the players reported to be cooperating directly in the renewed federal probe.

I was aware of the curtain being drawn around the Cuban big leaguers shortly after the season shut down. I had hoped for an official chat with José Abreu in the off-season, but not to pry into his escape story, since I had always stayed off that topic with the players themselves. I simply wanted a better feel for Abreu's experiences as a big-league novice and to chat about personal and on-field adjustments he was forced to make. Although I had been friendly with Abreu for a number of years, I didn't want to contact him directly. My plan was to move through official chan-nels and thus avoid jeopardizing long-standing positive relationships with the Cuban baseball community on both sides of the Straits of Florida. Although Praver did not respond to several emails informing him of the book I was writing, I did receive a much-welcomed phone call from Abreu's business manager (who had been copied in my emails to Praver and Shapiro) apologizing for being unable to help under the current con-ditions but encouraging my efforts nonetheless. The message seemed to be that perhaps a year earlier there might not have been a problem, but now (after the April 2014 Puig revelations) "things were simply getting too tense and complicated regarding the whole Cuban player situation."

But if Praver was not going to arrange (or permit) an Abreu interview for me, he did not exactly shield his star franchise player from the press at large. Perhaps I was a bit of a risk since I had such visibility back in Cuba. Or perhaps I didn't have enough to offer in the way of potential media exposure for his client. A feature story in a slick Chicago magazine—like one that Praver would soon sign off on with a local Windy City writer—would likely spur Sox ticket sales and feed the fans' hunger for more details about their new slugging hero. And if there was now a supposed shield around the Cuban defectors, it turned out not to be a very tight one. Other players had recently been coming forth with some rather sensational details about their own personal Cuban escapes. Henry Urrutia (Baltimore Orioles) would soon be telling his story to ESPN cameras for a scheduled April 2015 *Outside the Lines* segment dedicated to the prospect of new Cuba-USA baseball relations. Nine-year veteran shortstop Yunel Escobar had also recently related a similar saga to the *Washington Post* after becoming a member of the Washington Nationals ball club.[22] These harrowing Cuban escape stories were now becoming somewhat regular media fare.

By early spring the story of how Abreu had left Cuba was now also out in the open. Rumors had been circulating for some time about a harrowing boat trip, and Jared Hopkins, writing in the *Chicago Tribune*, had reported in November on some of those rumors.[23] If the precise story remained something of a guarded mystery, that would soon change. Just in time to pique interest at the start of a new season, Michael Miller would publish a much fuller account in the April issue of *Chicago* magazine, and overnight the Abreu saga would be a guarded mystery no more.

If Praver had shielded his client's story up to this point, he was now willing to let Abreu sit down with Miller and divulge his full tale for the Chicago reading public. Praver himself was present at the interview, as Miller stresses; it was in fact staged at the luxury Coral Gables Riviera Golf Club, where Praver is a member.[24] The trip by boat to Haiti was hardly any different from similar journeys recently revealed by Henry Urrutia and a handful of others. The intrepid group departing in a small and barely seaworthy craft under cover of darkness sometime in late August consisted of the ballplayer, his fiancée (Yusmary), his parents, and also his sister and her husband. The two-engine, twenty-foot craft left Cuban shores at midnight, pressed on for more than twelve hours through fifteen-foot waves, and somehow reached the welcoming coastline of

Haiti without being either capsized or broken in two by any of the huge trawlers and cargo steamers that often traverse the same sea route.

Abreu did indeed risk his own life and the safety of several accompanying family members, but it was a risk he was clearly willing to take. And it was an escape route that had apparently been decided on as early as the World Baseball Classic trip to Japan in 2013. There would even be later speculation that the injury suffered early in the July Rotterdam tournament had been purposely exaggerated in order to delay his presence at the late August preseason training sessions of his Cienfuegos league team. It was by Abreu's own account (offered to Miller) that while in Fukuoka and Tokyo he had already decided to test himself against the world's best players in the major leagues.

José Abreu was only in the early stages of his assault on the American League rookie record book when news leaked out of Cuba that yet another potential prize was already MLB-bound. Powerful outfield speedster Yasmany Tomás had just completed his sixth National Series season with the popular Havana Industriales club and, like all but one of those seasons, it had been a campaign shortened and muted by a series of small nagging injuries. Tomás had built a reputation for awesome power displays, although his numbers were never exceptionally lofty and he had not ranked among league leaders in any individual category. His six-season home run total (37) barely outstripped Abreu's numbers for several individual campaigns. In short, the power hype all seemed based more on potential than actual achievement. And his biggest drawback seemed to be a free-swinging approach to hitting that displayed little in the way of plate discipline. Over the final two Cuban seasons the muscular outfielder had struck out every fifth official trip to the plate; he owned only one season of home run double figures (16), and his .284 lifetime batting average paled in a league that regularly produces dozens (sometimes as many as 30) .300-plus batters annually.

But clearly the pie-in-the-sky search was now on for the next Abreu, and a hefty long-ball threat with a potent bat seemed sure to pique plenty of interest in front offices and press circles alike. If the Industriales slugger was not another Abreu, he might at least be another Céspedes, or at the very least a toned-down version of Yasiel Puig. Plenty of MLB scouts had noticed Tomás on brief display in the Japan segment of the 2013 World Baseball Classic, and he had not failed to impress with a .375 six-game batting mark (hits in all six games) plus five RBIs. A part-time outfield starter as a last-minute addition to the squad, he whacked an impressive three-run homer in the second-round rout of Taiwan and then, in the crucial final showdown match with the Dutch, Tomás almost became the island's latest "hero of the moment." A lead-producing clutch base knock in the eighth seemed about to launch Cuba into the final-four round in San Francisco, until pitching collapsed (Norberto González yielding a fateful homer to Andrelton Simmons) and the Cubans let the do-or-die game slip away.

A second showcase that summer had not been quite so impressive. Manning right field for a Cuban B squad that won a World Port Tournament crown in Rotterdam, Tomás displayed sloppy and even lackadaisical play in right field that generated negative buzz among many of the two dozen scouts on hand. He did make a crucial game-saving, wall-climbing grab against the host Dutch, but that play resulted mostly from raw athletic skill. A month later, during the Midwest and East Coast tour for the renewed USA-Cuba Friendly Series, Tomás had replaced the injured José Abreu at first base and he didn't look exceptionally smooth there either. And his rather undisciplined free swinging at the plate certainly didn't pad his resume.

The not-so-surprising defection of Yasmany Tomás less than a year after that 2013 USA series was colored with the normal measure of mystery and intrigue, and there was more than a little negative fallout as well. It didn't take long for stories to hit the Miami press that several Cubans back on the island had been rounded up and charged with aiding the ballplayer's first effort at illegal exit, which was now being reported as occurring in April 2012, nearly a full year before Tomás was selected for the Japan-bound WBC squad. (This was also more than two years before Tomás successfully fled to Haiti in June 2014, accompanied by a cousin, Yasiel Rodríguez, and a longtime friend, Carlos Damas.) The earlier unsuccessful attempt had apparently been considered an odd kidnapping effort by Cuban authorities, and while Tomás himself had been fully exonerated, eight others were reportedly now serving Cuban prison terms as a consequence.[25] Tomás would not comment on any of those reports; he would later claim that his decision to leave home didn't have much at all to do with baseball but rather was related to his girlfriend's earlier legal immigration to the United States.[26] It was admittedly a rather hard story to swallow.

Whatever the backstories of this latest defection might have been, Tomás was soon garnering plenty of interest not only from big-league clubs, but also from the stateside sporting press fascinated with breaking stories about the next blockbuster Cuban find. There were feature articles

Yasmany Tomás with Team Cuba at Japan's Tokyo Dome during the 2013 World Baseball Classic. Courtesy of Peter C. Bjarkman.

with headlines like "Yasmani Tomás Capturing MLB Imaginations as Next Great Cuban Slugger" (Scott Miller, the *Bleacher Report*) or "Cuba's Next Big Thing Ready to Impress Scouts" (Jesse Sanchez, MLB.com).[27] His showcase workouts in the Dominican impressed the gathered scouts, and the media buzzed in the late fall with reports of a bidding war for the services of this latest chaser of the American Dream. The Arizona D-Backs would eventually come out on top in late November, landing the slugger in an astounding $68.5 million deal. So rapidly had the market already elevated, based largely on pure speculation, that Tomás was now going to be paid more than twice what the Reds invested in Chapman four years earlier, twice what the Dodgers had gambled on Puig two years back, and even more than the White Sox had recently handed out for newly crowned American League rookie-of-the-year José Abreu.

Tomás proved to be very much a work in progress during his first spring training. The D-Backs were attempting to transform him into a third baseman and essentially to do it at the major-league level. The bold effort received decidedly mixed reviews. The hitting side of his game was progressing as expected and in twenty-four spring games he posted a pair of homers, a dozen RBIs, and a barely respectable .257 BA. But he certainly hadn't torn up spring training in the manner that many a high-profile rookie often does. And there were definitely visible rough spots when it came to "hot corner" play.

Once the league season began, the jury was still out on Tomás. He opened the year with AAA Reno, where his five-game offensive numbers were hardly eye-catching (consisting of a single homer and a sub–Mendoza Line .190 BA). But the D-Backs apparently couldn't endure a lengthy wait for a much-needed potential bat in their struggling lineup, and by April 15 Yasmany was called back to the parent club. There he made an adjustment that might have surprised even some of his strongest supporters.[28] Splitting time between the outfield and third base, the high-priced rookie wasted little time proving he could indeed hit big-league pitching. And it certainly wasn't all about power. At the end of six weeks in the majors Tomás had socked only a single homer. But he was hitting the ball at a near .350 clip and was an anchor of a D-Backs offense that was suddenly one of the most productive in the National League. It was still early, but there were some clear signs already that Tomás might be capable of rivaling Dodgers fast-starting rookie slugger Alex Guerrero for National League rookie-of-the-year honors. If such were to transpire and either was to keep up a torrid early-season pace beyond the post-July "dog days," we might well be witnessing the third consecutive season with one of these hotshot Cuban imports walking away with a coveted first-year outstanding player award.

7

NO RESERVATIONS FOR CUBA

To grow up under communism is to live forever in the present.
—Slavenka Drakulic, *Café Europa*

The world of Cuban baseball was thrown open to numerous television viewers across North America via a most unlikely source when celebrity chef Anthony Bourdain and his Zero Point Zero production crew filmed their long-anticipated episode for the Travel Channel's popular *No Reservations* series in March 2011. Bourdain had been attempting to visit the communist nation for half-a-dozen years but had been repeatedly rebuffed by suspicious Cuban officials leery of any North American commercial television documentary that might expose the capital city's rather shabby exteriors. Bourdain's announced visit promised a novel insight into Havana's long-hidden cultural ambiance; in the end it turned out to be everything promised and then some.

One of Bourdain's Zero Point Zero producers, Phil Boag, contacted me via email less than a month before the planned shooting. Boag wanted some coaching on potential filming sites, famed Havana bars and eateries, "local color" characters to be pursued as on-camera subjects, and above all, recommendations for a centerpiece ballpark visit. Bourdain, it turned out, was a devoted baseball fan, a lifelong New York Yankee booster, and the celebrity chef had done his homework well. He wanted to get right to the heart of the subject, which meant he wanted to focus his shoot on Cuban baseball. He also wanted me in tow as his expert guide to the Havana baseball scene.

At the time I knew preciously little about Bourdain or his wildly popular Travel Channel series, but it all seemed like an excellent opportunity for yet another visit to the island—this time on someone else's dime and with an ego-boosting television gig thrown in for good measure. I had not previously been a Bourdain fan and his apparent popularity in the electronic media had never fallen on my radar. I had neither read the best-selling *Kitchen Confidential* nor even witnessed a single episode of a series that had become something of an international cult favorite. But when I heard precisely what Bourdain had in mind, this seemed just too good an opportunity to pass up. What better way might there be to expose something of Cuban baseball to a wider North American audience? And before it was all over, the Bourdain excursion would turn out to be quite an adventure indeed.

Bourdain's "No Reservations Cuba" (first aired on July 13, 2011) provided a unique window on Cuba's national sport, perhaps the first glimpse for most in the mainstream American television audience. The show's three baseball segments may indeed now stand among the best and most revealing episodes of the entire seventh season of the Bourdain series.[1] In the final editing, the "No Reservations Cuba" film was largely dominated by its three baseball episodes, and the colorful portrait offered was entirely fair and exceptionally well balanced. It opened with a sequence devoted to a little-league city championship featuring ten-year-olds wearing the colors of Havana's Cerro and Tenth of October neighbors. The segment delightfully captured much about the passion of the game on the island and had Bourdain exclaiming "it's hard to imagine (American) urban soccer moms shaking their asses between pitches" and also admitting he was personally "scouting for a future shortstop to fill a hole in the Yankee roster." Exquisite filming (including highly artistic slow-motion sequences) captured the young athletes in action and revealed an adoring overflow crowd focused as intently on the neighborhood contest as on any national team performance. If Cuban officials had earlier harbored suspicions about Bourdain and his network crew, there appeared to be "no reservations" once we were on the ground in Havana. Access provided by Cuban handler Tony Diaz (an INDER public relations chief) proved to be surprisingly accommodating and completely unrestricted. And that remarkable opening little-league scene captured the very essence of the island's true baseball passions as perfectly as any I have yet witnessed.

Author Peter Bjarkman explaining Cuban baseball to host Anthony Bourdain during the filming of the Travel Channel's "No Reservations Cuba." Courtesy of Peter C. Bjarkman.

Also included was a pivotal episode in which Bourdain visited the famed Esquina Caliente ("Hot Corner") and debated baseball in Old Havana's Central Park with some of the city's most knowledgeable street-corner fans. That second four-minute episode would also contain a rather interesting backstory. The Esquina Caliente itself is frequently reported but very little understood by visiting media searching for the heart of Cuban baseball culture. In truth it is a rather chaotic street-corner verbal free-for-all and no video crew stumbling unprepared upon the scene is likely to capture the true nature of the infamous daily event. What they encounter instead is a rowdy and often intimidating screaming match among usually inebriated self-appointed experts spouting often unintelligible gibberish. The popular Esquina Caliente is not actually the daily Central Park session that most journalists have in mind when they envision knowledgeable exchanges among Havana's reputedly savvy ballpark aficionados.

There are in fact two distinct groups that call the park home, and only one is what the foreign media typically has in mind. Ironically the group of serious debaters frequently mentioned in the press is not the actual "Hot Corner" group at all, but rather a much more knowledgeable segment of Cuba's fandom. The true debaters are a few-dozen members of Havana's formally recognized Peña Deportiva (literally "sports circle"), a government-sanctioned baseball debating club that indeed does occasionally meet in Havana's Central Park, holds regular functions in the adjacent Kid Chocolate Sports Center building, and claims a special section of seats behind the first-base dugout at Latin American Stadium.[2] This is Cuba's approximation of a stateside chapter of the Society for American Baseball Research, the group that spawned American baseball's sabermetrics craze. It was this special contingent of fans that promised to provide an enlightening segment for the Bourdain documentary.

I arrived on the scene early on the day of a scheduled film shoot and rounded up a small group of Peña regulars for the desired Bourdain episode. It would be necessary to capture what I knew Bourdain wanted and what it was important for the American viewing public to experience—lively, informed, and intelligible insights into the passions and concerns of Cuba's baseball fandom. The resulting segment proved one of the show's more memorable highlights. It also revealed a corner of Cuban fandom that broke down many potential stereotypes. While Bourdain was interested in probing baseball on the island, the Cubans themselves wanted to talk about their own handful of expatriate heroes now playing in the big leagues. The sequence did leave some misconceptions, such as the notion that Cubans could only debate publicly on street corners with the sanction of a government license.[3] But it also revealed the rather surprising connections of Cuba fans with players like Aroldis Chapman, Alexei Ramírez, and El Duque Hernández, who were supposed to be taboo subjects on the island.

Cuban fans have over the past decade been increasingly drawn to the players who have migrated north. They take great pride in these former locals and follow their exploits religiously despite limited media access, but it is only those former stars that have played in the National Series that hold their rapt attention. José Canseco and Rafael Palmeiro (despite their island birth) are of virtually no interest to the Cuban fan. It is rather those that have emerged from their own league that they now see as carrying the prideful banner and demonstrating just how good the Cubans truly are. For Havana fans it is Viciedo, Ramirez, Contreras, and Liván and El Duque (later Abreu, Puig, and Chapman) who have carried the national reputation onto the big-league stage. And ironically, instead of being shunned as the traitors the government has so long portrayed them to be, they have instead emerged as the new national heroes.

Even the Cuban media has somewhat changed its once depressingly repetitious tune. For years the "traitors" were never mentioned in official media outlets, even if the fans knew of their North American exploits. But the ban wasn't as strict as some North American writers visiting the island would report. Michael Lewis in his *Vanity Fair* article mentions names being stricken from the annual record books, even though his fellow traveler and guide Kit Krieger had told him it was not that way at all.[4] As early as 2001 I was interviewed for a live studio Havana television sportscast and was briefly stunned by several questions directed at me about the handful of departed stars who had become big leaguers. But even at the time of Bourdain's visit the topic was not general Cuban sports–talk radio fare.

A decade later (post-Bourdain) the scene had shifted rather drastically. The common mantra that Cubans have no Internet access is a distortion, like so much misinformation about the island. It is true that the Internet is not widespread, and this has as much to do with economics and communications infrastructure as with any government repression. By spring 2015, against the backdrop of President Obama's efforts at renewed diplomatic relations, NPR would devote an evening report by Robert Siegel to the paucity of Havana Internet connections.[5] But the truth is that the Internet is a rapidly growing presence on the island, and if there are no public Internet cafes, there are hotel hot spots used by a growing clan of wired Cuban youth. Two Cuba-based blogsites operating outside official government support (but nonetheless permitted to exist) provide outspoken and uncensored views on the issues surrounding the Cuban League. *Zona de Strike* (a personal blogsite of Ibrahim Sánchez based in Granma Province) is widely accessed inside and outside the county. And the *Universo Béisbol* blog and monthly digital magazine produced in Holguín by photojournalist Reynaldo Cruz provides surprising sophistication in design and content. These emerging media fronts today already far outstrip the official baseball reports in the government-run digital press.

There is still official resistance to acknowledging ballplayer departures, as was revealed during my September 2013 Parque Central visit with ESPN's Paula Lavigne. While filming a discussion with a similar group of fans in the Parque Central, Paula asked about players (especially Puig and Céspedes) that were now headlining in the big leagues. The topic quickly shifted to recently inaugurated weekly broadcasts of big-league games that had begun on Cuban national television earlier that same summer. A universal complaint from the group was that their beloved Cubans were never shown; selected games only featured those teams without Cuban defectors. Paula asked if they were anxiously waiting to see Puig in the World Series. The immediate response was that this would simply not be allowed. The World Series and other postseason games would only be available, as in the past, to those lucky enough to crash tourist bars in Old Havana hotels and thus glimpse pirated Spanish-language *ESPN Deportes* broadcasts available exclusively for visiting foreign guests.

So much current focus on celebrated defectors provides at least one explanation for an increase in young players leaving home. For several decades the national team stars were unquestionably the biggest heroes on the island. It was easy enough in that earlier era to appreciate why Omar Linares could still boast he would rather have a million hometown fans than a million foreign dollars. But times were changing rapidly as the new millennium progressed. For one thing, the national team was no longer invincible (it didn't win every tournament as in the past) and as a result had slid from its onetime lofty pedestal among long-spoiled island fans. There was increased grousing at home that the top stars were not nearly as good as those from previous generations. At the same time, young players who had abandoned the homeland were drawing ever-bigger headlines abroad that the increasingly plugged-in Cubans were now fully aware of. The dreams for many young islanders could now once again be centered on big-league celebrity, with all its vaster perks, rather than on shining locally on the poorly rewarded home front. This was increasingly true even if that dream held many roadblocks and dangers along the tortuous route to fulfillment.

In the wake of Chapman, Puig, and finally Abreu, the true island heroes had suddenly become the departed big leaguers and not the loyalists like Cepeda, Gourriel, and Despaigne, who were still donning Team Cuba jerseys. The big leaguers clearly had several undeniable advantages.

Each home run struck or new strikeout record set against the best in the world was demonstrating Cuban quality and stoking nationalist pride. The huge salary windfalls were certainly also a large part of the bulging Cuban big-league image, even if average Cubans at home could hardly appreciate the difference between $30 million and $60 million or $100 million. The general wisdom along the streets of Havana was capsulized somewhat as follows: "If our players are drawing so much cash, this must prove they are the best or at least equal to the best. . . . Perhaps we don't so easily win with Team Cuba in Olympic play anymore, but we are now instead striking better pay dirt in an even bigger arena." But in the end, of course, it was all about national pride, which had always been the heart and soul of Cuban baseball.

Bourdain's 2011 episode culminated with a filmed visit to historic, if now rather ramshackle, Latin American Stadium to witness a Cuban big-league game. That visit would contain a surprise moment that would later hold unexpected significance. Bourdain and I had barely settled in our grandstand seats behind the first-base home team dugout when the game's first batter for Ciego de Avila stroked a soaring fly into the left-field bleachers. The event is highlighted in the final cut of the episode and has me throwing up my hands and exclaiming to the chef-turned-baseball fan—"Well, that didn't take long!" The camera briefly focuses on Ciego's leadoff batter, wearing number 38, in the middle of his home run trot. I would later take delight in pointing out to viewers of the episode that the unnamed number 38 was outfielder Rusney Castillo, an emerging league star at the time who in less than two years would be inking the richest MLB contract ever handed to an international free agent prospect.

* * *

Two years later the same Rusney Castillo would be an engaging headline story in the US sporting press. Within mere weeks of his surprise arrival in the United States, Castillo would sign a $72.5 million deal with the Boston Red Sox that would make him not only the wealthiest Cuban defector so far to strike instant big-league gold, but also the highest-paid international free agent in MLB history. If any further signals were needed that things were now spinning out of control with the over-the-top spending on Cuban free agents, then Rusney Castillo would have to occupy top billing as the poster boy for the ever-expanding rags-to-riches Cuba defector saga.

Why the Red Sox would saddle themselves with a contract of this gargantuan size for a largely untested and already twenty-seven-year-old prospect raises many questions, for which there are only a handful of largely unsatisfying answers. If Castillo was impressive in his late-July Florida showcase, his international career was indeed quite short when compared to that of, say, Céspedes, or certainly Abreu. And his five-year Cuban League career (containing only two injury-free full seasons of action) was also something of a mixed bag. Boston writer Ben Lindbergh was able to offer some explanations that might shed at least partial light on both the specific Castillo signing and also the overall Cuban free agent phenomenon.

Lindbergh (writing for Grantland.com on August 26, 2014) was able to sort out some of the intricacies. And it would indeed take some sorting to explain just why anyone thought this new arrival was worth a bigger bundle of cash than recent rookie island sensations Puig and Abreu, or even a much younger domestic stud like 2012 AL Rookie of the Year Mike Trout, who now owned a six-year $144 million deal but was originally inked as a teenager for a mere $1.2 million bonus check. The Boston club already owned a corps of promising young outfielders (the best being Mookie Betts) and had just dealt for Cuban slugger Yoenis Céspedes, but Lindbergh reasoned that all those other prospects carried questions about health, consistent offense, and especially youth. The latter concern didn't signal much, given Castillo's own advanced age. According to Lindbergh, it all seemed to come down to physical tools and the prospect that Castillo had the profile to become the club's regular center fielder. He was a speedy runner and excellent contact hitter, and possessed only slightly less foot speed (6.5-second 60-yard dash) than did the newly arrived Céspedes.

But why did Castillo command so much more cash than the best previous Cuban free agents? It all seemed to be a matter of the new market realities on the MLB scene. Teams were literally rolling in excess revenues due to inflated television deals and, to quote Lindbergh, there were "fewer appealing players on whom to spend those spoils." There was the inflation factor that inevitably and continually rewrites all free agent spending records. And then there were new spending restrictions governing annual stateside amateur player drafts that had been instituted by the new collective bargaining agreement. With even small-market clubs now willing to gamble on offering early contract extensions to their younger emerging stars, fewer attractive players in the midtwenties age range were becoming available. In brief, Castillo happened to be in just the right place at just the right time.

Such an investment on the part of the Boston club was especially surprising given that outfit's recent transaction history. They had indeed tentatively entered into the Cuban market when they pursued and inked a young shortstop named José Iglesias, who also carried tons of apparent promise but little experience on his home island. Iglesias had been a whiz on the junior-level national team and did flash both offensive (.322 BA) and defensive brilliance in the National Series as a raw seventeen-year-old. He would then jump the Cuban squad in July 2008 at the Edmonton AAA Junior World Championships along with southpaw hurler Noel Argüelles, a Cuban League Habana Province teammate who would soon be inked by Kansas City. Iglesias developed slowly at Pawtucket, where he struggled as a sub-.250 hitter for parts of three seasons, and the question remained whether he could hit big-league pitching. But when he finally did arrive in Beantown he proved a most pleasant surprise, stroking the ball at an impressive .330 clip through late July. Then Iglesias was suddenly dealt away during the 2013 stretch pennant run in a three-cornered move that brought hurler Jake Peavy to Boston and sent Avisail García to Chicago. It was a move that would appear highly questionable only a few months down the road. The Sox would indeed claim a World Series title that October, but without much aid from Peavy, who lost his only postseason decision. The next two years would find Peavy laboring out in San Francisco and Boston also laboring in the American League Eastern Division basement.

Iglesias, for his own part, seemed to thrive during his brief late-season 2013 opportunity with Detroit. He flashed in the postseason with stellar glove work and proved something of an offensive force as well in a losing effort against his old teammates during the six-game American League Championship Series. Then, in the early spring of 2014, disaster struck for Iglesias and the Detroit Tigers. Not merely one but two leg fractures would keep the young shortstop sidelined for the entire campaign, a huge blow to the club's growing championship aspirations. One year later Iglesias was back in the Detroit lineup, and in the early weeks of the campaign he was poking the ball at a .340-plus clip and playing a significant role in a highly potent Tigers lineup (now also featuring Yoenis Céspedes). By mid-season he was one of only three Cubans to snag an

All-Star Game berth. One still had to wonder if the Red Sox had pulled the plug far too early on Iglesias and thus themselves scuttled their first Cuban recruiting experiment.

What was most surprising about Boston's signing of Castillo, and their foreign free agent recruiting approach in general, was that they would invest so heavily in a second Cuban prospect only weeks after shoring up their sagging offense and their outfield defense by acquiring high-profile slugger Yoenis Céspedes. Boston paid a high price for Céspedes, who had made headlines only weeks earlier with a second All-Star Home Run Derby crown but had also been fading badly in Oakland. The price paid was ace lefthander Jon Lester, assumed to be on his way to testing free agent waters at year's end and thus a likely loss to the club at any rate. But Lester might have brought many other prizes from pennant contenders with excess talent to deal. As it worked out, Lester was not quite able to fill the pennant-pursuit role Oakland had hoped for, and Céspedes didn't seem to fit the bill in Boston either. After hitting a mere .269 and producing little power (5 homers and 33 RBI in 51 games) Céspedes would soon be following Iglesias to Detroit. With the Castillo signing and several earlier roster moves (the 2013 debut of twenty-two-year-old Jackie Brantley Jr. and the mid-season 2014 call-up of twenty-one-year-old Mookie Betts) the Boston outfield was getting exceptionally crowded.

Castillo had experienced a brief and uneven career back home in Cuba. He had not landed a spot on his hometown Ciego de Avila Tigers until the fairly advanced age (by Cuban League standards) of twenty-two, and he then played only sparingly (72 games and 142 ABs) his first two campaigns. But if he saw moderate early action he did hit well enough (.317) and was a valued fill-in on a quality league team composed of veteran stars. Never on the radar at the junior provincial level, Castillo seemed to be a prototypical late bloomer. But then came a truly surprising reversal during the Golden Anniversary 2010–2011 National Series, in which he put up impressive offensive numbers, with a .320 BA (including postseason games), 22 homers, and 95 RBI for a team that charged all the way to the championship finals. It was at the tail end of that same campaign that he also made his brief cameo on the Bourdain *No Reservations* episode. The single breakout season was enough to earn a first national team selection for the summer World Port Tournament in Holland, where he proved the team's second leading batsman (sandwiched between future defectors Yoilan Cerce and Yasiel Puig). That inaugural Team Cuba performance on a B-level squad was next parleyed into a starting role with the elite national club for the September World Cup in Panama and October Pan American Games in Mexico.

There was one moment when Castillo first caught the eyes of MLB scouts. He exploded on the scene like an unexpected thunderclap at the Panama World Cup matches. The spotlight had been expected to fall on established stars like Abreu, Despaigne, Gourriel, and Cepeda. But it was Castillo that carried the team on his shoulders in the early going, with vital extra-base hits in each of the opening four games. It was an old story in Cuba, with new national stars always fortuitously emerging at the very moments when most needed. As a power-packed leadoff slugger, Rusney wowed big-league scouts who had arrived with a list of other names to target and were caught off guard by the new phenom with a cannon arm and exploding bat. Posting a final .489 tournament-best hitting mark (four doubles, a pair of triples, and also a pair of homers), Castillo walked off with treasured hardware as a consensus all-star outfield selection, and his performance was the one true bright spot in an event that brought yet another title-game gold medal disappointment for the Cuban camp.

The stellar fall 2011 international performances were followed by another high-octane National Series campaign as part of a Roger Machado–managed Ciego squad that marched all the way to its first-ever league championship. Rusney again stood among the league leaders in a number of different categories: notably first in doubles (28), third in total bases (205), and fifth in homers (22). He appeared a lock at age twenty-five as the next big national team star and an apparent center-field fixture for the foreseeable future.

Then everything quickly went south for Rusney back home in Cuba. He traveled with a national squad for exhibition matches in Taiwan during the fall of 2012 as part of preparations for the upcoming third edition of MLB's World Baseball Classic. Unconfirmed reports suggested that he was injured in training on that trip, perhaps suffering torn muscles during excessive weight lifting routines. Whatever might have transpired, upon the opening of a new National Series in November, Rusney's performance went into an immediate tailspin. He played only two-thirds of the season's schedule, and his power numbers sagged (6 homers and 29 RBIs). He was, not surprisingly, left off the roster for the Classic scheduled to open on Japanese soil in Fukuoka and Tokyo in March. One stateside report suggested the reason for exclusion was a suspected defection attempt. But poor National Series performance alone would have been enough to explain his absence from the thirty-two-man pre-selection Cuban squad.

The pre-WBC defection story simply held no weight for another reason. Rusney played in the post-WBC second round of the new National Series league format. He performed well enough and raised his average from his earlier season slump—from .250 in his first 43 games to .317 in 25 second-round games. He almost certainly would not have been banned from the Classic for an extreme disciplinary infraction (attempted illegal emigration) and yet allowed to play domestically in the championship series. It was seemingly a familiar tale of observers outside Cuba speculating that defection attempts were always the reason for not making national team rosters. It was a story du jour that had been dragged out in other cases, such as those involving Aroldis Chapman and Yoenis Céspedes.

If there was a preliminary defection attempt, it came only after the 2012–2013 National Series had closed down. By the time a pair of national squads traveled to Rotterdam and then on to the USA for a renewal of their ongoing series with USA Baseball, Rusney had disappeared from the scene and was a truly forgotten presence. Castillo's actual defection came in December 2013, on th˙ heels of the departures of Abreu, Arruebarrena, and Raisel Iglesias a few months earlier. It was a capstone to the most dramatic short stretch of talent drain in the island's post-revolution history.

Castillo enjoyed a fast-track route to the big time that had not been available to many earlier defectors, who often languished through months of third-country residence. As the flood of defectors expanded and their market value soared, the MLB/OFAC restrictions seemed to be loosening. Castillo had already been cleared by OFAC for MLB signing in early June. Within a month he had departed from Dominican soil, bound straight for Miami, where he impressed more than three dozen eagle-eyed scouts during two separate staged Florida workouts. The Detroit Tigers were reported to be front-runners in the Castillo chase, but Boston also seemed truly desperate to fill outfield gaps with a seasoned big-name recruit. By August 23 Rusney was securely locked into the Boston fold and rumors suggested the Sox aimed to showcase him in Fenway Park before season's end. The surprising fast track continued with a brief three-week conditioning session at a Florida minor-league camp and then a ten-game trial run with the parent club which began only twenty-four days after the historic signing.

With the opening of the 2015 MLB campaign, neither Céspedes nor Castillo would be patrolling the outfield pastures for Boston. Despite all the hype and enthusiasm on the Bosox Cuban front, there would be no islanders in the Opening Day Beantown outfield.[6] Céspedes had been dealt away to Detroit, where he joined Iglesias, formed a lethal middle lineup one-two punch alongside Miguel Cabrera, and bolted out of the gate with nine homers in the first sixty-five games; he also continued to grab headlines with his rifle-like throws from left field. Castillo would be back in Pawtucket for more seasoning, bumped from the outfield rotation by Shane Victorino's return from the disabled list and the free agent signing of Alejandro De Aza. But a fast AAA start in April and the hefty $72 million contract seemed to demand he wouldn't stay there long, no matter how crowded the Boston outfield stable might be.

* * *

Several weeks before Castillo would make an initial early appearance in Boston (and four days after the attention-grabbing signing) his arrival would be paralleled and even slightly upstaged by another coveted Cuban outfield prospect somewhat longer in the molding. After a celebrated 2012 signing for a then eye-popping but now pedestrian $30 million, and a couple years of somewhat rocky minor-league seasoning in the Chicago Cubs organization, controversial fly-chaser Jorge Soler arrived in Wrigley Field with a thud and a bang. In his first big-league at bat Soler slugged a home run and thus became the second Cuban (and the 117th player overall) to manage this rare stunt. Among Cubans only Bert Campaneris had pulled off a similar feat while debuting with Kansas City several decades back. Soler's eventual arrival had been long anticipated by Cubs fans, and it played out against a rather uneven and admittedly checkered background.

Soler had defected back in 2011 after a stellar stint with the junior team and an all-too-brief National Series sojourn. At the 2010 World Junior Championships in Thunder Bay, Ontario, he had batted over .300 and slugged over .500 for the third-place Cubans; in two seasons as a teenager with a strong Habana Province Cuban League team he got into only a dozen games and failed to hit above the Mendoza Line (sub-.200). After his mysterious flight from his homeland, he took up residence in Haiti, reportedly worked out in the Dominican Republic, and was unblocked by OFAC the following year (specifically on June 2, 2012). And it all happened with some controversy attached, as Ben Badler would report early on in the pages of *Baseball America*. There were definitely residency issues involving the Cuban's Haitian documents.[7] And then there was further controversy about a possible arranged deal between Soler's agents and the Chicago Cubs.

The Soler circus continued during his early minor-league sojourn in the Chicago organization. Starting the spring 2013 season with Daytona's Advanced A-level club, Soler was involved in an on-field fight that escalated into an ugly bat-wielding episode. And then there were further questions about his playing style and hustle, as reported by Evan Altman for the *Cubs Insider* online journal only sixteen days before Soler's eventual summons to Wrigley Field.[8] But his on-field performance was solid enough over two full summers of minor-league seasoning (mostly with Daytona and the AA Tennessee Smokies) and he arrived in late 2014 as one of a quartet of highly touted Cubs prospects that also included infielders Kris Bryant and Javier Baez and outfielder Albert Almora. Of the four, Soler would be the first to implant his presence in the big-league lineup, where he would open the 2015 campaign as the anointed right fielder. Jorge Soler had taken more than a few years to get off the ground, but by April 2015 he seemed ready to steal some of the thunder and "stellar rookie" hype from the slightly older and considerably wealthier Rusney Castillo over in Boston.

Back in Boston a promising rookie season on the horizon for Rusney Castillo was not the only story unfolding during a frenzied off-season "hot stove league" that brought a new flurry of activity destined to keep the Beantowners very much in the headlines when it came to Cuban ballplayer recruitment. It would soon be revealed that the Boston front office brass were far from finished with the idea of expanding their own Cuban connection. In fact it would soon land what was to appear perhaps the heftiest prize of the entire 2014–2015 winter-season deal-swinging enterprise. If it was not the biggest off-season free agent signing, it was certainly the one likely to generate the most media buzz, both in Boston and all around the rest of the North American baseball universe.

The latest refugee from Castro's disintegrating baseball empire now on Boston's radar was nineteen-year-old switch-hitting infielder Yoan Moncada, perhaps the most unusual Cuban free agent to appear on the scene so far, and one that—given his apparent tools and teenage years—

might also be the biggest find and the soundest investment. But at the same time, a mysterious flight from Cuba, substantial personal baggage, and the distinct lack of measurable experience in the professional or even top-level amateur ranks all combined to make Moncada at best a considerable gamble.

Moncada's personal story quickly proved to be one of the most convoluted—outstripping even the celebrated escape tales of Puig or El Duque Hernández when it came to full-blown drama, a touch of political intrigue, and the potential specter of illegal smuggling activities. Most intriguing was the fact that Moncada had not escaped Cuba via a harrowing speedboat ride or with the aid of any network of crime syndicate smugglers after the fashion of so many of his predecessors. Nor had he walked away from any junior or senior national squad traveling in Asia, Europe, Mexico, or North America. He had instead blazed a new trail, one not entirely unprecedented, but also one only rarely followed. By all indications he had somehow managed to secure a legal exit visa from the Cuban government, and at least as far as any illegal emigration was concerned, he most surprisingly had not technically defected at all.

Moncada had popped scouts' eyes in Mexico on two separate occasions as a fifteen- and sixteen-year-old. The first showcase came in October 2010 at the COPABE Junior Pan American Championships. The teenage switch-hitter provided the biggest buzz of the tournament by flashing the same kind of all-around brilliance seen from Dayan Viciedo and Yasiel Puig in earlier editions of the same event. Less than a year later, in August 2011, he was turning heads on Mexican soil during the 16U World Championships, where he was again tabbed as tournament all-star third baseman. Tampa Bay international scouting boss Carlos Alfonso was on the scene that summer in Lagos de Moreno and had some glowing words to share with this author about Moncada's performances and his obvious outsized talent. Alfonso was impressed enough during that initial viewing to arrange a visit to Rotterdam in June 2013 specifically for the purpose of double-checking Moncada's progress during a first scheduled showcasing with a senior national team. And he would be only one among dozens converging on Rotterdam for that very same purpose.

It was at the junior level that Moncada made his biggest impact on the domestic scene back in Cuba. During the summer of 2011 he dominated the country's 16U provincial league play as the island's top hitter, posting gaudy figures with a .500 BA, .643 on-base percentage (OBP), and .918 slugging percentage (SLG) mark across 158 plate appearances. These were all league-leading numbers, as were his 8 homers, 37 free passes, and 15 stolen bases (in only 15 tries). One year later he stepped up to the country's 18U provincial tournament, where he again posted stratospheric league-best numbers. This second dominant season included rarified batting totals (.434/.543/.648) in 152 trips to the plate, as well as 20 thefts on the base paths, this time in a mere 24 attempts. Moncada was seemingly playing in a different universe than the rest of his competition, and doing so in a youth league that was capable of producing one of the world's leading national squads.

Like those of Puig and Chapman before him, Moncada's defection story would begin in Rotterdam during the same World Port Tournament event that seemed to hold so many pitfalls for the beleaguered Cuban baseball establishment. The strapping youngster would make his first appearance on a senior-level national squad at the July 2013 Rotterdam event, and it was his presence more than anything that accounted for the bulk of the fifty-plus MLB bird dogs flocking to the Dutch port city to drool over still another new crop of rising Cuban talent. The Cubans were fresh off a disappointing elimination at the World Baseball Classic in Tokyo several months earlier and seemed bent on recouping some sagging prestige against the host Dutch, who had sent them packing in the Tokyo Dome. The Cuban squad this time around was a mixture of front liners (Abreu, Arruebarrena, Yasmany Tomas, Yulieski Gourriel) and promising youngsters (headed by Moncada, hard-throwing bullpen ace Raisel Iglesias, and promising nineteen-year-old infielder Andy Ibáñez). It was Moncada that most of the talent hunters wanted to see.

As it turned out, Moncada did not provide much of a showcase. He was used only sparingly, pinch-hitting on three occasions and filling in as a defensive second-base replacement for two innings of a one-sided romp over Curaçao. It was Ibáñez instead who was able to flash considerable talent, smacking three hits in the opener as the starting second baseman. The youngster from Isla already seemed a few steps ahead of Moncada in the Cuban pecking order. He had earlier made the WBC team traveling to Japan in March, although he saw little game action there (appearing in five contests but batting only once). Given the chance to start in Rotterdam, however, Ibáñez came up big on the offensive end, collecting six

Boston Red Sox nineteen-year-old prospect Yoan Moncada may prove a test case for the lavish spending on unproven Cuban talent. Courtesy of Jay Vandevoort.

hits and three RBIs in nine official at bats. At the same time Moncada languished on the bench.

Rotterdam again proved to be a mixed experience for the Cubans. Before the games begun, pitcher Odrisamer Despaigne had bolted camp at the Paris airport for a prearranged reunion with his expatriate father, who had earlier taken up residence in Spain. That single defection left the team desperately short of pitching and nearly compromised their tournament hopes. There was also a somber note added by the opening game ceremonies honoring the memory of 2011 World Port Tournament hero Yadier Pedroso, who had been tragically killed in an automobile accident only three months earlier. On the field of play José Abreu was injured in the second contest and remained inactive on the sidelines for the remainder of the week. What was unknown at the time was that this would be Abreu's last appearance in a Team Cuba uniform. Yasmany Tomás earned his first serious playing time after only limited use in Tokyo as a last-minute addition to the WBC squad. But Tomás struggled defensively and did little to impress the scouting corps with his seeming inability to track fly balls; a game-saving catch versus the Dutch was overshadowed by generally shoddy outfield play. Perhaps the biggest upside for the Cubans was the bullpen work of Raisel Iglesias, who saved three of the four victories with a flawless 0.00 ERA. It was the budding national team closer who slammed the door on the host Dutch in the finale and in the process exacted some much-needed revenge for the Cuban squad managed by Victor Mesa.

It was in Rotterdam nonetheless where the serious recruitment of Moncada began. It was also there that much of the rather bizarre circumstances surrounding one of Cuba's most coveted young prospects would start to unfold. The setting for the Rotterdam event is unique, even among the second tier of international baseball events. Four or sometimes five teams, the small press corps (usually only this author and a handful of others not connected directly with the Dutch media), tournament officials including umpires, MLB scouts (usually at least a dozen, with a few more camped out in Amsterdam), and a small contingent of non-local fans and groupies all crowd into the same four-story luxury hotel located on the city park grounds shared by Neptunus Family Stadium (the most impressive baseball facility in the country and a close match for almost any Class A or AA park in the States) and the sprawling Diergaarde Blijdorp, one of Europe's finest zoos.

It was from this same Van der Valk Hotel—newly opened on the eve of the 2009 Rotterdam tournament—that Aroldis Chapman made his bolt to freedom (chapter 4). Both Holland tournaments—the Rotterdam event (odd-numbered years) and the Haarlem Baseball Week (even years)—provide unparalleled opportunities for fans to mingle intimately with the Cuban ballplayers, who are never under tight security lockdown, as so many rumors and press accounts have always suggested. My own access has always been rather special, but in Rotterdam it is no more privileged than that enjoyed by just about any tournament attendee. The Cuban players wander in and out of the ballpark during games that they are not playing, often hawking cigars to earn a bit of spending money for a scheduled open-date shopping trip. They hang out in the hotel lobby and cafeteria day and night and wander the hotel grounds with the contingents of fans and groupies that regularly follow the "rock star" Cuban players on their annual European tours. It is also not that unusual at the Dutch venues for Cuban players to sit in the stands during opponents' games and talk baseball with some of the big-league scouts in attendance.

While a handful of established agents (and even a few wannabes hoping to break into the potentially lucrative representation game) lurk in the background, it is a little-kept secret they are also repeatedly attempting contact with targeted potential defectors, often with the aid of certain "undercover employees" masquerading as doting fans. It was such a situation that led to the first notable appearance of a woman known as Nicole Banks.[9] Banks was a constant evening presence on the floor occupied by the Cuban squad. This was not a rumor, but something I was personally quite aware of, since my own room was on a corner of the same floor, a few doors away from quarters occupied by Moncada and his Cienfuegos teammate Erisbel Arruebarrena. At first I didn't pay a lot of attention, although a British friend and regular Team Cuba follower (Gawain Owen) mentioned a couple of juicy tidbits that eventually did catch my notice.[10] Nicole Banks was one of my own numerous Facebook friends, and she was rumored to be working behind the scenes for agent Jaime Torres (also a presence in the Rotterdam grandstands for a handful of games). She seemed to have her sights fully aimed at the pair of coveted Cienfuegos roommates.

Whatever relationship had developed between Nicole Banks and Moncada in Rotterdam, it did not result in any immediate flight by the heralded prospect or by any of his teammates. None of the Cuban players left the squad during or after the event. But Banks would soon become a rather obvious presence lurking in the background of a number of rather mysterious events that would take place around Yoan Moncada back on Cuban soil during the succeeding months.

When the Cubans arrived in the States for an exhibition series with the USA Baseball Collegiate All-Stars a month later, Moncada was not on the scene with Team Cuba. He was playing in Asia in the 18U World Championships. Ibañez was also absent, but without any official explanation. I had been told in Rotterdam by manager Victor Mesa (also scheduled to make the USA tour) that Ibáñez would not travel because he was about to be given some time off for his upcoming wedding. Moncada and Ibáñez would both soon quit their National Series teams in the fall of 2013 on the eve of a new season, but they would surprisingly do so without departing from the country. Their moves were largely unprecedented and little understood at the time. A new means for expressing dissatisfaction seemed to be blossoming among young Cuban ballplayers.

At the very time that Moncada and Ibáñez were quietly informing Cuban officials that they had no further taste for Cuban domestic baseball, I was again setting foot in Cuba, this time accompanying ESPN reporter Paula Lavigne, her producer Andy Lockett, and a two-man film crew on a mission to interview Tony Castro, son of Fidel, former baseball team doctor, and current vice president of both the Cuban sports ministry (INDER) and the IBAF-replacement now known as the World Baseball and Softball Confederation. That same month would witness historic news concerning radical changes in INDER policies governing overseas player assignments, although no one yet knew this when we arrived in Havana. On a more depressing note, this would also prove to be the month of greatest player attrition to date, since within those same early weeks of September the potent WBC squad that had stumbled in Tokyo earlier in the year was largely being gutted by a rash of new and still-hidden defections. Abreu would turn out to be the biggest loss, but Arruebarrena and Iglesias were also about to flee (and may already have been outside of Cuba at the time of our arrival). Although the cases of Moncada and Ibáñez had not yet come to public light, by the time they did, they were no longer either the biggest story in Miami or the biggest headache in Havana.

Vice Sports reporter Jorge Arangure would eventually produce an Internet piece delving into details of the Banks-Moncada "affair" (which now seem to involve both readings of the term) and the little that was known about the ballplayer's extraordinary methods of escaping Cuba. Reports of a subsequent romantic involvement back in Cuba included news of a baby that was apparently born in September 2014. But there were also plenty of contradictions over the location of the birth as well as an indication that a birth certificate originally listing both parents was subsequently altered to remove the father's name. Banks was also reported by some sources to be acting as Moncada's business agent while he was still in Cuba. By the time of Arangure's article (December 2014), Moncada was being managed by Florida CPA David Hastings, a St.

Petersburg accountant who had never before claimed a ballplayer client. The Cuban athlete was reportedly already in Florida after reaching an undisclosed third country in June (perhaps Argentina, where Banks supposedly had citizenship), then being secretly sequestered (with a surrounding contingent of bodyguards) in Guatemala while Hastings awaited the US visa that would allow Moncada to be showcased for scouts without the safety concerns that might well exist in Central America.[11]

A further November report by MLB.com writer Jesse Sanchez blew the lid off any plans laid by Hastings and Banks by exposing Moncada's Guatemala hideout. A hastily arranged Guatemala showcase was then arranged for November 12, drawing nearly 100 scouts and MLB executives, as well as a few unwelcomed interlopers such as partners of rival agent Scott Boras. It took place with an armed guard on the field and seemed amateurishly managed, since no quality pitchers could be found for a live batting session. The country's only live arms were reportedly in Mexico with the national team, participating in the Central American Games (an event fittingly won by Cuba).

There are now details beyond those provided by Arangure, but there are also still unanswered questions. In May 2015 a personal friend of this writer (and here is one case where I honor a request for anonymity) quite fortuitously stayed at the same private rental home (*casa particular*) in Cienfuegos where Moncada and Banks one year earlier had spent thirty-five days awaiting his Cuban exit visa. The rental had been arranged by the owner's former student, who was apparently a personal acquaintance of Moncada. Accompanying the couple was Banks's six-year-old son from a previous relationship. The owner repeated the very same stories (apparently common knowledge in Cienfuegos) about Banks going to Rotterdam "to target Moncada" and confirmed that she had also followed him a month later to the 18U tournament in Asia. The property owner's wife further confirmed that Banks was pregnant at the time, although she seemed skeptical about any legal marriage.

My personal contact also reported further discussions with the property owner's wife, who had stayed in touch with Banks, and she suggested that Banks had later complained in her letters that Moncada wasn't spending much time with her and the boys (she reportedly gave birth in September) once he reached Florida. The letters suggested that the new baby's name was Robinson, and my friend also reports witnessing Moncada a year earlier at a workout in Havana wearing a "number 42" wristband in honor of his apparent role model, Jackie Robinson. Admittedly there is quite a bit of circumstance and pure speculation in these reports, and thus there is still enough mystery to cloud any specifics. But a circulating photo of Moncada at the March 2015 Boston spring-training facility in Fort Myers with Nicole Banks and her baby (presumably the infant Robinson) in tow adds at least reasonable credence to much of what has been reported.

If there is consistency, it lies in the fact that all sources report Moncada's exit from Cuba to have been legal. If Banks was the mastermind of the exit strategy, there seems little to suggest that she might have violated any provisions of the Helms-Burton Cuba embargo. The plot may have been aided by his "marriage" to Banks, who reportedly holds both US and Argentine citizenship. What appears to be the case is that Moncada (with apparently some coaching and a carefully hatched plan) simply retired from Cuban baseball, then applied through newly existing legal channels in Cuba for an exit permit. The entire process remains obscure, but we can speculate that since the athlete did not embarrass Cuban officials with defection, and since it was clear he would no longer play there, the process was expedited.

Moncada was not the only player recently granted permission to leave Cuba legally. Two decades earlier Ariel Prieto (chapter 5) had pioneered the radical idea by faking several injuries and performing poorly on the mound, a gambit that then allowed him to secure an exit visa within thirteen months and pursue his big-league dream after arriving as a political asylum refugee in Florida. But this type of deception lay dormant for twenty years before Moncada's Cienfuegos teammate Pavel Quesada also took that same route (actually leaving a matter of weeks before Moncada), as did Isla's Andy Ibañez at approximately the same time. Nearly a year before this more celebrated recent wave, catcher Yenier Bello (married to an Ecuadorian) took a similar route, as have more than a half-dozen other discouraged National Series players over the past fourteen months.[12] In one of the most unusual cases, Matanzas pitcher Jorge Alberto Martinez was recently aided by US Homeland Security's 2007 Cuban Family Unification Parole Program after an application for US residence was made on his behalf by his Miami-based expatriate Cuban father-in-law.[13]

New OFAC and MLB regulations would also soon have a direct impact on teams pursuing Moncada. Because he had neither played a required five seasons at home nor claimed the minimum of three appearances in senior international tournaments, Moncada would fall under a condition now requiring any team signing him for more than the allotted minimum to also hand over to MLB coffers a penalty fee equal to the contract amount itself. It would be an expensive deal—say in the range of $60-plus million—that few clubs would likely be willing to risk.

But the process was sped up and some complications removed when MLB and OFAC policies shifted suddenly in early February. While OFAC had long required a process of "unblocking" Cuban players (by requiring them to prove residence outside Cuba in accordance with embargo regulations), it had also long suggested that no specific licensing was required and ballplayers could qualify by merely signing a "general license" waiver. The MLB commissioner's office had always held to more rigid demands that players needed to apply for specific written license approval, a process that often delayed free agency for months if not years. Now MLB was relenting just in time for an early Moncada feeding frenzy to begin.

Moncada's eventual signing came on the heels of Cuba's landmark victory in the San Juan based Caribbean Series. MLB signing penalties were not enough to deter Boston's significant gamble of $32.5 million plus an equivalent amount in penalty fees. Boston's rush to land Moncada whatever the cost thus seemed just as clear a signal of continued uncontrolled spending as was the deal earlier handed to Yasmany Tomás or the one about to be offered to Héctor Olivera. But this case was perhaps the most stunning. At least Tomás had performed well at the last WBC and had made minimal waves as a potent slugger in the domestic league while playing four-plus full seasons with Industriales. And Olivera had been a major star in Cuba even if he had lately been slowed by career-threatening injury. In the case of Moncada there was nothing more to go on than raw speculation based on a handful of staged workouts measuring the physical skills of a still-developing but unproven teenager.

If newly instituted rules governing international player signings had already impacted the Moncada case, Moncada himself had only barely escaped one of the new provisions that might have blocked his direct and lucrative path to the majors. He had beaten a September 1, 1995, birthdate requirement making him eligible for signing during the 2014–2015 international draft pool period. Ben Badler, writing for *Baseball America*, elaborated on the situation in a discussion of future prospects surrounding a pair of young Cuban pitchers who had recently come on the scene.[14] A new MLB requirement for international signings governed players who had not yet turned twenty before a September 2015 registration deadline for that year's signing period and thus effectively pushed their eligibility back to the 2015–2016 pool. Two test cases on the horizon were those of underage pitchers Yadier Alvares and Vladimir Gutierrez. MLB rules on this matter are far more complex and convoluted than need be explained here. But as Badler suggests, there may also soon be a new policy of exemptions for Cubans that would free up their signing eligibility on the basis of complications they now face regarding the mandate of a third-country residence. These latest cases were almost certain to impact the future of such Cuban signings, given the increasing number of underage players recently leaving the island.

Gutierrez had bolted in Puerto Rico at the Caribbean Series and was reportedly already working out somewhere in Mexico only a couple of months later. He had not yet showcased and there did not seem to be pressure by his agents to have him immediately signed. But Alvares was working out in the Dominican, already being showcased, and on an apparent fast track to third-country residence. The issue was meeting the registration deadline. Since, as Badler noted, there appeared to be some loopholes in the new regulations, it was now possible that the Alvares case might test such potential exceptions. And if it did so, then some important precedents regarding future Cuban defector signings might lie just around the corner.

Moncada for his own part would begin his professional career in the low-level minors (Greenville, South Carolina, in the Class A South Atlantic League) and do so with much fanfare but little sign of big-time readiness. There were certainly questions about how advanced he was as a player, especially when it came to infield defensive finesse and offensive consistency. The youngster appeared to have all the needed tools, even if some had not yet been well honed. But he lacked experience and also fell short on maturity, since in the aftermath of the celebrated signing there were still many unsolved questions about the young Cuban's personal life. Issues surrounding his rather odd exit from Cuba and the role in that adventure played by the mysterious Nicole Banks had not gone away. And neither had many questions about the readiness of the young man to seriously approach the workload and sacrifices necessary to play major-league baseball.

* * *

The ink was hardly dry on Yoan Moncada's windfall contract when attention shifted to still another new Cuban supernova. A new National Series (number 54) opened a bit earlier than normal, the Federation again having deemed it necessary to jerry-rig domestic-league play to accommodate the winter's heavy schedule of international tournament action. The Central American Games in Mexico would necessitate a first stoppage of play in mid-November. And then the Caribbean Series was again on tap for February, an event Cuba was taking seriously this time around after the long-awaited return to the event a year earlier in Venezuela had proven such a disaster.[15]

The season opened the final week of September (nearly two months early) and promised to feature another intense battle for eight qualifying championship-round slots to be decided in the first forty-five games. But the earliest surprises and most of the street-corner buzz among island fans had to do with the continued leakage of star players. Matanzas, a team that reached the finals one year earlier under flamboyant manager Victor Mesa, was immediately hard hit by the unexpected departures. In a controversial move, Mesa had tried to arrange the transfer of top Santiago pitcher Dany Betancourt to his own roster, but that plan was blocked by vociferous protest from Santiago's provincial INDER commission. Then star outfielder Guillermo Heredia—a starter on the 2013 WBC national squad—was notably missing from camp and rumored to have either fled or suffered a hushed-up suspension. News also quickly broke that two additional national team performers from Matanzas had departed, this time with less successful results.

José Miguel Fernández had for a couple of years been considered one of the island's biggest potential prizes. The smooth left-handed hitter had barely missed a batting title in National Series 52 and then anchored second base on the World Baseball Classic team in Japan. Fernández was reputed to be an excellent contact hitter; he played shortstop and batted clean-up for his league team, but he was not noted for either long-ball power or exceptional range in the middle infield. Paula Levine had interviewed him during our ESPN visit in September 2013 and he had cautiously expressed an expected party line: he would love to test his skills at the highest level but his only true interest was in playing for family and community back home on the island.

Twenty-four months later Fernández either had succumbed to temptation or decided he had had enough of Victor Mesa's managerial style. He reportedly attempted to escape the island with teammate Lázaro Herrera, a catcher who had also tasted brief overseas play with Team Cuba during the July 2013 Friendly Series versus USA Baseball's collegians in Omaha, Des Moines, and Durham. Details again were sparse as always but the pair were apparently apprehended and disappeared behind a wall of disciplinary action. Reports would soon emerge that Herrera's wife had been removed from the government housing the ballplayer had received for his athletic service.[16] The two players would remain in limbo for a number of months, but by spring reports were circulating that they had executed a second and finally successful flight, this one landing them in the neighboring Dominican Republic.

A far bigger surprise at the outset of the new Cuban National Series season was a story that prized infielder Héctor Olivera had also left his Santiago ball club during the opening weeks of play. It was the timing of Olivera's flight that seemed to provide the largest chunk of pure mystery. Several years earlier the talented infielder had been one of the hottest properties on the island in the eyes of most big-league bird dogs with a bead on Cuba. But he had never left home despite what had to be obvious temptations, given flourishing rumors of bonus potential in the millions of dollars. When a rare blood disorder surprisingly sidelined Olivera in early 2012, it appeared that the window had slammed on big-league aspirations and that a brilliant domestic career had come to a sad and premature ending. Olivera had been entirely written off as a story of "what might have been" but now simply would not be.

Héctor Olivera had once been the brightest star on the Cuban horizon. In 2007 he was the talk of scouts in Rotterdam at the five-team World Port Tournament, the first such event I covered as senior baseball writer for the newly established BaseballdeCuba.com. That Cuban team, managed by Victor Mesa, was especially stocked with top young prospects, several of whom would eventually become true national team megastars. Several others were destined to emerge as notable defectors. Catcher Yosvany Peraza made his first impact there, as did tournament MVP first baseman Jose Julio Ruiz. Yadel Marti—who had already shown brilliance the previous March as a starter in the semifinals of the first World Baseball Classic—was a pitcher on that squad, and outfielders Alfredo Despaigne and Alexei Bell were making their Team Cuba debut that summer in Rotterdam. But it was Olivera who turned heads among the teeming population of scouts.

Momentum would build across the next several seasons for the top-draw infield prospect. His career high .353 BA of 2007 remained level at .346 and then .322, and he pounded 16 homers and knocked home 71 runs for a stellar 2008 Santiago club that walked off with a second straight league title. The sinewy youngster also carried a notable baseball lineage, since his father (Héctor Olivera Sr.) had been a star performer of the late 1970s and early 1980s before being struck down early by a career-ending leg injury after thirteen productive campaigns. The full irony of the younger Olivera's own destined bout with physical trauma was not apparent in those earliest days. It was, in fact, his full blossoming by the time of the November 2007 IBAF World Cup in Taiwan that had made Alexei Ramirez expendable as a national team second baseman and may have indirectly lead to Ramirez's own premature departure from Cuba.

A true showcase for the emerging Santiago star came in the 2009 second edition of the World Baseball Classic. There he combined with shortstop Luis Navas, a Santiago teammate, to form a dynamic double-play combo whose string of flashy twin killings were repeatedly featured on ESPN *SportsCenter* recaps. Olivera was also a mainstay that same fall during IBAF World Cup action in Europe, striking a late game-winning blow to ice a key win over Canada and vault Cuba into an expected finals showdown with the potent Americans. But joy quickly changed to despair as a rare pitching meltdown by Pedro Luis Lazo and Olivera's own pair of throwing errors highlighted a seventh-inning defensive collapse that opened the door on a disappointing 10–5 gold-medal game defeat at the hands of Team USA.

Olivera's career would suffer a brief setback with the September 2011 Panama IBAF World Cup, still another bitter championship near miss in which Santiago's stellar infielder would once more play a pivotal role. This was the very same event at which Rusney Castillo would emerge on the horizon as the latest Cuban supernova prospect. But it would be Olivera in the end, and under the strangest of circumstances, once more coming within an eyelash of standing tall as the ultimate island hero. A painful leg bruise kept him out of action after the third game and forced Cuban manager Alfonso Urquiola to realign his infield corps, moving versatile Yulieski Gourriel over to second base and installing veteran Michel Enríquez at the hot corner.

A dozen days and nine games later, Olivera would reemerge just in time to play a key role during the final championship match with Holland. The climactic game was played under the worst of conditions during a day of constant heavy rain that washed out the bronze-medal contest and delayed the start of the championship finale for more than five hours. Eventually the sky cleared long enough for action to commence. Once the weather broke the evenly matched rivals locked in a classic pitchers' duel that found the Dutch nursing a 2–1 lead into the final frame. Loaded with island talent from Curaçao and Aruba, Holland had been the surprise team of the event and had already edged Cuba 4–1 in a preliminary-round match. The soggy rematch stretched to the wire, and in the bottom of the ninth Cuba was poised for a thrilling miracle victory. Summoned to pinch-hit with one out remaining and the winning runs aboard, Olivera lashed a vicious liner that was blindly stabbed for the final out by Dutch third-sacker Jonathan Schoop. Another inch of elevation and the ball would have landed deep in the left-field corner, sending Gourriel and Enríquez scampering home with the precious victory. But again Lady Luck had singled out Olivera as the ill-starred victim in a second painful World Cup gold-medal setback.

Fate was soon to strike a much crueler blow. Shortly after returning home, Olivera was diagnosed with a rare blood disorder that would put his ball-playing career, if not his life, in serious jeopardy. A condition preventing proper blood clotting meant that any blow from a pitched or batted ball that caused internal bleeding might well trigger a fatal stroke. The dire situation would cost him the entire 2011–2012 campaign. He was suddenly a largely forgotten man on the international scene, while José Miguel Fernández emerged as the new national team second sacker on the eve of the 2013 World Baseball Classic. Yet with a year-plus of painstaking rehabilitation and unspecified experimental drug treatments (a renowned Cuban specialty), Olivera was already working himself back into playing fitness, and by National Series 52 he was again a regular in the Santiago lineup, playing a nearly full schedule (73 of 90 games) and putting up sound numbers (batting above .300) despite a noticeable drop in power production. Nevertheless he had by now obviously lost his earlier coveted role with Team Cuba.

Then in September 2014, precisely a year after the mass exodus that included Abreu, Iglesias, and Arruebarrena, Olivera would also surprise by suddenly leaving home in the first week of the new season without suiting up for a single game. Arriving on Dominican shores, he would overnight find himself on a fast track toward the major leagues. The only question marks now were his slightly advanced age (he was only six months shy of thirty) and his health. Had the rebound been strong enough to meet big-league standards? Answers were quick in coming, as intensive workouts before hungry scouts in the Dominican during the early winter months seemed to verify Olivera was now actually quite healthy and thus worth a substantial gamble.[17] And there was no shortage of immediate suitors, with the Padres, Athletics, Braves, and especially the Dodgers all receiving prime billing as the hottest pursuers.

The pursuit would not prove lengthy. On the eve of 2015 spring training Moncada would already be making his own ballyhooed appearance in the Red Sox Florida rookie camp and grabbing considerable attention after Boston was willing to risk spiraling salary cap penalties to sign him. Yasmany Tomás was learning a new position (third base) with the D-Backs, showing unexpected maturity when it came to developing patience at the plate, and he was thus being touted as the next big overnight sensation, likely the next Puig or Abreu. Yet before spring training had ended it was Olivera who was again grabbing the bulk of the headlines with a somewhat surprising $62 million offer from the Dodgers, whose infield was already stacked with talent, including two other Cubans on whom a ton of cash had already been spent. The signing, now dwarfing the club's earlier investment in Puig, clearly signaled the Dodgers' belief that Héctor Olivera was indeed injury-free and a ready-made big-league starter.

In late May Olivera would finally receive his long-delayed visa for US entry and arrive in the States, accompanied by another recent signee, pitcher Pablo Millan Fernández, a veteran of seven National Series seasons with Holguín. The two would pass physicals and finally officially ink their Dodgers contracts; Fernández had picked up a minor-league pact spiced with a reported $8 million signing bonus. These latest signings had further underscored the Dodgers recent heavy encroachment into the Cuban market. Early in the spring Alex Guerrero had returned to the parent club, and by the end of May he was still posting fabulous offensive numbers as a pinch hitter and part-time second baseman.[18] If he kept producing as spring rolled into summer, there would likely be talk of a third straight Cuban rookie-of-the-year winner (especially with Arizona's Yasmany Tomás also in the running). It was a bit of an irony, in fact, that Puig was no longer the highest-paid Cuban on the LA roster, since Guerrero had inked a deal ($28 million but spread over only four years) that made him an even heavier investment than the more publicized Yasiel. [19]

But if the Dodgers had struck it rich with Puig and Guerrero and were still harboring high hopes for both Olivera and Fernández, another investment had not only failed to pay off, but was beginning to look like living proof that there was indeed a danger in all this wild speculation on the high-profile Cubans. Erisbel Arruebarrena had tasted a cup of coffee early in the 2014 season but spent almost the entire year in the Los Angeles minor-league system, including a brief twenty-six-game stint at AAA Albuquerque which began well enough but ended in disciplinary disaster. [20] By December the Dodgers were already having second thoughts, and the high-investment prospect (five years at $25 million) was designated for assignment but managed to clear waivers, largely due to the heavy price tag he bore. After again failing to make the big club or even a high minor-league roster in spring training, the problem-child shortstop was offered and accepted assignment to the club's Arizona Rookie League club for extended spring training.

If the signing of Moncada (for only half the price tag of Abreu or Tomás) suggested at least some sanity might be returning, the furor surrounding Olivera was a clear indication that the lavish spending frenzy directed toward Cubans was still very much in vogue. [21] Something needed to give, of course, and there was now much talk about the need for some sort of worldwide amateur player draft. That might be how MLB and the American media were now viewing things. But Cuba's baseball brain trust probably had a much different perspective. The winds of change might for the first time be blowing in a direction more favorable for the Cuban baseball establishment than for those bent on raiding its shores. The days of wild signings might already be much closer to an end than most were speculating.

8

GO EAST, YOUNG MEN, GO EAST

The closer one is to an issue the more difficult it is to gain objectivity. Cuba is so close to the United States that US policy makers, like a physician trying to diagnose a family member's ailment, have been unable to see it objectively. They have asked the wrong questions and inevitably have come up with faulty diagnoses of the problem.—Saul Landau

In the autumn months of 1966, Japanese newspaper magnate and Yomiuri Giants team founder Matsutaro Shoriki was already envisioning fulfillment of his long-cherished dream to stage a true "world series" between his powerhouse Central League champions and the pennant winners of the North American major leagues. The dream would be frustrated at seemingly every turn, however, as then MLB commissioner Ford Frick repeatedly scuttled any budding plans by the overanxious Japanese to turn annual Asian barnstorming visits by big-league clubs into anything more than what they had always been meaningless exhibitions in which American baseball stars and their families frolicked as vacationers, enjoying Nippon's popular tourist sites and shopping attractions and taking the dozen or so ballyhooed ball games (which American clubs regularly and easily swept) with only mild seriousness.

If the Japanese fans and promoters were temporarily (and also quite falsely, in retrospect) encouraged in the pipe dream that their own best clubs could compete on an equal footing with top American pros—egged on by the shoddy performance of the National League champion Los Angeles Dodgers in November 1966—they would soon have a rude awakening. The Dodgers club that sleepwalked through a break-even eighteen-game tour in which they dropped four of seven to Shoriki's powerhouse Yomiuri Giants was, after all, playing without its dynamic mound duo, Sandy Koufax and Don Drysdale, who had refused to make the postseason trip. Any false expansion of Japan's baseball self-image would be totally deflated over the next handful of years. Within twenty-four months the St. Louis Cardinals, featuring ace Bob Gibson and speed-sters Lou Brock and Curt Flood, and owning consecutive National League crowns, punctured Nippon hopes with a convincing romp over their hosts that found the crack Tokyo club capturing only two of ten contests.

Shoriki died within less than a year of the Cardinals convincing sweep though Japan. Two years later, in 1971, the budding Japanese plans for "beating the Americans at their own game" suffered an even more convincing blow. The Baltimore Orioles—not exactly reeling from a recent seven-game World Series setback at the hands of the Pittsburgh Pirates—thoroughly embarrassed the still-champion Giants in a powerful display of dominant pitching (by Jim Palmer, Dave McNally, and Pat Dobson—who tossed a no-hitter) and awe-inspiring slugging (Boog Powell, Frank Robinson, Brooks Robinson, and Paul Blair). The Nippon press corps lamented that "the biggest Japanese stars looked like pygmies compared with the Orioles."[1]

Shoriki's dream of a true baseball "world series" might well have been an unworkable fantasy back in 1966, when he first conceived it. But precisely forty years later, it would finally come to at least partial fruition when Major League Baseball decided to adopt the façade of international-izing the "American national pastime" with a new commercial venture known as the World Baseball Classic. The novel effort would be modeled after wildly popular "World Cup" events that had long been filling the coffers of FIFA (international soccer's governing body) and now seem-ingly promised to lock up MLB's ownership of the global sport.[2] When the first WBC was staged in March 2006, however, the MLB brain trust did not quite achieve what it was anxiously anticipating. The event drew but mild fan interest in North America, although it gripped fans across Latin America and throughout Asia. Perhaps more surprising still was the fact that after three weeks of elimination play, the two national squads that took the field for the championship match were teams representing a pair of longtime outliers in the baseball universe—Japan and Cuba. The

American big leaguers, sporting the likes of Derek Jeter, Ken Griffey Jr., Roger Clemens, Chipper Jones, and Alex Rodriguez, were not even among the four squads reaching the semifinals in San Diego.

The first MLB World Baseball Classic may not have seemed anything like a legitimate "world championship," since it still maintained all the trappings of a mere exhibition series at best or glorified spring-training exercise at worst. Some MLB team owners such as George Steinbrenner—apparently oblivious to any patriotic flag-waving—groused about the event interfering with spring pennant preparations for their own big-league clubs. The event was in fact played during early spring-training weeks, when big leaguers were clearly not in midseason physical and mental form. It also appeared that high-paid pros (especially the Americans) were not, in most cases, truly motivated to throw themselves into doing battle for something as intangible as national pride. But if there is indeed a baseball heaven, then Shoriki-san had to be broadly smiling. The inaugural "true World Series"—for all its potential illegitimacy—surprisingly provided a showcase triumph for the Japanese leaguers whose national game had always been considered a peg or two below the American professional version.

And for those plotting the WBC as a celebration of American baseball ownership, there was another unpleasant surprise in store. Also left standing for the championship match was that other "outlier" rival, communist Cuba, whose entire baseball enterprise also had been geared up for four decades to undermine North American claims about ownership of the shared game. Cuba had at first wanted no part of an MLB-sponsored event that it saw as simply another crass commercial spectacle of the type long rejected by its socialist sports model. But in the end the temptation had been too great; the potential challenge, perhaps even potential payoffs in moral victories, if not in Yankee dollars, loomed as too attractive to ignore. Cuba, like Japan, could now claim at least a symbolic victory by momentarily staking a claim atop baseball's true world championship pile. For both of these non-MLB, baseball-loving countries, the WBC would prove to be something of a perfect storm.

Not only were the Americans and haughty Dominicans upstaged in San Diego during March 2006, but the surprise finale at MLB's inaugural World Baseball Classic would also provide Cuba with an additional perk. There was now an obvious rationale for the Cubans to welcome Japan as a legitimate partner in an alliance potentially providing salvation for their own sagging national game. Japan was anything but a second-tier base-ball operation and was certainly a huge step up from the AAA Mexican League or various less-prestigious European leagues where the Cubans had previously offered player and coaching exchanges. And there had already been a precedent set four years earlier, when Cuba's biggest-ever star, Omar Linares, had been allowed to cap his brilliant career with a brief (though disappointing) cup of coffee in the top Nippon pro circuit.

And for the Cubans, it also seemed that something had to be done to deflect latent MLB claims that the US pros offered the only viable future for Cuba's struggling game. When Cuban officials made their move, however, in September 2013—only months after a new North American furor surrounding Cuban talent had been unleashed with Yasiel Puig's dramatic debut in a Dodgers uniform—the American press was all too eager to celebrate what appeared to be a reversal of strategy from an arch-conservative and avidly anticapitalist Cuban sports ministry. It would take some time for those much closer to the scene to send out the message that Cuba was in reality traveling in a different direction than the one popularly assumed in Miami, in Washington, and in the New York office of MLB commissioner Bud Selig.

In what turned out to be an improbable case of accidental good timing, ESPN had sent a crew consisting of reporter Paula Lavigne, a producer, and a pair of veteran cameramen to Havana in the very week Cuba was poised to unveil a scheme for potential international player exchanges. The ESPN plan had been to interview INDER vice president Antonio Castro about the rapidly changing baseball scene in Cuba. This writer was invited along as a go-between to help guide the ESPN visitors through the tangled maze of the Cuban baseball hierarchy. Lavigne had also inter-viewed national team manager Victor Mesa earlier that same summer (during Team Cuba's visit to Omaha as part of the annual Friendly Series with USA Baseball) and had plans to talk in more depth with the outspok-en ex-superstar and current Matanzas manager about his own visions of Cuba's future, especially vis-à-vis MLB relations and the issue of grow-ing defections.

The ESPN interview sessions turned out to far exceed expectations, in filmed content as well as the surprising degree of free access. Tony Cas-tro provided some most quotable observations and some remarkably lib-eral positions regarding Cuba's own need to drift away from past policies. He spoke in comfortable English for more than an hour before cameras

Legendary Omar Linares was the first Cuban League star loaned to the Japanese leagues when he played for the Chunichi Dragons in the early 2000s. Courtesy of Jay Vandevoort.

on the picturesque National Hotel grounds overlooking the city's north side seafront; later he chatted with Lavigne for a couple hours off-camera.[3] A day later in the empty grandstands of Victory at Girón Stadium in Matanzas, Victor Mesa also provided a valued insider's view on how things were playing out in Cuba and where developments might lead. Castro and Mesa spoke on similar themes. The biggest problems for island baseball (in their shared view) all came down to the odious US embargo; Cuba was indeed open to some of its players reaching the big leagues, but only if the right conditions were met (mainly Cuba maintaining control of those players and having them return home for winter-league action); and the island might benefit heavily if former stars like José Contreras or El Duque could freely return home with both their much-needed wealth and their acknowledged popularity, factors that might inspire new generations of ball-playing island youth. It was a surprisingly positive stance, even if one had to admit that such upbeat rhetoric seemed to either ignore or miscalculate the true complexities blocking any smooth passage toward actual baseball détente.

The talks in Havana focused exclusively on MLB, as might have been anticipated. There was no mention of Japan or of any possibility of Cuba solving its problems by turning to Mexico or Europe or maybe even Canada. Big-league opportunities were clearly now the focus of defecting Cuban players, and working some arrangement with the MLB hierarchy seemed the only order of business—at least for Tony Castro and Victor Mesa. It was somewhat ironic that at the very time these interviews were being held, other upper-echelon INDER officials were about to launch plans that Castro and Mesa never mentioned and may not have been fully aware of. And it was more ironic still that during the very week we were on the ground in Havana, the Cuban League was quietly experiencing what would turn out to be its single biggest month of big-name player losses to date.

A first interview session with Tony Castro had been held at Changa Mederos Stadium on the grounds of Havana's sports academy training center, immediately before a practice game between hometown Industriales and visiting Cienfuegos. I had noted almost immediately that Abreu, Arruebarrena, and Moncada were all missing from the field, and when I asked several Cienfuegos ballplayers about the absences during a pre-game dugout visit I was assured that all three were merely nursing injuries. (It would later remain unclear if these teammates were actually unaware or perhaps spouting a rehearsed position on the matter.) But my suspicions were aroused further when Tony Castro privately told me, moments before starting his filming session with Lavigne in the bleachers, that there were indeed circulating rumors about several important player absences and also more concrete signals that some top stars had only that week fled the island.

The trip concluded with a third major interview, this one with national team third-baseman Yulieski Gourriel. That session, during which I served as off-camera translator for Lavigne and her crew (as I had for interviews with Victor Mesa in Matanzas), turned out to be the most informative of all. Yulieski was joined by his father, Lourdes, a major national team star two decades back, and both spoke frankly about Cuban pay scales (Yulieski himself received bonuses of several hundred convertible pesos monthly as a national team star), about some salary changes that they had been informed were about to be implemented, and about the younger Gourriel's hopes and dreams of someday reaching the majors, but of doing so only with permission of his government's highest officials.[4] Skeptics might suggest that Gourriel would always spout the government line about loyalty due to constant intimidation, and that his words might therefore not be genuine. But I had known Yulieski for years—chatting with him openly in both Cuba and on the road in Europe and Asia—and personally held no doubts about his sincere loyalties to the Cuban baseball system that had raised and trained him.

The interviews nonetheless revealed to some degree just how unrealistic the persisting Cuban view actually was. Yulieski was hoping that he could reach MLB via some unlikely miracle just around the corner. Mesa saw the only real roadblock to player exchanges as being the hated and all-too-easily-blamed embargo. Tony Castro could not envision any reasons why Cubans in MLB couldn't also still play back home. All were idle dreams, of course. But the sessions also shed light on the unfolding crisis and the actual realities of contemporary Cuban baseball.

In the end ESPN would drop the ball and fail to use filmed material that might have shed considerable light on the current Cuban baseball scene and thus stripped away many of the misconceptions surrounding events that were about to unfold. The story filmed by Paula Lavigne, for all its insights, was not the story that ESPN programmers apparently wanted to tell. They desired a far different saga, one that had played well on the home front but was now growing a bit stale. The program, eventually aired on the eve of the October World Series, would fail to reach beyond a repetitive mantra of "how can we get those coveted Cuban players into the big leagues where they belong?"[5] ESPN producers missed out entirely on a rare opportunity to explain the real complexities of Cuban baseball, explore the true crisis the island was currently facing, and examine just how complex USA-Cuba baseball relations might have to remain for some time to come. That was a story they deemed of little interest to stateside fans, and in the end they likely were sadly correct, at least from their own narrow MLB-affiliated perspective.

* * *

The timing of Cuba's dramatic shift in course regarding treatment of its ballplayers was somewhat ironic, since that news broke at precisely the moment ESPN was on the ground attempting to portray (or at least assess) Cuba's current baseball crisis. News of the INDER plan would in fact break while our small crew was landing in Miami on our return. I was still in the airport when I received some surprise emails from my wife back in Indiana inquiring about the gist of a story she had just caught over the airwaves on NPR. Immediate overreaction in the US press apparently had twisted the story rather significantly. It was being reported that Cuba had abandoned long-standing policies and was about to release ballplayers for service abroad, which could only mean the American big leagues. Most commentators rushed to predict a flood of Cuban players freely coming north for the first time in decades. It was a prediction that would be repeated again fifteen months later with Obama's December announcement of efforts to reopen diplomatic relations. And it was no truer the second time than it was the first.

In reality the Cuban policy shift was something very different from what most were writing and most wanted to hear. It should have been clear at the outset what Cuba's baseball officials, as well as their Communist Party superiors, now had in mind. The agenda as it was laid out in the formally released INDER press announcement contained several provisions. Ballplayer salaries would be raised to the smallest extent possible. As Victor Mesa had emphasized to Paula Lavigne and her cameras that same week, the Cuban Federation would love to pay its players more, but this was simply not an economic possibility for a government-run baseball program that raised almost no cash revenue and that struggled in a current US embargo–driven national economic downturn.

In addition to modestly increased salaries at home, there would now also be opportunities for at least some players to be loaned out abroad and earn additional salaries when the domestic season wasn't in progress. There was no hint that any Cubans would suddenly be free agents released to move anywhere they pleased or negotiate their own deals. Perhaps few would have such opportunities offered to them in the foreseeable future, since the plan would have to begin as a modest experiment. But it was a start and some doors were being opened. Japan and other Asian and European leagues were mentioned as distinct possibilities.[6] But there was no specific mention of MLB and no reason to assume that long-standing objections to business with the American pros were now softening.

The Cuban plan, at least in something of an experimental form, had actually been launched a full six months earlier with the shipping of a first batch of veteran players to the Mexican League Campeche Pirates. Slugger Alfredo Despaigne had been first to benefit from the changing scene and had already enjoyed a banner summer with Campeche. Biggest headlines came when the Granma "Caballo de los Caballos" ("The Big Stallion") equaled a batting feat of Martin Dihigo, the celebrated black-ball-era star and Cuba's greatest ball-playing legend. In mid-July Despaigne banged out six hits (one homer and five singles) in six at bats during his team's victory over Saltillo, matching an historic September 18, 1936, performance by Dihigo.

The convenient Mexican connection was not exactly a novel one for Cuban baseball. Victor Mesa—perhaps the island's most colorful player in the '80s and '90s and certainly its most colorful manager in the 2000s—himself had already enjoyed a brief sojourn there as part of his own hiatus from the Cuban League. But that particular venture neither lasted very long nor ended very well. When Mesa's abrupt firing as Veracruz manager was announced in the midst of the 2010 season, it was badly misreported in the pages of Miami's Spanish-language *Nuevo Herald* as a personality conflict.[7] The actual reasons for the discord involved the Mexican team's signing of defector Yadel Marti, an event which caused INDER officials to reverse course and summon home both Mesa and former slugging star Agustin Marquetti, who had also been loaned out as the team's hitting instructor. The Cubans were not ready to allow any of their coaching personnel to work and fraternize with players who had blatantly abandoned the revolution. Things had not yet turned a corner as far as INDER's view of baseball "traitors" was concerned.

Mesa would return to Cuba with a new assignment and a new stature as a still-controversial but suddenly highly effective skipper. He would rapidly revamp sagging fortunes for a doormat Matanzas club, leading that team to its first of several postseason appearances in the club's near-quarter-century history. He would then take over the national team in time for the 2013 World Baseball Classic in Japan, where his charges would suffer a disappointing second-round ouster at the hands of eventual semifinalist Holland. While Mesa surged at home, he would be replaced in Mexico by Pinar del Río's Jorge Fuentes—another celebrated former national team skipper who had fallen in and out of favor back home.[8] Fuentes's Mexican tenure was also painfully brief, but for different, if somewhat mysterious, reasons. Taking the reins in Campeche (the team that had received Despaigne and two additional Cuban stars on loan the previous summer), Fuentes lasted little more than a month and was then sacked in the wake of a breaking sexual abuse scandal involving several Pirates players. The newly arrived Cuban manager was reportedly let go for failure to maintain proper disciplinary control over his club.

Other Cuban stars also had been finding their way to Mexico with government sanction for post-career service and some needed extra cash. Pedro Luis Lazo was the most notable and his story perhaps the most typical. At the end of a brilliant career Lazo was rewarded with a chance to coach abroad, again in Campeche, during the summer 2012 season. Lazo had finally hung up his spikes earlier that spring after a stellar twenty-year tenure that had left him Cuba's all-time winningest pitcher (257–136). His Campeche assignment would turn out to involve more than just sideline or bullpen coaching, as soon he was also pitching again on a part-time basis. Before the year was out Lazo would see limited duty as a thirty-nine-year-old Campeche reliever and also a spot starter for the winter-season Mexican Pacific League club based in Los Mochis. Pedro Lazo had ultimately reached professional baseball action overseas, even if it was under rather belated and odd circumstances. Longtime national team catcher Ariel Pestano also served a short 2013 winter coaching stint in Mexico (as an instructor with Campeche's minor-league club in Coatzacoalcos), as did retired shortstop Eduardo Paret. Lazo enjoyed the most productive and personally rewarding Mexican sojourn as semiretired ballplayer-coach, and his experience abroad was obviously an overdue INDER perk being gifted to the best Cuban pitcher of the generation, a loyalist who had stayed home while Pinar teammate Jose Contreras had fled to the big leagues.

Other retired or about-to-be-retired players were simultaneously loaned out to more distant European leagues. Three such notable travelers were Granma hurler Ciro Silvino Licea (France), Cienfuegos southpaw

Norberto González, and fence-busting Las Tunas slugger Joan (pronounced Juan) Carlos Pedroso (the latter two both shipped to Nettuno in Italy). All enjoyed a degree of success and Silvino Licea guided his Division I French squad (Templiers de Sénart) to a league championship. A year later the thirty-nine-year-old was still pitching out of the bullpen for Granma and ringing up some National Series milestones, including a 200th career win that elevated him to sixth place in league annals. Joan Carlos Pedroso and Norberto González would also both soon find their way to the Mexican Pacific League with the Los Mochis Cane Growers. But that pair, like Lazo, Pestano, and Paret, were already finished in Cuba as active ballplayers.

Pedroso's case was a particularly odd one. He had been one of Cuba's truly great sluggers of the modern era, although he never tasted much success with the national team. Pedroso was the first to top 200 home runs in the wooden bat era (post-1999) and the country's leader in that department over the previous fifteen seasons. He was also at times a source of rather unfair derision at home because of his abject failures on offense during several national team trials; nonetheless he had been an unsung hero of the first WBC if only for his stellar defensive play at first base. At career's end Pedroso was approaching numerous milestones and had finally reached the coveted 300–home run plateau (ninth all-time). But the plug was pulled by INDER after sixteen seasons and before he could claim any final home run landmarks (he stood only a dozen short of the number six slot). It was reminiscent of similar action that forced Orestes Kindelán into retirement in 2002 when the Santiago star was a mere thirteen long balls away from the charmed 500 circle.

The shipping out of players like Pedroso, Norberto, and Lazo—all of them finished at home—was not to be seen as part of any newfound player development formula. These were instead cases of providing bonuses to acknowledged loyalists in a tradition launched when Linares, Pacheco, and Germán Mesa went to Japan in the early 2000s. Perhaps this was also calculated to encourage mid-career players to remain loyal to the system. The summer of 2013 also saw Michel Enríquez and Yordanis Samón join Despaigne in Campeche. But both those trials suffered a quick and ignominious ending. Enríquez was damaged goods before being shipped off to Mexico, or at least that was the reading and reaction of the Campeche club. Suffering a leg injury, Enríquez was promptly shipped home after failing a Campeche team physical. Ironically, though, he would recover quickly enough to win a second Cuban league batting title the following winter. Samón also failed to perform up to expectations (two hits in eighteen at bats) in his brief trial and was quickly sent packing back to Cuba, where he too revived on home cooking over the next couple winters.

Ingenious as it might have seemed at the time, the budding Mexican plan would quickly blow up directly in INDER's face. The goal had been to train players in higher-level international leagues while assuring they would remain free from the clutches of MLB teams. But there was a factor that the Cubans simply had not considered, one that would quickly come back to bite them. As a AAA circuit loosely in the fold of organized baseball, the Mexican League fell under regulations governing Cuban player contracts in the eyes of both MLB and OFAC (US Treasury Department) guardians of Helms-Burton embargo legislation. Those hoping to sabotage Cuba's plans didn't have far to look for their potential weapon of mass destruction.

The fallout came in the summer of 2014 and turned on the return to Campeche of Alfredo Despaigne, Cuba's biggest star and a top gate attraction for the Mexican club. Cepeda had already gone to Tokyo and Gourriel had quickly followed as the summer campaign began. Campeche nonetheless wanted Despaigne to return there and INDER clearly wanted to keep that door open, even if a Japanese accord was now solidly in the making. But MLB-related forces had a trump card to play in Mexico, even if there was none available in Japan. It had to do with the restrictions on Cuban ballplayer signings imposed by OFAC and governing all teams and leagues living under the MLB thumb. Despaigne or any other Cuban playing in Mexico was in clear violation of those policies that mandated Cubans establish third-country residence, thus guaranteeing that no monies would return to the island or be placed in the hands of any Cuban nationals. By playing in Mexico, not only was Despaigne receiving a large salary, but 20 percent of the take was being shipped directly to INDER. Despaigne was a big-enough cog in the Cuban player-loaning scheme for those bent on sabotaging that strategy to notice and finally exploit this letter of the law.

The bombshell dropped when Dominican-based ESPN reporter Enrique Rojas almost gleefully broke the story that Despaigne had apparently been playing in Mexico for several weeks with a falsified Dominican passport.[9] The Campeche club had become aware of the infraction of

OFAC policies and had tried to cover its tracks with a poorly planned subterfuge. A dandy soap opera of events would quickly follow and the eventual fallout was that Despaigne would be sent home from Mexico and summarily banned for life from Mexican League play. The Mexican League had to save face and had come down hard on Campeche team officials for their indiscretions. Meanwhile INDER bosses repeatedly (and, some thought, rather hollowly) claimed that neither they nor the player were in any way involved in the passport-rigging operation. When the smoke cleared, North American organized baseball had won a major propaganda victory. But it was one with a sour aftertaste. One could only wonder what the outcry might have been stateside if FIFA (soccer's governing body) took a similar stand on USA soccer players because of a dislike of USA foreign policy—demanding they renounce their USA citizenship for third-country residence. What in the end appeared most sordid were not indiscretions by the Mexican ball club, but rather the illogical and archaic OFAC policies that had forced the deceptions in the first place.

* * *

When the Mexican door slammed shut, the Japanese portals were flung open, wide and inviting. It was perhaps subtly ironic but also transparently appropriate that Cuba would seek to mold its novel working arrangement with the Nippon leagues in a framework that at least in broad outline resembled the "posting system" approach that Nippon Professional Baseball had already worked out as early as 1998 with MLB. INDER officials would designate a handful of players as being available and invite Japanese clubs to send scouts, examine the available talent in tryout camps, and bid for the services of a few selected and coveted players.

There were, of course, marked differences in the Cuban approach. Players would be loaned out piecemeal and in small numbers rather than sold outright; the design was obviously to protect the domestic league and the showcase national team from any further rapid talent depletions. The notion behind it all was the admitted need to begin retaining these star players by handing them much-needed opportunities to earn larger salaries, but at the same time keeping them safely in the INDER fold. And there was also the added and considerable advantage of better preparing national team stalwarts by exposing them to considerably higher levels of professional competition. To an outsider it was a bit of a Pollyanna scheme, since the bulk of top league prospects might have to wait years for their number to be called and the exposure to Japanese competition would likely never be handed to enough national team regulars to make much of a change in tournament readiness.

Cuba had long enjoyed a hospitable baseball connection with Japan. This was not surprising, since the two countries were the bastions of international baseball and also the two prongs of an alternative baseball universe existing entirely outside MLB and organized baseball. An earlier and more limited interchange saw Omar Linares and a handful of other veterans visit Japan in the early 2000s, mostly in the role of coaches or industrial league players. Linares largely floundered in his three seasons of limited service (2002–4) for the Central League's Chunichi Dragons, but there were few surprises there, since the aging star was already at the end of his career rope. Linares had merely been handed a much-deserved reward for long loyalty to the revolution, and the move also took Cuban officials off the hook and allowed an overweight and now unproductive veteran to be quietly replaced on the national team. [10]

This time around the plan would have a somewhat different aim. The goal now would be to upgrade Cuban star power and not merely to send it off to pasture. If a few select stars were again being singled out for late-career reward, the goal was also to preserve and even upgrade those players. The first high-profile signee in Japan was Freddie Cepeda, long-time national team captain and perhaps the best hitter the island had produced since Linares himself. Cepeda was certainly the best I had seen during dozens of visits to the island and to Team Cuba's international venues; he was the focus of most pro scouts and perhaps, in truth, better even than Linares, given that he had been tested against professional arms while swinging wooden bats. Cepeda's choice for the pioneering role was a most fitting move, but also one that signaled just how Cuba would now be handling its placement of privileged players in foreign leagues.

Cepeda made history with his Japanese League contract (announced at US$1.5 million), becoming the first non-defecting Cuban baseball millionaire. The outfielder-turned-designated-hitter had long been the heart of Cuban baseball and was easily the nation's most beloved sports personality. There was no better role model for Cuban baseball than Freddie Cepeda, who reacted to newfound wealth by humbly pronouncing that he had "always been a millionaire since I have always had the love and respect of 11 million Cuba fans who loyally follow my career."[11]

Slugger Freddie Cepeda became the Cuban League's first million-dollar ballplayer after inking his 2014 contract with the Japanese League Yomiuri Giants. Courtesy of Peter C. Bjarkman.

MLB scouts had long been universal in their claims that Cepeda was the top offensive performer on the Cuban side of the international scene. A switch-hitter possessing awesome power but even more impressive plate discipline, Cepeda never dominated league statistics at home. But time and again he singlehandedly won games with timely slugging at the most dramatic moments of international action. Australian team manager John Deeble capsulized the top Cuban slugger when he once remarked to me that "Cepeda is the one who year-in and year-out has always killed us (the Australians)." Few knowledgeable in MLB's international scouting operations would hesitate to say that Cepeda likely would have "busted the MLB bank" (as Linares might also have done) long before Abreu or Chapman had he ever chosen to turn his back on the revolution and its socialist sports system. Any list of his incredible eleventh-hour heroics—stretching from the 2003 Havana World Cup (where two late solo homers clinched a gold medal) to the recent 2015 Caribbean Series (where he singlehandedly crushed the favored Venezuelans)—reads almost like a fanciful storybook account.

Cepeda's selection as the first among the new wave of players sent to Japan was also something of an overdue redemption. Despite his impeccable stature as showcase performer and model citizen, even this icon had eventually been victimized by the baseball system he had so long championed. It all unfolded during an unfortunate incident a few years back that would highlight the ugliest side of Cuba's internal baseball struggles. The elite Cuban squad competing in a September 2010 Pre-Mundial (World Cup Qualifier) tournament in San Juan had been placed under strict orders not to communicate with earlier defectors who might show up attempting to contact former teammates. Hard-line control of Cuban players was very much still the norm and San Juan was seen as a particularly dangerous venue, given its proximity to Miami, its designation as official American territory, and its expected onslaught of scouts, harassing player agents, and both local and visiting anti-Castro demonstrators. There had been more than a little trouble there during the 2006 World Baseball Classic and the Cubans had not returned since. The extended state security regimen was most likely an unnecessary overreaction, but it was one that would have severe consequences for Cepeda, the most unlikely of unintended victims.

It all played out during a surprise visit to the team's Sheraton Hotel lodgings by Maels Rodríguez. His own sensational, if truncated, Cuban career and ill-fated defection saga were recounted in chapter 4. Rodríguez, Cepeda, and the Gourriels had grown up side by side in rural Sancti Spíritus and had been both constant childhood companions and eventual National Series teammates. Maels, now a resident of Miami and finished with any professional baseball ambitions, seized the opportunity afforded by the Cubans' San Juan stopover to risk a brief visit at the heavily guarded Sheraton. He managed to sneak into the room shared by his two former teammates for an innocent few moments of warm greetings and well wishes and little more—there was no talk of defections, nor any veiled attempts to entice old neighborhood companions into abandoning their island loyalties.[12] Innocent as the brief encounter was, the fallout would be severe for the Cuban team captain who was expected to toe the line and set an example, not violate team security policies.

The surreptitious visit was noted by ever-vigilant Cuban security, then promptly reported to Higinio Vélez. On the return flight to Havana Cepeda was informed by the iron-willed commissioner that he was being suspended for his infraction and would thus not accompany the Cuban team to upcoming Intercontinental Cup matches in Taiwan. (That this was largely a symbolic act was obvious from the fact that there had been no such punishment meted out to Gourriel.) Public embarrassment was one thing. But banishment from an upcoming trip to Taiwan was also an economic setback, since players relied on such rare opportunities for an increased paycheck to supplement miniscule National Series incomes. [13]

Cuba's best and most loyal soldier had fallen accidental victim to a hard-line policy that soon left him in temporary disgrace and isolation. It was a severe blow and one that soon caused considerable outcry among fans back home on the island. When pre-season rosters were announced two weeks later, Cepeda had also been dropped from his Sancti Spíritus club. Only after continued uproar over the matter in Havana and elsewhere around the island, and also a reported behind-the-scenes intervention by the influential Tony Castro, would Cepeda eventually be quietly reinstated just in the nick of time for a new National Series pennant chase. In due course he would also be allowed to resume his unfairly besmirched role as the most reliable among national team heroes. The bitter aftermath of this entire sad affair persisted in collective memory, and by early 2014 (more than three years later) it was apparently time to smooth any lingering hostility with a lucrative assignment in Japan.

Unfortunately the first year in Tokyo would not turn out anything like what Cepeda or his legions of Cuban fans might have wished. He experienced a surprisingly slow start at the plate and continued to struggle mightily against Japanese pitching. As he would later privately tell me (and also formally admit to other interviewers) he had been initially optimistic that he would be joining Japan's top club as a valued regular. When that proved not to be the case and he was assigned the lesser role of occasional pinch hitter or spot DH, he was never able to find a comfortable rhythm while withering on the bench. There were a few highlights (a game-winning grand slam-homer was one), but these were overshadowed by a lengthy slump from which he could never manage to recover. The batting average slid drastically, and since he was on board as a prized DH, the failure to produce at the plate was fatal. Before the year was out Cepeda was demoted to the Giants top farm team, subsequently bouncing back and forth to the parent club, where in fifty-two games he produced only six homers, eighteen RBI, and an anemic .194 batting mark. The abysmal showing wouldn't even match Linares's surprise swoon with Chunichi a dozen seasons earlier. It was all a huge embarrassment for one of Cuba's proudest and most talented players. Skeptics were also suggesting that this was indeed Linares all over again and that it didn't bode well for any future Cuban plans regarding a productive Japanese pipeline.

On-field failures aside, there were other issues regarding Cuba's first showcase player rented out for Japanese service. Cepeda's new contract stirred controversy, especially among fans in Miami who wanted to see an MLB pipeline and not an NPB solution to Cuba's growing baseball isolation. The pact might be substantial, but it was nothing like what big-league clubs might have offered another top Cuban slugger. It paled when compared to compensations that Puig, Céspedes, and Abreu (or soon Tomás and Olivera) were demanding. There was considerable commentary about this discrepancy in the US press and in numerous blog posts. But as always there was also much distortion of the underlying facts. Cepeda's payday was huge by Cuban standards and would provide him a luxury status in his hometown that was rarely if ever enjoyed by a post-revolution Cuban citizen (top government officials included). It would make him one of the nation's wealthiest residents. And it was in Cuba that Cepeda clearly wished to remain.

What was sometimes also missed by US press accounts was that IN-DER had indeed changed policy and the 80/20 salary split between government and player now had been reversed. And those who still complained that the communist government should not get any cut of the ballplayers' earnings were simply out of touch with contemporary economic realities. MLB players earning multimillions pay a far larger portion to the US government in the form of federal income taxes. They also are responsible for often complex state and city taxes and fees. And then there are agents waiting for their own take, perhaps 10 percent of a player's total earnings and assorted signing bonuses. The Cuban player working in Japan indeed seems to come off quite well, especially in light of any desires that athlete might have to continue living at home.

Another side of this story involves the true realities of MLB pay scales, a matter hidden from today's fans by obsessive media focus on soaring compensations paid to our celebrity-addicted culture's most heavily promoted icons, whether they be athletes, movie and television actors, recording artists, or other high-profile pop culture performers. The sordid saga of how baseball players and other pro athletes are often treated by

North American franchises also has historic roots that almost entirely escape our view. Current astronomical base salaries aside, Major League Baseball can hardly point to a glorious history when it comes to the compensation paid its athletes. Before the dawn of free agency in the mid-1970s, most big leaguers were treated largely as reasonably compensated slave laborers. No opportunities existed to sell their services on the open market; they were owned outright by their clubs like tradable commodities and enjoyed only minimal shares of the game's overall revenues. The odious "reserve clause" in effect for nearly a century (1879–1975) meant big leaguers could be traded, sold, or released at an owner's or general manager's whim; their one leverage was to hold out at contract renewal time and refuse to play unless minimal demands were met. Once a strong players union and a rapidly changing social scene brought liberation in 1975 (when arbitrator Peter Seitz struck down reserve clause conditions in celebrated cases involving pitchers Andy Messersmith and Dave McNally), ballplayer salaries for the first time soared astronomically. But MLB owners were, the truth be told, dragged kicking and screaming into a new era of ballplayer free agency.

But have things changed that drastically for baseball players in general under a revamped free agent–era MLB umbrella, or only for those who climb to the apex of the pecking order? A recent story published originally in the *Toronto Star* reveals disturbing discrepancies between organized baseball's pay scale for franchise stars and the slave-labor wages still being doled out to minor-league journeymen. It turns out that MLB and its supporting structure of lower-level leagues treats many of its players just as poorly, or perhaps worse, than does the Cuban socialist baseball system.

The details of minor-league contracts are in fact quite startling. As Brendan Kennedy points out in his revealing *Toronto Star* report, A-level minor leaguers are paid a standard $6,300 for their five-month season, only about two-thirds of what Toronto Blue Jays star José Bautista currently makes for each inning on the field. Since 1976, minor-league salaries have increased a reported 75 percent, while big-league salaries have hiked more than 2,000 percent over the same span. While a handful of top minor leaguers do pocket huge signing bonuses, many sign for less than $5,000. In short, most minor leaguers are compensated well below the federal US poverty line, which was set at $11,670 for 2014. How, asks Kennedy, does MLB's $9 billion industry get away with exploiting its minor leaguers by dangling often futile dreams of a possible big-league career before their eyes in exchange for a cheap sub-poverty-level labor pool? [14]

It should be stressed here that while US minor leaguers on average don't make a reasonable living wage while pursuing their American Dream, Cuban Leaguers (who all agree are minor leaguers and not major leaguers) are paid well beyond the salary of an average Cuban worker. This is a comparison never made in Miami, and one lost in all the hype about the $30 million contract for Chapman or the $60 million deal for Abreu.

An impetus for breaking stories regarding the minor-league salary gap was the accompanying revelation that thirty-four current or former minor leaguers filed a February 2014 lawsuit against all thirty big-league clubs and former commissioner Bud Selig contending they had not received minimum wages mandated by federal and state laws. [15] It is instructive to compare these revelations about minor-league paychecks to the constant complaints about miniscule Cuban League salaries. In the case of the Cubans the low pay is understandable, since the structure of Cuban baseball has nothing to do with any business models or corporate ball-club profits. But in North America, where baseball is nothing more than high-profit business, it is harder perhaps to understand (certainly harder to justify) this kind of athlete exploitation once it is revealed. It turns out that here at home, in our bastion of rampant corporate capitalism, mistreatment of journeymen professional athletes is far more egregious than in communist Cuba.

* * *

Cuba's most celebrated and coveted star, Yulieski Gourriel, would soon follow longtime Sancti Spíritus teammate Freddie Cepeda to more lucrative and polished playing conditions in Japan. Gourriel had long been a potent slugger of the same magnitude as Cepeda, even if not always quite as idolized by fans or as popular in Cuban press circles. [16] He had been a fixture at either second or third base for the national team since the early 2000s. The pair had played side by side for a dozen years before a recent controversial move had transferred the three Gourriel brothers to the more popular Havana Industriales ball club in the fall of 2013. Gourriel came from a celebrated baseball family that had long displayed firm loyalty to the Cuban system. His father, Lourdes Sr., was a major batting star and national team icon across the 1980s and early

1990s. Older brother Yunieski had never been a national team member but displayed consistent talent as one of the league's more adept defensive center fielders. Younger brother Lourdes Jr. (popularly known as Yunito) had in the last two years emerged as a major prospect at shortstop and was seen in many quarters as potentially the best among the ball-playing Gourriel clan.

A decade back, during an inaugural MLB World Baseball Classic, Yulieski Gourriel was the seemingly "off-limits" Cuban prospect all MLB scouts had their eyes and video cameras most firmly fixed upon. Not yet twenty-two at the time, he was an agile infielder and a slugger of pronounced skills. There were some notable gaps in his game, especially an issue of plate discipline and knowledge of the strike zone. But he did nothing in San Juan and San Diego during Cuba's 2006 run to the WBC finals to indicate that he was anything short of a budding big league star. For starters he launched the clutch three-run blast during an opening game against Panama that effectively ignited Cuba's unlikely journey to a championship showdown with Japan. I myself had written a short pre-tournament essay for *Béisbol Mundial* magazine touting Gourriel as "the best player who nobody north of Miami knew anything about." If there was one player that spring that "defection talk" swirled around, it was definitely Yulieski Gourriel.

Over succeeding years Gourriel's rising star would tarnish a bit. He didn't seem to mature as rapidly in the batter's box during international competitions as some scouts had anticipated. His overall game seemed to level off considerably and the weaknesses in his offensive approach lingered. He also suffered from some bad timing in big games that unfairly soured his reputation at home. Notably he made the final out of the WBC title match with Japan, and two years later he hit into a game-ending double play during the Beijing Olympics gold medal match with the winning runs marooned on base. He even became an object of considerable derision among Industriales fans (while still playing for rival Sancti Spíritus), who marked him rather unfairly as an overrated failure with an inflated reputation. Such is the curse of unlimited potential. But Gourriel, for his own part, did nothing but continue to amass numbers that put him at the top of many career lists and elevated him among the greats of island baseball history. [17] As years passed it also became more than obvious that despite occasional guarded comments to foreign journalists about secret big-league dreams, Gourriel certainly would never seek to depart his homeland without government sanction.

Cepeda may have been the inevitable choice to pioneer in Japan under the new working agreement, but Gourriel was hardly a surprise selection either when he also was tabbed for a contract with the Yokohama DeNB BayStars of the Central League on May 11, 2014. Once given his shot in Japan, Gourriel easily had the edge over Cepeda when it came to on-field performance and adjustments to the intricacies and pressures of the Asian game. His 2014 salary (reported at $980,000) fell a bit short of what Yomiuri had thrown at Cepeda, but it was a windfall nonetheless. Arriving in Yokohoma in late May with the season well underway, Yulieski would immediately shine with the DeNB BayStars, while Cepeda's considerable struggles continued with the more celebrated Tokyo Giants. Over his truncated season (which included some initial conditioning with Yokohama's farm club), Gourriel put up respectable numbers (a .305 BA, 11 homers and 30 RBIs, and a .536 slugging mark across 62 games) that seemingly justified the hefty investment by the Japanese team.

If Cepeda disappointed the Giants in Tokyo while Gourriel rewarded the BayStars in Yokohama, it was late-arriving Alfredo Despaigne (signed on July 15, 2014) who rapidly became the poster boy for the new Japan-Cuba accord. Despaigne, for his part, would not languish in disgrace long after the Mexican League passport fiasco. The fireplug-shaped Granma slugger and Cuba's most consistent hitter (233 career homers and a lifetime .348 BA after eleven seasons) was corralled at mid-season by the Chiba Lotte Marines, Metropolitan Tokyo's second team and a longtime powerhouse in the Pacific League. Before the summer was out it was Despaigne who was having the biggest immediate impact in Japan. His raw numbers were impressive (11 homers, 33 RBI, .311 BA, and .627 slugging in only 45 games), and his quiet demeanor and personal work ethic meshed perfectly with a traditional Japanese ball-playing style. On the heels of his strong first-year showing, Despaigne also became the most rewarded Cuban recruit. In December 2014 it was announced that he would be welcomed back with a new two-year deal at a reported $6.5 million (800 million yen plus incentives), dwarfing the contracts gambled on Cepeda and Gourriel and thus also establishing him overnight as easily one of the wealthiest men back in his Cuban homeland.

There was also another Cuban Leaguer quietly performing in Tokyo that first summer of the exchange, although his lesser presence was overshadowed by the big three. Nineteen-year-old Héctor Mendoza—a hot prospect perceived as a future national team reliever with a blazing 95-plus-mph fastball—had been a surprise selection (signed by the Giants on July 17), since he did not fit the profile of a long-tenured veteran receiving overdue perks at career's end. Mendoza was merely a raw youngster with a very short Cuban League resume featuring three seasons of limited bullpen duty in Isla de la Juventud. His selection not only signaled the obvious potential the Japanese scouts saw in his talents, but also indicated some novel thinking on the part of the Cubans. Perhaps the motive was to keep Mendoza in the fold, forestalling any attempts at defection, or perhaps the idea was to groom a new national team closer. Either way the experiment had some immediate payoffs. The youngster would see limited duty with Yomiuri's Eastern League farm club (four appearances with a 1.59 ERA), but by the time the Caribbean Series rolled around in February 2015 Mendoza was already entrenched as a highly effective national team bullpen stopper.

The Cubans on loan by INDER were not the only ones present on the Nippon circuit. They were joined by a handful of earlier defectors headed by Leslie Anderson and Bárbaro Cañizares, both of whom had recently given up on their stalled big-league dreams in the States. Anderson smacked fifteen homers for Yomiuri despite missing a large chunk of the season with injuries; Cañizares appeared in a mere eight games for the Fukuoka Softbank Hawks. Less successful were nine-season MLB veteran Yunieski Betancourt, who hit below the Mendoza Line (at .141) in brief duty with the Orix Buffaloes, and Michael Abreu, the 2013 Pacific League home run king who was released by Hokkaido's Ham Fighters after his season was sabotaged by back problems. That these two sets of Cubans (four defectors and an equal number of loyalists) would now play side by side represented yet another shift in INDER policy back home. A similar scenario had forced Victor Mesa's sudden recall in 2010 from Mexico once the Mexican League Veracruz outfit he was managing inked 2008 defector Yadel Marti to strengthen its pitching staff.[18] If Cuba wanted a Japan connection, it was now in no position to entirely dictate the terms.

By most measures, the first full year of Cuba's new Japan exchange might be deemed an overall success.[19] But by the time a second year would roll around there were already some noticeable cracks beginning to show in the seams of the system. The new campaign was expected to bring substantial expansion of the alliance. Japanese scouts were now being invited to Havana to audition ballplayers at Latin American Stadium, something that will likely continue to be denied to MLB bird dogs for at least the foreseeable future. Optimism was initially high on both sides of the budding partnership. But when the 2015 roster of players assigned to Japan was finally announced in February, it contained only the original four plus a single addition—the youngest member of the Gourriel clan, twenty-one-year-old Lourdes Jr. Obviously things were moving rather slowly—perhaps the Asians were finding the available Cuban talent a bit thin—and a Japan connection wasn't proving to be an immediate panacea.

Japan wasn't the entire solution, even if it was perhaps the only viable one in the short term. There would be a handful of other Cubans heading overseas for the 2015 summer season, but the location didn't promise much in the way of a salary haul for the players or many prospects of improved training for national team stars at a higher level of competition. The third Gourriel brother, Yunieski, had spent part of the previous summer with the Quebec City Capitales in the low-level Can-Am independent league. Joining him for 2015 would be Santiago outfielder Alexei Bell, Holguín shortstop Yordan Manduley, and Sancti Spíritus pitcher Ismel Jiménez, a trio of well-seasoned veterans. This latest move might have held a small incentive salary-wise for the ballplayers involved, but it was in truth a demotion in terms of league quality. It also was transparently another reward being handed to the loyalist Gourriel family, since Yunieski could hardly be considered either a league star most deserving of overseas opportunities or a prospect most in need of protecting with the lure of overseas summer employment.

The first tangible demonstration of advantages to be culled from these new arrangements came when league play resumed in Cuba. Each of the four players on recent loan to Japan would make large contributions to a surprising resurgence for Cuba in international tournament events over the winter months. This was a large part of the plan as INDER officials had envisioned it from the start. An initial demonstration came with the November Central American and Caribbean Games staged in Veracruz, Mexico. After several embarrassing recent outings topped by an early ouster at the Caribbean Series nine months earlier, the Cuban selection reversed expectations and ran roughshod over the opposition with five straight victories to claim a face-saving gold medal. This was not a win over especially strong opposition—Nicaragua, Puerto Rico, Mexico, and the Dominicans did not field elite teams. But it was a much needed boost after several years of exasperating near misses and embarrassing failures. Three months later there would be stronger evidence of resurgence put on display during a triumphant return to the Caribbean Series in San Juan.

Three of the Japanese recruits were destined to play central roles in San Juan. MVP Cepeda stole the show with a rally-producing triple and a bases-clearing double in the semifinal win over previously unbeaten Venezuela. Gourriel chipped in with a victory-clinching homer in the tense finale versus Mexico and earned a tournament All-Star nod for his weeklong labor. Perhaps more vital still was the clutch performance of Héctor Mendoza, whose flawless relief work bailed out the Cubans in all three do-or-die victories down the stretch run to a surprising gold medal victory. Few even at home had given the Cubans much chance in San Juan in light of the embarrassing early elimination that had darkened their historic 2014 return to Caribbean Series action after a fifty-five-year hiatus. Fewer still glimpsed any hope after three opening-round losses again left them on the doorstep of near-certain elimination. In the end the San Juan championship was arguably the most important international triumph for the islanders since their shocking performance at the 2006 World Baseball Classic.

The quartet of part-time Japanese leaguers jointly displayed that Cuba was indeed back in the limelight as an international force. Despite two more defections in San Juan, the ship had, in some measure at least, now been righted.[20] When the triumphant Cubans returned to Havana, Cepeda was already en route back to Japan and had thus been scratched from the championship round of domestic-league play. Cepeda's Yomiuri club in Tokyo was hoping that an extended spring training would facilitate his resurgence from a disastrous Japanese debut. The other three, plus the latest young recruit, Lourdes Jr., would all return to finish out the winter season on the home front. But some negative signs were also beginning to emerge. Yulieski faded badly down the stretch and perhaps the stresses of year-round play were largely to blame. Despaigne was also suffering from nagging injuries (most prominently a leg strain that hampered running). Mendoza experienced minor arm stress, although he recovered in time for postseason service with a Cinderella-like Isla de la Juventud ball club that reached the league finals for the first time in its history. Lourdes Jr. had been injured in the weeks leading up to the Caribbean Series, saw no action in San Juan, and was reinjured in the final weeks of the Cuban campaign when he was struck on the wrist by an errant fastball. Perhaps there was a glitch in the new scheme that the Cuban brain trust had not quite anticipated.

Then overnight the whole Japanese experiment seemed to hit a huge pothole. It was the issue of injuries to not only Yulieski (thigh strain) but also Lourdes (bruised wrist) that triggered a chain of events destined to unravel nearly everything being built between the two baseball federations. In the aftermath of a disappointing late-season sag, Gourriel had not reported to Yokohama as expected, and neither had brother Lourdes. When alarmed BayStars officials began inquiries, they were told the pair were still recuperating from late-season injuries and needed rehabilitation time back in Cuba. But this was hardly a rationale for a Japanese ball club that believed any contract was to be understood as the letter of the law. [21]

The Japanese club quickly dispatched a top official to Havana with orders to fetch the malingering players immediately. Yulieski, who had inked a $3 million (359 million yen) renewal, was the prime concern. Yulieski and his brother Lourdes both persisted in their injury claims and insisted they needed further treatments at home before departure. It may well have been merely a case of the Cubans now desperately holding out for much-needed rest. But the Japanese weren't buying it, and suddenly Gourriel's contract was canceled. An angered BayStars spokesman—team general manager Shigeru Takada—suggested that "perhaps this will teach the Cubans what contracts mean," and he had a valid point, since contracts were not a reality for Cuban players and certainly not for beleaguered Cuban baseball officials. [22]

Cuban authorities were at first silent, which only added to the firestorm building among island fans, who enjoyed much more access to breaking news than popularly assumed. Social media in Havana (limited as it was), and Miami as well, was abuzz with angry responses to the silence of Cuban officials. After three weeks a belated INDER press release finally appeared and amounted to a good deal of face-saving ironically more in tune with Japanese ethos than any Cuban style. According to the Cuban sources, it was all merely a misunderstanding (one that had cost both INDER and the Gourriel family a healthy piece of change) and the contract cancellation was portrayed as a mutual agreement between the two federations. Even so, it appeared that any arrangement for continued player exchanges might now be in jeopardy. Was the same story that had played out a year earlier with the Mexico fiasco now about to repeat under equally bizarre circumstances? The immediate aftermath for the Cubans would fortunately prove less toxic than might have been expected. Despaigne and Mendoza reported promptly to their respective Asian clubs despite their own nagging minor injuries and the Japanese authorities seemed willing to let the issue drop, at least temporarily.

The Gourriel saga would soon hold another rather interesting and unexpected ramification. Overnight the story broke in Miami that Gourriel was, in fact, on his way to the Yankees, and that the Japanese contract fiasco was somehow all part of a carefully orchestrated plan to land a far bigger contract with the Americans. The Spanish-language *Miami Nuevo Herald* not only broke the story online but even reported confirmation from a top Havana official, none other than longtime commissioner Higinio Vélez himself. The spur again had been Gourriel's televised comments about his love for the Yankees, sound bites obviously taken out of context, but enough to anchor hopes for the always-blooming Miami anti-Castro fantasies. The story was, from the first, rather absurd on its face. No big-league club was free to negotiate with Cuban athletes under MLB's own existing procedures. And any such agreement under the watch of Higinio Vélez also defied logic. The whole affair once again reflected journalistic tactics that were prevalent in Miami. This time MLB would even be goaded into a formal response, which came from public relations officer John Blundell, who informed the *Nuevo Herald* by email that all such circulating reports were wild rumors and nothing more.[23]

If the Gourriel affair indicated anything, it seemed to underscore the pitfalls now surrounding the Cuban Federation's hopes for a viable long-term solution in Japan. The biggest flaw perhaps was INDER's rather unrealistic expectations of having its stars perform year-round at the highest levels without a single respite from taxing game action. Gourriel's injury was the first signal of the difficulties imbedded in such a scheme. MLB clubs would never allow such an arrangement, and that was the main stumbling block to any arrangement with the big-league teams. In today's baseball universe, where lengthy long-distance air travel and myriad night games—to say nothing of more serious off-season conditioning—take such a toll, the era in which players performed from January through December is simply no longer a viable possibility. Today's salary structures have also eliminated a world in which twelve-month ball playing was an athlete's only means of financial survival. It is perhaps here that Cuba is most out of step with baseball realities that have left its own system on the outside looking in.

In the end the Japanese plan is likely to be, at best, a short-term solution for a Cuban League that is still facing numerous challenges. Star players have continued to defect in larger numbers than ever since the project was launched in September 2013 (see appendix 2), and there doesn't seem to be any immediate end to the bleeding of talent. Explanation for the player drain doesn't any longer seem quite so easily reduced to a mere issue of money. Playing conditions, fan enthusiasms, and ballplayer morale have now sunk to all-time lows. It has become increasingly obvious on the streets of Havana that the national team heroes are no longer the island's biggest news, or even its biggest stars. The sustaining dream seems to have radically shifted for athletes and fans alike to the luxuries and celebrity attached to careers offered only in the North American big leagues.

More than ever before, publicized successes and sensational contracts nabbed by defectors—daily fodder still ignored by the Cuban press but spreading like wildfire across a highly effective Cuban grapevine—were occupying fans in the streets of Havana during my most recent visits. And if there was any doubt remaining about this new reality, it was erased when Gourriel's contract plight in Japan and the associated rumors of his imminent flight to the Yankees were suddenly more popular "hot corner" topics than the current Cuban League finals between Isla de la Juventud and Ciego de Avila—a gripping series matching perennial underdogs that under other circumstances might have provided the best Havana storyline in years. That dramatic shift in fan priorities now seems to be just as evident in the streets of Havana as it obviously is on the "Little Havana" street corners in Miami.

Gourriel remained in the headlines as this book went to press in mid-August. His ongoing saga is likely to take more than one additional twist or turn before this volume finally appears in print. The latest bulletin had to do with the reversal of an earlier rumored decision to request legal exit from Cuba with the clear intention of pursuing a coveted big-league career. This was a much-cherished fantasy among Miami exiles. Now, on the eve of a new National Series set to open in late August, Gourriel was reportedly rejoining the Industriales roster. At age thirty-one, Cuba's biggest star would remain on home soil.

There was also a constant stream of rumors circulating among Cuba sports bloggers and across social media that a November meeting in Havana was now to be anticipated (had in fact secretly been agreed to) between top MLB officials and INDER authorities. One theory was that such historic talks would focus on MLB's repeatedly stated desire to stage spring-training exhibitions in Havana's Latin American Stadium, perhaps as early as next March. A more fantasy-laced version of these reports suggested that Yulieski Gourriel's return to the Industriales club had all been a thinly veiled ploy designed to set the stage and open the door for a far more significant announcement—that the Havana slugger would be released in November to become the first Cuban League player cleared for legal transfer to a big-league ball club. Only time will tell, of course. Such rumors have long since become a regular part of the landscape in both Havana and Miami. If anything is certain it is only that change will inevitably have to come. And when it does arrive somewhere down the road, it is also a reasonable bet that the Cubans themselves will have the ultimate say in just how it all plays out.

9

THE UNSUSTAINABLE DREAM

Why, sometimes I've believed as many as six impossible things before breakfast.—The White Queen to Alice, *Alice in Wonderland*

Winds of change may well be blowing, but so far they remain little more than a tepid spring breeze. A full decade after legendary Cuban strongman Fidel Castro was finally felled by illness and forced to cede power to his octogenarian brother Raúl, Cuba remains a festering thorn in the side of Washington policy makers. It also lingers as a persistent nightmare for the shrinking Miami phalanx of Old Guard Cuban exiles. There seemed little hope for any significant thaw in the half-century-old cold war between an American behemoth and its pesky communist neighbor that has managed for decades to dominate Western Hemisphere political and economic realities while fostering what one scholar has labeled "America's internalized allergic reaction to Cuban socialism."[1] In the wake of the fiftieth anniversary of the Cuban Revolution (celebrated on the eve of Barack Obama's 2009 inauguration as America's first black president), the two countries appeared as firmly as ever trapped in a cycle of mutual hostility. This cycle displayed few signs of resolution, no matter what steps a post-Fidel Cuban government might be making toward gradual, if ultimately significant and radical, overhauls of its state-controlled economic and political machinery.

That little had so far materialized from flickering hopes for a revamped Cuban policy under a more liberal Obama administration was not itself all that surprising. The US government's position has long remained chiseled in granite under eleven different presidents of varying political stripes. There would be no change as long as any member of the Castro clan remained in power. The prime requisite for any détente, from Washington's rigid perspective, was still what was euphemistically known as "the biological solution"—the death of Fidel Castro—and perhaps other long-cherished contingencies as well, like American-style "democratic" elections, a US-model two-party system, prospects for immediate return to lucrative full-scale American corporate business investments, and perhaps even total financial reparations for all those Cuban Americans still fostering dreams of reclaiming their lost homeland. From a Washington perspective it has always remained the same fixed mantra—do it our way or stay off the highway.

What was surprising—even somewhat shocking—was the rapidity with which the Obama administration would suddenly reverse field concerning Cuba on the eve of the "lame duck" American president's final twenty-four months in office. Obama's earthshaking, unanticipated Rose Garden announcement of December 17, 2014, was, after all, fulfillment of a seismic policy shift that think-tank scholar Daniel P. Erikson had envisioned only a handful of years earlier when he wrote that given the history of US recalcitrance regarding Fidel Castro, "any attempt to change course and seek a rapprochement with Cuba will be the equivalent of making a train jump off the tracks."[2]

Erikson had not been far off the mark with his 2008 speculations. The sudden shift in course did indeed have a front-page impact usually reserved for catastrophic natural disasters or acts of savage international terrorism. The story broke with the impact of a political bombshell on the eve of normally news-light Christmas-season festivities.[3] President Obama was remarkably enough confronting the recalcitrant Miami Cuban lobby and on his own initiative (Congress be damned) reopening long-frozen dialogue with a still much-maligned and distrusted Cuban government, now in the hands of Fidel's only slightly more pragmatic brother Raúl. For the most part, the reactions north of Miami bordered on pure euphoria. America's two-generation-plus hard-line stance on Cuba had admittedly lost popular support from most Americans over at least the past decade. Washington's decision to finally abandon fifty-four years of failed policy directed unsuccessfully at sabotaging an evil-empire Castro-led Cuban government was celebrated just about everywhere outside of a rapidly aging and still-embittered exile community in Miami. And it was big-enough news to sweep any latest round of global terrorist threats occurring in Afghanistan, Palestine, Syria, or Yemen off the front pages and out of the prime-time reports of every US media outlet.

Yet for most Americans the breaking news simply meant increased prospects for unimpeded travel to a long-forbidden yet compellingly mysterious land lurking ninety miles off the Florida coast and beckoning with its Siren call of rum, cigars, sensuous women, pristine beaches, intoxicating musical rhythms—and, of course, baseball. Many started mentally packing for the long-fantasized trip before the ink was even dry on the evening headlines.

My own personal email box and public Cuban baseball–oriented Facebook page were immediately lit up with Cuba travel inquiries. "When can we see Cuban baseball in the quaint ballparks of Havana or Cienfuegos or Matanzas?" "Is the league still in progress in January and how do I book a ticket to Havana before the final pitch of the winter season?" "Is the spectacle really as wonderful as you have been describing it in your Internet writings?" "Are Cuban ballparks actually a true time-warp trip recalling the minor-league parks of decades past?"

Such were the questions I was suddenly fielding like so many hot infield bouncers. If Cuba meant anything to most Americans, it seemingly meant a much-coveted travel destination—a beckoning paradise perhaps so magnetic for so many simply because it had been long denied to Americans by their own somewhat hypocritical "freedom-trumpeting" government. For two decades envious friends had been confiding that they too longed to catch a firsthand glimpse of Cuba and its brash experiment in socialist living before it went the way of the dinosaur.

Overnight Cuba was back in the news, back on everyone's lips, and perhaps for the first time in decades actually within physical reach of the mobile American public. If not quite yet a tangible reality, the island nation of Castro, salsa, cigars, and baseball was coalescing as something a bit more solid than a mere mythical presence. In truth hordes of Americans had been skirting embargo restrictions and voyaging either legally or illegally to Cuba for years, and of late doing so in increasing numbers—perhaps as many as 950,000 in the past twelve months.[4] But this announcement, dropped out of the blue, seemed suddenly to promise a true sea change of possibilities—for expansive tourism, for unfettered American business investment, for perhaps finally scuttling the odious reign of those arch-enemy Castro brothers, and for American baseball.

A sports-crazy American nation of rabid baseball fans had been recently intrigued by the rags-to-riches tales of Cuban imports like Yasiel Puig, José Dariel Abreu, Yoenis Céspedes, and the rumored phenom Yoan Moncada swinging such heavy bats and demanding multimillion-dollar paychecks. Now here was a breakthrough allowing major-league baseball—the official custodian of the sanctioned American national pastime—to ravenously harvest much of Cuba's seemingly endless supply of diamond talent just as it had so long been harvesting talented ballplayers from the Dominican Republic, Venezuela, and sometimes even from Japan, Korea, and Taiwan. Wasn't this now a clear signal that Cuba—the long off-limits home to the sport's top-ranked international powerhouse squads—would at last begin to "play ball" with the bosses of organized North American professional baseball? The speculations flew wildly—this was an immediate "game-changer" in the view of one quoted former player agent.[5] Seemingly every major print and electronic news outlet raced to speculate on these apparent new and welcomed guarantees of a virtual Cuban-talent windfall coming soon to a big-league ballpark near you. It was heady stuff, long awaited by both casual and fanatic American ball fans alike—and unfortunately all of it was a bit premature.

How, then, had it all come about, so suddenly and so unexpectedly? There was an important backstory buried behind the enthusiasm of the headlines. The Obama announcement was accompanied by the somewhat surprising news that American political prisoner Alan Phillip Gross was to be immediately freed on humanitarian grounds by relenting Cuban authorities, who had been holding him for five years on serious espionage charges. A USAID subcontractor, Gross had been arrested (back in December 2009) and subsequently convicted of illegally transporting (without the required Cuban license) satellite phones and computer equipment to members of Cuba's Jewish community. The American press painted a picture of an innocent victim of Cuban hard-line repression; the Cubans claimed Gross was openly working for American intelligence agencies and plotting to aid a group overtly bent on government overthrow. Three-plus years into a fifteen-year prison term, Gross was reportedly now in declining health, and a number of American political figures (Jesse Jackson and several congressmen among them) had lately traveled to Havana to lobby for his release.[6] The *New York Times* issued renewed calls for some kind of exchange only weeks before Obama's steps toward détente.

If the Americans (especially the anti-Castro Miami contingent) wanted to secure Alan Gross's freedom, the Cubans had their own long-standing crusade to resolve. This involved the much-ballyhooed Cuban Five, who had long been a celebrated cause stoked at home by the Castro regime. In the United States these men were viewed—much like Gross in Cuba—as evil foreign agents and a threat to American security. But there was a distinct difference, despite the belated 2001 admission in Havana that the group had indeed consisted of undercover agents. They were spying on what Cuba considered the South Florida "exile Miami mafia" (an organization behind several bomb plots on the island) and not directly on the US government. Three had earlier been released after decade-long Miami prison terms. In the end a deal had been quietly struck and Gross (along with an unnamed American agent held in Havana) was being swapped for the remaining three members of the Cuban Five. An exchange was unceremoniously made on the morning of Obama's December 17 announcement, and both sides simultaneously scored a long-awaited political victory.

But if there were pragmatic prisoner exchanges underpinning the December announcement, there also seemed to be much more motivating both sides in seeking a workable dialogue. A tipping point had perhaps finally been reached. Obama was seeking some elements of true legacy at the end of a stormy eight-year presidency more tarnished than propped up by battles over health-care reform, border security, and bungled executions of the endless war on terrorism. The Castro government was seeking to improve its own downward economic spiral and recognized that an end to the US embargo was the key element. It was time for a strong renewed overture from Raúl Castro, who was approaching the home stretch in his own tenure. As chapter 3 of this volume discusses, this was not the first overture from the Castro regime—there had been many others over the years from Fidel himself, most of them never reported to the American public.[7] But this was perhaps the best timed. It was certainly the biggest news to rattle entrenched conservatives in Miami's Little Havana since a recent ballyhooed, if more casual, ceremonial December 2013 Raúl-Barack handshake at the funeral of Nelson Mandela.

Obama's plan announced—or at least hinted at—some seemingly major changes in travel and trade restrictions—the definition of cultural exchanges was broadening and commerce opportunities for American firms might not any longer be entirely banned. What was in the offing was not at all a sanction of open tourism, but rather a rolling back of restrictions for Cuban-American families wishing to pay annual visits to families, and also for scholars or journalists aiming to do research or file reports from within Cuba. In essence we would return to pre-2003, when the Bush administration had tightened requirements for most sanctioned travel.

Of course the 1996 Helms-Burton legislation was not yet going away, and with a Republican-controlled Congress invading Washington in the spring, there was not a lot of room for optimism that trade embargo policies would actually be lifted while Obama was still in the White House. When specific changes were spelled out in January, they didn't quite measure up to most of the December hype. In reality the Obama policy changes on Cuba were minimal and largely cosmetic. The largest substantive move would be the reestablishment of a formal US embassy presence in Havana.[8] There was at the very least an emerging dialogue between the rivals, and that was certainly healthy. But if there was any heightened optimism that a new era had actually arrived, that optimism was quickly proving excessive, if not entirely misplaced.

Developments of December 2014 and the Obama initiative to ease relations also led overnight to a resulting flurry of highly optimistic assumptions about new certainties for MLB's immediate inroads into long-forbidden Cuban territory. Everyone was quickly conjuring up long-repressed visions of MLB scouts racing down to Havana, Dominican-style academies being hastily constructed all across Cuba in perhaps a matter of months, and an immediate spate of new legal signings, with a resulting flood of Cuban stars into the majors. It would quickly turn out to be far more familiar fantasy than any revamped reality.

For many Cuba baseball watchers in the media, who often seemed as much in the business of making news as reporting it, this was simply too good a fantasy to pass up. Stories about immediate change looming on the horizon were flooding the sporting press as well as the mainstream political press, renewing a favored mantra about possibilities of USA-Cuba baseball diplomacy.

Ben Badler, a self-styled Cuban baseball expert, was in the forefront of such optimism. Badler had recently been making a habit of reporting on the Cuban game for *Baseball America* and had emerged as that magazine's reigning authority on the topic. He rushed into print his sophisticated new amateur talent rankings, detailing scouting-book strengths and weaknesses for Cuban prospects that might now be falling in the scope of MLB talent hunters and armchair fantasy baseball geeks. He also elaborated in one overview piece on details of what it was actually like to watch Cuban baseball and explained precise "ins and outs" of the Cuban game (the batting strategies, pitching weaknesses, and stadium ambience).[9] It all rang a bit hollow, since there was no accompanying evidence that Ben Badler had actually witnessed any live games in Cuba (versus catching them occasionally on Internet television). His credibility took a further hit when Badler failed to show up to watch the Cuban club playing at the latest edition of the Caribbean Series in nearby San Juan.

Writers like Badler were not known for doing their homework. Often their bold pronouncements reveal sparse firsthand knowledge of the actual contemporary Cuban scene. And now the pattern was only being ramped up a notch. A better understanding or deeper familiarity might provide more balanced assessments of pitfalls that might lie ahead. One indication of the perception gap came during the Caribbean Series staged in San Juan in early February. When two Cubans (young pitcher Vladimir Gutiérrez and veteran shortstop Dainer Moreira) walked away from the team hotel during the third day of action, ESPN rushed a crew to the scene to exploit the breaking story for an upcoming edition of *Outside the Lines* with longtime anchor Bob Ley. Reporter Tom Farrey was able to land a hoped-for press box interview with the newly appointed Cuban baseball commissioner Heriberto Suarez Perera.[10] Farrey pressed the novice commissioner for pointed responses to the latest round of disturbing defections and also for his take on exploding rumors surrounding possibilities for new business dealings with MLB. Suarez's responses slammed the door on any premature optimism and indicated just how little anything had really changed on the Cuban side of the equation.

When asked about the recent defectors, Suarez provided an all-too-familiar party line that reflected decades of similar responses: "They have abandoned the battle and we simply don't talk about them, don't even mention their names."[11] The Cuban press might have been relaxing its hard-line stance in recent years, but the official INDER baseball spokesmen were not. Comments offered by the commissioner regarding intercourse with the North American big leagues were carefully crafted and more telling still. When prompted by Farrey about possible business deals with MLB, Suarez was especially concise on that issue: "We build our own academies and train our athletes for the glory of the country. We are very patriotic. . . . But if training is in Cuba, of course we will be the ones in control."

Obviously Cuba would stick religiously to its long-standing assumptions about owning its own national sport and its own baseball resources. Any novel revamped plan that was based upon MLB's economic dominance, with little offered in return, was simply off the table. Cuban officials (INDER officials or Communist Party leaders) obviously would in no way be interested in any "globalization" of Cuba that left MLB totally in control, or even ceded any partial claim to ownership of Cuban baseball and its coveted resources. The impasse seems as thorough and the gulf as wide as ever before.

Whether the subject is tourism or baseball prospects, American journalists have maintained a tendency to view USA-Cuba relations as if they were a narrow one-way street. On the tourist front, there has long been a belief that as soon as the embargo laws went away Havana would almost overnight revert to the Caribbean pleasure palace and preferred vacation destination it was during the final opulent pre-Castro years. Nothing could be further from the truth. Cuba may well have replaced fading sugar and tobacco markets with a fledgling tourism industry, but the awkward reality is that Cuban tourism infrastructure is already overtaxed and stretched nearly to the breaking point. If the embargo and the accompanying travel restrictions imposed on Americans by Washington were dropped tomorrow, there would be little immediate change in the offing. Havana hotels would not be prepared for any immediate upsurge in business. Havana's Jose Marti International Airport (third world by any standard, despite the single cramped new terminal hastily erected with Canadian dollars just in time for Pope John Paul II's historic 1998 visit) could not be retrofitted overnight for a surge in commercial flights from Miami, Los Angeles, and New York. Building the necessary Cuban infrastructure on which wide-open US tourism depends constitutes an arduous project to be measured in many years—perhaps several decades—and certainly not in months or weeks.

The Cuban side of the story is rarely given even passing consideration, let alone balanced or accurate reporting. This is especially true regarding the tourism elements of the equation. It is true enough that tourist dollars have now become Cuba's essential survival mechanism. The country lives almost exclusively off free-spending visitors who arrive regularly from Europe and Canada. But Cuba is not resort-filled Jamaica, and Old

Havana is only a slightly more dingy version of spiffy Old San Juan. Decades of American embargo restrictions and Cuba's own internal mismanagement have left the nation's economy and infrastructure in near-total shambles. Cuba is not ready for any overnight facelift and the raw truth of the matter is that Cuba simply cannot fling open welcoming doors to any massive influx of anticipated American tourists.[12] There simply is no additional hotel space to be had in dilapidated Havana, and there will not likely be any for some time to come.

Easing of Cuban travel as it is now prescribed in Washington will only continue a trend that has been ballooning for some time. Americans in increasing numbers now visit Cuba each year for thinly veiled tourism under the relaxed rubric of humanitarian missions or educational exchanges. More American visitors sneaking through the embargo has simply meant spiraling requests for scarce hotel rooms and therefore spiraling prices attached to available Havana lodging. American-style capitalism, with its inherent principles of marketplace value hinged on consumer demand, is already creeping steadily onto Cuba's socialist doorstep. But an open avenue to the island is not likely to unleash any immediate surge of ugly American tourists onto the streets of Old Havana any more than it is likely to refill big-league dugouts with dozens of new showcase José Abreus, Aroldis Chapmans, and Yasiel Puigs.

* * *

All misconceptions concerning any immediate boosts in potential tourist trade or corporate commerce aside, the reigning misunderstandings surrounding Cuban baseball have quickly proven even more tenacious and intractable. Far too many journalists have been viewing the purported American "national pastime" only through rosy MLB-tinted blinders. An overarching MLB mentality regarding the existing baseball universe and the jingoistic American prerogatives attached to that universe have apparently been firmly entrenched in the American psyche.

Our assumptions as fans remain simple and unchallenged, just the way we like them. Cuba is an enticing wellspring of awe-inspiring big league–level talent. Cuban ballplayers, like athletes the world over, deserve unbridled freedom to cash in on God-given ability, and to do so at any level the international market might bear. American-style big-league baseball is the only game in town, after all, and filling MLB rosters to the maximum degree seems a logical imperative. Should we be at all concerned about long-term health for baseball in other lands that have co-

opted what we claim as our own national sport? Should we trouble our-
selves one iota about MLB reducing its current "globalization" practices
to just another misguided form of ugly Yankee imperialism? Those are
questions perhaps a bit too complex or uncomfortable to tackle when all
we wish to do is "root, root, root for the home team." It is never easy to
see matters from the other side of the fence.

The reality remains that Cuba cannot simply be willed into turning
itself into another version of the Dominican Republic—another ripe-for-
exploitation base of operations housing MLB academies designed to
strip-mine the tropical landscape of all its invaluable baseball resources.
A thriving national sport is far too important to Cubans for the Castro
government to hand it over "lock, stock, and batting cages" and without a
substantial struggle. As today's richest remaining domestic resource,
baseball stands at the very crux of Cuba's six-decade resistance to all
returning vestiges of US capitalist manipulation. Baseball remains a last-
standing source of Cuban national pride and Cuban national identity.

Cuban authorities understand the full impact of decades of MLB inroads into neighboring Caribbean countries. They have watched the Do-

**Team Cuba celebrates a surprise championship at the 2015 Caribbean Series in
San Juan, Puerto Rico. Courtesy of Peter C. Bjarkman.**

minican Republic and Venezuelan and especially Puerto Rican winter leagues fade to mere shadows of what they were in their heyday, when top-flight native big leaguers returned each winter season not merely to hone rusty batting swings or tune lame arms, but to entertain local fans and stimulate local pride in a homegrown game played by homegrown stars. They have watched those neighboring countries across the past three or four decades relinquish their native baseball resources in a fashion that now eerily mirrors the very manner in which big-league "farm system" policies were already sucking local control out of the fifties-era Cuban winter leagues at the time of Fidel Castro's sudden rise to power.[13]

In brief, baseball is far too ingrained in Cuban society and far too important an instrument for building both domestic societal cohesion and an effective foreign policy propaganda machine to now be abandoned by a socialist regime struggling for survival and for continued popular legitimacy. The handwriting nonetheless seems clearly enough plastered on the wall. Cuba must somehow modify its baseball to accommodate encroaching realities, just as it must begrudgingly overhaul its sagging model of state-controlled and centralized national economy.

On the baseball front we might anticipate a Japanese-style posting system similar to one already hinted at in the previous chapter. The Cubans already claim warm relations with Japanese professional baseball (Omar Linares finished his career there in 2002–4) and they have already demonstrated an appreciation of certain advantages offered by unique Asian approaches to an inherently North American and Caribbean sport. In recent decades the Cubans have both adopted and adapted many of Japan's on-field strategies and tactics (the effective style of "small ball" that seems key to success in international tournament play) as their own. The sacrifice bunt, as one example, is now a staple Cuban League offensive weapon. The next logical step might be wholesale adoption of a Japanese-style business model honed for survival in an increasingly MLB-centric baseball universe.

The "posting system" that has warded off MLB intrusions into Japan requires some further elaboration here.[14] It is a practical business accord that has remained far off the radar for the bulk of American fans who pay limited, if any, attention to the Asian game. It is also the mutually arranged pact now existing between NPB (Nippon Professional Baseball) and MLB that has allowed over the past seventeen seasons only a minor trickle of top Japanese stars such as Ichiro, Hideki Matsui, and Daisuke

Matsuzaka to reach US shores. And it is a system that now works fully to the benefit of the Japanese and less so to the interests of American big-league clubs. It is not an exaggeration to view this system as being the very salvation of contemporary Japanese baseball.

Japan's unique posting system came about in December 1998 as direct fallout from the celebrated case of Hideo Nomo, star pitcher for the Osaka-based Kintetsu Buffaloes of the Japanese Pacific League, who had escaped his NPB contract on a clever technicality three years earlier. The agreement as it was worked out between NPB and MLB front offices was part and parcel of a last-ditch effort to salvage deteriorating relations between the two leagues that had begun with the saga of a first Japanese big-league import back in 1964. Initial accords had held up across the sixties, seventies, eighties, and nineties, but had unraveled with the case of Nomo and a new fix was desperately needed.

The first Japanese player to test MLB waters was a diminutive south-paw hurler named Masanori Murakami (known popularly as Mashi), who enjoyed a brief and largely undistinguished career with the San Francisco Giants in the mid-1960s. A noteworthy late-season bullpen call-up in 1964 (1.80 ERA in nine relief appearances), Murakami lasted one additional campaign (where he saved nine games and won four of five decisions) before retreating to the obscurity of the Japanese Pacific League under a considerable cloud of diplomatic controversy.

Mashi's off-the-field saga was indeed much more important than his brief fifty-four-game sojourn in the National League. Lent to the Giants by the Nankai Hawks under an odd contractual arrangement that the Japanese ball club apparently didn't quite understand, Murakami had surprisingly opted to honor his new big-league contract and remain in the United States after his unexpected 1964 cup of coffee. Nankai had sent him to America for some additional pro seasoning under a novel "friendly agreement" with the San Francisco club, but never assumed their prospect might actually make the big time and thus be retained by the National Leaguers (as the fine points of his contract allowed). What followed was two years of heated tensions that not only threatened NPB-MLB relations, but ruffled US-Japanese political relations as well. Mashi was first pressured by his despairing father (he was an only son) during an off-season visit home to remain with the Nankai club, but Giants owner Horace Stoneham, backed by MLB commissioner Ford Frick, intervened and eventually prevailed in forcing Murakami back to San Francisco for the 1965 campaign.

The issue loomed vital to MLB team owners, since they saw the Nankai club's failure to honor the loaned player's MLB contract as a threat to the time-honored major-league reserve clause. A dangerous precedent might be set here, since if the Japanese player skirted the rules and failed to abide by his deal with the team holding his rights, then this might actually open the door for American big leaguers to do the same. Eventually Japanese League commissioner Yushi Uchimura came up with a compromise plan (Mashi would indeed play for the Giants in 1965, but then be free to return home) that was accepted by Stoneham and Frick, and order between the warring leagues was finally restored.

Peace seemed to hold for nearly three decades, until Nomo decided to test the waters. For four decades there had been only a couple of ways Japanese players could leave home for the majors. They could be granted an outright release, or they could complete the nine-year service term required by their NPB contracts. Nomo found a loophole in this system and, with the aid and encouragement of his renegade Japanese-American agent Don Nomura, fully exploited it. Only a five-year veteran, Nomo surprisingly announced his retirement, which, according to Nomura's careful reading of standard player contracts, left him free to entertain big-league offers. It appeared that loose wording in those contracts adopted by NPB decades earlier blocked signing with other Japanese clubs (but not foreign clubs) in possible cases of voluntary early retirement. When an independent arbitrator eventually ruled in Nomo's (and MLB's) favor, the voluntary retirement escape ploy became infamously and widely known as the "Nomo clause."

In winning his case and jumping to the Los Angeles Dodgers, Hideo Nomo would become Japan's first baseball defector. Nomo would be initially labeled in the Japanese press as an ingrate, troublemaker, and even traitor. But the negative tune quickly changed when "Nomomania" set in during the 1995 National League season and the first true Japanese big-league star suddenly captured his nation's imagination as a vital emblem of national pride. Tensions were once again near the breaking point between NPB and MLB for several more years as Alfonso Soriano (a young Dominican recruit playing for the Hiroshima Carp) and Hideki Irabu (fastballing pitcher for the Lotte Marines) also escaped Japan for lucrative big-league deals (both with the Yankees). It was Soriano's odd

case (he earned freedom via the technicality of an illegal underage signing) that finally broke the back of the 1967 post-Murakami "working
agreement" with MLB (ironically despite the fact that Soriano was not
Japanese). The posting system, however, would finally put a permanent
end to the NPB talent drain, since it outlawed the "Nomo clause" and
effectively ended NPB defections.

Under the December 1998 arrangement, big-league clubs were now
allowed to bid on NPB players whose Japanese clubs opted to put them
up for auction in advance of the required nine-year service period. Some
NPB clubs might desire to do this when the promised harvest of MLB
dollars might outweigh the option of forcibly retaining a player whose
eyes and heart were already set on the American leagues. Such postings
of freed players would occur during the November–March off-season and
MLB teams would have four days to enter sealed bids with the MLB
commissioner. A bid represented the amount to be paid to the Japanese
club if the player actually signed with his MLB suitor.

The difference between Nomo and his more recent Cuba counterparts
was rather large and the term "defector" never got used much in Nomo's
case. The Japanese player might abandon his league affiliations and in
some eyes sabotage his native baseball institutions, but he would never
have to abandon his native country. There was no required third-country
residence here, no official government branding, no banned return to
family and the lost homeland. And there were no published fantasies in
American press accounts about athletes rebelling against the Japanese
political system. Japanese players turning their backs on homeland teams
were admittedly seeking better competition for their ball-playing skills
and upgrades in pay scale, but they were not escaping reported "slave-
labor status" or bolting from communist oppression in noble search of the
American Dream.

American press treatments of players fleeing Japan and Cuba also
offer a most interesting contrast. Robert Whiting suggests, but then
quickly dismisses, a notion that there may have been pressures on MLB
in the wake of the 1965 Murakami case to back off recruiting plans in
Japan for the sake of preserving healthy relations between the two countries. It is hinted there might have been a de facto ban on recruiting NPB
stars in the form of US government pressure spurred by a fear from
Japanese leaders that Americans would soon hijack their sacred game.
Japan was needed to support American foreign policy and shore up

American defense interests across Asia.[15] Yet with Cuba it has always been the reverse. Incursions by MLB into Cuban baseball are most often championed by the US media (if not quietly cheered in Washington) as part of the ongoing campaign to bring down a hated Castro regime repeatedly charged with sponsoring international terrorism and threatening American Western Hemisphere hegemony.

The Japanese posting system has been an uncomfortable arrangement for MLB and there have been occasional issues raised by big-league bosses about its legality. Many would see it as violating US antitrust law, and cries have been heard about infringing on human rights by blocking athletes from cutting their own best deals. The same cry is now echoed in support of Cubans seeking to defect to big-league clubs. So far the Japan accord has not been legally tested, perhaps largely because MLB owners likely don't want to push relations with a vibrant Japanese League to the near-breaking point. There are potential future markets envisioned for MLB in Asia's top baseball hotbed that might be jeopardized with any strong anti-NPB stance potentially alienating the masses of Japanese baseball fans.

The system is also one that works against both the players and the agents riding on their coattails; big-league suitors have to pay twice (dishing out both the player contract and the posting fee) to land a prized NPB star. But the Japanese players have not raised much of a fuss either. There are not that many Nippon stars clamoring to leave home; while MLB contracts are heftier, the salary gap is not today what it was a quarter-century back. The required lifestyle transition is also far greater for Japanese players, both in cultural and baseball terms, than it is for Latin-bred athletes. The game is played far differently in Japan than it is in Caracas or Havana, and there are large welcoming Spanish-speaking communities in most US cities. Japanese players are also not exactly suffering at home economically.

It remains to be seen what version of the Japan model Cuban authorities might opt to institute. Will it perhaps involve forming contracts with players that require a certain service (say nine years) before free agency? Or will the Cubans be willing, like the Japanese, to make a few players each year available for sale to high-bidding MLB ball clubs? Either approach will limit the current bleeding by restricting the number of yearly departures to a bare minimum. In taking either route, however, Cuba will have to give up any remaining dreams of seeing its players, once sold off to MLB, regularly returning for any domestic-league winter service. As seen in the previous chapter, requiring double duty (perhaps 200 or more games a year) from Cuban stars hasn't worked well under the current Japanese player exchange (for either Cuban authorities or Japanese ownership) and would be totally off the radar for big-league clubs.

Any accord with MLB that involves a posting plan will almost certainly once again raise issues in MLB quarters concerning legalities. The argument will likely be made about antitrust violations and unfair restraints on players' rights to free agency. The MLBPA (players union) can be expected to weigh in on these issues. But if MLB is to seek any progress with Cuba under new diplomatic accords now on the horizon, its hands may be effectively tied on all these issues. Owners will not likely wave the antitrust campaign banner too visibly in light of the sport's own jealously guarded and controversial antitrust status. And Washington is likely to come down heavily on any MLB actions that might threaten efforts at compromise with the Cubans as part of the new détente arrangements.

The issue of free agency for Cuban players is not one likely to raise much hue and cry from big-league owners for yet another rather transparent reason. Such protests run against the grain of the owners' own long history of economic player al uses and thus raise specters of possible renewed antitrust debates (now focused on issues of franchise relocations, since the reserve clause has vanished) that owners don't want back on center stage. Through much of the game's history MLB owners fought free agency tooth and nail while hiding behind privileged antitrust status of their own (exemptions from Sherman Act antitrust legislation preventing price-fixing in interstate commerce) underpinning an infamous reserve clause condition that kept ballplayers permanently bound to a single club. MLB owners became champions of free agency only once it was forced down their throats by an arbitrator in the mid-1970s and they were left with no other option.

In the wake of 1975 arbitration cases involving Andy Messersmith and Dave McNally, owners (at least the wealthiest, like George Steinbrenner and a few others commanding major media markets) stumbled on some unexpected advantages. Rampant free agency could be used by the richest clubs to horde the best players and parlay their own economic advantages into yet further windfalls. Mark Armour and Daniel Levitt (*In*

Pursuit of Pennants) recently examined this development as a prime example of one of the true tipping points of big-league history. [16]

We find an eerie and telling parallel in Japanese professional baseball. Long anathema to NPB club owners (mostly corporations relying on the sport as an advertising crutch), free agency came about for the Nippon leagues in 1993 under parallel, if somewhat divergent, circumstances. Here it was not the ballplayers (or a players union) that forced it into reality, but rather all-powerful Yomiuri Giants owner Tsuneo Watanabe. Faced with ebbing TV ratings brought on by his proud club's sagging performance, as well as the sudden popularity of a new pro soccer league, the all-powerful mogul, easily able to manipulate other NPB owners, hit upon a scheme that would allow him almost exclusively to stuff his Giants roster and thus rebuild the club's waning popularity. Controlling unlimited financial resources, Watanabe could easily corral top players who were interested both in improving their financial lot and also enhancing their personal profiles by playing with NPB's historically beloved team. Free agency meant wholesale star player–hoarding by the league's richest ball club and thus made Watanabe the single biggest winner.

Free agency becomes a rallying cry for club owners only when they realize it is a key to quick profits. It is easy enough to want players to choose their own destinations if one knows he holds all the top economic resources and thus can attract talent by simply outbidding any competitor. It is for this reason alone that MLB clubs and the MLB commissioner's office now trumpet the message of free-market rights for Cuban stars. The talent flow can only move in one direction and the cards are all stacked for big-league clubs. Should some hypothetical rival suddenly offer better deals (now an unlikely scenario, but once seen with Jorge Pasquel's Mexican League uprising in 1945) the popular MLB tune would alter radically.

Any open-arms policy now extended to Cuban athletes has always been all about strategies to improve big-league profits and the financial health of major-league franchises. All the lip service paid to the notion of Cuban players deserving inalienable rights to exercise personal freedom in the choice of their employer rings hollow against the lengthy history of stances taken by big-league club owners themselves regarding the free agency rights of players on their own rosters. For a full century big-league clubs held their own players in servitude (in the service of ball-club profits) with no possibility of true free agency and no ability to sell their services to the highest bidder (the very thing that MLB moguls now claim should be the privilege of Cuban players). If one is to argue that Cuban players have been slaves in service of the political agendas of Fidel Castro, one cannot do so without acknowledging that for decades during baseball's reputed golden age, big leaguers were mere slaves to the profit motives of Connie Mack, Branch Rickey, John McGraw, and legions of other American League and National League club owners.

Once big-league players finally hit on an avenue for overturning decades of economic abuse in the 1970s by forcing a modern free agent system upon MLB club ownership, the innovation was grudgingly accepted by the owners only if it might also require the players to serve out an initial contract obligation of six years. Free agency was thus something of a compromise allowing owners certain safeguards for protecting their investments in recruiting, signing, and training players in the first place. Quite obviously Cuba's own claims on its players result from similar desires to maintain control over athletes in which the government-run sports machinery has heavily invested.

If the Cubans were now suddenly to put in place some system requiring their players to honor contracts committing them to similar six-year commitments at home before the door to free agency and possible big-league contracts were to open, would this not be a case of the Cuban Baseball Federation requiring the same form of self-preservation tactics that MLB itself has long demanded for its own operations? To argue against the rights of Cuban baseball officials to protect their initial investment in ballplayers while at the same time requiring it for their own talent reserves would seem the height of disingenuousness on the part of big-league owners. But the world of corporate management operating in the realm of organized baseball has never been a business model noted for the highest level of ethical practice.

The history of the Japanese posting system can be rather easily oversimplified when reduced to its basics. Details might well vary in any agreement worked out with the Cuban authorities, and perhaps those need not trouble us here. The requirement of playing through a lengthy period of service keeps the top players at home. It maintains a vibrant league and lively fan interest surrounding established stars. But it does open the door for some players to test big-league baseball and, in the process, to demonstrate the high quality of the system that originally produced them. Even with the option of departure, many of the best domestic players opt to stay home, at least in Japan, where salaries are now (unlike back in the 1960s or 1970s) relatively high and the culture is familiar and comfortable. When a few do choose to leave, the league and its teams stand to reap huge financial benefits.

Such a change, if adopted in Havana, would greatly benefit the Cuban baseball establishment. It would solve most of the problems the Cuban League now faces. Certain leading figures in Cuba, like INDER vice president Tony Castro and national team manager Victor Mesa, both of whom have spoken publicly of their desire to work with MLB, don't always necessarily represent the voices of men wielding the true decision-making powers. The expressed views of some Cuban League spokesmen have also at times appeared somewhat naïve. Speaking in front of ESPN cameras in September 2013 (chapter 8), both Castro and Mesa voiced a shared and deeply felt view that it was the US embargo policy alone which had handcuffed Cuban baseball, that players shuttling back and forth between the Cuban League and the majors would provide the best of both worlds, and that they envisioned such changes to be lurking around the next corner. But it seemed at the time that neither truly understood the motives or plans of MLB officials plotting for a foothold on the Cuban baseball scene.

If a posting system emerges, it will solve two of Cuban baseball's biggest headaches. Players will still be developed at home in their own training centers and will serve the system for a reasonable period of time. They will not be kept forever, but the attrition will be far slower and league deterioration will be stemmed in the main. An improvement of sagging league competition and upgrading of playing conditions will itself increase the motivation for young players to ply their trade on their native island. Once players do leave, the government (and read here the national baseball administration and not just central government functionaries, as so often portrayed) will reap large financial payoffs. This, in turn, will likely improve player salaries at home, again stemming dissatisfaction.

If the scenario plays out along these lines, the biggest losers will be MLB and perhaps the next wave of top Cuban ballplayers themselves. Despite the headaches surrounding human-trafficking issues, MLB clubs have had it all their way of late. Without diplomatic relations there has been no need to respect Cuban law. If a star player (say Héctor Olivera) or even a top prospect (say Andy Ibáñez) departs from the island, he is

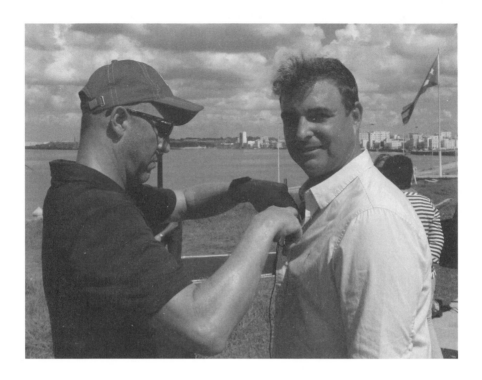

INDER vice president Antonio (Tony) Castro is interviewed by ESPN on the grounds of Havana's Hotel Nacional in September 2013. Courtesy of Peter C. Bjarkman.

fair free agent game, available for plucking by the highest bidder. And all these current free agent signings can also be conveniently cloaked in the American flag. Players breaking free from apparent unjust slavery are painted as lucky beneficiaries of American freedom and American democracy, and that is an easy message to sell to the sports-loving stateside public. Little attention is paid to hundreds who don't make the grade and are abandoned by the system. And few questions are ever asked about long-range implications of a current system that destroys one budding rival baseball universe after another for the instant gratification of a present generation of North American fans alone.

EPILOGUE

"The United States never remembers and Latin America never forgets" is a well-known Latin American aphorism. It succinctly explains the depth of Cuban distrust about the United States and the continuing surprise North Americans manifest about Cuban behavior.—Philip Brenner

In the end we are well served to revisit questions posed and issues raised in this volume's opening pages. What is the final or lasting impact of the "Cuban defector story" for both Cuban baseball (the apparent loser) and major league baseball (an apparent winner)? What is the downside, if any, to these heroic flights of refugee ballplayers escaping a decaying homeland in which they remain blocked from harvesting any deep financial rewards—even fair minimum wages—from their phenomenal ballplaying talents? Why aren't all the world's pro sports leagues governed by free-market principles identical to those being showcased here in the Land of the Free and Home of the Brave? And why should North American fans—prepared to shell out the hefty price of admission—not savor the world's best performers? In brief, is there any possible negative side to this much-publicized mad rush northward by underprivileged and overtalented Cuban baseball stars now fleeing Castro's dying communist camp? As true patriotic, flag-waving American baseball fans, shouldn't we all heartily cheer on a much-delayed happanstance that finally sinks the rickety Castro ship and upgrades our own beloved big-league spectacle?

Perhaps most central of all, if the dawn of player free agency and dismantling of the long-standing reserve clause in the mid-1970s truly launched American big-league baseball's apex era of financial health and competitive pennant races, then how can international free agency not be merely the next logical step in growing the sport as a true global phenomenon?

These are all intriguing and challenging questions, to be sure. For some—especially those among MLB's brain trust, or those cheering on MLB's market policies—perhaps these are also questions far more uncomfortable to ponder than they are difficult to answer.

Yes, the hefty long-term salary deals now being casually tossed at runaway Cubans may be spiraling far out of control, but won't the uninhibited free-market system eventually take care of that problem? It might be somewhat more troubling (especially to those who campaign for tightening our Mexican borders) that before ever setting foot on a big-league diamond some renegade Cuban Leaguers are now demanding windfall multimillion-dollar deals that far outstrip what is available to comparable or maybe even better homegrown prospects who have paid proper dues by working their way through our domestic collegiate ranks or minor-league systems. But then again hasn't American big-league baseball always been far more business than sport, and hasn't the game always come down to money issues in the end? And if hints or even broad evidence of illicit human trafficking lurk in the background, can such evils really be blamed on MLB bosses or their hordes of underlings, who so far have displayed no traceable evidence of any involvement in plotting, encouraging, or underwriting such tactics?

We might easily agree that human-trafficking issues are a huge negative and perhaps even represent the true elephant in the room. And the seemingly out-of-whack MLB salary structure remains a plague on the game's long-term economic health. But there do appear to be viable solutions that MLB is already pursuing. The prospect of a long-awaited USA-Cuba relations thaw may soon erase the smuggling issue. And some type of global drafting system for amateur free agents will likely soon enough abate most existing salary inequities. Given such prospects, it is hard for most fans to comprehend anyone casting aspersions on current forms of corporate baseball that lure the world's best players into the world's top leagues. And only supporters of rigid and repressive socialist sports enterprises might be expected to bemoan the dismantling of baseball structures in such rogue-nation outposts as communist Cuba—or even in the sport's struggling outlying colonies spread across the Dominican Republic, Korea, Taiwan, or Venezuela.

Nonetheless there are troubling issues surrounding today's one-way flow of baseball talent out of Cuba. We argue extensively in the preceding chapters that there are indeed identifiable downsides to this conundrum that our sports-crazed North American media outlets so far have displayed little enthusiasm for exposing, exhaustively analyzing, or even rigorously reporting. From a rarely touched alternative perspective, the current Cuba phenomenon threatens MLB on numerous counts just as much as it threatens Cuba itself. Plenty of potential for disaster can be found in MLB's historic program of baseball imperialism, a strategy that has long been the game's hidden calling card. Admittedly that problem is not often so easy to see, since it is effectively masked by the glow of MLB's current box-office successes. But there are foreboding signals on the horizon.

We might begin by asking if the state of Major League Baseball today—the front office business as well as the on-field spectacle—is truly all that healthy. After all, the sport is stagnating globally, especially when compared to the behemoth of world soccer, or an increasing worldwide popularity for pro basketball, or even the recent encroachments of NFL-style football into Mexico and parts of Europe. MLB, for all its exploding revenues (mainly from ubiquitous cable television deals), has indisputably lost its grip as America's favored national pastime. It falls further and further behind as fewer inner-city youngsters play or even watch the sport and as NASCAR continues to mount its own challenges to the nation's older and now primary sporting pastimes—NFL and NCAA football. And the efforts baseball now makes to hold on to its title of anointed "national pastime" by becoming just another made-for-television spectacle seem only to have a reverse effect.[1] They merely transform a pastoral nineteenth-century game from what once made it unique (its pace, its rhythms, its spaces for contemplation and reflection, its deep symbolic content) into what now seemingly only renders it quite indistinguishable from a myriad of other made-for-TV sports productions it so desperately seeks to overhaul by imitation.

If the sport has failed to keep pace at home, it has failed even more completely on a worldwide stage. The MLB brainchild known as the World Baseball Classic did not globalize baseball in any sense, but only served in the end to underscore all the reasons why it is not actually an international game. With only MLB-eligible athletes drawn only from countries where the game already produces big leaguers, MLB's veiled imitation of soccer's World Cup exposed itself for what it truly was—just another recruiting tool designed for the benefit of big-league clubs. It sent the clear message that other ball-playing nations could never actually compete against the Yankees, Cardinals, or Dodgers in a true "World Series" but rather might only hope to ship their top stars off to the big-league folds in search of an elusive American Dream. As long as MLB continues to mirror the American nation itself in a greedy imperial pursuit of worldwide ownership, rather than posing as a true partner in global growth, its future cannot be all that bright.

Baseball's current crisis with Cuba may in the long run ironically offer one of the last opportunities to reverse the current course and instead pursue a global baseball strategy actually founded on true cooperation and partnership. One potential avenue would be a strategy that not only preserves but actually improves the health of the game in one of its last rival strongholds. Propping up Cuba's domestic game—rather than ruthlessly strip-mining it for any remaining talent—also entails reviving the Olympic version (the rationale for funding the game in many nations) and encouraging international competitions actually geared to enlivening baseball in those nations now struggling to keep it afloat. Here might be found at least one healthy alternative to staging showcase events like the World Baseball Classic, designed only for propagandizing the MLB brand in a handful of nations already welcomed into the family.

But so far few if any of the signs seem positive. MLB now talks of inroads into Cuba as something to be celebrated simply because they provide new talents for big-league stadiums and because Cuba seems a promising market for MLB products. At this point one has to agree with author Robert Elias (*The Empire Strikes Out*), who warns us so persuasively that our one-time national game, just like the very nation that houses it, is at long last dangerously close to finally striking out.

* * *

The corporate business of Major League Baseball has slowly been consuming the baseball universe for more than a full century. Intimate connections both historical and practical between the American national pastime as business model and the calculated foreign policy agendas of Washington have been effectively traced by political science scholar

Robert Elias in his engaging 2005 study, *The Empire Strikes Out*. Professor Elias has constructed a persuasive argument that organized baseball's century-and-a-half-long and rather sordid history of racism, jingoism, unbridled militarism, and blatant insensitivity to other cultures has, from the late nineteenth century on, been an undeniable overseas "quasi instrument" of our overarching American foreign policy. In carrying the newly anointed "national pastime" into the hinterland ports of Latin America and Asia in the 1860s, 1870s, and 1880s, American sailors, merchants, missionaries, and educators were first and foremost engaged in spreading American democratic ideals and cultural attitudes. Baseball was, from the start, a vital tool at the heart of a young and self-confident nation's ambitious plans for expansive economic and militaristic globalization.

The Americans were not alone in this effort at cultural diffusion through bat and ball diplomacy. In his rich history of baseball's historical evolution throughout Asia, Joseph Reaves (*Taking in a Game: A History of Baseball in Asia*) demonstrates how the Japanese—having entirely revamped a "foreign" sport foisted upon them by American naval adventurers in the earliest years of Japan's Westernization—would spread their own brand of cultural hegemony via military occupation throughout the homelands of their Asian neighbors—Korea, China, Taiwan, and even the more distant Philippines. The culturally proud and long-isolationist Japanese first "Japanized" the baseball they had been handed by the Americans at the dawn of the twentieth century, replacing American notions of joyous play and rugged individualism with Japanese principles of relentless work and dedicated group harmony. They made it their own unique product instilled with their own cultural identity. And they then utilized the game as a convenient method of "Japanizing" the rest of neighboring Asia.

But the process did not stop there. Korea would eventually use the game to resist Japanese colonization, to strike back on the baseball field at unwelcomed Japanese masters in the same fashion that the Cubans had once employed the sport to "beat the Yankees at their own game." Taiwan was also forced to adopt Japan's sacred game and in turn enthusiastically tweaked it to construct a unique national identity. In the hands of each new convert, baseball became both an ideal tool for fostering cultural hegemony and also a powerful weapon for resisting it. Mainland communist China would belatedly employ bats and balls in the shadow of the Cultural Revolution to rekindle friendship and regain credibility with neighbors across Asia and also in the West. The Philippines had its own means of adapting the sport while reshaping homeland culture during early twentieth-century efforts at Westernization forcibly fostered by their American colonial occupiers.

Cuba and Japan adopted the game of baseball under similar circumstances; the sport was viewed as a paragon of modernism (Westernization for the Japanese) and thus a viable method of imitating the values and achievements of a much-admired American society. For the Cubans, that shining model to the north provided a promising alternative to decades of oppressive colonial rule at the hands of the Old World Spanish. Allen Guttmann has labeled the process "the motive of imitation" and sees it as the key to the game's successes in both Asia and Latin America. And Cuba, like Japan at the same period in history, also adapted the sport to its own cultural ideals and was soon busy spreading its own unique cultural hegemony with the aid of the popular bat and ball sport. The Cubans, and not the Americans, were the undeniable apostles of baseball throughout the Caribbean region. Cubans first carried baseball to nearby Puerto Rico (via a Spanish diplomat transferred from Havana to San Juan in the early 1890s), Venezuela (through expatriot Cuban ballplayer Emilio Cramer in 1895), the Dominican Republic (with groups of sugar plantation owners fleeing disruptive 1890s independence struggles), and likely also Mexico (by Havana families also fleeing the independence wars and landing in the Yucatan region during the same decade); the best research to date brands Cubans as the sport's zealous Caribbean missionaries.[2] And it was the distinct Cuban style of ball playing that persisted in becoming a model to be imitated throughout neighboring Caribbean countries.

If American missionaries—political and business types, as well as purveyors of muscular Christianity—have used the "American" sport to sell American values, big-league baseball moguls have of late held a slightly different goal in mind. MLB views of "internationalization" articulated by the commissioner's office (under several different tenants) have seemingly been all about growing the game in line with economic incentives, as a new, profitable branch of the ever-expanding MLB business model. The innovative World Baseball Classic launched in 2006 was the latest proof of that scenario. If FIFA (soccer) could enjoy a television bonanza with its universally beloved World Cup matches, then why couldn't MLB also parlay growing worldwide baseball interest into a similar windfall. Of course there were some serious miscalculations along the way—mainly an assumption that baseball had anything beyond the most minimal "global" appeal. But that the true interest was in profits pure and simple could be seen in the ticket structures and made-for-television orientation. And the limiting of entrants to a handful of baseball supernations was not at all in line with growing the sport on a worldwide basis. There were most certainly other motives at play here.

Elias is just as insightful in spelling out apparent motives for this new MLB project under the guise of "globalization" as he is in documenting the massive history of the sport's compliant pact with American politicians and military leaders for spreading American cultural and political dominance to all corners of the globe. The World Baseball Classic (WBC) was conceived in the mid-2000s by the Office of the Baseball Commissioner as a clever venture aimed superficially at spreading the game's global appeal, but there was little here to hide the thinly veiled motive of establishing MLB Inc.'s ownership of the entire outlying baseball universe.

Unlike a now-dormant Olympic tournament or the faltering IBAF Baseball World Cup, this new event would be owned and run exclusively by organized baseball (MLB). Coming at a time of sagging US popularity worldwide, the event might also have a much-valued additional perk of serving as a "foil to American unilateralism and xenophobia."[3] There was also a perhaps rather unrealistic hope of cornering a televised spectacle that might someday provide huge economic windfalls, just like FIFA's wildly popular soccer extravaganza. The event would prove anything but an immediate financial success, with games played in half-empty stadiums during each of the first three editions, little American fan interest due largely to failure of the American squad ever to reach the finals, and only lukewarm support from many of the league's most powerful owners. George Steinbrenner, for one, groused that a springtime WBC not only interrupted his team's preseason preparations but also undercut the traditional luster of an MLB "World Series," on which his Yankees staked special historical claim.

But as Elias explains it, the WBC became an immediate case of "win by losing" strategy. Although the American-born stars forming Team USA did relatively poorly (only once reaching the semifinals in three tries), that could be turned into a plus of sorts. The message seemed to be: "that's okay, American fans, because all these showcased imported stars will soon enough be back performing on your favorite teams in big-league cities near you." Interest would hopefully also peak among fans abroad, who would soon enough become TV consumers of MLB games once their heroes returned to ballparks on American soil. MLB's iron-fisted ownership was fully enforced when Japan's attempt to control opening-round games on its own soil was quickly blocked. The message was loud and clear. If baseball is now becoming a global sport, it is still owned and controlled entirely by the American nation and by a powerful American corporation known as Major League Baseball. No bottom-up globalization appeared on the horizon, with numerous partner nations sharing the rewards. Again we would have only all-too-familiar American baseball imperialism posing in a thin cloak of globalization—a system imposed from the top down by a single reigning self-appointed owner of what was only being reinforced as America's national game.

The fact that the World Baseball Classic offered little room for growing the sport internationally was revealed most transparently by its structure. To stage a short-span competitive event, the field had to be limited to only sixteen of the world's top baseball nations. It rewarded only the baseball "haves" and ignored the "have-nots," the very nations that are the true frontier and necessary future of the game. Unlike the IBAF Baseball World Cup it was replacing—a tournament more than willing to tolerate lopsided mismatches and a chaotic schedule in order to include upwards of thirty competing teams—this new event did nothing for fans in all those countries that housed weak domestic versions of the game and provided no major leaguers. There was nothing here for present or future fans and players in neophyte baseball-playing outposts like Croatia, Greece, Sweden, the Czech Republic, the Philippines, or a host of African nations that have only recently taken up the game.

That MLB should pursue soccer's World Cup competition as a model for its own latest approach to globalization carries its own special ironies. Soccer is indeed a global sport, a fact springing perhaps less from its history and more from its structural simplicity and small economic demands: it can be played by groups of almost any number and demands no equipment other than a single ball. Those factors make it especially appealing in poorer nations worldwide. While it shares English origins with baseball, it has no single national or regional center; nor was it imposed on large parts of the world by any planned imperialist program as were its British cousins, cricket and baseball. Soccer has no epicenter of control resting in a single nation or professional league. From the earliest years of its nineteenth-century global spread, it has been perceived as a world game and not an American or Japanese or Brazilian or English game. MLB-centered baseball is just the opposite in its expansion history and in its present global strategy. It therefore seems to offer scant possibility for true globalization, at least in its present form.

If the plan being hatched by MLB bosses was indeed to take over ownership of a true world championship from a fading IBAF, it was only the latest such incursion into competing baseball realms. MLB's plan for total dominance began on the home front. Over the years MLB has successfully sold its adoring fans a notion that Baseball with a capital B means no more than MLB. That idea has been so long and firmly implanted through clever and ceaseless marketing campaigns that it today seems part of the public consciousness. We never think of basketball as meaning the NBA exclusively; for many the college game holds far great er appeal. Football is not simply the NFL, nor hockey the NHL (even in Canada). In much of Asia it is scholastic and collegiate baseball that most thoroughly rivets both the Japanese and Koreans, but here alone baseball has somehow become irreparably entrenched as little beyond the corporate business of MLB. If you are identified as a baseball fan, then a single question will always follow—"which team?" The assumption is always that your interest must be the major leagues. The same marketing campaign (boosted, if not initiated, when coverage went from newspaper to radio to television) that has established this view has been only one part of a long-entrenched strategy by generations of big-league owners to squelch all possible competition both at home and abroad. As Robert Elias suggests, if MLB has long aligned itself as the cheerleader and active partner in US imperialist adventurism around the globe, it has also always maintained effective imperialist strategies of its own.

Negro-league baseball first fell by the wayside. Once integration was rammed down the throats of team owners in the shadow of World War II, the potential of black talent on big-league clubs soon meant wholesale raiding of leagues that were once dismissed as outlaw baseball and left untouched only because of the racial divide itself. Long a vital institution in major North American black metropolitan centers, those "outlaw" black leagues and Negro barnstorming teams had enjoyed a checkered history in the first half of the twentieth century. When integration finally wiped away MLB's greatest atrocity in 1947, however, the event also destroyed another vital cultural institution. While a few black stars struck it rich in the majors, thousands more had no leagues left to play in. And destroyed as well was a thriving support system that was the economic backbone of black communities in many major US cities. No one would argue that integration was not needed, but the consequence was the killing off of baseball as both occupation and leisure-time preoccupation for many Americans of color.

The minor-league system was virtually dismantled as well in the decade of the fifties. There were dozens of minor leagues and hundreds of league teams thriving in the years immediately following World War II. The number of active minor-league circuits shrank from a high of 59 in 1949 to 33 by 1955 and only 28 a year later. When television became the prime medium, it was MLB that quickly ruled the landscape; the local ballpark didn't hold the same allure when one could dial in more glamorous big-league stars from the comfort of the family den. Admittedly minor-league baseball is today a big business once more—perhaps thanks as much to family entertainment promotions like dizzy-bat races and buried infield treasure hunts, the frenetic between-innings antics of colorful acrobatic mascots, and other such gimmicks as to the on-field game itself—but it is no longer the heart and soul of the sport as it was a couple of generations back. And that loss may have much to do with the disappearance of the sport as a true national pastime.[4]

Pasquel's upstart Mexican League, with its piecemeal raids on big-league stars in the shadows of World War II, also could not be tolerated as a potential rival. The "Mexican League War" that resulted—consisting mainly of Happy Chandler's threatened lifetime bans on Pasquel's small cadre of recruits—was short-lived and also affected the winter season baseball landscape in Cuba (chapter 2). But the powers of MLB were quickly able to squash an overly ambitious Mexican tycoon's attempts at constructing anything that might resemble a rival pro-baseball universe.

Japan long remained a holdout from MLB hegemony, but itself has only become more MLB-like over the years. By the second half of the last century the Caribbean nations, as well as those in Asia, would eventually be seen by MLB bosses as potential overripe markets—sources for both players bought cheaply and television rights sold dearly. There have been strong MLB efforts to crack into Japan, though that has proven only a partial success, and only since the mid-1990s (on the heels of modern "defectors" like Nomo, Irabu, and finally Ichiro Suzuki). Japan has erected a protective wall around a game it sees as its own. Cuba is now next in line. That is most obvious not only from the rush to sign up dozens of defecting island stars but also from the recent words of a new MLB commissioner, who quickly announced possible Havana spring-training matches in the wake of Obama's December 2014 overtures toward USA-Cuba détente. Most telling was the precise phrasing of Commissioner Manfred's press releases, which intoned that "Cuba provides a great potential market for us [MLB]." The choice of words was telling and it was clear that the top MLB executive was not merely speaking in metaphors.

Again it is Elias who best articulates the downsides of MLB's moves toward globalization and best elaborates why many see that process as far from benign.[5] Elias points to the differences between globalization that is experienced from the bottom up (with all parties benefitting) and that imposed from the top down, with only one party exploiting all the benefits. The first is true "globalization" and the latter is better termed imperialism. Elias cites David Fidler as drawing pointed parallels between the actions of MLB in opening markets to reap talent and sell memorabilia (or media programming rights) and earlier neocolonial activities of US companies throughout Central and South America. When it comes to MLB inroads into Cuba, it is hard to put any other face on it. Constant platitudes about rights of beleaguered or oppressed Cuban ballplayers to find the American Dream of economic freedom might well be taken as merely an effective smokescreen obscuring true MLB motives for enriching team coffers.

Elias makes a final telling observation by suggesting that the desperate needs of MLB to exploit these newly emerging (and perhaps rapidly diminishing) talent sources may well result from the fact that the game has been so poorly tended at home. The "immediate profits at the expense of the future" mentality behind skyrocketing player salaries, surrender of the game to television, and soaring ticket prices may well be losing future generations of fans—and also the next generation of homegrown ballplayers. Baseball is no longer the game played on every street corner. It has virtually died in the inner cities. The wealth of black ballplayers that accounted for the baseball boom of the fifties and sixties has dissipated. One result is that America no longer produces the world's best ballplayers, or at least not the wide bulk of them. Available overseas markets for talent—exploited quickly and thoroughly—has become a desperate priority for big-league clubs.

Cuba will likely be able to resist such incursions for only so long. If there is a cautionary tale here for the Cubans, it is to be found in developments throughout the once-proud baseball communities of their Caribbean neighbors. Here again the economic realities of the MLB model have meant a death knell for the domestic sport all across Latin America. Winter circuits featuring homegrown big leaguers were once a thriving winter season spectacle. But today's pro salary structures no longer require (or allow) top players to perform during off-season months in their homelands. The result has been collapse of fan support in Puerto Rico, the Dominican, Venezuela, and to a lesser degree in Mexico. The onetime showcase Caribbean Series in turn quickly became a talent-barren sham. It was the latter collapse that finally resulted in overtures to Cuba in a last-ditch effort to upgrade and even salvage the competition. MLB has meanwhile moved its off-season focus to the Arizona Fall League, where it has more control over management and profits. And the Caribbean nations have become little more than talent farms, fertile plantations where the entire player talent pool might be sucked wholesale into MLB ball clubs and their minor-league feeder systems.

Mostly through accidents of political history, Cuba alone has remained, until recently, mostly immune to the inroads and encroachments of MLB. Post-revolution Cuba provided a true alternative baseball universe—arguably the only one still standing. The downside, perhaps, was the loss of opportunity for two generations of North American fans to witness first-hand so much great talent. And Cuba's own loss—one it was stubbornly willing to live with—was that its abilities to showcase its baseball talent and heritage had to remain restricted to obscure corners of the evolving international baseball scene. The epicenter of the game remained North America's professional diamonds, where the Cuban presence was only an occasional small blip or fading memory—a handful of mid-level refugee pitchers in the late 1990s and early 2000s and the periodic Old-Timers Day ceremonial appearances of bygone heroes Orestes Miñoso, Tony Perez, Tony Oliva, or perhaps Camilo Pascual. A newly minted MLB World Baseball Classic—especially Cuba's shocking 2006 near-championship—began to change all that. And the recent exploding "defector" phenomenon has now put Cuba squarely back in the baseball headlines.

External pressures now fomenting around Cuba and its baseball enterprise are increasingly complicated by internal breakdowns in the Cuban baseball machinery itself. It was possible, even easy, to keep star players homebound and satisfied when the island nation was isolated from all but minimal contact with an outside baseball world and when international triumphs were boringly regular, a source of huge national pride, and highly valued at home even if sometimes rather hollow in content. Now the younger players no longer see stardom back home as the highest pinnacle of achievement. The true heroes for ballplayers themselves and for fans on street corners have overnight become the very athletes government officials still attempt to brand as traitors. In an age of exploding social media and electronic access, fans in Cuba are no longer quite so isolated. And they no longer are buying standard government propaganda. Increasingly an American model of baseball—one based on the idea of playing for personal economic windfall and not simply for community pride or love of sport—has seeped onto the island and has turned the heads of fans as much as those of promising young ballplayers.

There is also the issue of deteriorating physical conditions across the island. Stadiums are crumbling and playing fields no better than crude and shoddy—the roof covering Havana's seven-decade-old Latin American Stadium displays gaping holes, grandstand seats are often cement slabs or portable folding chairs, and dugouts at more than a few parks are cooled with hundred-pound blocks of melting ice. Playing conditions in the best ballparks (perhaps Victoria de Girón Stadium in Matanzas) are substandard, as are balls, gloves, and uniforms. The system survives on gifts from abroad: touring national team players barter with rivals for Louisville Slugger bats, batting gloves, and MLB-quality warmup jerseys; National Series team members request gifts of top-quality mitts or MLB balls from visiting tourists and often trade team jerseys for such items. Open business with the United States may now hold promise for easing some domestic financial stress. The Cuban government line has long been that dropping the embargo is the one pressing need for a Cuban economic revival. But an influx of American dollars from the coffers of MLB might be the shot in the arm actually needed to salvage the national sport, even if that revenue source might come at a terrible price (loss of Cuba's treasure trove of ballplayers that are the league's main rationale). Of course the rebuilding of Cuban infrastructure will be a massive undertaking and baseball stadiums may not be the highest priority, especially if the final vestiges of cold war tensions disap-

Gaping holes and missing sections of the grandstand roof, as well as torn backstop nets, reveal the decaying status of Havana's once-proud Latin American Stadium. Courtesy of Peter C. Bjarkman.

pear and international tournament victories are no longer such a touted propaganda tool.

* * *

From the viewpoint of most American fans and a majority of stateside journalists, the single option now on the table for Cuba's baseball management seems patently obvious. Selling off ballplayers rather than merely letting them slip away, with no compensation for the country that nurtured them, seems like a no-brainer solution from any capitalist orientation. But that all-too-easy reading of the situation never considers Cuba's rich baseball legacy, or the vital connections of the national sport to a communist social experiment that has been Cuba's lot for six decades. Cuba is far more similar to Japan than to the Dominican Republic or any of its other Caribbean neighbors. Baseball is more cultural anchor than mere entertainment spectacle or potential revenue source. The national sport remained so important to cultural cohesion in the halcyon days of the revolution that admission fees were never charged for games during the showcase National Series (indeed all sporting events were free of admission charges before the devastating Special Period in the Time of Peace of the early nineties).

The Japanese posting system discussed in the previous chapter might produce a much-needed influx of cash for Cuban baseball, but that quite obviously could not happen overnight. Such a system would be a long-range project; even if instituted immediately it would not begin producing free agent players for perhaps half-a-dozen years. In the interim the currently evolving Japanese connection might well be the best and perhaps the only quick fix, and that solution has not so far proven all that beneficial to either Cuban or Japanese interests. At the very best it seems to be a stopgap measure, and one laced with numerous pitfalls. It is not reasonable, for one thing, to expect that top Cuban stars will be able (or even willing for very long) to play year-round seasons that might contain well over 200 games.

Many complex questions remain and few easy solutions are apparent. Potential compromises cannot be expected to unfold smoothly. But what seems most certain is that this two-headed phenomenon involving escaping Cuban ballplayers that has captivated the imagination of fans and press in recent years will not continue much longer at its present pace. And it may not continue at all if Obama's promised détente agenda becomes a reality as rapidly as many are hoping. Two often-asked questions have been: (1) how much more talent is there in Cuba? and (2) are there enough potential big leaguers waiting in the wings to keep a Cuban pipeline open? A recent flood of new high-quality prospects (more than a dozen in May 2015 alone) seems already to have answered those questions—the supply does at the moment seem almost endless. One former player agent, Joe Kehoskie, believes that if doors to the communist island miraculously swing open in the foreseeable future, Cuba will indeed dwarf the Dominican Republic as a big-league talent source.[6] It does seem rather unlikely that the current talent pool will quickly evaporate entirely. But there will be other factors to likely alter the current dynamic. That which has resulted from a full half century of cold war policies will fade only once those policies themselves have finally disappeared from the scene.

There is a final coda to this story. The saga unfolded here has focused on an explosion of Cuban talent on the big-league scene over a recent handful of years. Two background tales prop up that main storyline. One is the diminishing quality of Cuban domestic-league baseball now apparent as more talented island players choose to flee the system that raised them. Another is the saddest tale of all—the one true tragedy—and this involves the hundreds of young athletes who over the past half-dozen years have fled the island in droves, only to find their big-league dreams to be yet another false hope and vague illusion. MLB scouts are presently wrestling with precisely how to handle the flood of players temporarily residing in the Dominican and across Central America who are all-too-quickly finding profit-minded agents and hastily arranging showcase tryout sessions in hopes of landing instant riches and lives of imagined big-league glory. A sad truth is that the great majority of these prospects have little hope of grasping that elusive dream. They might have been better served staying at home and enjoying lesser domestic baseball rewards in the comfort of supportive family and adoring local fans. Many will be quickly abandoned along the way; hundreds already have been. It is a tale of tears that at some point will likely require its own volume-length treatment.

One can only imagine how strong Cuban baseball would be today if all these now-exiled sluggers and hurlers had remained home to feed the domestic system—no matter what feelings one might have about the policies of Cuban communism that sustain and exploit that system. The mere loss of numbers has been equally as big a blow to the domestic Cuban League as has the flight of top-draw stars, since the latter always seem to be rather quickly replaced. It is the thinning talent pool—coupled with a sagging economy—that is now forcing INDER officials seriously, if also reluctantly, to consider contracting the traditional Cuban League to perhaps eight teams or less. But if recent events underscore the quality of lost talent, they have also unveiled the remarkable resilience of a baseball culture still surviving on the island that may have been severely damaged and repeatedly assaulted but hardly pushed into anything that might resemble a true death spiral.

What has remained the most remarkable chapter in this tale has been the always-underestimated resilience exhibited by the island's favorite sport. Fidel may have wildly exaggerated when he once boasted that invading North American scouts might steal as many of his players as they could and yet equal replacements would always quickly be substituted. But he was not wrong by all that much, even in an emerging millennium that has witnessed ballplayer defections at a rate Fidel never could have imagined. The winter season of 2014–2015—bookended by strong showings at both the Central American Games in Veracruz and the Caribbean Series in San Juan—has made that fact abundantly clear. One should neither celebrate nor mourn prematurely any overnight disappearance of the muscular Cuban baseball that we have so long known.

Cuban baseball and its proud national team have been sent reeling of late. The string of automatic gold medals was ended by the middle of the past decade. The other "Big Red Machine" has rarely been invincible since the first loss of Olympic gold at Sydney back in September 2000, although it remains highly competitive and a magnet for adoring international fans and MLB scouts wherever it travels. In recent months a new roster of stars among the remaining loyalists has even provided some surprising face-saving victories.

One came in the November Central American Games when an all-star squad under controversial manager Victor Mesa breezed through mediocre opposition in a manner reminiscent of past decades. Another emerged with the March Caribbean Series, where a stunning pair of dramatic come-from-behind final-weekend wins over favored Venezuelan and Mexican professionals seemed for the moment to nullify yet another batch of disruptive player defections that had grabbed all-too-predictable headlines during the tournament's earliest days. Both those triumphs were also keyed by the very players—Cepeda, Gourriel, and Héctor Mendoza—now farmed out for summer duty in Japan. Given such ongoing losses (off-field defections) and renewed triumphs (on-field wins) one is reminded of the prophetic words of S. L. Price (*Pitching around Fidel*), who once observed that "Cuba is the worst place on the globe to be an athlete today . . . it is also the best."[7] Cuba remains (as when Price penned his observation more than a decade back) both the very worst and the very best place to be a talented baseball player.

If there is one certainty, it is that the story related here may well have taken new twists and turns by the time this book first reaches the marketplace. The story of Cuba's current baseball crisis is now evolving almost daily, with regularly added chapters playing out both on big-league diamonds and on the high seas between Cuba, Haiti, and the Dominican Republic. For a frustrating span of years, even decades, not much changed regarding Cuba and its cold war stalemate with Washington and

Miami, and therefore any seemingly dramatic current shifts or novel episodes have to be taken with extreme caution. The story is ever-evolving.

In the final months of writing this book, developing events seemed to
be spinning around me at a disturbing breakneck clip. There were new
media outlets jumping onto the bandwagon daily with requests for fresh
print and on-camera interviews that interrupted writing sessions on a
weekly and sometimes almost an hourly basis. And there were constant
new revelations that altered either the direction or tenor of the story that I
was struggling to craft. One such development was a fast-breaking April
rumor that the New York Yankees were about to land prized infielder
Yulieski Gourriel. It was the kind of fanciful if irresistible speculation
regularly planted in the Miami Spanish-language press and always guaranteed to take on a life of its own.

In the wake of Gourriel's rather mysterious contract fiasco with the
Yokohama ball club (chapter 9), it was now suddenly being reported that
perhaps the whole matter had been somehow orchestrated by the Industriales star himself as part of a thickly laid plot to land a more coveted deal
with a big-league club of his dreams.[8] The source for such a potential
bombshell would turn out to be nothing more than the player's own
repeated comments to foreign journalists that he would indeed someday
like to perform in pinstripes alongside his hero Alex Rodríguez. The
Miami Nuevo Herald even went so far as to report that it had confirmation directly from former Cuban League commissioner Higinio Vélez
himself. It was all pure fantasy, of course, and it ignored the obvious—
that MLB policy on Cuban signings would never allow such dealings
with any single American or National League ball club. The rush to print
such a bald-faced yarn revealed simultaneously both how little things had
actually changed on a wishful-thinking media front, and also how ram-
pantly and explosively renewed Cuban baseball fantasies were now
emerging.

There will almost certainly be more stories like this in coming months.
The list of new defectors is guaranteed to grow, perhaps even exponen-
tially, by the time this book is in readers' hands (two more flashed across
my computer screen as I typed these exact pages only this morning).
Some of the issues laid out in these chapters may be largely, if not
entirely, resolved by the time the volume lands on bookstore shelves. But
any assumption that Cuba will have already been turned into yet another
MLB plantation—a new mother lode of talent free for the plucking—

Yulieski Gourriel stirred controversy when he failed to report to the Yokohama DeNa BayStars in April 2015 and forfeited a million-dollar-plus contract. Courtesy of Byron Motley.

remains little more than an idle dream. If history teaches us any lasting lessons, the past half-century of contentious Cuba-USA cold war baseball dealings should have prepared us to expect that Cuba will steadfastly remain the jealous owner of its own domestic baseball destiny.

APPENDIX I

193 Cuban-Born Major Leaguers

This list of all Cuban-born major leaguers is complete through September 2015 and includes only native Cubans born on the island nation. Those who also played in the post-revolution Cuban National Series (i.e., all those except Bárbaro Garbey, who was expelled from Cuba during the Mariel Boatlift and technically did not "defect") and therefore should be considered Cuban baseball "defectors" are indicated below in **boldface** (59 players). Post-1961 Cuban big leaguers not in boldface are players born on the island that immigrated to the United States at an early age and later developed their baseball-playing skills in North America and not in Cuba. The list of true "defectors" now totals 59 (31 percent of the total number, 193, of Cuban big leaguers). The symbol SA in the far-right column (MLB Games) indicates the player was still an active major leaguer in September 2015 (or an active professional who might return to big-league action).

Pre-Modern Era, 1871–1903 (2 Players)

Player	Debut Date	Debut Team (League)	Position	MLB Games
1) Enrique Esteban Bellán	May 9, 1871	Troy (NA)	Infield	60
2) Pedro (Chick) Pedroes	August 21, 1902	Chicago (NL)	Infield	2

Pre-Revolution Period, 1911–1960 (86 Players)

Player	Debut Date	Debut Team (League)	Position	MLB Games
3) Armando Marsans	July 4, 1911	Cincinnati (NL)	Outfield	655
4) Rafael Almeida	July 4, 1911	Cincinnati (NL)	Outfield	102
5) Miguel (Mike) González	September 28, 1912	Boston (NL)	Catcher	1042
6) Merito (Baldomero) Acosta	June 15, 1913	Washington (AL)	Outfield	180
7) Jacinto (Jack) Calvo	September 15, 1913	Washington (AL)	Outfield	34
8) Adolfo (Dolf) Luque	May 20, 1914	Boston (NL)	RHP	550
9) Manolo (Manuel) Cueto	June 25, 1914	Cincinnati (NL)	Outfield	51
10) Angel (Pete) Aragón	August 20, 1914	New York (AL)	INF/OF	32
11) Emilio Palmero	September 21, 1915	New York (NL)	RHP	41
12) José (Joseito) Rodríguez	October 5, 1916	New York (NL)	Infield	58
13) Oscar Tuero	May 30, 1918	St. Louis (NL)	RHP	58
14) Eusabio González	July 26, 1918	Boston (AL)	Shortstop	3
15) Ricardo Torres	May 18, 1920	Washington (AL)	Catcher	22
16) José Acosta	July 28, 1920	Washington (AL)	RHP	55
17) Pedro Dibut	May 1, 1924	Cincinnati (NL)	RHP	8
18) Ramón (Mike) Herrera	September 22, 1925	Boston (AL)	Infield	84
19) Oscar Estrada	April 21, 1929	St. Louis (AL)	LHP	1
20) Roberto (Tarzán) Estalella	September 7, 1935	Washington (AL)	INF/OF	680
21) Fermín (Mike) Guerra	September 19, 1937	Washington (AL)	Catcher	535
22) René Monteagudo	September 6, 1938	Washington (AL)	LHP	46
23) Gilberto (Gil) Torres	April 25, 1940	Washington (AL)	Infield	44

25) Roberto (Bobby) Ortiz	September 6, 1941	Washington (AL)	Outfield	214
26) Salvador Hernández	April 16, 1942	Chicago (NL)	Catcher	90
27) Napoleón (Nap) Reyes	May 19, 1943	New York (NL)	Infield	279
28) Mosquito (Tony) Ordeñana	October 3, 1943	Pittsburgh (NL)	Shortstop	—
29) Tomás de la Cruz	April 20, 1944	Cincinnati (NL)	RHP	34
30) Santiago (Carlos) Ulrich	May 3, 1944	Washington (AL)	RHP	31
31) Rogelio (Roy) Valdés	May 3, 1944	Washington (AL)	Hitter	—
32) Preston (Pedro) Gómez	May 5, 1944	Washington (AL)	Infield	8
33) Luis Suarez	May 28, 1944	Washington (AL)	3B	1
34) Oliverio (Baby) Ortiz	September 23, 1944	Washington (AL)	RHP	2
35) José Zardón	April 18, 1945	Washington (AL)	Outfield	54
36) Jorge Comellas	April 19, 1945	Chicago (NL)	RHP	7
37) Armando Roche	May 10, 1945	Washington (AL)	RHP	2
38) Isidoro (Sid) León	June 21, 1945	Philadelphia (NL)	RHP	14
39) Adrian Zabala	August 11, 1945	New York (NL)	LHP	26
40) Regino (Reggie) Otero	September 2, 1945	Chicago (NL)	1B	14
41) Moin (Ramón) García	April 19, 1948	Washington (AL)	RHP	4
42) Angel Fleitas	July 5, 1948	Washington (AL)	Shortstop	15
43) Orestes (Minnie) Miñoso	April 9, 1949	Cleveland (AL)	Outfield	1835
44) Julio (Enrique) González	August 9, 1949	Washington (AL)	RHP	13
45) Luis (Witto) Aloma	April 19, 1950	Chicago (AL)	RHP	116
46) Conrado Marrero	April 21, 1950	Washington (AL)	RHP	118
47) Sandalio Consuegra	June 10, 1950	Washington (AL)	RHP	248
48) Rogelio Martínez	July 13, 1950	Washington (AL)	RHP	2
49) Julio (Jiqui) Moreno	September 8, 1950	Washington (AL)	RHP	73
50) Carlos Pascual	September 24, 1950	Washington (AL)	RHP	2
51) Rafael (Ray) Noble	April 18, 1951	New York (N_)	Catcher	107

52) Willy Miranda	May 6, 1951	Washington (AL)	Shortstop	824
53) Francisco Campos	September 11, 1951	Washington (AL)	Outfield	71
54) Héctor Rodríguez	April 15, 1952	Chicago (AL)	3B	124
55) Raúl Sánchez	April 17, 1952	Washington (AL)	RHP	49
56) Sandy Amoros	August 22, 1952	Brooklyn (NL)	Outfield	517
57) Miguel Fornieles	September 2, 1952	Washington (AL)	RHP	432
58) Camilo Pascual	April 14, 1954	Washington (AL)	RHP	529
59) Carlos Paula	September 6, 1954	Washington (AL)	Outfield	157
60) Pedro Ramos	April 11, 1955	Washington (AL)	RHP	581
61) Roman Mejias	April 13, 1955	Pittsburgh (NL)	Outfield	627
62) Wenceslao González	April 13, 1955	Washington (AL)	LHP	2
63) Juan Delis	April 16, 1955	Washington (AL)	Infield	54
64) Vicente Amor	April 16, 1955	Chicago (NL)	RHP	13
65) Lino Dinoso	June 18, 1955	Pittsburgh (NL)	LHP	2
66) José Valdivielso	June 21, 1955	Washington (AL)	Shortstop	401
67) Julio Bécquer	September 13, 1955	Washington (AL)	1B	488
68) Lázaro (Cholly) Naranjo	July 8, 1956	Pittsburgh (NL)	RHP	17
69) Chico Fernández	July 14, 1956	Brooklyn (NL)	Shortstop	856
70) Evelio Hernández	September 12, 1956	Washington (AL)	RHP	18
71) René Valdéz	April 21, 1957	Brooklyn (NL)	RHP	5
72) Tony (Antonio) Taylor	April 15, 1958	Chicago (NL)	Infield	2195
73) Panchón (Juan) Herrera	April 15, 1958	Philadelphia (NL)	1B	300
74) Fernando Rodríguez	April 19, 1958	Chicago (NL)	RHP	8
75) Osvaldo (Ozzie) Alvarez	April 19, 1958	Washington (AL)	Infield	95
76) Daniel (Dan) Morejón	July 11, 1958	Cincinnati (NL)	Outfield	12
77) Orlando Peña	August 24, 1958	Cincinnati (NL)	RHP	427
78) Rodolfo (Rudy) Arias	April 10, 1959	Chicago (AL)	LHP	34

Player	Debut Date	Debut Team (League)	Position	MLB Games
81) Tony (Antonio) González	April 12, 1960	Cincinnati (NL)	Infield	1559
82) Eduardo (Ed) Bauta	July 6, 1960	St. Louis (NL)	RHP	97
83) Miguel (Mike) de la Hoz	July 22, 1960	Cleveland (A-)	Infield	494
84) Leo (Leonardo) Cárdenas	July 25, 1960	Cincinnati (NL)	Infield	1941
85) Joe (Joaquín) Azcue	August 3, 1960	Cincinnati (NL)	Catcher	909
86) Borrego Alvarez	September 18, 1960	Cincinnati (NL)	1B	17
87) Leo (Leopoldo) Posada	September 21, 1960	Kansas City (AL)	Outfield	155
88) Héctor Maestri	September 24, 1960	Washington (AL)	RHP	2

Post-Revolution Period, 1961–2015 (105 Players)

Player	Debut Date	Debut Team (League)	Position	MLB Games
89) Dagoberto (Bert) Cueto	June 8, 1961	Minnesota (AL)	RHP	7
90) Manuel (Manny) Montejo	July 25, 1961	Detroit (AL)	RHP	1
91) Orlando McFarlane	April 3, 1962	Pittsburgh (NL)	Catcher	124
92) Octavio (Cookie) Rojas	April 10, 1962	Cincinnati (NL)	Infield	1822
93) José Tartabull	April 10, 1962	Kansas City (AL)	Outfield	749
94) Diego Segui	April 12, 1962	Kansas City (AL)	RHP	639
95) Orlando (Marty) Martínez	May 2, 1962	Minnesota (A-)	Infield	436
96) Héctor Martínez	September 3, 1962	Kansas City (AL)	Outfield	7
97) Tony (Pedro) Oliva	September 9, 1962	Minnesota (A-)	Outfield	1676
98) Tony (Gabriel) Martínez	April 9, 1963	Cleveland (AL)	Infield	73
99) José Cardenal	April 14, 1963	San Francisco (NL)	Infield	2017
100) Marcelino López	April 14, 1963	Philadelphia (NL)	LHP	171
101) Aurelio Monteagudo	September 1, 1963	Kansas City (AL)	RHP	72
102) Chico (Hiraldo) Ruiz	April 13, 1964	Cincinnati (NL)	Infield	565
103) Luis Tiant Jr.	July 19, 1964	Cleveland (AL)	RHP	573
104) Bert Campaneris	July 23, 1964	Kansas City (AL)	Shortstop	2328
105) Tony (Atanasio) Perez	July 26, 1964	Cincinnati (NL)	Infield	2777

Name	Date	Team (League)	Position	Games
106) Sandy Valdespino	April 12, 1965	Minnesota (AL)	Outfield	382
107) Tito (Rigoberto) Fuentes	August 18, 1965	San Francisco (NL)	Outfield	1499
108) Jackie Hernández	September 14, 1965	California (AL)	Shortstop	618
109) Paul (Paulino) Casanova	September 18, 1965	Washington (AL)	Catcher	859
110) Minnie Rojas	May 30, 1966	California (AL)	RHP	157
111) José Ramón López	August 21, 1966	California (AL)	RHP	4
112) Hank Izquierdo	August 9, 1967	Minnesota (AL)	Catcher	16
113) Jorge Lauzerique	September 17, 1967	Kansas City (AL)	RHP	34
114) José Arcia	April 10, 1968	Chicago (NL)	Infield	293
115) Chico Fernández	April 20, 1968	Baltimore (AL)	Infield	24
116) José Martínez	June 18, 1969	Pittsburgh (NL)	Infield	96
117) Minnie Mendoza	April 9, 1970	Minnesota (AL)	Infield	16
118) Oscar Zamora	June 18, 1974	Chicago (NL)	RHP	158
119) Orlando González	June 7, 1976	Cleveland (AL)	1B	79
120) Bobby (Roberto) Ramos	September 26, 1978	Montreal (NL)	Outfield	103
121) Leo Sutherland	August 11, 1980	Chicago (AL)	Outfield	45
122) Bárbaro Garbey	**April 3, 1984**	**Detroit (AL)**	**Outfield**	**226**
123) José Canseco	September 2, 1985	Oakland (AL)	Outfield	1887
124) Rafael Palmeiro	September 8, 1986	Chicago (NL)	1B	2831
125) Orestes Destrade	September 11, 1987	New York (AL)	1B	237
126) Nelson Santovenia	September 16, 1987	Montreal (NL)	Catcher	297
127) Tony (Emilio) Fossas	May 15, 1988	Texas (AL)	LHP	567
128) Israel Sánchez	June 7, 1988	Kansas City (AL)	LHP	30
129) Ozzie Canseco	July 18, 1990	Oakland (AL)	Outfield	24
130) Tony Menéndez	June 22, 1992	Cincinnati (NL)	RHP	23
131) René Arocha	**April 9, 1993**	**St. Louis (NL)**	**RHP**	**124**
132) Ariel Prieto	**July 2, 1995**	**Oakland (AL)**	**RHP**	**67**

135) Liván Hernández	September 24, 1996	Florida (NL)	RHP	519
136) Elieser (Eli) Marrero	September 3, 1997	St. Louis (NL)	Catcher	724
137) Rolando Arrojo	April 1, 1998	Tampa Bay (AL)	RHP	158
138) Orlando Hernández	June 3, 1998	New York (AL)	RHP	219
139) Vladimir Núñez	September 11, 1998	Arizona (NL)	RHP	254
140) Michael Tejera	September 8, 1999	Florida (NL)	LHP	111
141) Jorge Toca	September 12, 1999	New York (NL)	Infield	25
142) Eddie Oropesa	April 2, 2001	Philadelphia (NL)	LHP	125
143) Adrian Hernández	April 21, 2001	New York (AL)	RHP	14
144) Danys Báez	May 13, 2001	Cleveland (AL)	RHP	533
145) Alex Sánchez	June 15, 2001	Milwaukee (NL)	Outfield	427
146) Bill (Willy) Ortega	September 7, 2001	St. Louis (NL)	Outfield	5
147) Hanzel Izquierdo	April 21, 2002	Florida (NL)	RHP	20
148) Juan Carlos Díaz	June 12, 2002	Boston (AL)	1B	4
149) José Ariel Contreras	March 31, 2003	New York (AL)	RHP	299
150) Michel Hernández	September 6, 2003	New York (AL)	Catcher	45
151) Brayan Peña	May 23, 2005	Atlanta (NL)	Catcher	SA
152) Yuniesky Betancourt	July 8, 2005	Seattle (AL)	Shortstop	1156
153) Kendrys Morales	May 23, 2006	Anaheim (AL)	1B	SA
154) Alay Soler	May 24, 2006	New York (NL)	RHP	8
155) Yunel Escobar	June 2, 2007	Atlanta (NL)	Shortstop	SA
156) Alexei Ramírez	March 31, 2008	Chicago (AL)	Shortstop	SA
157) Alberto Castillo	April 28, 2008	Baltimore (AL)	LHP	74
158) Yoslan Herrera	July 12, 2008	Pittsburgh (NL)	RHP	25
159) Francisley Bueno	August 13, 2008	Atlanta (NL)	RHP	SA
160) Juan Miranda	September 18, 2008	New York (AL)	1B	111
161) Bárbaro Cañizares	June 11, 2009	Atlanta (NL)	1B	5

162) Raúl Valdés	April 11, 2010	New York (NL)	LHP	95
163) Dayan Viciedo	June 20, 2010	Chicago (AL)	INF/OF	SA
164) Aroldis Chapman	August 31, 2010	Cincinnati (NL)	LHP	SA
165) Yonder Alonso	September 1, 2010	Cincinnati (NL)	Outfield	SA
166) Yunieski Maya	September 7, 2010	Washington (NL)	RHP	16
167) José Iglesias	May 8, 2011	Boston (AL)	Shortstop	SA
168) Amaury Sanit	May 12, 2011	New York (AL)	RHP	4
169) Leonys Martin	September 2, 2011	Texas (AL)	Outfield	SA
170) Yoenis Céspedes	March 28, 2012	Oakland (AL)	Outfield	SA
171) Yasmani Grandal	June 2, 2012	San Diego (NL)	Catcher	SA
172) Eddy Rodríguez	August 2, 2012	San Diego (NL)	Catcher	2
173) Adeiny Hechavarría	August 4, 2012	Toronto (AL)	Shortstop	SA
174) José D. Fernández	April 7, 2013	Miami (NL)	RHP	SA
175) Yasiel Puig	June 3, 2013	Los Angeles (NL)	Outfield	SA
176) Henry Urrutia	July 20, 2013	Baltimore (AL)	Outfield	SA
177) Onelkis García	September 11, 2013	Los Angeles (NL)	LHP	SA
178) Alex Guerrero	March 22, 2014	Los Angeles (NL)	INF/OF	SA
179) José Dariel Abreu	March 31, 2014	Chicago (AL)	1B/DH	SA
180) Adrian Nieto	April 2, 2014	Chicago (AL)	Catcher	SA
181) Roenis Elias	April 3, 2014	Seattle (AL)	LHP	SA
182) Erisbel Arruebarrena	May 23, 2014	Los Angeles (NL)	Shortstop	SA
183) Odrisamer Despaigne	June 23, 2014	San Diego (NL)	RHP	SA
184) Jorge Soler	August 27, 2014	Chicago (NL)	Outfield	SA
185) Miguel A. González	September 3, 2014	Philadelphia (NL)	RHP	SA
186) Rusney Castillo	September 17, 2014	Boston (AL)	Outfield	SA
187) Raisel Iglesias	April 12, 2015	Cincinnati (NL)	RHP	SA
188) Yasmany Tomás	April 15, 2015	Arizona (NL)	INF/OF	SA

190) Adonis García	May 19, 2015	Atlanta (NL)	Outfield	SA
191) Dariel Alvarez	August 29, 2015	Baltimore (AL)	Outfield	SA
192) Héctor Olivera	September 1, 2015	Atlanta (NL)	Infield	SA
193) Raudel Lazo	September 5, 2015	Miami (NL)	LHP	SA

APPENDIX 2

Cuban Baseball Defectors

The list given here of Cuban baseball "defectors" includes most (but likely not all) of the players who appeared on the rosters of Cuban League National Series teams, developmental league teams, and senior- and junior-level national teams. Eventual major leaguers are listed in **boldface** print, while an asterisk (*) indicates players who legally emigrated. Those departing during the Mariel Boatlift are marked with a pound sign (#). Players also born in Cuba but leaving with their families as youngsters (such as major leaguers José Canseco, Rafael Palmeiro, Eli Marrero, or Adrian Nieto) and later developed as ballplayers in the United States (or outside of Cuba) are not considered here as "defectors" and thus not included in this listing. Also, former National Series stars (like Manuel Hurtado, Rigoberto Betancourt, and Antonio Pacheco) leaving Cuba legally or illegally long after their playing careers had ended are not included here. This list is complete through late 2015, and players are listed chronologically by known/assumed date of defection.

As this book went to press, the flow of defectors from the Cuban baseball system continued to expand almost weekly and any accurate accounting of actual numbers became increasingly difficult to achieve. Any list such as the one in this appendix was doomed to be obsolete even before the ink was dry. Estimates from various Cuban Internet and press sources placed the total for 2015 alone at somewhere between 100 and 150 (including numerous young hopefuls with no experience in either the

National Series or on junior-level national and provincial teams). This list was completed in late fall 2015 and was already dated when the book went to press; the grand total across thirty-five years is now likely closer to 400 than the 369 documented here. Notable defectors in early 2016 would include longtime national team slugger Alexei Bell and the brothers Yulieski and Lourdes (Yunito) Gourriel, who fled a team competing in the February Caribbean Series in the Dominican Republic. The departure of the long-loyal Gourriels was especially significant as it sent a strong signal that the anxiously anticipated accord between the Cuban Baseball Federation and Major League Baseball was no longer on the immediate horizon. In short, the decision of the Gourriels (now often spelled Gurriel) to leave Cuba seemed again to underscore the dominant theme of this book's final chapters—that no MLB-Cuba détente is likely for the foreseeable future.

	Name	Pos	Year	Team	Notes
1)	Eduardo Cajuso	IF#	1980	Industriales	Tigers minor leagues
2)	Julio Soto	IF#	1980	Habana	South Atlantic League
3)	Román Duquene	1B#	1980	Habana	No professional contract
4)	Julio Rojo	P#	1980	Habana	No professional contract
5)	Carlos M. Pérez	C#	1980	Unknown	No professional contract
6)	Roberto Salazar	OF#	1980	Habana	No professional contract
7)	**Bárbaro Garbey**	**OF#**	**1980**	**Industriales**	**3 MLB seasons (Tigers)**
8)	**René Arocha**	**P**	**1991**	**Metropolitanos**	**4 MLB seasons (Cardinals)**
9)	Iván Alvarez	P	1992	Industriales	Giants minor leagues
10)	Osmani Estrada	IF	1992	Industriales	Rangers minor leagues
11)	Alexis Cabreja	OF	1992	Industriales	Rangers minor leagues
12)	Lázaro González	1B	1992	Unknown	No professional contract
13)	Rafael Rodríguez	P	1993	Villa Clara	No professional contract
14)	**Rey Ordóñez**	**SS**	**1993**	**Industriales**	**9 MLB seasons (Mets)**
15)	**Eddie Oropesa**	**P**	**1993**	**Citrícultores**	**4 MLB seasons (Phillies)**
16)	**Alberto Castillo**	**P**	**1993**	**Cuba U-18**	**4 MLB seasons (Orioles)**
17)	Osvaldo Fernández	P	1993	Metropolitanos	Mariners minor leagues
18)	Luis Alberto Alvarez	OF	1993	Mineros	Angel's minor leagues
19)	**Hanzel Izquierdo**	**P**	**1994**	**Cuba U-18**	**1 MLB season (Marlins)**
20)	**Michael Tejera**	**P**	**1994**	**Cuba U-18**	**5 MLB seasons (Marlins)**
21)	Euclides Rojas	P	1994	Industriales	Marlins minor leagues
22)	**Alex Sánchez**	**OF**	**1994**	**Cuba U-18**	**5 MLB seasons (Tigers)**
23)	**Ariel Prieto**	**P**	**1995***	**Isla de la Juventud**	**6 MLB seasons (Athletics)**
24)	**Osvaldo Fernández**	**P**	**1995**	**Holguín**	**4 MLB seasons (Giants)**
25)	**Liván Hernández**	**P**	**1995**	**Isla de la Juventud**	**17 MLB seasons (10 teams)**
26)	Larry Rodríguez	P	1995	Habana Province	D-Backs minor leagues

27) Vladimir Núñez	P	1995	Habana Province	9 MLB seasons (4 teams)
28) Juan Carlos Díaz	1B	1995	Habana Province	1 MLB season (Red Sox)
29) Rolando Arrojo	P	1996	Villa Clara	5 MLB seasons (2 teams)
30) Yalian Serrano	C	1996	Cuba U-18	Tampa Bay contract
31) Osmani Fernández	P	1996	Cuba U-18	Tampa Bay contract
32) Ramon Valdivia	SS	1996	Cuba U-18	No professional contract
33) Josué Pérez	OF	1996	Habana Province	Dodgers minor leagues
34) Michel Hernández	C	1996	Industriales	3 MLB seasons (D-Rays)
35) William Ortega	OF	1996	Industriales	1 MLB season (Cardinals)
36) Jesús Ametller	IF	1996	Industriales	Cardinals minor leagues
37) Roberto Colina	1B	1996	Industriales	Mexican League
38) Francisco Santiesteban	C	1997	Industriales	Mariners minor leagues
39) Nestor Pérez	SS	1997	Matanzas	Devil Rays minor leagues
40) Osmany Santana	OF	1997	Cienfuegos	Indians minor leagues
41) Orlando Hernández	P	1997	Industriales	9 MLB seasons (2 teams)
42) Alberto Hernández	C	1997	Holguín	Taiwan professional league
43) Jorge Luis Toca	1B	1998	Villa Clara	3 MLB seasons (Mets)
44) Maikel Jova	OF	1998	Villa Clara	Blue Jays minor leagues
45) Jorge Olano Díaz	IF	1998	Villa Clara	Independent league
46) Angel López	C	1998	Villa Clara	Marlins minor leagues
47) Osmany García	IF	1998	Villa Clara	Rangers minor leagues
48) Alain Hernández	P	1998	Villa Clara	No professional contract
49) Brayan Peña	C	1999	Cuba U-18	11 MLB seasons (4 teams)
50) Miguel Pérez	P	1999	Holguín	Mets minor leagues
51) Danys Báez	P	1999	Pinar del Río	10 MLB seasons (6 teams)
52) Vladimir Hernández	IF	1999	Industriales	Mets minor leagues
53) Julio César Villalón	P	1999	Holguín	Devil Rays minor leagues

	Pos	Year	Team	Outcome
56) Alexis Hernández	C	1999	Industriales	Independent league
57) Adrian Hernández	**P**	**2000**	**Industriales**	**3 MLB seasons (2 teams)**
58) Mario Miguel Chaoui	P	2000	Havana University	No professional contract
59) Juan Chávez	P	2000	Industriales	No professional contract
60) Neylán Molina	1B	2000	Habana Province	No professional contract
61) Juan Carlos Muñiz	IF	2000	Metropolitanos	Marlins minor leagues
62) Mayque Quintero	P	2000	Industriales	Mets minor leagues
63) Evel Bastida	IF	2000	Industriales	Mariners minor leagues
64) Agustin Marquetti, Jr	P	200	Industriales	Independent leagues
65) Andy Morales	IF	200	Habana Province	Yankees minor leagues
66) Rolando Viera	P	200	Industriales	Red Sox minor league
67) Yolexandry Reina	P	200	Cuba U-18	Independent league
68) William Plaza	C	200	Cuba U-18	Yankees minor leagues
69) Gary Gálvez	P	2002	Cuba U-18	Red Sox minor leagues
70) José Ariel Contreras	**P**	**2002**	**Pinar del Río**	**11 MLB seasons (5 teams)**
71) Adrian Cruz	P	2003	Camagüey	Independent league
72) Maels Rodríguez	P	2003	Sancti Spíritus	No professional contract
73) Yobal Dueñas	IF	2003	Pinar del Río	Yankees minor leagues
74) Lázaro Costa	P	2003	Pinar del Río	No professional contract
75) Roberto Noriega	P	2003	Metropolitanos	Spanish professional league
76) Raúl Valdés	**P**	**2003**	**Habana Province**	**5 MLB seasons (5 teams)**
77) Alay Soler	**P**	**2003**	**Pinar del Río**	**1 MLB season (Mets)**
78) Yunieski Betancourt	**SS**	**2003**	**Villa Clara**	**9 MLB seasons (3 teams)**
79) Zaidel Beltran	P	2003	Villa Clara	Yankees minor leagues
80) Roberto Sotolongo	P	2003	Habana Province	Cubs minor leagues
81) Walter Frías	SS	2003	None	No professional contract
82) Reynar Díaz	NA	2003	None	No professional contract

Name	Pos	Year	Team	League/Destination
83) Michel Abreu	OF	2004	Matanzas	Mets minor leagues
84) **Bárbaro Cañizares**	C	2004	Industriales	**1 MLB season (Braves)**
85) **Amaury Sanit**	P	2004	Industriales	**1 MLB season (Yankees)**
86) Yosandy Ibáñez	P	2004	Industriales	Giants minor leagues
87) Maikel Nininger	P	2004	Metropolitanos	Nicaragua pro league
88) Raidel Costa	P	2004	Pinar del Río	No professional contract
89) Ramiro Chamizo	OF	2004	None	South Atlantic League
90) Edisbel Benitez	P	2004	Pinar del Río	Nicaragua pro league
91) Alexis Fonseca	C	2004	Camagüey	Mariners minor leagues
92) Yunior Sardiñas	1B	2004	Matanzas	No professional contract
93) Serguey Linares	P	2004	Pinar del Río	Pirates minor leagues
94) **Kendrys Morales**	IF	2004	**Industriales**	**9 MLB seasons (3 teams)**
95) **Francisley Bueno**	P	2004	**Industriales**	**5 MLB seasons (2 teams)**
96) Yoankis Toriño	P	2004	Industriales	Independent league
97) Allen Guevara	P	2004	Habana Province	No professional contract
98) Osmany Massó	IF	2004	Industriales	No professional contract
99) Osbeck Castillo	P	2004	Industriales	D-Backs minor leagues
100) **Yunel Escobar**	SS	2004	**Industriales**	**9 MLB seasons (3 teams)**
101) Yamel Guevara	P	2004	Industriales	Independent league
102) José Angel Cordero	P	2004	Metropolitanos	Twins minor leagues
103) Joel Pérez	OF	2004	Isla de la Juventud	Yankees minor leagues
104) Johan Limonta	OF	2004	Industriales	Mariners minor leagues
105) Rafael Galbizo	P	2004	None	Marlins minor leagues
106) Yunieski Sánchez	SS	2004	Matanzas	D-Backs minor leagues
107) Alejandro Zuanzanbar	P	2004	Metropolitanos	Mets minor leagues
108) Oscar Macias	IF	2004	Habana Province	Independent league
109) Roberto Alvarez	OF	2005	Matanzas	Braves minor leagues

	Pos	Year	Team	Status
112) Aylen Ortiz	OF	2005	Metropolitanos	No professional contract
113) Donell Linares	IF	2005	Industriales	Braves minor leagues
114) Omar Llapur	IB	2005	Industriales	Dominican summer league
115) **Juan M. Miranda**	**IB**	**2005**	**Pinar del Río**	**4 MLB seasons (2 teams)**
116) Amaury Cazañas	OF	2005	Matanzas	Cardinals minor leagues
117) **Yoslán Herrera**	**P**	**2005**	**Pinar del Río**	**2 MLB seasons (2 teams)**
118) Yohannas Pérez	IF	2005	Matanzas	Brewers minor leagues
119) Hassan Peña	P	2005	Industriales	Nationals minor leagues
120) José Cano	IF	2005	Metropolitanos	Independent league
121) Joel Galarraga	C	2005	Industriales	Mexican League
122) Reinier Bermúdez	P	2005	Industriales	Indians minor leagues
123) Roberto Sabates	C	2006	Industriales	Cubs minor leagues
124) Kenny Rodríguez	P	2006	Habana Province	Blue Jays minor leagues
125) Yusdel Tuero	P	2006	Habana Province	Cubs minor leagues
126) Leovet Cardoso	P	2007	Cienfuegos	Independent league
127) Ryde Rodríguez	OF	2007	None	Cardinals minor leagues
128) **Alexei Ramírez**	**SS**	**2007**	**Pinar del Río**	**8 MLB seasons (White Sox)**
129) Maikel Peña	OF	2007	Holguín	No professional contract
130) **José D. Fernández**	**P**	**2008**	**None**	**3 MLB seasons (Marlins)**
131) **Dayan Viciedo**	**OF**	**2008**	**Villa Clara**	**6 MLB seasons (White Sox)**
132) Juan Carlos Moreno	SS	2008	Isla de la Juventud	No professional contract
133) **José Iglesias**	**SS**	**2008**	**Habana Province**	**4 MLB seasons (2 teams)**
134) Noel Argüelles	P	2008	Habana Province	Royals minor leagues
135) Raydel Sánchez	P	2008	Cuba U-18	Dodgers minor leagues
136) Dimitri Camareno	P	2008	Holguín	Independent league
137) Felix Pérez Cardoso	OF	2008	Isla de la Juventud	Reds minor leagues
138) Lester Benavides	IF	2008	Villa Clara	No professional contract

139) Yosmany Guerra Febles	IF	2008	Metropolitanos	Marlins minor leagues
140) Sergio Espinosa	P	2008	Isla de la Juventud	Devil Rays minor leagues
141) Alexei Gil Pérez	P	2008	Industriales	Puerto Rico winter league
142) Yasser Gómez	OF	2008	Industriales	Braves minor leagues
143) Yadel Martí	P	2008	Industriales	Mexican League
144) Deinys Súarez	P	2009	Industriales	Independent league
145) José Julio Ruiz	1B	2009	Santiago de Cuba	Devil Rays minor leagues
146) Maikel Torres	P	2009	Metropolitanos	No professional contract
147) Luis Yadiel Fonseca	OF	2009	Isla de la Juventud	Mexican League
148) Joan Chaviano	C	2009	Isla de la Juventud	No professional contract
149) Israel Soto	P	2009	Isla de la Juventud	No professional contract
150) Aroldis Chapman	**P**	**2009**	**Holguín**	**6 MLB seasons (Reds)**
151) Yadil Mujica	SS	2009	Matanzas	Yankees minor leagues
152) Rubi Silva	OF	2009	Habana Province	Cubs minor leagues
153) Yunieski Maya	**P**	**2009**	**Pinar del Río**	**3 MLB seasons (Nationals)**
154) Adeiny Hecevarría	**SS**	**2009**	**Santiago de Cuba**	**4 MLB seasons (2 teams)**
155) Leslie Anderson	OF	2009	Camagüey	Devil Rays minor leagues
156) Ronnier Mustelier	IF	2009	Santiago de Cuba	Yankees minor leagues
157) Jorge Padrón	OF	2009	Pinar del Río	Red Sox minor leagues
158) Reinier Robal	P	2009	Santiago de Cuba	Giants minor leagues
159) Ricardo Estévez Pozo	P	2009	Camagüey	Arizona Fall League (Cubs)
160) Adalberto Ibarra	IF	2009	Camagüey	Red Sox minor leagues
161) Yoannis Negrin	P	2009	Matanzas	Cubs minor leagues
162) Juan Carlos Linares	OF	2009	Habana Province	Red Sox minor leagues
163) Yaniel Cabezas	C	2009	Habana Province	Cubs minor leagues
164) Rafael Valdés	IF	2009	Pinar del Río	Cubs minor leagues
165) Juan Yasser Serrano	P	2009	Villa Clara	Cubs minor leagues

168) Mayke Reyes	OF	2010	None	Cubs minor leagues
169) Duniesky R. Flores	P	2010	Metropolitanos	Puerto Rico winter league
170) Joan Socorras	P	2010	Industriales	No professional contract
171) Leguim Barroso	SS	2010	Industriales	Independent league
172) Javier Monzón	IF	2010	None	Spanish professional league
173) Yasiel Balaguert	OF	2010	Cuba U-18	Cubs minor leagues
174) Osdanis Montero	C	2010	Las Tunas	Mexican Pacific League
175) Reinier Roll	P	2010	Industriales	Unsigned free agent
176) Jorge Zaldivar	SS	2010	Holguín	No professional contract
177) **Roenis Elias**	**P**	**2010**	**Guantánamo**	**2 MLB seasons (Mariners)**
178) **Leonys Martin**	**OF**	**2010**	**Villa Clara**	**5 MLB seasons (Rangers)**
179) **Onelkis García**	**P**	**2010**	**Guantánamo**	**2 MLB seasons (2 teams)**
180) Kenen Bailly	OF	2010	Guantánamo	Blue Jays minor leagues
181) **Raudel Lazo Blanco**	**P**	**2010**	**Pinar del Río**	**1 MLB season (Marlins)**
182) Rafael Valdés Casola	IF	2010	Pinar del Río	Cubs minor leagues
183) **Adonis García**	**OF**	**2011**	**Ciego de Avila**	**1 MLB season (Braves)**
184) Gerardo Concepción	P	2011	Industriales	Cubs minor leagues
185) **Yoenis Céspedes**	**OF**	**2011**	**Granma**	**4 MLB seasons (3 teams)**
186) **Henry Urrutia**	**OF**	**2011**	**Las Tunas**	**2 MLB seasons (Orioles)**
187) Armando Rivero	P	2011	Industriales	Cubs minor leagues
188) Dael Mejias	P	2011	Las Tunas	Unsigned free agent
189) Carlos Martínez-Pumarino	P	2011	Industriales	Cubs minor leagues
190) Alex Cantalpiedra	OF	2011	Isla de la Juventud	Unsigned free agent
191) Victor Rivas	1B	2011	Isla de la Juventud	Unsigned free agent
192) **Jorge Soler**	**OF**	**2011**	**Habana Province**	**2 MLB seasons (Cubs)**
193) **Yasiel Puig**	**OF**	**2012**	**Cienfuegos**	**3 MLB seasons (Dodgers)**
194) **Dariel Alvarez**	**OF**	**2012**	**Camagüey**	**1 MLB season (Orioles)**

195) Aledmys Díaz	IF	2012	Villa Clara	Cardinals minor leagues
196) Omar L. Rodríguez	P	2012	Sancti Spíritus	Yankees minor leagues
197) Orestes Solano	IF	2012	Metropolitanos	Unsigned free agent
198) Yuseff Amador	IF	2012	Metropolitanos	Unsigned free agent
199) Alejandro García	OF	2012	Villa Clara	Unsigned free agent
200) Rafael Hildalgo	IF	2012	Granma	Unsigned free agent
201) Josué Franco	C	2012	Ciego de Avila	Unsigned free agent
202) Roberto Carlos Ramírez	SS	2012	Metropolitanos	Unsigned free agent
203) Yuniesky Lagart	P	2013	Metropolitanos	Unsigned free agent
204) Osbeidy Pérez	OF	2013	None	Unsigned free agent
205) Julio Rivera	C	2013	None	Unsigned free agent
206) Erian Rojas	OF	2013	None	Unsigned free agent
207) Alex Guerrero	**IF**	**2013**	**Las Tunas**	**2 MLB seasons (Dodgers)**
208) Dalier Hinojosa	**P**	**2013**	**Guantánamo**	**1 MLB season (2 teams)**
209) Miguel Angel González	**P**	**2013**	**Habana Province**	**1 MLB season (Phillies)**
210) Misael Silverio	P	2013	Villa Clara	Mariners minor leagues
211) Yenier Bello	C	2013*	Sancti Spíritus	Braves minor leagues
212) Odrismar Despaigne	**P**	**2013**	**Industriales**	**2 MLB seasons (Padres)**
213) Yozzen Cuesta	1B	2013	Ciego de Avila	Unsigned free agent
214) José Dariel Abreu	**1B**	**2013**	**Cienfuegos**	**2 MLB seasons (White Sox)**
215) Erisbel Arruebarrena	**IF**	**2013**	**Cienfuegos**	**1 MLB season (Dodgers)**
216) Raisel Iglesias	**P**	**2013**	**Isla de la Juventud**	**1 MLB season (Reds)**
217) Daniel Carbonell	OF	2013	Camagüey	Giants minor leagues
218) Orlando Pérez	IF	2013	Industriales	Unsigned free agent
219) Lednier Ricardo	C	2013	Camagüey	Unsigned free agent
220) Iriat Chirino	OF	2013*	Industriales	Unsigned free agent
221) Yandy Díaz	IF	2013	Villa Clara	Indians minor leagues

Name	Pos	Year	Province	Status
224) Alexis Leyva	OF	2013	Holguín	Unsigned free agent
225) Angel Tamayo	C	2013	Holguín	Unsigned free agent
226) Yolian Cerce	IF	2013	Guantánamo	Red Sox minor leagues
227) Daron Varona	OF	2013	Camagüey	Devil Rays minor leagues
228) Leonardo Lafitta	SS	2013	Las Tunas	Unsigned free agent
229) Yosvani Hurtado	1B	2013	Santiago de Cuba	Unsigned free agent
230) Yunier Leyva	P	2013	Cienfuegos	Unsigned free agent
231) Ernesto Molinet	1B	2013	Mayabeque	Mexican League
232) Dayán García	IF	2013	Artemisa	Unsigned free agent
233) Pedro William Castillo	OF	2013	Mayabeque	Unsigned free agent
234) Yoelkis Vera	P	2013	Guantánamo	Unsigned free agent
235) Orandy Abascal	C	2013	Mayabeque	Unsigned free agent
236) Yoan López	P	2013	Isla de la Juventud	D-Backs minor leagues
237) Jorge Hernández	P	2013	Cienfuegos	Unsigned free agent
238) Rusney Castillo	**OF**	**2013**	**Ciego de Avila**	**2 MLB seasons (Red Sox)**
239) Raysel Plutin	P	2014	Isla de la Juventud	Unsigned free agent
240) Roberto Baldoquin	IF	2014	Las Tunas	Angels minor leagues
241) Yoan Moncada	IF	2014*	Cienfuegos	Red Sox minor leagues
242) Pavel Quesada	IF	2014*	Cienfuegos	Unsigned free agent
243) Yasmany Tomás	**OF**	**2014**	**Industriales**	**1 MLB season (D-Backs)**
244) Jorge Despaigne	P	2014	Isla de la Juventud	Unsigned free agent
245) Jorge Alberto Martínez	P	2014	Matanzas	Puerto Rico winter league
246) Diosdany Castillo	P	2014	Villa Clara	Mexican League
247) Yasmani Hernández	P	2014	Villa Clara	Unsigned free agent
248) Ariel Miranda	P	2014	Mayabeque	Orioles minor leagues
249) Andy Ibáñez	IF	2014*	Isla de la Juventud	Rangers minor leagues
250) Héctor Olivera	**IF**	**2014**	**Santiago de Cuba**	**1 MLB season (Braves)**

251) Pedro Luis García	P	2014	Matanzas	Unsigned free agent
252) Darián González	SS	2014	Cienfuegos	Unsigned free agent
253) Yoasniel Emilo Pérez	OF	2014	Cienfuegos	Unsigned free agent
254) Michel Rodríguez	IF	2014	Artemisa	Unsigned free agent
255) Guillermo Heredia	OF	2014	Matanzas	Unsigned free agent
256) Angel Miguel Fernández	SS	2014	Isla de la Juventud	Unsigned free agent
257) Alejandro Jaime Ortiz	IF	2014	Isla de la Juventud	Unsigned free agent
258) Gelkis Jiménez	IF	2014	Santiago de Cuba	Unsigned free agent
259) Adriel Labrada	IF	2014	Santiago de Cuba	Unsigned free agent
260) Carlos Manuel Portuondo	P	2014	Santiago de Cuba	Unsigned free agent
261) Edwin Vassel Pedroso	IF	2014	Cienfuegos	Unsigned free agent
262) Javier González	P	2014	Cienfuegos	Unsigned free agent
263) Dian Toscano	OF	2014	Villa Clara	Braves minor leagues
264) Eddy Abel García	P	2014	Industriales	Unsigned free agent
265) Pablo Millan Fernández	P	2014	Holguín	Dodgers minor leagues
266) Raimar Navarro	P	2014	Holguín	Unsigned free agent
267) Pedro Luis Marquez	OF	2014	Cienfuegos	Unsigned free agent
268) Yadier Alvarez (Alvares)	P	2014	None	Dodgers minor leagues
269) Yasiel Mederos	1B	2014	Camagüey	Orioles minor leagues
270) Danny Hernández	P	2014	Cienfuegos	Unsigned free agent
271) Carlos Olexis González	P	2014	Holguín	Unsigned free agent
272) Lerys Aguilera	1B	2014	Holguín	Unsigned free agent
273) Yanis Quiala	P	2014	Holguín	Unsigned free agent
274) Royman Hernández	NA	2014	None	Unsigned free agent
275) Alexander Gambe	NA	2014	None	Mexican semipro league
276) Lorenzo Quintana	C	2015	Pinar del Río	Unsigned free agent
277) Julio Alfredo Martínez	P	2015	Pinar del Río	Unsigned free agent

280) Osniel Madera	OF	2015	Pinar del Río	Unsigned free agent
281) Lázaro Alfonso	1B	2015	Pinar del Río	Unsigned free agent
282) Yoel Rojas	C	2015	Pinar del Río	Unsigned free agent
283) Vladimir Gutiérrez	P	2015	Pinar del Río	Unsigned free agent
284) Dainer Moreira	SS	2015	Matanzas	Unsigned free agent
285) Orlando Barroso Gómez	P	2015	Santiago de Cuba	Unsigned free agent
286) Luis Alberto Valdés	SS	2015	Pinar del Río	Suspended in Cuba
287) Yosvani Peraza	C	2015	Pinar del Río	Suspended in Cuba
288) Yandy Fernández	P	2015	Villa Clara	Unsigned free agent
289) Yunieski García	P	2015	Artemisa	Unsigned free agent
290) Joaquin Carbonell	OF	2015	Santiago de Cuba	Unsigned free agent
291) Alain Tamayo	P	2015	Granma	Unsigned free agent
292) Leinier Rodríguez	P	2015	Mayabeque	Unsigned free agent
293) Victor Muñoz	OF	2015	Artemisa	Unsigned free agent
294) José Norbelis Betancourt	P	2015	Mayabeque	Unsigned free agent
295) Victor Ernesto Baró	P	2015	Ciego de Avila	Unsigned free agent
296) Rudelis García	C	2015	Ciego de Avila	Unsigned free agent
297) Osmel Aguila	OF	2015	Camagüey	Unsigned free agent
298) Yuniet Flores	OF	2015	Villa Clara	Unsigned free agent
299) Raidel Orta Ortiz	P	2015*	Industriales	Unsigned free agent
300) Dairon Blanco	OF	2015	Industriales	Unsigned free agent
301) Yosibel Castillo	P	2015	Granma	Unsigned free agent
302) Yordan Alvarez	OF	2015	Pinar del Río	Unsigned free agent
303) Julio Pablo Martínez	OF	2015	Isla de la Juventud	Unsigned free agent
304) Alay Rafael Lago	3B	2015	Artemisa	Unsigned free agent
305) Moises Esquerre	SS	2015	Cuba U-18	Unsigned free agent
306) Julio Chibás (Chivás)	OF	2015	Artemisa	Unsigned free agent

	Pos	Year	Team	Status
307) Enríque Bicet	IF	2015	Santiago de Cuba	Unsigned free agent
308) Lázaro Hernández	IF	2015	Artemisa	Unsigned free agent
309) Roland Bolaño	P	2015	Mayabeque	Unsigned free agent
310) Aribal Sierra	IF	2015	Pinar del Río	Unsigned free agent
311) Bárbaro Urquiola	NA	2015	Pinar del Río	Unsigned free agent
312) Mario Luis Cosme	OF	2015	Artemisa	Unsigned free agent
313) Carlos Viera	P	2015	Las Tunas	Unsigned free agent
314) Omar Estévez	IF	2015	Matanzas	Unsigned free agent
315) Dayan González	OF	2015	Artemisa	Unsigned free agent
316) Misael Villa	P	2015	Artemisa	Unsigned free agent
317) Diosbel Arias	IF	2015	Artemisa	Unsigned free agent
318) Navid Luis Cosme	P	2015	Artemisa	Unsigned free agent
319) Raidel Chacón	OF	2015	Mayabeque	Unsigned free agent
320) Rogelio Quesada	P	2015	Mayabeque	Unsigned free agent
321) Elian Leyva	P	2015	Mayabeque	Unsigned free agent
322) Yosuan Hernández	P	2015	Mayabeque	Unsigned free agent
323) Henry Quintero	IF	2015	Camagüey	Unsigned free agent
324) Dary Bartolomé	1B	2015	Camagüey	Unsigned free agent
325) Damian Leyva	IF	2015	Camagüey	Unsigned free agent
326) Raiko Olivares	IF	2015	Industriales	Unsigned free agent
327) Fidel Romero	P	2015	Camagüey	Unsigned free agent
328) Henry Pantoja	OF	2015	Santiago de Cuba	Unsigned free agent
329) Yusnier Efrain Díaz	OF	2015	Industriales	Unsigned free agent
330) Yordanis Linares	OF	2015	Villa Clara	Unsigned free agent
331) Yasiel Sierra Pérez	P	2015	Holguín	Unsigned free agent
332) Ramón Lunar	IF	2015	Villa Clara	Unsigned free agent
333) José Miguel Fernández	IF	2015	Matanzas	Unsigned free agent

336) Yohandris Portal	P	2015	Industriales	Unsigned free agent
337) Jesús Balaguer	P	2015	Industriales	Unsigned free agent
338) Ernesto Iglesias Blanco	P	2015	Industriales	Unsigned free agent
339) Alberto Díaz Martínez	C	2015	Santiago de Cuba	Unsigned free agent
340) Cionel Pérez	P	2015	Matanzas	Unsigned free agent
341) Eddy Julio Martínez	OF	2015	Las Tunas	Unsigned free agent
342) Alfredo Rodríguez	SS	2015	Isla de la Juventud	Unsigned free agent
343) Norge Luis Ruiz	P	2015	Camagüey	Unsigned free agent
344) Maikel Serrano	OF	2015	Pinar del Río	Unsigned free agent
345) Yosviel Vilaú	P	2015	Pinar del Río	Unsigned free agent
346) Randy Arozarena	IF	2015	Pinar del Río	Unsigned free agent
347) Jorge Oña	OF	2015	Industriales	Unsigned free agent
348) Yadiel Hernández	OF	2015	Matanzas	Unsigned free agent
349) Luis Yander la O	IF	2015	Santiago de Cuba	Unsigned free agent
350) Yanio Pérez	IF	2015	Artemisa	Unsigned free agent
351) Adrian Morejon	P	2015	U-15 National Team	Unsigned free agent
352) Yusnier Aguilar	OF	2015	U-18 National Team	Unsigned free agent
353) Pedro Duran	P	2015	Industriales	Unsigned free agent
354) Jorge Luis Bravo Ramírez	P	2015	Santiago de Cuba	Unsigned free agent
355) Lazarito Armenteros	OF	2015	U-15 National Team	Unsigned free agent
356) Jonatan Machado	IF	2015	U-15 National Team	Unsigned free agent
357) Yokist Luis Rodríguez	IF	2015	None	Unsigned free agent
358) Mario Miranda	IF	2015	Isla de la Juventud	Unsigned free agent
359) Numberto Castellano	OF	2015	None	Unsigned free agent
360) Juan Oviedo	P	2015	None	Unsigned free agent
361) Ramón Ernesto Perez	P	2015	None	Unsigned free agent
362) Julio Montesino	P	2015	Industriales	Unsigned free agent

363) Rodry Castello	P	2015	Pinar del Río	Unsigned free agent
364) Noel Ortiz	P	2015	Matanzas	Unsigned free agent
365) Luis Periche	SS	2015	Guantánamo	Unsigned free agent
366) Freddy Portilla	C	2015	Holguín	Unsigned free agent
367) Adrian Moreno Rondon	SS	2015	Granma	Unsigned free agent
368) Urmani Guerra	OF	2015	Granma	Unsigned free agent
369) Miguel Vargas	IF	2015	U-18 National Team	Unsigned free agent

NOTES

PROLOGUE

1. My first trip to Cuba occurred in February 1997, when Mark Rucker and I began research for the coffee table book *Smoke: The Romance and Lore of Cuban Baseball*. Cuba and its baseball soon became a personal passion and I have since visited the island every year except 1998, sometimes as many as three times. My total Cuba visits now number more than 50.

2. English-language biographies penned by Robert E. Quirk (*Fidel Castro*, 1993) and Tad Szulc (*Fidel, A Critical Portrait*, 1986) are the most highly recommended. Neither of these books, nor any of the other standard biographies, have anything substantive to say about Fidel's connections to baseball, a disappointing oversight likely related to the long-reigning prejudice against baseball as a serious academic topic.

3. John Walker, "The Bay of Capitalist Pigs" (*Newsweek*, May 15, 2015). To quote Walker further: "The Cuban invasion is at last taking place, on a limited basis (and on the bases). The soldiers are not clad in olive fatigues but in Dodger blue and Cincinnati red. The weapons are not missiles, but long balls and 100 mph fastballs. And because of the trade embargo between the United States and Cuba that dates back to 1962, the soldiers leading this invasion are contraband."

4. Brian Costa, "Why Baseball Is Losing Its Grip on Cuba" (*Wall Street Journal*, June 9, 2015). Costa refers to "a generational shift that highlights the global nature of the threat to baseball's future," and, while he focuses on Cuba, he also points to a similar phenomenon in North America and elsewhere in the Caribbean (Puerto Rico) and Asia (Japan).

5. The full saga of Jorge Pasquel's raids on big-league talent is recounted by John Virtue (*South of the Color Barrier*) whose treatment also reveals just how

Pasquel's challenges may well have hastened big-league integration as an immediate aftermath.

6. John McGraw, for one, on more than one occasion compared Cuba's top pitcher of the century's first decade, José Méndez, to his own New York Giants ace hurler Christy Mathewson. The National Baseball Hall of Fame (Cooperstown), on its current website page for 2006 inductee Méndez, quotes McGraw as saying "If Méndez was a white man I would pay $50,000 for his release from Almendares" (his Cuban League club). He also said that Méndez (known as Cuba's "Black Diamond") was "Walter Johnson and Grover Alexander rolled into one."

7. Ron Fimrite, "In Cuba Its *Viva* El Grand Old Game" (*Sports Illustrated*, June 6, 1977). A similar report from the outlying frontiers of Cuban baseball was penned by Thomas Boswell for his 1987 volume *How Life Imitates the World Series* ("How Baseball Helps the Harvest or What the Bay of Pigs Did to the Bigs"). It is intriguing that Boswell's report, penned almost five full years later, is based largely on his visit to the same Cuban ballpark toured by Fimrite, Pinar del Río's Capitan San Luis Stadium in Cuba's westernmost province.

8. Eugene McCarthy ("Diamond Diplomacy"), 12. McCarthy apparently buys the Fidel-as-prospect myth wholesale and cites an unsourced scouting report that Fidel "didn't have a major league fastball."

I. THE ESSENCE OF "PUIGMANIA"

1. Jayson Stark ("Detailing Yasiel Puig's Historically Great Run"), June 3, 2014.

2. At the 2008 World Junior Championships in Edmonton (Canada), Puig earned honors on the tournament all-star squad after leading Cuba to a bronze medal victory over Australia. His final game performance included a three-for-four batting display and three runs scored.

3. There has also been speculation that it was disciplinary issues and possibly an early defection attempt (not injury at all) that keep Puig on the sidelines during that second season. Jesse Katz ("Escape from Cuba: Yasiel Puig's Untold Journey to the Dodgers") speculates on the disciplinary causes and mentions some reported no-shows at team practices. Katz also reports a Puig quotation in the local *Cinco de Septiembre* newspaper. "I watched the next season from the bench for having behaved good in practice" is the direct translation of Puig's possible tongue-in-check comment to a local journalist.

4. Two years later (2013), during All-Star Game festivities celebrated in Sancti Spíritus, another promising Cienfuegos novice named Yoan Moncada

would capture these same two exhibitions during his own single appearance at the mid-season classic.

5. The strength of the Rotterdam team was in part explained by the fact that Cuba was preparing for the upcoming September IBAF World Cup games in Panama and had divided more than seventy pre-selection candidates into three separate training squads destined for summer participation in Rotterdam (World Port Tournament), Caracas (ALBA Games), and Canada (World Baseball Challenge).

6. Torres was prominent in the grandstand on the afternoon of the opening game between Cuba and Curaçao but quickly disappeared from Rotterdam once he had his one defector, Gerardo Concepción, securely in tow.

7. A greater obsession with shopping by Cuban ballplayers in Holland (as opposed to trips to higher-level events like the World Baseball Classic or World Cup) might be explained by the fact that many of the players traveling to the World Port Tournament are not regular national team stars and might see the occasion as a rare opportunity not to be missed.

8. Tight Cuban security is something of a myth, as suggested elsewhere in these pages. Although Cuban authorities may have relaxed ever so slightly on this issue in recent years (especially on familiar stomping grounds like the Netherlands), there is sufficient evidence that the notion of iron-clad security was always overplayed. This can be seen in Fainaru and Sanchez's reports throughout *The Duke of Havana* about how easy the access to players was for agents like Joe Cubas and Tom Cronin. Players often departed team hotels (although usually in secrecy and with considerable caution) to visit with the American agent Cubas and his pals, friendly high rollers willing to provide beer and food at nearby hotels or bars. Some players with no intentions of defection—Fainaru singles out Lázaro Valle—often took part and accepted handouts when they were available.

9. He had, however, sold a spare Cienfuegos jersey, something I can personally verify since I witnessed the transaction, which had taken place in my own hotel room the previous evening.

10. The Dutch Federation paid all expenses for the Cuban teams attending both the Rotterdam and Haarlem events. This would later result in a surprise development at the 2012 Haarlem Baseball Week when the Venezuelan team, wanting the same arrangement, was a last-minute "no show" after tournament action had already started. Venezuela didn't arrive on time, then promised to come a few days late, but only if fully funded like the Cubans. The request was denied and the tournament went on with one fewer team and a revamped schedule.

11. One subsequent development seems to argue in favor of the shoplifting story. After weeks of speculation surrounding Puig's absence from the Cienfuegos squad at the start of the 2011–2012 season, it was announced in Cienfuegos

Province (but not much publicized in the rest of the country) that he had done his penance (suggesting a charge less serious than attempting to defect) and was being reinstated on the reserve squad, making him eligible to be activated after twenty-five games. But he never surfaced, perhaps due to still another defection effort. This same revelation also feeds another contrary theory. Scott Eden ("No One Walks Off the Island") suggests that Puig may have struck a deal with government officials to cooperate in fingering actual or potential smugglers working to entice ballplayers. There would eventually be a Miami lawsuit (discussed later) suggesting that Puig indeed had given up the name of at least one innocent victim in order to purchase the good graces of officials and cover yet another plot for his own escape.

12. Gwen Knapp ("Puig: A Hollywood-Style Rookie"), June 17, 2013.

13. Jordan Ritter Conn ("From Cuba with Heat: Marlins Rookie Pitcher Jose Fernández on His Journey from Cuban Defector to MLB All-Star"), July 16, 2013.

14. Jesse Katz ("Escape from Cuba: Yasiel Puig's Untold Journey to the Dodgers"), April 13, 2014.

15. The case that Miami lawyer Avelino González would build against Puig (with help from the testimonies of Yunior Despaigne) involved a Cuban-Dominican named Miguel Angel Corbacho Daudinot, who received a seven-year Cuban prison term for human trafficking, which he later claimed resulted from false testimony by the ballplayer. While visiting Cuba, Corbacho had made the mistake of driving an acquaintance to Cienfuegos to meet with Puig. The pair were arrested and tried after Puig supposedly reported them both to authorities as potential traffickers. The suit in the Corbacho case also alleges that Puig had earlier become "a serial informant" and that, after supposedly being suspended at the end of his rookie year for a first defection attempt, he had purchased favor and reinstatement by turning in the two young men who had accompanied him in that initial failed *lanchero* escape effort. This claim is based solely on the Despaigne testimony and involves the same Puig suspension during his second league season that has so many other explanations attached to it. It is therefore uncertain how true any of these charges are.

16. Peter C. Bjarkman ("MLB's Next Headache: Cartels, Gangsters, and Their Cuban Superstars"), April 18, 2014.

17. Scott Eden ("No One Walks Off the Island"), April 17, 2014. Eden corrects two important errors that mar the Katz article. The first involves the date of the defection: Puig and his companions departed from the coast of Cuba in late April 2012, not June as Katz asserts. A June departure would have made the entire chronology of the events impossible, since it was in June that Puig signed his Dodgers contract in Mexico City. Also Katz fails to grasp Cuban geography and asserts that Puig and his party headed to the northern province of Matanzas

to meet their *lancheros*. This suggests a departure from the north coast. But the province of Matanzas stretches all the way to the southern coast and includes the famed Bay of Pigs invasion landing site. As Eden clarifies, the group departed from the jungle coastline of the Ciénaga de Zapata, a vast swampland to the west of Playa Girón (the Bay of Pigs).

18. Eden ("No One Walks Off the Island") quotes a Cuban indictment document in the Soriano case, obtained by Despaigne, that names Puig and Raúl Pacheco as co-conspirators trying to entice one of Puig's former Cienfuegos teammates (supposedly either Noelvis Entenza or Erisbel Arruebarrena) into leaving the island. This document, if legitimate, provides evidence of Cuban officials formally charging Puig with human trafficking. Eden's version is that Puig may have been angered by Despaigne's providing of information to the Miami lawyer building a case for the Corbacho suit. The speculation follows that Puig may have targeted Despaigne's family by sending money to Cuba to be delivered to Cienfuegos pitcher Entenza and urging Soriano to deliver it, knowing he would be caught. In other words it was some kind of prearranged trap or informal sting operation.

19. Jeff Passen, Charles Robinson, and Rand Geitlin ("Leonys Martin Lawsuit Details Allegations of Cuban Baseball Player Smuggling"), December 6, 2013.

20. Ibid.

21. James Wagner ("Yunel Escobar's Long and Winding Road to the Big Leagues"), May 7, 2015.

22. The five players accompanying Escobar were pitchers José Cordero, Rafael Galbizo, and Yamel Guevara (his cousin), outfielder Joel Pérez, and first baseman Johan Limonta. None of the others would ever reach the big leagues but all would play at least briefly in the minor leagues. Yamil Guevara injured his arm in one of many pre-draft tryouts and remained unsigned and relegated to playing low-level independent league baseball.

23. Jorge L. Ortiz ("Hechevarria Reflects: Marlins Shortstop Recalls Harrowing Trip from Cuba"), May 16, 2015.

24. The two phases known as the "Joe Cubas Plan" and the "*Bolsa Negra*" did have some overlap. While Cubas was never involved directly in illegally smuggling players off their home island, he did arrange to remove the families of Rolando Arrojo and Ozzie Fernández from Cuba by that method.

25. Scott Eden ("No One Walks Off the Island"), April 17, 2014.

26. Susan Slusser and Demian Bulwa ("While the Cuban Defector Broke In with the Oakland A's, His Family Endured a Harrowing Struggle to Reach the U.S."), July 30, 2014. The interview with Céspedes was actually conducted on May 31, 2014.

2. CUBA'S HIDDEN "*BÉISBOL PARADISO*"

1. Thomas Carter (*The Quality of Home Runs*), 41. The original passage is drawn from Giamatti's 1989 volume *Take Time for Paradise: Americans and Their Games*.

2. Peter C. Bjarkman (*A History of Cuban Baseball, 1864–2006*), 318–19; Roberto González Echevarría (*The Pride of Havana*), 90.

3. González Echevarría (*The Pride of Havana*), chapter 4 ("A Cuban *Belle Epoque*").

4. The full story of baseball's origins in Cuba is told in my own work (*A History of Cuban Baseball, 1864–2006*) and also in González Echevarría's *The Pride of Havana*.

5. González Echevarría (*The Pride of Havana*), 86; and Bjarkman (*A History of Cuban Baseball, 1864–2006*), 82.

6. Joseph Reaves (*Taking in a Game*), 17. Reaves here cites Allen Guttmann's suggestion (*From Ritual to Record*, 114–15) that the rapid spread of baseball (under the influence of American soldiers, sailors, educators, and missionaries) to Canada, Asia, and the Caribbean in the late nineteenth and early twentieth centuries had much to do with the fact that those regions were "strongly and favorably impressed with the United States as a model of modern civilization."

7. Bjarkman (*A History of Cuban Baseball, 1864–2006*), 321–22.

8. Early barnstorming tours of Havana are documented in Bjarkman's *A History of Cuban Baseball, 1864–2006*, especially in chapter 6 ("Cuba's Blackball Doubleheaders on the Dark Side of the Moon").

9. Bjarkman (*A History of Cuban Baseball, 1864–2006*), chapter 6. This chapter provides a listing and discussion of the sixteen Cubans who were both big leaguers and Negro leaguers between 1904 and 1953.

10. Bjarkman (*A History of Cuban Baseball, 1864–2006*), chapter 1 ("Martín Dihigo—Baseball's Least-Known Hall of Famer"). A more expansive version is also found in my essay on Martin Dihigo for the online SABR Baseball Biography Project.

11. González Echevarría (*The Pride of Havana*), 345–46.

12. Nicholas Dawidoff ("The Struggles of Sandy A"), July 1989. While the story related by Dawidoff is undoubtedly truthful in the main, it remains sketchy, since it contains only Amoros's own slim account of what transpired.

13. The new Havana-based Cuban Hall installed in its inaugural class five icons of the revolutionary era (1961–2015): Omar Linares, Luis Giraldo Casanova, Orestes Kindelán, Braudilio Vinent, and Antonio Muñoz. In recognition of the earlier pre-revolution epoch the following five were also enshrined: Esteban Bellán, umpire Armado Mastri, Conrado Marrero (recently deceased at age 103),

Camilo Pascual, and Orestes Miñoso. The old-timers group was restricted to those players and officials not already appearing on the pre-revolution-era plaque that has long hung in Latin American Stadium.

14. Preston Gómez's personal association with Fidel came directly through Fidel's fellow guerrilla warrior, personal secretary, and reported lover Celia Sánchez. Gómez (born Pedro) and Celia were schoolmates in the Preston sugar mill town located in Cuba's Oriente region, the location responsible for the future ballplayer's adopted name. Celia and Preston remained close friends while the latter was managing the 1959 Sugar Kings and the former was first installed in Havana alongside Fidel. Celia reportedly often invited Preston for postgame visits in the apartment she shared with Fidel.

15. The Miami association was appropriately and revealingly named the Federation of Exiled Cuban Professional Ballplayers (Federación de Peloteros Profesionales Cubanos en Exilio).

16. For the history of baseball's Amateur World Series (known as the Baseball World Cup after 1988) see Bjarkman (*A History of Cuban Baseball, 1864–2006*), chapter 7; and (*Diamonds around the Globe*), chapter 10.

17. Bjarkman (*A History of Cuban Baseball, 1864–2006*), chapter 7.

18. Elaborate parallels between American baseball and American military adventurism provide the central theme of Robert Elias's *The Empire Strikes Out*. Similar Japanese, Chinese, Taiwanese, and Korean uses of baseball are detailed by Joseph Reaves in *Taking in a Game*. I elaborate on the treatments by both authors elsewhere in this volume.

19. Bjarkman (*A History of Cuban Baseball, 1864–2006*), chapter 7 ("Havana as Amateur Baseball Capital of the World").

20. One such report was a June 1977 *Sports Illustrated* article penned by Ron Fimrite; another was a chapter in Thomas Boswell's 1987 book *How Life Imitates the World Series*. Both are mentioned in the prologue.

3. SUGAR CANE CURTAIN FIASCOS

1. Manfred's comments were made at a March 9, 2015, spring training visit press conference in Jupiter, Florida, and widely circulated in an online Associated Press news release.

2. Cuban players, employed by a government-run league and not by corporate teams, do not currently have contracts of a type widely recognized in other professional baseball leagues. It has also become quite clear that Cuban sports officials, operating within a communist-socialist government framework, have little understanding of contract law as it exists in a capitalist free-enterprise system. This fact became clear in late April 2015 when INDER officials chose to

ignore details of Yulieski Gourriel's Japanese contract, a mistake that ended in the cancellation of Gourriel's lucrative deal with the Yokohama DeNA BayStars club of the Japanese Central League.

3. Higinio Vélez, a strict disciplinarian and Communist Party hard-liner suspicious of almost any foreign contact with Cuban ballplayers, has never been popular with national team players, either as manager (where he was respected but not necessarily admired) or more recently as the head of the traveling team delegations. Vélez is renowned for keeping players confined to their hotel rooms (or at least to the team's hotel floor) and restricting contact with fans, media, and hotel visitors.

4. Julia Sweig and Michael Bustamante ("Cuba After Communism"), 1.

5. Margaret Randall (*To Change the World: My Years in Cuba*), 2, correctly notes that "freedom for Cuba" is always a rallying cry capable of attracting votes from the Cuban exile community and that "Cuban exiles still mostly hope for their country's return to 'democracy'—whatever their idea of democracy may be." The skeptic might assume that it mostly means the return of long-ago confiscated properties to Miami residents and the return to power on the island of Miami exiles, and little more.

6. The most impactful of the American-sponsored (or at least American-supported) attacks on Cuban soil was the unsuccessful Bay of Pigs invasion of April 1961. Less publicized in the US media was the bombing sabotage of a Cuban airliner (Cubana Airlines flight 455 bound from Barbados to Jamaica) on October 6, 1976, which killed all seventy-three passengers. Former CIA terrorist operative Luis Posada Carriles has long been implicated in the plot but remains free in South Florida exile. The same Posada Carriles latter admitted organizing a string of 1997 Havana hotel bombings (including the Nacional, Meliá Cohiba, Capri, and Copacabana), one of which took the life of an Italian tourist in the Copacabana bar. Also, reported plots on Fidel's life (some involving James Bond–like tactics) have been numerous but remain, in most cases, thinly documented and quite fuzzy in detail. Two sources for tracing these events are Jon Elliston (*Psywar on Cuba*) and Jane Franklin (*Cuba and the United States: A Chronological History*).

7. Randall uses United Nations statistics for her comparisons and emphasizes percentages and per capita figures rather than somewhat misleading total dollar amounts.

8. Randall (*To Change the World: My Years in Cuba*), 2–3. Randall also catalogs other pronounced hypocrisies of the official American stance on Cuba, especially during the recent eight-year Bush administration.

9. Randall admits personal misgivings about heavy-handed Cuban government tactics. But she does nonetheless find a rationale: "To defend itself the revolution has often taken measures strongly criticized by a succession of US

administrations (and also by some of us who love the revolution), such as clamp-
ing down on protests, imprisoning dissidents, restricting travel, and controlling
internet and other communication with the outside world" (3). Another source
detailing the disillusionment of many early Castro supporters is Patrick
Symmes's book-length portrait of Fidel's 1930s and 1940s Jesuit schoolboy days
in Santiago (*The Boys from Delores*).

10. Roberto González Echevarría (*The Pride of Havana*), 352, puts the matter
in perspective by suggesting "it is as if Franco had been deeply and visibly
committed to the fate of bullfighting in Spain throughout his long rule and
donned the *traje de luces* once in a while to try a few passes."

11. David Truby ("Castro's Curveball"), May 1989; Kevin Kerrane (*Dollar
Sign on the Muscle*); Michael and Mary Oleksak (*Béisbol: Latin Americans and
the Grand Old Game*).

12. The myth has been fully dismantled in this author's own Cuban baseball
history volume (chapter 9) and also by Roberto González Echevarría (*The Pride
of Havana*), chapter 9. Two novels exploiting the theme take very different
approaches nonetheless. Tim Wendel (*Castro's Curveball*) expands the myth
(even if he may not believe it) by providing a full-blown fictionalized account of
Fidel's nascent pitching career. Randy Wayne White (*Cuban Straits*) more recently builds his own twisted storyline around the concept of Cuban authorities
guarding the notion of the Comandante's baseball prowess in order to protect a
vital national myth. White completely distorts reality, since Fidel's one known
game with the Havana University law school team was indeed a baseball match
and not a mere softball match, as White fictionalizes. But the bottom line that
gives the lie to White's account is the fact that the Cubans have never been
behind the legend but only laughed off those reports, which were a creation of
American writers and not Cuban reporters.

13. Everardo J. Santamarina ("The Hoak Hoax"), 29–30.

14. Gary Joseph Cieradkowski (*The League of Outsider Baseball: An Illustrated History of Baseball's Forgotten Heroes*), 2015. Cieradkowski also writes
on his Castro ball card in that volume (one reproduced online as part of his
"Infinite Baseball Card Set") that "this was the extent of Castro's baseball career
which Cuban propaganda has greatly exaggerated." Again a distortion.

15. The detailed history of INDER's birth is best told by Paula Pettavino and
Geralyn Pye in their book *Sport in Cuba: The Diamond in the Rough*, (especially
chapters 1 and 3).

16. Fidel's presence at the center of the national sport was already established
during the final two seasons of organized baseball's professional winter league,
which found him throwing out the first pitch of the penultimate 1959–1960
season, the first league opening day after his rise to power.

17. González Echevarría (*The Pride of Havana*), 353. Those critics of the Cuban system who discredit the Castro regime's use of baseball victories as a propagandistic or nationalistic tool should remember that MLB also has a long history of utilizing the sport to spread American ideals, policies, values, and cultural domination. Those unaware of this element of America's national pastime are urged to read *The Empire Strikes Out*, Robert Elias's evaluation of more than a century of American baseball diplomacy as being thinly disguised American baseball imperialism.

18. William LeoGrande and Peter Kornbluh (*Back Channel to Cuba: The Hidden Story of Negotiations between Washington and Havana*).

19. LeoGrande and Kornbluh (*Back Channel to Cuba*), chapter 2. The authors of this revealing study trace in great detail virtually hundreds of communications and secret negotiations between Cuban officials and eleven successive American presidential administrations (including that of Barack Obama).

20. LeoGrande and Kornbluh (*Back Channel to Cuba*), 96–97. Castro, seeking once more to smooth the waters, secretly requested a meeting with Washington officials before the Warren Commission report on the Kennedy assassination was published. The subsequent meeting with Commission lawyer and later Secretary of Transportation William T. Coleman Jr. was held in mid-summer 1964 on Castro's private yacht off Cuba's northern coast. Coleman would later report to Chief Justice Earl Warren he could find no evidence of Castro's or Cuba's involvement in the Kennedy assassination.

21. "*Béisbol* Diplomacy: Declassified Documents from 1975 Reveal Secret U.S.-Cuba Negotiations for Exhibition Games" (The National Security Archive Electronic Briefing Booklet No. 12). A more detailed discussion of USA-Cuba baseball détente efforts and a chronology of specific attempts at baseball diplomacy can be found in Bjarkman (*A History of Cuban Baseball, 1864–2006*), chapter 12, 415–16.

22. Milton Jamail (*Full Count*), 126–27.

23. My frequent Cuba travel companion Robert Weinstein played an instrumental role in transporting several crates of Louisville Slugger bats to Havana in mid-March 1999. International tournament play was scheduled to introduce both wooden bats and professional ballplayers in time for the July–August Pan American Games in Winnipeg, and the Cubans were shifting to the new "lumber" in the middle of their own post-season playoffs in preparation for this new reality. Cuba's slow start in Winnipeg (they eventually defeated the Americans for the gold medal, after losing several preliminary round games) was largely attributed to the difficult adjustment to wooden bats by sluggers like Omar Linares and Orestes Kindelán, who had played nearly their entire careers with aluminum artillery.

24. The Federal Aviation Administration (at the urging of MLB) had also cleared airspace around the Camden Yards ballpark in anticipation of possible attempts to repeat an unsuccessful effort by one Miami-based pilot and Bay of Pigs veteran to breach Cuban airspace and drop anti-Castro leaflets over Latin American Stadium during the earlier March contest.

25. The lone Cuban jumping ship in Baltimore was former national team pitcher Rigoberto Betancourt, a southpaw of modest stature who had played eight National Series seasons during the sixties and achieved only slightly more than modest success. He owned a 38–27 career record and twelve career shut-outs. He had more recently been a youth league coach and was accompanying a 300-strong Cuban delegation of former athletes brought to Baltimore as belated reward for long and loyal service to the revolution. Betancourt was immediately portrayed in US media accounts as a top national team pitching coach, something he clearly was not. The ex-coach's story would soon involve a strange twist and sad outcome. Within six months his name would reappear as the subject of a Miami magazine story detailing at least one defector's subsequent disillusion-ments with the touted "American Dream." Betancourt told *Miami New Times* correspondent Lissette Corsa ("The Cuban Coach,"), August 30, 2001, that he had been promised work in organized baseball (coaching for the Boston Red Sox) but was still wasting away unemployed in Florida (Hialeah) and now very much regretting his decision to abandon his native land and former life. "I lived well in Cuba," he reflected, "I had a car, a large house . . . a good job, and the opportunity to travel abroad. I had prestige. And I left everything." The Boston job had been lost when paperwork for a US work permit was delayed, and he was subsequently abandoned by his agent and handler Joe Cubas. Betancourt was one apparent example of the risks inherent in any attempts by Cubans to trade home-land, family, and relative island security for the elusive lure of riches somewhere within America's coveted Promised Land.

4. NINETY MILES OF SEA, ONE HUNDRED MILES OF "HEATER"

1. The final pair of spring-training games in Havana's Latin American Sta-dium on the immediate heels of the 1959 revolution were played between the Los Angeles Dodgers and Cincinnati Reds on March 20–21, three months after Fidel Castro had come to power.

2. One of my most eye-opening moments at the beginning of my two-decade Cuban baseball sojourn occurred on the field in Winnipeg less than an hour before the gold medal game. I had approached the Cuban dugout to extend best wishes to then-commissioner Carlitos Rodríguez and was exchanging pleasant-ries when Carlitos received a cell phone call and excused himself while retreat-

ing to the dugout. I heard enough of the conversation from a distance to know that the voice on the other end of the line was definitely Fidel. There are many tales about Fidel Castro micromanaging the Cuban national team and now I had my own direct evidence.

3. For the record, Maels posted a 2.34/1 strikeouts/walks ratio in his admittedly brief six-year career. This compares favorably to the long tenures of Nolan Ryan (2.04), Bob Feller (1.46), Randy Johnson (3.26), and Walter Johnson (2.57). But Maels's single-season (2000) 3.46/1 ratio is one of the best found anywhere. That stellar season he led the National Series in both Ks (263) and free passes (76).

4. Dueñas was not the only defector to come to a sad end. In February 2015 former Pinar del Río pitcher Serguey Linares, who had failed in a 2007 trial with the Pittsburgh Pirates, shot and killed his girlfriend in a Miami beauty parlor and then turned the gun on himself. Details are found in Sergio Candido ("Oscuro final para ex pelotero cubano que intentó asesinar a su pareja"), February 9, 2015.

5. Jorge Ebro ("La estrella cubana que nunca brilló en las Ligas Mayores"), October 20, 2014. In recent years Maels has worked in both Miami and Tampa, training young pitching prospects, most notably collaborating with respected coach Orlando Chinea at the latter's academy in Tampa (where one of the early clients was future Marlins star José D. Fernández).

6. Moncada would play that same November at the U-18 tournament in Taiwan, but would never again suit up for a senior-level Cuban team.

7. The hotel was first known as the Domina but soon renamed the Vander Valk Blijdorp, and it would remain the Cuban team headquarters for future tournaments in Rotterdam (2011, 2013, 2015). It sits adjacent to the sprawling Rotterdam Zoo (Blijdorp) in a spacious park on the city outskirts that also houses the baseball grounds known as Neptunus Family Stadium. The Neptunus ball club is the local team in the Dutch Professional Baseball League.

8. Arangure would provide some of the best and earliest details on Chapman's defection in a piece written for ESPN ("New World of Hope Awaits Chapman"), November 1, 2009.

9. My three-part interview on the prospects of newly signed Aroldis Chapman was published on a Cincinnati Reds fan blog known as "Red Letter Daze" during the final week of January and first week of February 2010. The same question-and-answer interview sessions were republished simultaneously on the www.BaseballdeCuba.com website maintained by Ray Otero.

10. Chapman's first defection attempt in March 2008 (exactly one year before the World Baseball Classic in Mexico and San Diego) is revealed by Jorge Arangure as part of his post-defection interviews with the pitcher in Barcelona ("New World of Hope Awaits Chapman"). The botched attempt at Playa Blanca

on the north coast of Holguín Province ended with a police raid. Arangure reports that Chapman was summoned in the aftermath to a direct meeting with president Raúl Castro, where he was surprisingly only suspended for the remaining weeks of the National Series and also from the Beijing Olympics squad, but then reinstated for the following season and the 2009 World Baseball Classic. There is, of course, a discrepancy between Arangure's account and the fact reported above that Chapman was part of a pre-selection Olympic team auditioning in June at the Huelga Tournament in Havana.

11. Scott Eden ("No One Walks Off the Island") suggests that "most members of the national baseball team that travel abroad are informants for the Cuban government" and asserts that "several Cuban defectors now playing in major-league farm systems affirmed to me that state security makes an active effort to turn players." While there may be some truth here, such claims seem to me to create a false impression. If some players have bought reinstatement by reporting on suspected traffickers, the majority are hardly untrustworthy secret agents. I am around these players constantly and their behavior has never suggested such a scenario. Also, the fact that Cuban officials would ask players to report those approaching them seems to me a reasonable line of defense by a country attempting to keep poachers from dismantling its baseball through illegal smuggling activities.

12. Tyler Kepner ("Pushing the Limits of a Sport, and a Budget—Aroldis Chapman Stretches the Reds' Budget, and the Limits of Pitching"), March 5, 2015.

13. Eli Saslow ("A World of His Own—Since He Lit up Baseball With His 105 M.P.H. Fastball, Reds Closer Aroldis Chapman Has Lived the American Dream"), February 17, 2014.

14. Iglesias provides another interesting case of discrepancies in Cuban ballplayer names. Since his signing with the Reds, his name has appeared consistently as Raisel. But in Cuba and even in the official MLB media guide for the 2013 WBC, the first name was spelled Rasiel (and pronounced Rah-see-el, not Ryesell). This is reminiscent of Dodgers minor leaguer Erisbel Arruebarrena, who dropped a *u* from his name (Arruebarruena) once he'd arrived on US shores.

15. Robert Whiting (*The Meaning of Ichiro*), 25–26.

16. Fainaru and Sánchez (*The Duke of Havana*), 52–53.

17. Sharon Robb ("Cuban Pitcher Defects to Chase Major-League Dream"), August 7, 1991.

18. John Grupp ("Pirates Bullpen Coach Rafted to U.S. from Cuba Seeking Freedom"), June 26, 2011.

19. Garbey was in fact not the only former player to arrive during the Mariel exodus, but only one of as many as seven. He was, however, the most notable and the only one to have any impact on North American professional baseball.

Of the remaining six, all were scouted in the spring of 1980 at a makeshift refugee relocation camp in Florida, and two (infielders Julio Soto and Román Duquesne) were actually signed by the Macon ball club of the independent South Atlantic League, then released later that summer after only short trials. The most prominent outside of Garbey was pitcher Julio Rojo, son of a star Negro-league pitcher of the same name, who had won a then-record eighteen National Series games a dozen seasons earlier. For a full list of known ballplayers involved in the Mariel exodus, see appendix 2.

20. Peter Richmond ("Cuban Star Fixed Games to Support His Family: Refugee from Mariel Still May Reach Majors"), May 22, 1983.

21. After formal interviews, Johnson placed Garbey on probationary status, which allowed him to continue playing with Evansville but made him ineligible for major-league call-up until a further investigation was completed. The situation quickly worsened a month later when Garbey assaulted a fan in Louisville after being heckled about his reported game-fixing past. That incident led to an additional thirty-day suspension. But Garbey was impressive enough during March 1984 spring training to finally be called to the championship-bound Tigers by manager Sparky Anderson. Details of the Garbey case are found in Bjarkman's *A History of Cuban Baseball, 1864–2006* (pages 262–63), and in Doug Hill's online biography of the ballplayer found at the SABR Baseball Biography Project website.

22. S. L. Price (*Pitching around Fidel*), 75–81.

5. BROTHERS IN EXILE

1. Robert Whiting (*The Meaning of Ichiro*), 205. Writing of the pioneering Japanese big leaguers, Whiting observes: "Americans liked them because of their belief, generally speaking, in the team ethos and their commitment to the idea that playing baseball was first and foremost its own reward—monetary considerations coming later. They were welcome additions to a game that seemed increasingly consumed by greed and ego."

2. Kenneth Shouler ("El Duque's Excellent Adventures"), March/April 1999.

3. Steve Fainaru and Ray Sánchez (*The Duke of Havana*), 308.

4. There have been two serious challenges to El Duque's record for career winning percentage. Enjoying a far longer career, Santiago's Norge Luis Vera retired in 2012 after seventeen seasons with a .721 mark (176–68); given the length of Vera's career, his ledger might appear a bit more impressive. Still-active Sancti Spíritus right-hander Ismel Jiménez briefly overcame El Duque a

few seasons back but has now slipped to third place on the career list at 113–47 (.706) across eleven seasons.

5. In what was rapidly becoming something of a comic opera, Paret would also be suspended one year after the Atlanta Games for allegedly speaking by telephone with recent defector Rolando Arrojo, his former Villa Clara teammate. But like Mesa, Paret (who sat out the 1999 Pan Am Games and 2000 Sydney Olympics) was eventually reinstated and manned the Team Cuba starting short-stop post between 2002 and 2009.

6. Hernández Nodar appears on the ESPN *30 for 30* documentary to candid-ly tell the story of his misadventures in his own words. He also earlier provided *Wall Street Journal* writer Christopher Rhoads ("Baseball Scout's Ordeal," April 24, 2010) with a lengthy interview detailing his misadventures in Cuba and expanding on his resulting prison experiences.

7. Milton Jamail (*Full Count: Inside Cuban Baseball*), 102–3.

8. Also included in the party were El Duque's cousin Joel Pedroso, Rome-ro's wife Geidy, and a last-minute add-on—Lenin Rivero—whom none of the others previously knew. Two unnamed partners of Romero had also served as crew but returned once the planned rendezvous point at Anguilla Cay had been reached. Cuban ballplayer Jorge Toca had also planned to accompany the group but failed to appear on time for the departure. Toca defected a year later and eventually played with both the New York Mets and Mexican League Tabasco Olmecas.

9. Details of those three days on Anguilla Cay are laid out by Fainaru and involve the refugees initially hiding from a first air search by Miami-based Brothers to the Rescue planes. The stranded Cubans thought the aircraft be-longed to the US Coast Guard and that if found they would be immediately sent back to Cuba. They did not know that Anguilla Cay belonged to the Bahamians and that the Bahamian government would therefore decide their fate. Readers wanting the full story of the escape adventure and details of the American wet-foot, dry-foot policies governing such refugees should read Fainaru and Sánchez (chapter 13).

10. Alberto Hernández was not as fortunate and his story is far more typical for Cuban defectors than the fairytale-like saga of El Duque. Alberto was shunted aside by Cubas and eventually picked up by agent Guz Domínguez, who could arrange nothing better than a $7,500-per-month deal with a team in Tai-wan. Alberto's career lasted only two seasons in the Taiwan pro league and he eventually returned to an exile life in Costa Rica.

11. El Duque would fall short of Liván's rookie postseason MVP achieve-ment, but he would reprise that feat a season later, when his two solid outings versus the Boston Red Sox would earn an ALCS MVP trophy.

12. In the immediate aftermath of El Duque and Mesa's suspensions (designed to intimidate players with similar ideas), first baseman Roberto Colina and four other members of El Duque's Industriales team defected during a tournament in Tabasco, Mexico.

13. Fainaru (*The Duke of Havana*, 91) quotes one Cuban sportswriter as complaining that "Liván is an imbecile. But he has more natural ability than his brother. El Duque would love to have Liván's fastball."

14. In June 2010, another half brother of El Duque, Gerardo Regalado, shot and killed four women in Hialeah, Florida, before taking his own life. Gerardo was the son of El Duque's mother, María Julia Pedroso, but not his father, Arnaldo, and therefore Gerardo and Liván were not related.

15. *The Duke of Havana*, 91. Fainaru relates this story about the television tube. When Liván was frustrated by unsuccessful efforts to obtain one for his broken set from local party officials, he related the incident to Joe Cubas on a team trip to Japan and the agent immediately bought the precious item. Supposedly the pitcher returned to Cuba and told his father, Arnaldo (the source of Fainaru's tale), that after receiving such help he had seen the light about life in Cuba and was ready to sign on with the agent.

16. Ozzie Fernández would settle for a $3.5 million deal with the San Francisco Giants, also orchestrated by Cubas. It wasn't, perhaps, as big a bonanza, but a windfall nonetheless.

17. Fainaru and Sánchez, *The Duke of Havana*, 62–63.

18. The 2004 smuggling incident was the same one reported on by Kevin Baxter ("Ballplayers from Cuba are Now Flee Agents") in the *Los Angeles Times* on July 7, 2007. The agent's conviction involving "harboring aliens" was overturned by the courts because there did not appear to be enough evidence that the athletes (unnamed in press reports) actively tried to avoid immigration officials when they landed in California. But Domínguez's smuggling conviction stood since the court deemed he both knew and recklessly disregarded the fact that the Cubans did not have permission to enter the United States.

19. Fainaru (*The Duke of Havana*, 85) suggests that Fernández had reached the tipping point over an issue of some confiscated beer in Holguín. Immediately before he left his hometown on the eve of his final trip to Millington, two local police officers seized several six-packs Ozzie had bartered for enjoyment with teammates in Havana. Like Liván's celebrated television tube, the event was a proverbial back-breaking straw. The fuller explanation was a building frustration existing for even privileged athletes during the years of the Cuban Special Period.

20. Jennifer Frey ("Deceptive Practices: Prieto Plays His Way Out of Cuba and Into the Major Leagues"), August 17, 1995.

21. *The Meaning of Ichiro*, 118–19. Whiting mentions published reports from the 1960s and 1970s of a de facto ban on recruitment of talent from the Japanese circuit. The idea (largely unsubstantiated) was that Washington politicos didn't want MLB clubs upsetting crucial Japan-USA cold war alliances by hijacking and denuding Japan's sacred game.

22. Jorge Ortiz ("Five Years After Defecting from Cuba, Morales Has Arrived"), October 9, 2009.

23. Morales had actually leaped into the throng of welcoming teammates with the intention of stomping on home plate and his awkward landing (due to the pile of teammates) caused the lower left leg fracture.

6. "THE BEST THERE EVER WAS"

1. The *Calle del Medio* publication was a truncated version of an interview Reynaldo Cruz had done with me more than six months earlier for his online magazine *Universo Béisbol*, where it had appeared in the September 2014 issue.

2. During a meeting with a dozen former National Series players and coaches (most from the 1960s and 1970s) at the press room of Latin American Stadium in late February 2015, Kit Krieger's Cubaball tour group raised numerous questions about the current status of the national sport. When asked about the greatest all-time Cuban player, two of the dozen old-timers mentioned Martin Dihigo in passing (a stock answer on the island) and several talked about Omar Linares. But to the surprise of most (especially this author), a clear majority named Yulieski Gourriel, explaining that Gourriel played against top pros in the modern post-1999 wooden bat era and thus had the clear edge over Linares or others who starred only against amateur-league opponents.

3. Robert Whiting (*The Chrysanthemum and the Bat*), chapter 8.

4. Puig's rookie-month achievements of June 2013—highlighted by his challenge to Joe DiMaggio's base-hits record—are summarized in chapter 1. Abreu's debut month contains a long list of unprecedented or rarely matched accomplishments, including the following: league leader for April 2014 in homers, RBIs, total bases, and extra base hits; tied DiMaggio, Williams, and Pujols for third-highest RBI total (32) for a big leaguer in his first 29 games; first player in MLB history with four 4-plus RBI games in his first 29 contests; third player in MLB history with two multi-homer efforts in his first ten games; and first big leaguer ever to sock ten homers in his April debut month. Abreu also joined Puig as only the second player in history to capture both rookie-of-the-month and player-of-the-month honors simultaneously.

5. Abreu's and Mike Trout's rookie seasons compare rather favorably. Trout paced the circuit only in runs scored and stolen bases, but he was admittedly also

seven years younger and more legitimately a "true" rookie (considering the Cuban's ten seasons of National Series service).

6. Yadier Pedroso (along with two companions) died in a violent late-night automobile crash only a few miles outside Artemisa center when the Lada in which he was riding collided with a stationary truck on a darkened stretch of two-lane country roadway. His death in the early hours of March 17 came only five days after the Cuban team's return from Japan and ten days after his final brief pitching performance against the Netherlands in the Tokyo Dome. I had visited with Yadier and Freddie Cepeda in their Tokyo hotel room only hours before the team departed for Narita International Airport and the fateful trip home. At the July 2013 World Port Tournament in Rotterdam, an emotional memorial tribute and moment of silence were observed on the evening of the opening contest, arranged at the urging of this author. Pedroso had been the MVP at the previous 2011 World Port Tournament event.

7. These same interview sessions between Paula Lavigne and Tony Castro are covered again in chapter 8.

8. Details concerning Moncada's odd Cuban League "retirement" are found in chapter 7.

9. Jonah Keri ("The Best Hitter You've Never Heard Of—José Abreu Is Putting up God-like Numbers in the Closed-off World of Cuba"), February 23, 2012.

10. During National Series 28 (1988–89), when separate leaders were listed for Occidental and Oriental league divisions, Santiago's Orestes Kindelán (Cuba's all-time career home run and RBI standard-bearer) did pace the Eastern Division in all three major batting categories; however, he was not the overall National Series pacesetter in either batting average or runs batted in that season, trailing the Western Division leader in both categories.

11. The nine Cubans debuting in 2014 actually comprised the highest number in history. The only post-revolution season to come close was 1962, with seven; eight Cubans also debuted in 1955 and again in 1960, with five other seasons boasting a total of six (1944, 1945, 1950, 1958, 2015).

12. Peter C. Bjarkman ("White Sox Renew Their Historic Cuban Connections"), June 2014. The White Sox also celebrated their 2014 Cuban players with an official Cuban Connection luncheon for press and selected guests at U.S. Cellular Field in late June.

13. On April 8, 1969, the Cleveland Indians opened the season in Detroit with the following Cubans in the starting lineup: José Cardenal (CF), José Azcue (C), Zoilo Versalles (3B), and Luis Tiant (P).

14. Tom Hoffarth's article ("Our Daily Bread: The 'Other' Ramirez in Glendale, Arizona," March 9, 2009) was published against the backdrop of the second World Baseball Classic. Ramírez would candidly speak out about the false

stereotypes often attached to Cuban athletes supposedly playing under constant threats back home, telling a *Chicago Sun-Times* reporter that "There is no pressure to play [in Cuba]; there are no guns pointed at you. There is just pure love of wanting to play the game . . . the difference between Cuban ballplayers and players from the United States is players here (USA) play because that's their job. Cuban ballplayers play because of the encouragement from the province they're from, the town they're from, the region they're from. There is a sincere pride and passion from playing for your province. But no pressure."

15. Another promising Villa Clara infielder who had also fled the constant harping of manager Victor Mesa was Yunieski Betancourt, who would eventually blossom as a big-league shortstop with the Seattle Mariners. Betancourt played three full seasons (ages 18–20) in Villa Clara and was a top prospect and one of the league's fastest base runners, but he performed mostly at second base, since teammate Eduardo Paret, who manned the shortstop post, was a national team standout. At the start of his fourth campaign (in December 2003) Betancourt also left Cuban shores via speedboat bound for Mexico. Betancourt was known in Cuba as Rikimbili, a colorful nickname coined by manager Victor Mesa to describe the youngster's exceptional running style. The slang term was originally used in the 1970s and 1980s to refer to imported Chinese bicycles that had been ingeniously rigged with small engines to motorize them.

16. Before he turned five, Nieto accompanied his parents and eighteen others on a twenty-foot boat and endured a thirteen-hour journey guided only by a small hand-held compass before being rescued by the US Coast Guard and returned to the US. refugee camp at Guantanamo Bay. There they remained for more than six months in late 1994 and early 1995 before being cleared for entrance into the United States. Nieto would provide these details in his February 2014 spring-training camp interview with MLB.com journalist Scott Merkin ("Long Days Part of Nieto's Journey to the Big Leagues," February 21, 2014).

17. Bjarkman ("Can Baseball's All-Star Game Be Saved?"), July 15, 2014.

18. This was only the second time two Cubans ever squared off in an MLB All-Star Game. The first came in Anaheim in 1967, when Mike Cuéllar struck out Tony Oliva in the eleventh inning of a dramatic contest ironically won by a fifteenth-inning homer off the bat of Cuban Tony Perez.

19. Star right-hander for the Tohoku Rakutan Golden Eagles of the Japanese Pacific League, Tanaka had one of the most spectacular seasons in Nippon baseball annals in 2013. His 24–0 record (the second perfect season in post-WWII Japanese baseball history) featured a twenty-eight-game uninterrupted victorious string that included his final four starts of the previous campaign and also surpassed the twenty-four-game big-league standard held by Carl Hubbell since 1937. Tanaka's 2013 ERA was also an impressive 1.27, and he was an easy winner of the Sawamura Award (Japan's Cy Young). An unblemished six-game

postseason record stretched the remarkable ledger to 30–0 by season's end in late October.

20. Barry Praver has represented all the following Cuban players (among others): José Abreu, Raisel Iglesias, Adeiny Hechevarría, Jorge Soler, Yunieski Maya, Erisbel Arruebarrena, and Dalier Hinojosa. Ironically Abreu would abandon the Praver-Shapiro Agency in May 2015 and sign on with Diego Bentz and Fern Cuza (Relativity Baseball). A more or less complete agent list for additional 2015 Cuban big leaguers is as follows: Boras Corporation (José Iglesias, José M. Fernández, Kendrys Morales, Dayan Viciedo), Relativity Baseball (José Abreu, Aroldis Chapman, Roenis Elias), Roc Nation Sports (Yoenia Céspedes, Rusney Castillo), Wasserman Media Group (Yasiel Puig), MDR Sports Management (Leonys Martin), Epitome Sports Management (Yasmany Tomás), Rudy Santin (Alex Guerrero), the Legacy Agency (Yasmani Grandal), Miami Sports Management (Yunel Escobar), MVP Sports Group (Yonder Alonso), DPX Sports (Odrisamer Despaigne), Kinser Sports Management (Brayan Peña), Jaime Torres (Alexei Ramírez), and Bart Hernandez (Henry Urrutia).

21. Scott Eden ("Feds Interviewing Cubans in U.S."), September 16, 2014. In August 2014 Eliezer Lazo (alleged head of a smuggling ring that had illegally brought as many as 1,000 Cubans into the United States) pleaded guilty in a Miami courtroom to extortion involving a number of migrants he had aided, including Texas Rangers outfielder Leonys Martin (as reported in chapter 1). In November Lazo (already serving a five-year sentence in an unrelated Medicare fraud case) was handed an additional fourteen-year prison term in the Martin case.

22. James Wagner ("Yunel Escobar's Long and Winding Road to the Big Leagues"), May 7, 2015.

23. Jared S. Hopkins ("How Did Jose Abreu Get from Cuba to Chicago? Details Remain a Mystery"), November 7, 2014.

24. Michael E. Miller ("Who Is Jose Abreu?—After Defecting from Cuba the Sox Slugger Had One of the Best Rookie Seasons Ever. Yet His Story Has Remained Largely a Mystery. Until Now."), April 2015. Miller explains the interview setting as follows: "He (Praver) normally controls the questions put to his client, but with a limited understanding of Spanish, he can only check his cell phone and sip his iced tea."

25. Luis Felipe Rojas ("Industrialista que se fuga deja 8 personas en prisión"), August 28, 2014. Rojas reported that eight individuals (including one woman) had been sentenced to 5–10-year prison terms in 2014 for the aborted "defection" attempt involving Tomás during April 2012. Apparently Cuban officials had somehow bought the ballplayer's story that he had been kidnapped and was not actually attempting a voluntary flight; either that or he had been pardoned in exchange for his cooperation in turning state's evidence against the eight accused

plotters. Rojas also quotes a cousin of Tomás's as suggesting that he never had accepted the kidnapping version as being an honest account. Whatever the scenario, Tomás was obviously cleared and less than a year later he was allowed to travel to Japan as a member of the Cuban team entered in the March 2013 World Baseball Classic.

26. Jesse Sanchez ("Cuba's Next Big Thing Ready to Impress Scouts"), September 18, 2014.

27. There were also naysayers like David Schoenfield ("¿Es posible que Yasmany Tomás sea el gran fracaso?"), April 9, 2015.

28. During the USA-Cuba Friendly Series in North Carolina (July 2015), I discussed Tomás and his rapid big-league progress with longtime friend Craig Shipley (now Arizona D-Backs special assistant to general manager Kevin Towers). We shared our equal amazement that Tómas had turned out quite the opposite of what we all had anticipated, not limiting his game to power slugging, adjusting rapidly to big-league pitching, and showing rather surprising discipline in his mature recognition of the big-league strike zone.

7. NO RESERVATIONS FOR CUBA

1. Bourdain's "No Reservations Cuba" episode is available on the *Anthony Bourdain No Reservations Collection 7* DVD, released in late 2011.

2. All major Cuban cities have their own Peña Deportivas that regularly meet in the local town square. The Havana branch also occasionally extends honorary memberships to a handful of foreigners deemed knowledgeable on the Cuban national pastime and I was accorded that honor during my earliest visits in the late 1990s.

3. A single unfortunate aspect of the popular Central Park scene was a somewhat distorted portrait of the nature of Peña Deportiva membership. When I displayed my own honorary membership card during filming, Bourdain commented on camera about the need for such fans to have an "official government license" to gather on the streets and discuss baseball, the suggestion being that they would otherwise be confused with political protesters and quickly rounded up by local law enforcement. Bourdain's description fed some unfortunate stereotypes about political repression in contemporary Cuba. The membership cards and club licensing simply permit the Peña to use government facilities like the Kid Chocolate Center for group activities and are not at all required for public assembly.

4. Michael Lewis ("Commie Ball: A Journey to the End of a Revolution"), July 2008.

5. The Internet segment presented by Robert Siegel as part of his weeklong NPR *All Things Considered* reports aired on March 23, 2015. An online search will locate it under the title "An Object of Desire: Hope and Yearning for the Internet in Cuba" (http://www.npr.org/sections/parallels/2015/03/23/394276385/an-object-of-desire-hope-and-yearning-for-the-internet-in-cuba).

6. Bill Nowlin ("Baseball Talent from Cuba, and How the Red Sox Have Benefitted"), April 2015. In anticipation of its 2015 Cuban presence, the team had commissioned Nowlin's story for their April ballpark program magazine.

7. Ben Badler ("Jorge Soler May Be Using Haitian Documents"), June 8, 2012. Badler reported that OFAC requirements demanded evidence of two permanent resident documents from a third country before any player might be cleared for signing. Apparently Soler's agent (Barry Praver) claimed to have such documents, but since Soler was rumored to be in Haiti at the time and document fraud was notorious in that country, issues were being raised about Soler's legal status. In this same article Badler also cited a February 2012 report in the *Chicago Tribune* that the Cubs might have had a secret deal in place to sign the Cuban, and that there was pressure to do so before a July 2 deadline. After that date the twenty-year-old prospect would be subject to new MLB regulations capping the amount teams could spend on international free agents, without additional penalties, at $2.9 million.

8. Evan Altman ("Cuban Hustle Crisis: The Curious Case of Jorge Soler"), August 11, 2014.

9. Jorge Arangure ("What Happens to the Cuban Ballplayers Who Never Make It"), October 1, 2014. Arangure mentions Nicole Banks in his story as the listed agent for four January 2013 defectors (including former Havana Metros pitcher Yunieski Lagart) among the large group of disappointed hopefuls who have never achieved a coveted US pro contract. Arangure also notes that Banks had earlier handled paperwork for at least twenty Cuban free agents between 2010 and late 2014.

10. Gawain Owen has developed close relationships with many Cuban players, chats with them regularly online, and also shares information that rarely, if ever, proves faulty. That Nicole Banks had earlier sent me a Facebook "friend request" was not insignificant in retrospect, since I post regularly about Cuban players and Cuban baseball matters and many readers follow my page as a source of updated information. On hearing from Gawain about Banks's possible motives, I had already deleted her from my Facebook list before leaving Rotterdam.

11. Jorge Arangure ("The Weirdest Cuban Defector Story You Will Ever Read), December 4, 2014.

12. The list of ballplayers emigrating legally out of Cuba contains at least the following: Yenier Bello (Sancti Spíritus) and Iriat Chirino (Industriales) in 2013; Ibáñez, Quesada, Moncada, and Jorge Alberto Martínez in 2014; Yoadris Portal

(Industriales), Jesús Belanguer (Industriales), Yordan Alvarez (Pinar del Río), Rafael Ortíz (Industriales), Pavel Pino (Industriales), and Carlos Sierra (Sancti Spíritus) in 2015.

13. John Walk ("Jorge Martinez: A Hidden 2014 MLB Draft Gem Playing Indy Ball?"), June 2, 2014; also Steve Sypa ("International Free Agent Profile: Pavel Quesada"), August 18, 2014.

14. Ben Badler ("The Importance of Yadier Alvares, Vladimir Gutierrez on the Future of Cuban Signings"), March 2, 2015.

15. Cuba (represented by 2012–13 National Series champion Villa Clara) won only one of four preliminary round games (the final one against Puerto Rico) and was thus the single team eliminated after pool play.

16. Daniel de Malas ("Verdades y Rumores: ¿José Miguel Fernández con Industriales?"), January 8, 2015.

17. Early reports at the time of Olivera's March signing suggested a possible elbow muscle tear and resulted in an additional clause in his contract specifying that the Dodgers could add a seventh year (at $1 million salary) to the deal if the ballplayer needed Tommy John surgery. When Olivera finally received clearance to travel to Arizona and formally ink his contract on May 19, a further physical exam indicated suspicions of a UCL tear were unfounded.

18. Guerrero began his rookie 2014 season with the parent club, but after a season-opening series in Australia versus the D-Backs he was optioned back to AAA Albuquerque. A bizarre injury would, however, curtail his action during that debut minor-league campaign. On May 20 in Salt Lake City Guerrero became involved in a dugout altercation with teammate Miguel Olivo, who, in the resulting scuffle, bit off a portion of the Cuban's ear, which then had to be reattached via complicated plastic surgery.

19. The top 2015 salary earners among Cubans (2015 season only, as reported by *USA Today*) were as follows: Céspedes (Detroit) $10,500,000; Alexei Ramírez (Chicago) $10,000,000; Abreu (Chicago) $8,666,666; Chapman (Cincinnati) $8,050,000; Kendrys Morales (Kansas City) $6,500,000; Guerrero (LA) $6,500,000; and Puig (LA) $6,214,000.

20. Arruebarrena initiated a widely publicized brawl during a Pacific Coast League game between the Albuquerque Isotopes and the Reno Aces on July 25, 2014, that led to the expulsion of nine players and also temporarily ended Arruebarrena's stay in AAA, since he was demoted to the Class A (California League) Rancho Cucamonga Quakes the very next day.

21. Weeks before this book went to press, the Olivera saga took an unexpected twist when the high-dollar prospect was dealt to the Atlanta Braves (July 30, 2015) as part of a multiplayer swap designed to shore up LA pitching at the expense of a glut of infield prospects. By season's end Olivera would finally experience a taste of big-league action with the Braves.

8. GO EAST, YOUNG MEN, GO EAST

1. Robert Whiting (*The Chrysanthemum and the Bat*), 235–44.

2. MLB's adoption of the name World Baseball Classic is explained by
Robert Elias (*The Empire Strikes Out*, 275–76) as a conscious decision not to
upstage its own year-end championships that were from the beginning misnamed
as baseball's "world series." This would explain "Classic" versus "Series" but
not "Classic" versus "World Cup"—perhaps an important distinction if MLB
was trying to imitate FIFA. The truth here was that the IBAF (amateur baseball's
own world-governing body) had beaten MLB to the punch with legal registration
of the name back in 1988.

3. Three additional filmed sequences with Tony Castro were completed at
the Changa Mederos Stadium (with a preseason exhibition game going on in the
background), on the streets of Old Havana (where Tony elaborated on the city's
impressive history and culture), and on a suburban rough-hewn ball field (where
eight to ten youth teams were holding an afternoon practice).

4. Varying numbers have appeared in US press accounts over the years when
the topic has been Cuban ballplayer salaries. A fair estimate is about $125 (US)
per month, although national team players do receive supplements and earn extra
tournament prize money. Players are also supplied with lodging, ranging from
apartments to lavish houses (and automobiles) in the cases of some top national
team veterans. Over the years I have studiously avoided the uncomfortable topic
of salaries with players I consider close friends, in an obvious attempt not to
appear as little more than another prying journalist.

5. The program's title would reveal ESPN's true interests: "Cuban Baseball
Talent and Big League Baseball Money . . . Are They Any Closer Together?"
Truncated clips from several hours of September filming were used, and they
consisted mostly of Tony Castro saying "we in Cuba have to change, otherwise
we will continue to lose all our great players . . . we will lose everything." There
was a review of recent big-name defections and recent signings like that of
Abreu. And then the bulk of the airtime was given to a Bob Ley–moderated
panel of four tabbed experts: player agent Jaime Torres, Cuban exile and former
big leaguer Orestes Destrade (one of the more outspoken anti-Castro and anti-
communist cheerleaders), ESPN baseball commentator Pedro Gomez (a Cuban-
American who has never visited the island), and myself. Attempting to salvage
something of her original mission in Cuba, Paula Lavigne fought for my inclu-
sion. But it was hardly the show any of us thought we were doing. The other
three panel members droned on about ways the Cubans could all be freed up to
play in the majors. My own attempts to steer at least some of the conversation
back to Cuban efforts to maintain a domestic league were repeatedly rebuffed.

6. Canada was also apparently becoming an option for the Cubans, although the working agreement there was not with any high-level league. One player (Yunieski Gourriel, Yulieski's older brother) would be sent to the Québec Can-Am League team in 2014, and then four would be sent (again including Yunieski) the following year.

7. Mesa had a second chance to manage in Mexico the following summer with the Minatitlan Oilers and again lasted only twenty-one games before receiving the axe. But this time it was the Mexican League club that canceled the deal, and the reason now was simply a difference of opinion over managerial philosophy.

8. Jorge Fuentes's highly successful managerial career—with both Pinar del Río (where he won three league titles and managed Linares, Pedro Lazo, and Contreras) and the national team—peaked with the 1996 Atlanta gold medal. When a ten-year Cuban victory skein came to an end a year later at the Intercontinental Cup matches in Barcelona, the resulting shake up cost Fuentes and other top INDER officials their jobs. He would later manage the Nicaraguan national team (on loan from INDER) during the 2005 IBAF World Cup. While many touted Fuentes as the best baseball mind in Cuba, rumors circulated that his managing style had never been appreciated by Fidel, a fact which apparently diminished the latter part of his career.

9. Enrique Rojas ("Despaigne juege como dominicano"), May 13, 2014.

10. A first plan for renting players to Japan and perhaps elsewhere in the early 2000s was orchestrated by then INDER president Reynaldo González. It had little impact on stemming defections at the time, since only veteran stars near the end of their careers were involved. In addition to Linares, three other fading heroes (Mesa, Pacheco, and Kindelán) also went to Japan in 2002 (but as coaches and amateur industrial leaguers). One buried motive was to force retirement on some aging stars (Lázaro Junco was another famed slugger involved) and open fresh roster spots on the national squad without causing public outcry. It was deemed necessary to clear national team slots for a number of emerging prospects like Gourriel, Cepeda, and Pestano, among others, before they might also seek to escape the island (as had, say, Rey Ordóñez, who was stuck behind Mesa and Paret as an emerging shortstop).

11. Elsa Ramos ("Frederich Cepeda: Siempre he sido millonario"), October 29, 2014.

12. Wilfredo Cancio Isla ("Maels Rodríguez: Si, me encontré con Frederich Cepeda en Puerto Rico"), December 27, 2010. In this remarkable interview with the Miami press, Maels would soon provide his own version of events in San Juan. But the story also had a purely personal twist for this author. Only two days before the incident I had transported two dozen Louisville Slugger bats to Cepeda's hotel room. These were a gift from a mutual friend well connected with

MLB and were intended to go to the Sancti Spíritus team and not to the Federation (which would likely have different plans for their distribution). Thus the delivery was made with cloak-and-dagger secrecy. When the story of Cepeda's suspension first broke my immediate fear was that it was the bats that were at issue and that I myself was embroiled in the scandal. There was great relief on my part when that proved not to be the case.

13. When we next met the following February, Cepeda would tell me that missing the Taiwan trip was the most bitter pill of his storied but sometimes arduous career. It would have been another desperately needed chance to shop for family necessities. Once Cepeda was sent to Tokyo on loan in May 2014 the situation would be altered rather drastically.

14. Brandon Kennedy ("Minor League Lawsuit Claims MLB Fails to Pay Minimum Wage to Minor-Leaguers"), December 3, 2014.

15. Jorge Ortiz ("Minor Leaguers Want Major Upgrade"), April 23, 2015.

16. Many in Cuba (especially Industriales boosters, before Yulieski joined that fan-favorite team) have been all too quick to deride Gourriel's failures at some key moments of international play (especially hitting into a fatal double play to end the Beijing gold medal quest). Yulieski, for all his skills, has often been a very convenient target for Havana fans, who always seem to need a scapegoat on the heels of any national team setback.

17. Gourriel's impressive fourteen-season numbers (217 homers, 902 RBIs, .330 BA) put him near the top of multiple Cuban League career lists. I was on the scene at Latin American Stadium in February 2015 when a group of touring Canadian fans met with a contingent of twelve Cuban League veterans (most from the earliest seasons of the National Series) and inquired about Cuba's best-ever players. Speaking from their knowledge of history, most immediately singled out Martin Dihigo. But when pressed about the past half century, only two names emerged—Linares and Gourriel. And several of the old-timers were quick to voice my own opinion that Gourriel had to have the edge since he played with wooden bats and against far superior competition.

18. The replacement of Mesa in Veracruz, as reported above, was originally explained in Miami as a firing, but it was actually a recall by INDER authorities. Hitting coach Agustin Marquetti was also recalled at the same time.

19. Wayne Graczyk provides an alternate analysis from the Japanese rather than the Cuban perspective. He suggests the plan might be on borrowed time and best viewed as a mere fad. But the second-year developments suggest that Graczyk's assessment might have been premature.

20. On the eve of a crucial opening-round game with host Puerto Rico, nineteen-year-old Pinar pitcher Vladimir Gutíerrez (a big-league prospect) and veteran shortstop Dainer Moriera (not a likely big leaguer) both abandoned the Cuban team hotel. Once again the attention seemed to shift away from the actual

performances of the Cuban team and to the hot-button topic of ballplayer defections. The news was barely hours old when ESPN already had two reporters and a camera crew en route to San Juan to exploit the breaking story.

21. Two decades earlier Japanese baseball officials had been stunned when star pitcher Hideo Nomo took advantage of a loophole in his standard Japanese player contract and formally declared his retirement, thus escaping as a free agent bound for the American majors. That incident had made Japanese baseball officials extremely sensitive to contract details. See Whiting, *The Meaning of Ichiro* (chapter 5).

22. "BayStars Void Gourriel's Contract" (April 2, 2015).

23. Jorge Ebro ("Grandes ligas niegan acuerdo con Cuba por Gourriel"), April 9, 2015.

9. THE UNSUSTAINABLE DREAM

1. Daniel P. Erikson (*The Cuba Wars*), ix.

2. Ibid.

3. Christmas season seems to hold a special penchant for false hopes surrounding the half-century Cuba-USA stalemate. It was during the Christmas season of 1997 that Fidel restored the holiday on the island, only to see former star pitcher Orlando (El Duque) Hernández defect on Christmas Day of that year (chapter 5). For fullest details see Steve Fainaru and Ray Sánchez (*The Duke of Havana*), chapters 12 and 13.

4. Julia E. Sweig and Michael Bustamante ("Cuba After Communism") suggest that much of that American "tourism" consists of Cuban Americans visiting relatives on the island. They note that in 2012 alone upwards of 400,000 American-resident Cubans returned to their homeland for family visits.

5. Former agent Joe Kehoskie, who once specialized in representing defecting Cuban ballplayers before turning to a full-time consulting business, expressed this view on camera for an ESPN *Outside the Lines* special entitled "Cuba on Deck?" (a program that first aired on April 5, 2015).

6. Alan Gross's wife would eventually outspokenly criticize the Obama administration for continuing a failed Cuba policy that led to her husband's suffering as an unwitting pawn in a US-Cuba standoff. In a March 2012 interview with the online journal *Politico*, Judy Gross claimed the Cuban trial of her husband wasn't actually about him, but rather it was about USAID and the repeatedly subversive Washington policies aimed at unseating the Castro government. See Tim Mak ("Wife's Plea for American Held in Cuba," March 13, 2012).

7. A full-blown history of hidden negotiations between Havana and Washington across eleven different American presidential administrations has now

been provided in the important recent book by Washington foreign policy insiders William M. LeoGrande and Peter Kornbluh (*Back Channel to Cuba*). The authors draw especially from recently declassified documents to demonstrate that Fidel Castro (especially in the years surrounding Kennedy's assassination) made repeated efforts at a détente with Washington and that it was indeed the United States policy makers who repeatedly rebuffed any true efforts at establishing some kind of workable and peaceable accord.

8. The main thrust of Obama's announced policy changes involved a "major loosening of travel and economic restrictions" and plans to open formal embassies in both countries and launch serious talks aimed at eventual normalization of diplomatic relations. One element demanded by the Cubans was the removal of their country from the US list of "nations sponsoring terrorism" (a US concession that was finally made in May 2015). While in Havana in March 2015, I chatted informally with the outgoing deputy head of the US Interests Section (the long-standing substitute for a formal embassy), Conrad Tribble, who foresaw the changes on that front coming quickly, although as of May the process still had not been completed. The change would be largely a formality, of course, since the current Interests Section already maintains a larger working staff (51 American diplomats and 400 Cuban staff employees) than any US embassy elsewhere in Latin America.

9. Ben Badler ("What It's Like to Watch Cuban Baseball"), August 26, 2014. Badler's account (with its hardly veiled criticism of the quality of Cuban League play, which he measures against big-league standards) doesn't ring very true for most anyone who has spent time watching and enjoying games on the island. For all its foibles, the Cuban game features a color and ambiance that Badler never captures (nor, in fairness perhaps, does he intend to capture them).

10. ESPN reporter Tom Farrey arrived at Hiram Bithorn Stadium in San Juan (a camera crew in tow) within several hours of the announcement that two players had defected from the Cuban hotel, a surefire magnet for an ESPN story. One of the cameramen happened to be ESPN veteran photographer Joe LoMonaco, who had worked with Paula Lavigne on our September 2013 visit to Havana for interviews with Tony Castro and Victor Mesa (chapter 8). When LoMonaco saw me in the press tent, he immediately called my presence to Farrey's attention. That led to a long discussion about the backdrop for continuing defections in the aftermath of the Obama efforts at détente and also to Farrey's decision to include me in their planned series of on-camera interviews that evening. Material gathered that day in San Juan became the basis for the eventual April *Outside the Lines* program.

11. Commissioner Suarez was interviewed in Spanish. The translation of his words here is my own and not the one provided by the caption writer for the *Outside the Lines* report. Cuban slugging star Alfredo Despaigne was also inter-

viewed on the field immediately after a crucial Cuban victory over Puerto Rico (one that staved off tournament elimination) and responded (paraphrasing here) that the defections were not important and that Cuba would play hard and win with the faithful players who had remained loyal to the team.

12. American groups traveling to Havana in recent months often pay premium rates to the Cuban tourist agencies for specified hotels (rates that have nearly doubled over the last fifteen months) and then arrive to find that they are either shuffled from one hotel to another during their stay, or split up into smaller groups and assigned to *casas particulares* (private homes licensed to rent rooms) at the original rates. This often causes major inconvenience to both the visitors (sometimes stuck in out-of-the-way locations with no hotel amenities such as restaurants or bars) and tour guides (who have to corral their group from various locations for each day's planned agenda of activities). This is just one ramification of current inadequate hotel facilities in Havana, others being sometimes limited food options, broken hotel elevators and nonfunctioning barroom ice machines, lack of regular hot water, and lack of functioning room safes for storing valuables. Travelers to Cuba have to be prepared for a third-world experience, albeit a most charming one in almost all cases.

13. The formal accord between the Cuban winter league and organized baseball (MLB) in the aftermath of the late-1940s "Mexican League Wars" (caused by Jorge Pasquel's raids on big-league talent) had placed the Havana winter circuit squarely under the control of the MLB commissioner's office and was already generating complaints during the final decade of that circuit about decreasing roster slots for native Cubans (as opposed to imported Americans). These changes in Cuban League management and the controversy that resulted are briefly discussed in chapter 2.

14. The fullest and most useful treatment of the Japanese League player posting system (its functioning as well as its origins) is found in Robert Whiting's *The Meaning of Ichiro* (2004), especially chapter 6.

15. See the discussion by Whiting (*The Meaning of Ichiro*) at the beginning of chapter 6.

16. Armour and Levitt list those historical "inflection points" for the MLB sport as being (1) creation of the general manager's role in the 1920s, (2) establishment of farm systems in the 1930s, (3) racial integration following Jackie Robinson in 1947, (4) introduction of an amateur player draft in 1965, (5) arrival of player free agency in 1976, and (6) the rise of baseball analytics (based on sabermetrics) in the 2000s.

EPILOGUE

1. An argument concerning baseball's self-transformation for the purpose of television marketing is expanded in the introduction to my earlier *Diamonds around the Globe: The Encyclopedia of International Baseball*.

2. Baseball's earliest inroads into various Caribbean and Latin American countries are traced in quite some detail in Bjarkman, *Diamonds around the Globe*. Also see Michael M. and Mary Adams Oleksak, *Béisbol: Latin Americans and the Grand Old Game* (chapter 1: "The Cuban Connection") and Rob Ruck, *The Tropic of Baseball: Baseball in the Dominican Republic* (chapter 1: "The Apostles of Baseball").

3. Elias (275) cites William Gould ("Baseball Classic Mirrors World Events") in explaining how MLB squandered any potential goodwill in this effort by designing WBC rules in a manner that favored the USA team. The assumption here was that the appearance of the American squad in the finals would boost television ratings and stadium ticket sales. Gould suggests that MLB in the end simply mirrored the country's defiance of international law during the ongoing Iraq War.

4. Joseph Reaves (*Taking in a Game*, 13) points out the prophetic 1969 observations of Marshall McLuhan, who only a decade after the sport's acknowledged golden-age fifties was already suggesting that baseball had lost its hold on the American public. Reaves reports McLuhan's comments in a *New York Times* interview where the celebrated cultural critic pronounced that baseball was doomed in what was now already an acknowledged "telegenic age."

5. Elias (*The Empire Strikes Out*), 286.

6. Kehoskie's comments were made on an ESPN *Outside the Lines* special program hosted by Bob Ley, produced and narrated by Tom Farrey, and first broadcast on April 5, 2015. This author is also featured as one of the "talking heads" on an episode that is entitled "Cuba on Deck?" and explores possibilities for Cuba-MLB rapprochement on the heels of the December 2014 thaw in USA-Cuba political relations.

7. S. L. Price (*Pitching around Fidel*), 7.

8. Jorge Ebro reported (perhaps even launched) the Gourriel rumors in a series of columns in *El Miami Nuevo Herald* in early April 2015.

REFERENCES AND SOURCES

BOOKS CONSULTED

Armour, Mark L., and Daniel R. Levitt. *In Pursuit of Pennants: Baseball Operations from Dead Ball to Moneyball*. Lincoln: University of Nebraska Press, 2015.

Bjarkman, Peter C. *Diamonds around the Globe: The Encyclopedia of International Baseball*. Westport, CT, and London: Greenwood Press, 2005.

———. *A History of Cuban Baseball, 1864–2006*. Jefferson, NC, and London: McFarland & Company Publishers, 2014 (2007).

Boswell, Thomas. *How Life Imitates the World Series*. New York: Doubleday, 1987. ("How Baseball Helps the Harvest or What the Bay of Pigs Did to the Bigs," 81–96.)

Bourne, Peter. *Fidel: A Biography of Fidel Castro*. New York: Dodd, Mead & Company, 1986.

Carter, Thomas F. *The Quality of Home Runs: The Passion, Politics, and Language of Cuban Baseball*. Durham, NC, and London: Duke University Press, 2008.

Cieradkowski, Gary Joseph. *The League of Outsider Baseball: An Illustrated History of Baseball's Forgotten Heroes*. New York: Simon & Schuster (Touchstone Press), 2015.

Corbett, Ben. *This Is Cuba—An Outlaw Culture Survives*. Cambridge, MA: Westview Press (Perseus Book Group), 2002.

Elias, Robert. *The Empire Strikes Out: How Baseball Sold U.S. Foreign Policy and Promoted the American Way Abroad*. New York and London: New Press, 2010.

Elliston, Jon, ed. *Psywar on Cuba—The Declassified History of U.S. Anti-Castro Propaganda*. Melbourne and New York: Ocean Press, 1999.

Erikson, Daniel P. *The Cuba Wars—Fidel Castro, the United States, and the Next Revolution*. New York and London: Bloomsbury Press, 2008.

Fainaru, Steve, and Ray Sánchez. *The Duke of Havana: Baseball, Cuba, and the Search for the American Dream*. New York: Villard Books, 2001.

Franklin, Jane. *Cuba and the United States: A Chronological History*. Melbourne and New York: Ocean Press, 1997.

Fuentes, Norberto. *The Autobiography of Fidel Castro*. Translated by Anna Kushner. New York: W. W. Norton & Company, 2010.

González Echevarría, Roberto. *The Pride of Havana—A History of Cuban Baseball*. New York and London: Oxford University Press, 1999.

Guttmann, Allen. *From Ritual to Record: The Nature of Modern Sports*. New York: Columbia University Press, 1978.

Halperin, Maurice. *The Rise and Decline of Fidel Castro: An Essay in Contemporary History*. Berkeley and London: University of California Press, 1972.

Jamail, Milton H. *Full Count: Inside Cuban Baseball*. Carbondale and Edwardsville: Southern Illinois University Press, 2000.

Kelly, John D. *The American Game: Capitalism, Decolonialization, Global Domination, and Baseball*. Chicago: Prickly Paradigm Press, 2006.

Kerrane, Kevin. *Dollar Sign on the Muscle—The World of Baseball Scouting*. New York and Toronto: Beaufort Books, 1984.

Klein, Alan M. *Growing the Game: The Globalization of Major League Baseball*. New Haven, CT: Yale University Press, 2006.

LeoGrande, William M., and Peter Kornbluh. *Back Channel to Cuba: The Hidden Story of Negotiations between Washington and Havana*. Chapel Hill and London: University of North Carolina Press, 2014.

Leonard, Thomas M. *Encyclopedia of Cuban–United States Relations*. Jefferson, NC: McFarland & Company Publishers, 2004.

Oleksak, Michael M., and Mary Adams Oleksak. *Béisbol: Latin Americans and the Grand Old Game*. Grand Rapids, MI: Masters Press, 1991.

Perez Jr., Louis A. *On Becoming Cuban: Identity, Nationality and Culture*. Chapel Hill and London: University of North Carolina Press, 1999.

Pettavino, Paula J., and Geralyn Pye. *Sport in Cuba: The Diamond in the Rough*. Pittsburgh: University of Pittsburgh Press, 1994.

Price, S. L. *Pitching around Fidel: A Journey into the Heart of Cuban Sports*. New York: Ecco Press (HarperCollins Publishers), 2000.

Quirk, Robert E. *Fidel Castro*. New York: W. W. Norton & Company, 1993.

Randall, Margaret. *To Change the World: My Years in Cuba*. New Brunswick, NJ, and London: Rutgers University Press, 2009.

Reaves, Joseph A. *Taking in a Game: A History of Baseball in Asia*. Lincoln and London: University of Nebraska Press, 2002.

Regalado, Samuel O. *Viva Baseball! Latin Major Leaguers and Their Special Hunger*. Urbana and Chicago: University of Illinois Press, 1998.

Rogosin, Donn. *Invisible Men—Life in Baseball's Negro Leagues*. New York: Atheneum Books, 1983.

Ruck, Rob. *The Tropic of Baseball: Baseball in the Dominican Republic*. Westport, CT: Meckler Books, 1991.

Senzel, Howard. *Baseball and the Cold War—Being a Soliloquy on the Necessity of Baseball*. New York and London: Harcourt Brace Jovanovich, 1977.

Symmes, Patrick. *The Boys from Dolores: Fidel Castro's Classmates from Revolution to Exile*. New York: Pantheon Books, 2007.

Szulc, Tad. *Fidel: A Critical Portrait*. New York: William Morrow and Company, 1986.

Thomas, Hugh. *Cuba: The Pursuit of Freedom*. New York: Harper and Row Publishers, 1971.

Virtue, John. *South of the Color Barrier: How Jorge Pasquel and the Mexican League Pushed Baseball toward Racial Integration*. Jefferson, NC, and London: McFarland & Company Publishers, 2008.

Wendel, Tim. *Castro's Curveball: A Novel*. New York: Ballantine Books, 1999.

White, Randy Wayne. *Cuba Straits—A Novel*. New York: G. P. Putnam's Sons, 2015.

Whiting, Robert. *The Chrysanthemum and the Bat: Baseball Samurai Style*. New York: Dodd, Mead and Company, 1977.

———. *The Meaning of Ichiro—The New Wave from Japan and the Transformation of Our National Pastime*. New York: Warner Books, 2004.

PRINT MEDIA ARTICLES

Bjarkman, Peter C. "American Baseball Imperialism: Clashing National Cultures and the Future of Samurai *Besuboru*" in: *Studies on Asia* 3:2 (Fall 2006), 123–40.

————. "Baseball and Fidel Castro" in: *The National Pastime: A Review of Baseball History* 18 (1998), 64–68. Cleveland, OH: Society for American Baseball Research.

————. "El major jugador que nadie conoce—Yulieski Gourriel, un tercer base de 22 años, es el Nuevo Linares de pelota cubana" in: *Béisbol Mundial* (February–March 2006), 16.

————. "Fidel on the Mound: Baseball Myth and History in Castro's Cuba" in: *Elysian Fields Quarterly* 16:3 (Summer 1999), 31–41.

————. "Las relaciones Cuba-EE.UU. sin mucho efecto en MLB (excerpted version)" in: *Béisbol Mundial* 6:60 (edición All-Star July 2015), 12–13.

————. "Las relaciones Cuba-EE.UU. sin Mucho efecto en MLB (parte I)" in: *Universo Béisbol* 6:59 (February 2015), 25–26.

————. "Las relaciones Cuba-EE.UU. sin mucho efecto en MLB (parte II)" in: *Universo Béisbol* 6:60 (March 2015), 29, 34.

————. "Prospect Spotlight: Cuba's José Abreu Is Baseball's Newest Slugging Sensation" in: *Baseball Digest* (July–August 2014), 32–35.

————. "Revisando la histórica temporada de novato de José Dariel Abreu" in: *Universo Béisbol* 5:55 (October 2014), 30–32.

————. "White Sox Renew Their Historic Cuban Connections" in: *White Sox* 23:2 (June 2014), 28–30, 33, 35.

Brioso, César. "Abreu Could Be Next Big Cuban Bat in the Majors—White Sox First Baseman Leads Latest Wave of Defectors" in: *USA Today Sports Weekly* (March 12–18, 2014), 10–11.

Carp, Daniel. "Abreu Acclimates Quickly for Sox" in: *USA Today Sports Weekly* (July 9–15, 2014), 21.

Cruz Díaz, Reynaldo. "Deserciones: Dos versiones de una misma historia" in: *Universo Béisbol* 6:58 (January 2015), 6–7.

Cruz Díaz, Reynaldo (with Peter C. Bjarkman). "Los jugadores cubanos de la ultima década: Los mejores de la historia" in: *La Calle del Medio* 82 (Febrero 2015), 12–13.

Cwiertney, Scott M. "The Need for a World-Wide Draft: Major League Baseball and Its Relationship with the Cuban Embargo and United States Foreign Policy" in: *Loyola of Los Angeles Entertainment Law Review* 20 (March 1, 2000), 391–428.

Dawidoff, Nicholas. "The Struggle of Sandy A—Sandy Amoros, a Hero of the '55 World Series, Was Foiled by Fidel" in: *Sports Illustrated* (July 10, 1989).

Fidler, David P. "Baseball in the Global Era: Economic, Legal and Cultural Perspectives" in: *Indiana Journal of Global Legal Studies* 8:1 (2000), 1–8.

Fimrite, Ron. "In Cuba It's Viva El Grand Old Game" in: *Sports Illustrated* 46:24 (June 6, 1977), 68–80.

Gould, William B. "Baseball Classic Mirrors World Events" in: *San Jose Mercury News* (March 21, 2006).

Granger, Grant. "Deconstructing the Castro Myth: Dictator 'Never Offered a Contract'" in: *Winnipeg Sun* (July 31, 1999), 25.

Kelly, William W. "Is Baseball a Global Sport? America's National Pastime as Global Field and International Sport" in: *Global Networks* 7:2 (May 2007), 187–201.

Keown, Tim. "What's Next for Yasiel Puig? On the Eve of His Second Season, the Dodgers Phenom Is Aiming for Something Bigger: Transcendent" in: *ESPN The Magazine* (February 17, 2014), 46–52, 54.

Lavigne, Paula. "Cuba Has to Budge: Antonio Castro—Son of Fidel—Believes the Future of Cuban Baseball Relies on Severing Ties with the Country's Political Past" in: *ESPN The Magazine* (February 17, 2014), 57–59.

McCarthy, Eugene J. "Diamond Diplomacy" in *Elysian Field Quarterly* 14:2 (Summer 1995), 12–15.

Mehta, Manish. "Uncovering Cuba's Secret—Sports Week's Manish Mehta travels to Cuba to Discover Mystery of Orlando 'El Duque' Hernandez" in: *New York Post Sports Week* (June 1–7, 2000), 10–13.

Mercano, Arturo J., and David P. Fidler. "The Globalization of Baseball and the Mistreatment of Latin American Baseball Talent" in: *Indiana Journal of Global Legal Studies* 6:2 (1999), 511–77.

Nowlin, Bill. "Baseball Talent from Cuba, and How the Red Sox Have Benefitted" in: *Red Sox.com* (April 2015), 52–55.

Ortiz, Jorge L. "Adversity, Promise Link Tomas, Lopez" in: *USA Today Sports* (March 9, 2015), 8C.

———. "Cuban Stars Poised to Cash In: Recent History Boon for Tomas, Moncada" in: *USA Today Sports* (November 18, 2014), 2C.

———. "Hechevarria Reflects: Marlins Shortstop Recalls Harrowing Trip from Cuba" in: *USA Today Sports* (May 16, 2015), 6D.

———. "Minor Leaguers Want Major Upgrade" in: *Indianapolis Star—USA Today Sports* (April 23, 2015), 9C.

Rhoads, Christopher. "Inside Baseball: This *Yanqui* Is Welcome in Cuba's Locker Room—Peter Bjarkman Is an Expert, a Go-Between, and, to Some Cuba-Americans, a Stooge" in: *The Wall Street Journal* (November 9, 2010), A1, A16.

Richmond, Peter. "Cuban Star Fixed Games to Support His Family: Refugee from Mariel Still May Reach Majors" in: *Miami Herald* (May 22, 1983), 1A.

Santamarina, Everardo J. "The Hoak Hoax" in: *National Pastime* 14 (1994). Cleveland, OH: Society for American Baseball Research, 29–30.

Saslow, Eli. "A World of His Own—Since He Lit up Baseball with His 105 M.P.H. Fastball, Reds Closer Aroldis Chapman Has Lived the American Dream" in: *ESPN The Magazine* (February 17, 2014), 60–64, 66.

Shouler, Kenneth. "El Duque's Excellent Adventures—How Cuba's Ace Pitcher Escaped Political Oppression to Become Part of a Great American Success Story" in: *Cigar Aficionado* (March–April 1999), 78–99.

Truby, J. David. "Castro's Curveball" in: *Harper's* (May 1989), 32, 34.

Walters, John. "The Bay of Capitalist Pigs—Cuba Is Being Stripped of One of Its Most Important Resources: Strong-Armed Fielders Who Can Go Deep" in: *Newsweek* 164:19 (May 15, 2015), 54–57 ("Cuban Moneyball" cover story).

Wertheim, L. Jon, and Don Yaeger. "Fantastic Voyage—Three Fellow Refugees Say the Tale of Yankees Ace Orlando (El Duque) Hernandez's Escape from Cuba Doesn't Hold Water" in: *Sports Illustrated* 89:22 (November 30, 1998), 60–63.

ONLINE SOURCES

"Admite Cuba que existio pasaporte falso de Despaigne" in: *Zona de Strike* (May 23, 2014).

Aguila, Alberto, and Wilfredo Cancio Isla. "Frederich Cepeda, reivindicado y rumbo a la cima beisbolera" in: *Café Fuerte* (April 14, 2011).

"Alexei Ramirez's Story Pokes Holes in Stereotypical 'Cuban Defector' Tale" in: *A View to the South* (March 9, 2009).

Altman, Evan. "Cuban Hustle Crisis: The Curious Case of Jorge Soler" in: *Cubs Insider* (August 11, 2014).

Alvarez, Carlos M. "Capturados Fernández y Herrera, no pudieron abandoner Cuba" in: *Swing Completo* (October 29, 2014).

Arangure, Jorge, Jr. "New World of Hope Awaits Chapman" in: *ESPN The Magazine* (November 1, 2009).

———. "The Weirdest Cuban Defector Story You Will Ever Read" in: *Vice Sports* (December 4, 2014).

———. "What Happens to the Cuban Ballplayers Who Never Make It" in: *Vice Sports* (October 1, 2014).

Arce, Raúl. "Pasaporte al profesionalismo: ¿Fin de béisbol en Cuba?" in: *Café Fuerte* (December 19, 2010).

Atkinson, Dillon. "Henry Urrutia: 'The Best Decision of My Life'" in: *OriolesUncensored.com* (January 15, 2015).

Badler, Ben. "The Importance of Yadier Alvares, Vladimir Gutierrez on the Future of Cuban Signings" in: *Baseball America* (March 2, 2015).

———. "Jorge Soler May Be Using Haitian Documents" in: *Baseball America* (June 8, 2012).

———. "Meet Yoan Moncada, the Next Cuban Baseball Star" in: *Baseball America* (August 22, 2014).

———. "MLB Changes Cuba Policy, Yoan Moncada Free to Sign" in: *Baseball America* (February 3, 2015).

———. "OFAC Sends Letters to Cuban Players, MLB Tells Team Don't Sign Them" in: *Baseball America* (January 31, 2015).

———. "One Big Problem for Teams with Yoan Moncada" in: *Baseball America* (November 14, 2014).

———. "Vladimir Gutierrez, Yadier Alvarez Can't Sign Until July 2" in: *Baseball America* (February 3, 2015).

———. "What It's Like to Watch Cuban Baseball" in: *Baseball America* (August 26, 2014).

Bautista, Julio. "Cuban Baseball: The Blockade and the Profits" in: *Progresso Weekly* (February 17, 2014).

Baxter, Kevin. "Ballplayers from Cuba Are Now Flee Agents—The Cottage Industry of Smuggling Exposes Lax Rules in the Big Leagues" in: *Los Angeles Times* (July 1, 2007).

"BayStars Void Gourriel's Contract" in: *Japan Times* (April 2, 2015).

Beaton, Andrew, and John W. Miller. "How an Open Door to Cuba Could Benefit Baseball—Thawing of U.S./Cuba Relations May Lead to Great Cuban Presence in Majors" in: *Wall Street Journal* (December 17, 2014).

Becnel, Thomas. "Rays Fans Ask, 'Who Is Leslie Anderson?'" in: *Tampa Herald Tribune* (February 28, 2013).

"*Béisbol* Diplomacy: Declassified Documents from 1975 Reveal Secret U.S.-Cuba Negotiations for Exhibition Games" in: *National Security Archive* (National Security Archive Electronic Briefing Booklet No. 12), George Washington University.

Berkow, Ira. "Joe Cubas Helps Cuban Ballplayers Defect" in: *New York Times* (August 15, 1996).

Bjarkman, Peter C. "The Amazing Debut and Untold Saga of Cuban Sensation Yasiel Puig" in: www.BaseballdeCuba.com (June 14, 2013).

———. "Can Baseball's All-Star Game Be Saved?" in: *Daily Beast* (July 15, 2014).

———. "Cuban League" in: *SABR Baseball Biography Project* (February 2011).

———. "Fidel Castro and Baseball" in: *SABR Baseball Biography Project* (August 2013).

———. "José Abreu's Big-League Debut in Chicago Proves Ringing Offensive Success" in: www.BaseballdeCuba.com (March 31, 2014).

———. "MLB's Next Headache: Cartels, Gangsters, and Their Cuban Superstars" in: *Daily Beast* (April 18, 2014).

———. "Reviewing José Abreu's Record-Book Rookie Big-League Season" in: www.BaseballdeCuba.com (September 30, 2014).

———. "Some Needed Historical Perspectives on Aroldis Chapman's Breakout Season" in: www.BaseballdeCuba.com (October 11, 2012).

———. "US-Cuba Thaw Is Not So Hot for MLB" in: *Daily Beast* (February 19, 2015).

Boudway, Ira. "Major League Baseball Might Miss a Closed-Off Cuba" in: Businessweek.com (December 23, 2014).

Bush, Karen. "The Continuing Adventures of Barbaro Garbey" in: *Detroit Free Press* (August 26, 2009).

Butler, Brin-Johnson. "Heroes for Sale: Teofilo Stevenson, Yasiel Puig, and the Agony of the Cuban Athlete" in: *SB Nation* (June 10, 2014).

Callis, Jim. "How Moncada Compares to the Top Middle Infield Prospects" in: MLB.com (February 11, 2015).

Camerato, Jessica. "In Cuba There Are Hardly Any Cars: Rusney Castillo Gears Up for Life in Boston" in: Boston.com (September 1, 2014).

Cancio Isla, Wilfredo. "Maels Rodríguez: 'Sí, me encontré con Frederich Cepeda en Puerto Rico'" in: *El Miami Nuevo Herald* and reprinted in *Desde Mi Palco del Fanático* (December 27, 2010).

Candido, Sergio. "Oscuro final para ex pelotero cubano que intentó asesinar su pareja" in: *El Miami Nuevo Herald* (February 9, 2015).
"Cerradas las puertas de LMB para los peloteros cubanos radicados en la isla" in: *Zona de Strike* (June 1, 2014).
"Condenada a prisión una empleada de la Academia de Béisbol por 'tráfico de illegal de deportistas'" in: *Cubaencuetro* (July 23, 2009).
Contreras, Michel. "Alfonso Urquiola: Estoy tan decepcionado que no vuelvo a dirigir" in: *Cubadebate* (April 27, 2015).
Corsa, Lissette. "The Cuban Coach" in: *Miami New Times* (August 31, 2001).
Coskrey, Jason. "Releasing Stubborn Gourriel Best Move for Bay Stars" in: *Japan Times* (April 3, 2015).
Costa, Brian. "MLB All-Star Game: The Cuban Baseball Invasion" in: *Wall Street Journal* (July 14, 2014).
———. "Why Baseball Is Losing Its Grip on Cuba" in: *Wall Street Journal* (June 9, 2015).
Crasnick, Jerry. "D-Backs Like What They Have in Tomas" in: MLB.com (March 11, 2015).
Cruz Díaz, Reynaldo. "Caso Gourriel-Yokohama: La historia del hombre que ahogó esperando a Dios" in: *Swing Completo* (April 2, 2015).
———. "Peloteros que desaparecen: ¿Qué pasa con ellos?" in: www.elpalcodelahistoria.com (March 17, 2015).
"Cuban Player Smuggler Pleads Guilty" in: ESPN.com (August 22, 2014).
"Defecting Cubans Likely Planned Ahead Baseball Agent Says" in: *Edmonton Journal* (July 31, 2008).
De Malas, Daniel. "Capturados Fernández y Herrera: No pudieron abandonar Cuba" in *Swing Completo* (October 29, 2014).
———. "La lista de peloteros Cubanos, de la que nadie quiere hablar" in: *Swing Completo* (March 17, 2015).
———. "Verdades y Rumores: ¿José Miguel Fernández con Industriales?" in: *Swing Completo* (January 8, 2015).
De Vries, Karl. "Major Leagues May Have to Wait for US-Cuba Thaw to Bring Island Talent" in: www.FoxNews.com (December 19, 2014).
Dokoupil, Tony. "Does Major League Baseball Exploit Latino Players?" in: NBCNews.com (October 21, 2014).
Ebro, Jorge. "Chapman llega a un acuerdo extrajudicial tras demanda" in: *El Miami Nuevo Herald* (November 17, 2014).
———. "Grandes ligas niega acuerdo con Cuba por Gourriel" in: *El Miami Nuevo Herald* (April 9, 2015).
———. "Julio Estrada, el moldeador de los talentos cubanos" in: *El Miami Nuevo Herald* (May 11, 2015).
———. "La estrella cubana que nunca billó en las Ligas Mayors" in: *El Miami Nuevo Herald* (October 20, 2014).
———. "La Leyenda de Bárbaro Garbey" in: *El Miami Nuevo Herald* (February 15, 2015).
Eden, Scott. "Feds Interviewing Cubans in U.S." in: ESPN.com (September 16, 2014).
———. "No One Walks Off the Island" in: *ESPN The Magazine* (April 17, 2014).
Edes, Gordon. "Plot Thickens on Yoan Moncada" in: *ESPN Boston* (March 14, 2015).
Farrey, Tom. "Paying the Price in Pursuit of Fame, Fortune" in: ESPN.com (July 9, 2001).
Fehrman, Craig. "The Enigma of Mr. 105" in: *Cincinnati* (CincinnatiMagazine.com) (March 1, 2013).
Frey, Jennifer. "Deceptive Practices: Prieto Played His Way Out of Cuba and into the Major Leagues" in: *Los Angeles Times* (August 17, 1995).
García, Anne-Marie. "Defections Prompt Call for Change in Cuban Sports" in: *Deseret News* (August 22, 2011).
García, Anne-Marie, and Michael Weissenstein. "Cuban Baseball Opening Runs into Trouble" in: *AP: The Big Story* (September 22, 2014).
García, Edmundo. "Peloteros cubans en Grandes Ligas: La verdad de la mentira" in: *La Patria Chica* (March 12, 2012).

Graczyk, Wayne. "Cuban Players Experienced Mixed Success This Season" in: *Japan Times* (October 18, 2014).

Grupp, John. "Pirates Bullpen Coach Rafted to U.S. from Cuba Seeking Freedom" in: *Pittsburgh Tribune* (June 26, 2011).

Gurnick, Ken. "Dodgers Wary in Pursuit of Moncada—Singing Cuban Prospect Would Come at a High Cost" in: MLB.com (February 6, 2015).

———. "Influx of Cuban Signees Set to Help Dodgers—Guerrero Excelling in Majors; Infielder Olivera, Pitcher Fernandez on Deck" in: MLB.com (May 19, 2015).

Hermoso, Rafael. "Baseball: Star Pitcher Has Defected from Cuba" in: *New York Times* (November 1, 2003).

Hill, Douglas. "Barbaro Garbey" in: *SABR Baseball Biography Project* (September 2010).

Hoffarth, Tom. "Our Daily Bread: The 'Other' Ramirez in Glendale, Arizona" in: *Farther Off the Wall with Tom Hoffarth* (www.insidesocial.com) (March 9, 2009).

Hopkins, Jared S. "How Did Jose Abreu Get from Cuba to Chicago? Details Remain a Mystery" in: www.chicagotribune.com (November 7, 2014).

"How Rene Arocha Turned Marlins Fans into Cardinals Fans" in: *Retro Simba* (June 14, 2013).

Katz, Jesse. "Escape from Cuba: Yasiel Puig's Untold Journey to the Dodgers" in: *Los Angeles* (April 13, 2014).

Kennedy, Brandon. "Minor-League Lawsuit Claims MLB Fails to Pay Minimum Wage to Minor-Leaguers" in: www.thestar.com (*Toronto Star*) (December 3, 2014).

Kepner, Tyler. "Pushing the Limits of a Sport, and a Budget—Aroldis Chapman Stretches the Reds' Budget, and the Limits of Pitching" in: *New York Times* (March 5, 2015).

Keri, Jonah. "The Best Hitter You've Never Heard Of—José Abreu Is Putting up God-like Numbers in the Closed-off World of Cuba" in: *Grantland* (February 23, 2012).

Knapp, Gwen. "Puig: A Hollywood Style Rookie" in: www.SportsonEarth.com (June 17, 2014).

Labott, Elise. "Obama Announces Historic Overhaul of Relations; Cuba Releases American" in: www.CNN.com (December 17, 2014).

Lamelo, Robert. "José Abreu: Cienfuegos siempre va a tener en José Dariel Abreu al Elefante Mayor" in: *Huffpost Voces* (October 14, 2014).

"Leonys Martin Ransom Case Detailed" in: *ESPN Dallas* (December 21, 2013).

Lewis, Michael. "Commie Ball: A Journey to the End of a Revolution" in: *Vanity Fair* (July 2008).

Lind, Dara. "Major League Baseball's Human Trafficking Problem" in: www.vox.com (March 15, 2015).

Lindbergh, Ben. "What the Red Sox Rusney Castillo Signing Means for the Player, the Team, and Future Cuban Free Agents" in: *Grantland* (August 26, 2014).

Longenhagen, Eric. "Seeing Red" in: www.SportsonEarth.com (June 29, 2014).

Longman, Jere. "Olympics: His Eye on Major Leagues, Top Cuban Pitcher Defects" in: *New York Times* (July 11, 1996).

Mak, Tim. "Wife's Plea for American Held in Cuba" in: *Politico* (March 13, 2012).

McDaniel, Kiley. "U.S. Government's New Policy May Help Cuban Ballplayers" in: *Fangraphs* (January 26, 2015).

McKinley, Jr., James C. "What Price Glory? A Special Report: Cuban Players Defect, But Often with a Cost" in: *New York Times* (April 25, 1999).

Merkin, Scott. "Long Days Part of Nieto's Journey to Big Leagues: Cuban Catcher Determined to Put Forth Effort and Take Advantage of Opportunity" in: MLB.com (February 21, 2014).

Miller, Michael E. "Who Is Jose Abreu?—After Defecting From Cuba the Sox Slugger Had One of the Best Rookie Seasons Ever. Yet His Story Has Remained Largely a Mystery. Until Now." in: *Chicago* (April 2015).

Miller, Scott. "Yasmani Tomas Capturing MLB Imaginations as Next Great Cuban Slugger" in: *Bleacher Report* (November 19, 2014).

Miroff, Nick. "Past Clashes with Present for Cuban Baseball" in: *Washington Post* (March 27, 2015).

Moncado, Arturo. "Posible escándolo con Yoan Moncada" in: *Swing Completo* (October 8, 2014).

Morosi, Jon P. "Red Sox's Moncada Comes from Cuba Shrouded in Mystery" in: www.FoxSports.com (March 13, 2015).

Morrow, Geoff. "What Shift in U.S.-Cuba Relations Means for Baseball—How Restored USA-Cuba Diplomacy Will Change MLB" in: www.FoxSports.com (December 17, 2014).

———. "When Baseball Hits Home: Hassan Pena Fled Cuba Five Years Ago for a Better Life in the U.S." in: www.Pennlive.com (July 25, 2010).

Murray, Mary, and Orlando Matos. "Cuban National Signs First Million Dollar Baseball Contract—Cuban Outfielder Frederich Cepeda Has Scored One for the History Books" in: www.NBCNews.com (April 23, 2014).

Nobles, Charles. "5 Cubans in Search of a Club" in: *New York Times* (June 2, 1993).

Olney, Buster. "Puig-mania Turning into Puig Backlash" in: MLB.com (July 10, 2013).

Ortiz, Jorge L. "Activist Uses Simple Methods to Help Cubans Defect" in: *USA Today Sports* (February 5, 2015).

———. "Baseball Impact of USA-Cuba Thaw May Take Years" in: *USA Today Sports* (December 17, 2014).

———. "Can Agreement with USA Fix Defects in Cuban Baseball?" in: *Louisville Courier-Journal* (February 4, 2014).

———. "Cespedes: Fellow Cuban Jose Dariel Abreu Is the Real Deal" in: *USA Today Sports* (August 13, 2013).

———. "Dodgers in Pursuit of Cuban Infielder Guerrero" in: *USA Today Sports* (September 9, 2013).

———. "Five Years After Defecting from Cuba, Morales Has Arrived" in: *USA Today Sports* (October 9, 2009).

———. "In Suing MLB, Minor Leaguers Want Minimum Wage for Maximum Effort" in: *USA Today Sports* (April 22, 2015).

———. "Two Lesser Cuban Defectors About to Cash In" in: www.FloridaToday.com (January 4, 2013).

———. "Yasmany Tomás, Yoan López Eye Big Future with D'Backs" in: *USA Today Sports* (March 8, 2015).

Palacios, Daniel. "Esclandolo: Expulsado Yosvani Peraza de la Serie Nacional por presunto tráfico de personas" in: *Swing Completo* (March 5, 2015).

Parlapiano, Alicia. "How America's Relationship with Cuba Will Change" in: *New York Times* (December 17, 2014).

Passen, Jeff. "Coast Guard Crew Reflects on Time with Yasiel Puig during Attempt to Defect to U.S." in: *Yahoo Sports* (July 2, 2013).

Passen, Jeff, Charles Robinson, and Rand Getlin. "Leonys Martin Lawsuit Details Allegations of Cuban Baseball Player Smuggling" in: *Yahoo Sports* (December 6, 2013).

Plaschke, Bill. "Back Story of Yasiel Puig's Journey to America Should Concern Dodgers" in: *Los Angeles Times* (April 15, 2014).

Powell, Michael. "For Cuban Players, No Embargo on Dreams" in: *New York Times* (December 23, 2014).

Ramos, Elsa. "Frederich Cepeda: Siempre he sido millonario" in: *Cuba Debate* (October 29, 2014).

Rhoads, Christopher. "Baseball Scout's Ordeal: 13 Years in Cuban Prison" in: *Wall Street Journal* (April 24, 2010).

Ringolsby, Tracy. "Cuban Defectors Enjoy Signing Freedom—Most Are Not Part of Draft and Can Choose between Major League Bidders" in: MLB.com (February 4, 2015).

Ritter Conn, Jordan. "From Cuba with Heat: Marlins Rookie Pitcher Jose Fernandez on His Journey from Cuban Defector to MLB All-Star" in: *Grantland* (July 16, 2013).

"Rob Manfred quiere realizer juegos de exhibición en Cuba" in: *Zona de Strike* (April 24, 2015).

Robb, Sharon. "Cuban Pitcher Defects to Chase Major-League Dream" in: *Chicago Tribune* (August 7, 1991).

Robertson, Linda. "What Will Become of Baseball's Decline in Cuba? The Field Might Open Further in U.S." in: *Miami Herald* (December 28, 2014).

Rodriguez, Claudio. "Excandolo: Caso Gourriel hace peligrar relaciones beisboleros Japón-Cuba" in: *Swing Completo* (March 31, 2015).

Rodríguez Otero, Claudio. "Análisis del Intercambio Cuba-NPB en 2014" in: BéisbolJapones.com (November 3, 2014).

Rojas, Enrique. "Despaigne juege como dominicano" in: ESPNdeportes.com (May 13, 2014).

Rojas, Luis Felipe. "Industrialista que se fuga deja 8 personas en prisión" in: martinoticias.com (August 28, 2014).

Romero, Francys. "Felix Pérez: 'Extraño de mi familia, mi isla y mi béisbol'" in: *On Cuba* (March 30, 2015).

Roza, Joel. "The Curious Case of Jorge Soler: How 19-Year-Old Cuban Outfield Sensation Could Alter Baseball's View of the Houston Astros" in: *Caller-Times* (February 23, 2012).

Rubin, Adam. "Cuban Starts Over as a Met: Soler Is in, as Rotation Turns to Defector" in: *New York Daily News* (July 8, 2004).

———. "For Valdes, a Long Journey to the Majors" in: ESPNNewYork.com (April 12, 2010).

Salisbury, Jim. "This Phillies Rookie Knows Pressure; Eddie Oropesa Defected from Cuba in '93. Opening-Day Jitters? Maybe. Tears? Definitely" in: Philly.com (April 2, 2001).

Sanchez, Jesse. "At Caribbean Series Gourriel Captures the Imagination" in: MLB.com (February 6, 2015).

———. "Cuban Pitcher Reportedly Seeks Asylum in Puerto Rico" in: MLB.com (February 6, 2015).

———. "Cuba's Next Big Thing Ready to Impress Scouts" in: MLB.com (September 18, 2014)

Schmidt, Michael S. "Opening of Relations Could Bring Cuban Stars to Major League Baseball" in: *New York Times* (December 17, 2014).

Schoenfield, David. "¿Es posible que Yasmany Tomás sea el gran fracaso?" in: *Swing Completo* (April 9, 2015).

Seidel, Jeff. "Tigers' Brayan Pena Defected from Cuba for Baseball, More" in: *Detroit Free Press* (February 14, 2013).

Siegel, Robert, and Eyder Peralta. "With Improved Relations Are the US and Cuba Ready to Play Ball?" in: www.NPR.org (March 24, 2015).

Slusser, Susan, and Demian Bulwa. "While the Cuban Defector Broke In with the Oakland A's, His Family Endured a Harrowing Struggle to Reach the U.S." in: *San Francisco Chronicle* (July 30, 2014).

Speier, Alex. "Red Sox Prospect Yoan Moncada's Pro Debut Quite an Event" in: *Boston Globe* (May 19, 2015).

Stark, Jayson. "Detailing Yasiel Puig's Historically Great Run" in: *Jayson Stark Blog* at MLB.com (June 3, 2014).

Strauss, Ben. "Cuban Slugger Brings Promise and Risk to the Plate" in: *New York Times* (September 17, 2013).

Sweig, Julia E., and Michael J. Bustamante. "Cuba After Communism: The Economic Reforms That Are Transforming the Island" in: *Foreign Affairs* (July–August 2013).

Sypa, Steve. "International Free Agent Profile: Pavel Quesada" in: *SB Nation* (August 18, 2014).

Victor, Philip J. "MLB Pitches Cuba Exhibition as Cuba Balks at Idea" in: *Al-Jazeera America* (March 22, 2015).

Vorkunov, Mike. "U.S. Opens Diplomatic Relations with Cuba but Benefits for MLB May Not Be Near" in: NJ.com (December 18, 2014).

Wagner, James. "Yunel Escobar's Long and Winding Road to the Big Leagues" in: *Washington Post* (May 7, 2015).

Walk, John. "Jorge Martinez: A Hidden 2014 MLB Draft Gem Playing Indy Ball?" in: mlbdailydish.com (June 2, 2014).

Walters, John. "Cuba's Been Losing Its Best Baseball Players to America" in: *Newsweek* (May 2, 2015).

Weaver, Jay. "Report: Texas Rangers Outfielder Leonys Martin and His Family Victims of Kidnapping and Extortion" in: *Dallas Daily News* (December 4, 2013).

INDEX

ABOUT THE AUTHOR

Peter C. Bjarkman is the recognized authority on Cuba's post-1961 revolutionary-era baseball. He is author of the seminal volume *A History of Cuban Baseball, 1864–2006* (2007) and coauthor (with Mark Rucker) of *Smoke—The Romance and Lore of Cuban Baseball* (1999). Bjarkman has witnessed domestic-league Cuban baseball firsthand on more than forty visits to the communist country since 1997 and has also followed the Cuban national team to international events in Latin America, Europe, Canada, and Asia since 1999. A former linguistics professor, Bjarkman is featured as celebrity chef Anthony Bourdain's Havana guide on the 2011 Travel Channel episode of "No Reservations Cuba" (season 7). A regular consultant on Cuban baseball for the North American media, his many television appearances include a featured role in the 2014 ESPN *30 for 30* documentary film "Brothers in Exile" (the story of Cuban pitchers Orlando "El Duque" Hernández and Liván Hernández).

Author Peter C. Bjarkman in Bayamo, Cuba, with Alfredo Despaigne, a top national team slugger loaned to the Japanese League in 2014. Courtesy of Peter C. Bjarkman.